Local Public Finance in Central and Eastern Europe

Local Public Finance in Central and Eastern Europe

Edited by

Željko Šević
University of Greenwich Business School, UK

Edward Elgar
Cheltenham, UK • Northampton, MA, USA

Published by
Edward Elgar Publishing Limited
The Lypiatts
15 Lansdown Road
Cheltenham
Glos GL50 2JA
UK

Edward Elgar Publishing, Inc.
William Pratt House
9 Dewey Court
Northampton
Massachusetts 01060
USA

A catalogue record for this book
is available from the British Library

Library of Congress Control Number: 2008927965

ISBN 978 1 84376 658 2

Printed and bound in Great Britain by MPG Books Ltd, Bodmin, Cornwall

Contents

Contributors

Svetlana Alexandrova is a Professor of International Financial Management and Capital Markets in the University of National and World Economy. She has been with the University since 1992. Professor Alexandrova was educated in Bulgaria, the US, Italy and Denmark. She has held consulting positions in a range of non-governmental organisations and governmental institutions on regional policy, public finance and European structural funds project management. Professor Alexandrova's current research interests are in public sector reform, public private partnership and EU project management at regional and local levels. She has worked on macroeconomic, finance and policy impact assessment issues under the auspices of different projects, financed by the World Bank, Open Society Fund, UNDP and the EU.

Anto Bajo graduated and received an MSc from the Faculty of Economics and Business, at the University of Zagreb; PhD from the Faculty of Economics, at the University of Ljubljana, Slovenia in 2006. He has attended professional courses in the USA (Harvard University, J. F. Kennedy School of Government), Hungary, South Africa, Japan and Slovenia. He is a researcher at the Institute of Public Finance in Zagreb and assistant professor at the Faculty of Economics and Business, at the University of Zagreb teaching courses in Public Finance and Local Government Finance. He is a member of the Advisory Council of Higher Education and Science Funding of the Ministry of the Science, Education and Sport, and editing board of the journal *Financial Theory and Practice*. He has published a number of scientific papers in Croatian and international scientific journals and books (*Financing Higher Education and Science*, 2003; *Budgetary System Management*, 2006), dealing with budget system and fiscal federalism. His main fields of interest include public finance management, budget system and fiscal federalism.

Djordjije Blažić is an Associate Professor and the past Dean at the Faculty of Public Administration and European Studies at the University of Podgorica, Montenegro. Dr Blažić is a former local government official, senior civil servant and distinguished promoter of the third sector in Montenegro. From 1993 to 2002 he served as the Assistant Minister of Justice, overseeing the local self-government system. Before that he was Chief Administrative Inspector and Secretary to the Municipality of Danilovgrad (one of the oldest settlements in Montenegro). He is primarily interested in legal aspects of decentralisation and local self-government, having published 14 books and numerous papers in several languages. Dr Blažić is well-known not only in Montenegro, but also in the Western Balkans region and is a regular speaker at professional and academic events. He has worked as an expert adviser on a large number of reform projects, not only in Montenegro, but also in other transitional countries. Dr Blažić is also an adjunct faculty member at the University of Novi Pazar, University of Belgrade and the Montenegrin Police Academy. He holds an LLB degree from the University of Montenegro (formerly the University of Titograd), and an LLM and a PhD in Law from the University of Belgrade.

Phillip J. Bryson is the Douglas and Effie Driggs Professor of Economics at the Marriott School of Brigham Young University in Provo, Utah, USA. From 1967 to 1988 he was at the University of Arizona and has been at BYU since 1988. He received his BA degree from the University of Utah and a PhD in economics from The Ohio State University in 1967. As a Humboldt Fellow and a Fulbright Fellow he conducted research and taught at the Free University of Berlin, the University of Munich, Marburg University and Duisburg University. He has published four books and many research papers on the East German and Soviet economies and on their disappearance. He has also written on the transition of some of the centrally planned economies to market orientation, including the German Democratic Republic, the former Soviet Union, the Czech Republic, the Slovak Republic, China, and Armenia.

Piotr Bury is a Professor of Economics at the Academy in Kielce where he serves as the Director of the Institute of Economics. Prior to joining the Academy Dr Bury was a Professor at the University of Łódź where he was the Chair of City and Regional Management. He is also a Professor at the Higher School of Public Administration in Łódź. Professor Bury specialises in public finance, city planning and regional management. He has a CSc and habilitation doctorate (Dr habil.) from the University of Łódź. He has participated in a number of international projects and has a widely known expertise in Polish local and regional finance.

Mark W. Chandler is a British economist, currently working for the UK Centre for the Measurement of Government Activity as Head of the Health and Adult Social Care Branch. Previously he spent four years at the Stockholm

School of Economics in Riga as an Assistant Professor, and at BICEPS, as a Research Associate, after eight years teaching at Vilnius University, Lithuania. His current work is to construct estimates of productivity in the British National Health Service and state funded adult social care. His main academic research areas are local public finance, the economics of education, and industrial relations. His publications include articles in *Public Finance Review*, and the *Journal of Education Finance* and as co-editor of a book for Routledge on tax policy in the new EU member states. He is also Managing Editor of the *Baltic Journal of Economics*. Current research projects include a study of unreported income in Lithuania. Mark first went to the Baltics in 1995, with the Civic Education Project. He received a doctorate in economics at the University of Connecticut in 1996 and continued working in the Baltics, joining EuroFaculty in 1997. Since then, in addition to teaching and purely academic research, he has carried out research projects funded by the EU, the Global Development Network and the Institut des Sciences du Travail.

Gary C. Cornia was recently named the new Dean of the Marriott School of Management. Dr Cornia, the Stewart Grow Professor of Public Management, had been serving as the Director of the School's George Romney Institute of Public Management since 2004. Professor Cornia earned a PhD in public finance from Ohio State University in 1979. In 2006, the National Tax Association presented him with its prestigious Stephen D. Gold Award. From 2002 to 2003 he served as the President of the National Tax Association. From 1990 to 1998 he was the Associate Dean of the Marriott School. In 1998, Dr Cornia was named the Marriott School Outstanding Faculty member, the highest award given by the School. He currently serves on the boards of three fixed income funds and one equity fund as well as with the Lincoln Institute of Land Policy in Massachusetts, the Land Reform Training Institute in Taiwan and the Utah Governor's Tax Review Commission.

Jadvyga Čiburienė is a Professor in the Department of Economics and International Trade at the Faculty of Economics and Management, Kaunas University of Technology (Lithuania). She is a member of a committee of doctoral studies at Kaunas University of Technology and a member of the Faculty Board. She holds a BA in Engineering Economics (Kaunas University of Technology, Lithuania, 1979), and a PhD in Social sciences (Economics) from the Sankt-Petersburg University, Russia, 1989. She has acquired a habilitation in Social Sciences (Economics) from the Kaunas University of Technology, Lithuania, 2006. Her research interests include fiscal and monetary policy and analysis, taxes and taxation, economic stabilisation policy, Economic growth. She has published many articles in these fields.

Borče Davitkovski is a Professor of Administrative Law at the St Cyril and Methodius University of Skopje (Republic of Macedonia) where he also served as Vice-Dean of the Faculty of Law. He also served as Student Rights Defender at the University of Skopje and for four years as the Chairman of the Board of the Macedonian TELECOM, a national telecommunication company. He is currently serving on the Macedonian Government Legal Council. He has published widely in the field of Administrative Law, having authored more than seventy publications. He holds LLB, LLM and PhD degrees from the St Cyril and Methodius University of Skopje.

Claudiu Doltu is a Professor of Economics at the Economics and Economic Policies Department, Academy of Economic Studies, Bucharest. He started his academic career in 1993, when he joined the Economics Department of AES, and he obtained a PhD in Economics in 1996. His teaching and research activity was complemented with consultancy for various international bodies including the World Bank, International Finance Corporation, European Commission, USAID, DFID and UNDP. He has also occupied various positions in the Romanian administration: economic advisor of the President of Romania (1999), senior adviser to the Governor of the National Bank of Romania (2000–2002) and Deputy Minister of Finance (2005–2006). He has experience in international financial institutions where he represented Romania in 2005 and 2006 at the IMF, as Alternate Governor, Black Sea Trade and Development Bank, as Vice-Governor, Council of Europe Development Bank, as member of the Administrative Council, International Investment Bank (Moscow) and International Bank for Economic Cooperation (Moscow), and as member of the Administrative Council. At present he is Alternate Executive Director of the Dutch Constituency in the World Bank Group. His current research interests include the transformation process in Eastern European economies (the road from planned economy to market based economy), monetary economics and financial policies. He has published five books, articles and brochures (analysing the developments of transition economies) and also two economics handbooks for students.

Artan Hoxha is the President of the Institute for Contemporary Studies (ISB), a policy research institute and in this capacity, manages and supervises the overall research activities of ISB. He has been involved in projects in various public policy areas including democratic institution reforms (public administration, decentralisation, parliament, judiciary), free market reforms (economic policies, public finance, trade, local and regional development), and public services (education, environment, social care, water and wastewater). He has provided training to central and local civil servants in areas of public management, performance management, policy development, law, accountability and transparency. He is currently Head of the Board of Directors of the Albanian Centre for Mediation and Arbitration, member of an ad hoc working group for simplification of tax and customs procedures and member of the group of experts for decentralisation (since 1999). Mr Hoxha holds a Masters degree in the Economics of Energy and Environment from Enrico Mattei School, Italy and a BS in Drilling Engineering from the University of Tirana, Faculty of Geology and Mining.

Eugeniu Hristev is an economist specialising in EU Accession issues with a masters degree in policy analysis and public finance from Indiana University. He has conducted research on legislative and regulatory reforms in budgeting and fiscal areas for various Moldovan think tanks, USAID, World Bank, and TACIS. He has played a key role in developing Moldovan policy for WTO negotiations drafting new legislation compatible with the EU and WTO agreements. Mr Hristev was also a member of the research team on fiscal decentralisation and helped draft laws on local public finance and budgeting process.

Ivana Jakir-Bajo is employed in the Croatian Ministry of Finance as the Head of Budget Analyses and Capital Projects Evaluation Department. She received a degree in Economics in Organization and Management at the University of Zagreb and is currently enrolled in a masters program at the Faculty of Economics and Business, University of Zagreb. Additionally, she has studied government budgeting issues at the John F. Kennedy School of Government at Harvard University and the Centre of Excellence in Finance in Ljubljana, Slovenia. She has authored and co-authored numerous papers on government budgeting and accounting and co-authored two books *Budgetary Accounting* (2001) and *Budgetary Planning and Accounting* (2003), published in Croatia, and *Accountability and Gauging Success: Performance Measurement in South Eastern Europe* (2003), *Local Government and Public Service Reform Initiative* in Budapest, Hungary. Her main research and professional interest is government budget accounting and public expenditure management.

Solvita Klapare is an Operations Analyst at the Sustainable Development Department of the Europe and Central Asia (ECA) Region of the World Bank.

Since 2005, she has been involved in carbon finance, agriculture reform and development operations since 2005. From 2000 to 2005 she worked at the World Bank's Urban and Water unit of the ECA region with a focus on municipal development operations, as well as projects for rehabilitation and operational and financial improvement of water and sanitation systems. Prior to joining the Bank, since 1996 she worked at the Latvia Municipal Development Fund as an Economist and later as a Fund Manager. During this time she actively participated in that country's process of decentralisation and local capacity building. She was a part-time trainer at the Centre for Municipal Training, where she delivered lectures on project development and public procurement to the government, municipal, and private sector participants. She also worked at the Foreign Economic Relations department of the Ministry of Economy of Latvia since 1995, before joining the Fund. Ms Klapare holds a Master's Degree in Economics and Management from the University of Latvia and Graduate Diploma in Law from BPP Law School in London, UK.

Yuri Krivorotko is Professor of Finance and Banking and Head of the Accounting, Analysis and Audit Department at the Belarus Institute of Jurisprudence. Dr Krivorotko is also a Senior Lecturer at the State Economic Regulation Department of the Academy of Management under the President of the Republic of Belarus. Previously he was the Head of Finance and Banking Department of the Higher School of Management and Business at the Belarus State Economic University (2002–2006). He is an alumnus of the Central European Summer University (2001) attending the programme Intergovernmental fiscal relations and local financial management. He is an expert in that sphere of local government finance at the non-governmental organization Lev Sapieha Foundation. His research interest focus on local financial management and intergovernmental fiscal relations. Professor Krivorotko has authored and co-authored seven books and more than forty articles and working papers. Yuri Krivorotko is currently concentrating on a new book on a financial toolkit for local government in Belarus.

Kenneth A. Kriz is an Associate Professor at the University of Nebraska at Omaha, USA and Extraordinary Professor at the University of Tartu, Estonia. Professor Kriz conducts research focusing on municipal debt economics and administration, government financial risk management techniques, economic development policy, and transportation finance, along with the use of simulation techniques in public finance. He has consulted with several public and non-profit organisations on financial and economic issues. Professor Kriz is a frequent presenter at budgeting and financial management conferences and has published papers in the areas of local government reserve funds, municipal bond economics and underwriting strategies, the effects of revenue limitation initiatives on state government borrowing costs, and tax increment financing.

Thomas Meekel is currently the Technical Secretary of the United Cities and Local Governments Committee on Local Finance and Development, a world network of mayors and national associations active in local finance. He worked in the Serbian Ministry of Finance on the area of local public borrowing and local finance between 2002 and 2005, setting up the Municipal Infrastructure Agency and also assisted in drafting the public debt law. He also assisted 11 South Serbian Municipalities and worked in the City of Belgrade to develop its Multiyear Investment Plan as a consultant for the EAR. He has practical experience in city management, having been the finance director and head of the economic development unit of the City of Montreuil France, between 1999 and 2002. He is a graduate of the Institut d'Etudes Politiques de Paris (France) and University of Paris I Sorbonne.

Juraj Nemec is a Professor of Public Finance and Public Management at the Faculty of Economics, Matej Bel University in Banska Bystrica, Slovakia. He is also Visiting Professor at the Masaryk University Brno, Czech Republic, the University of Bath, UK and at WSB Gdansk, Poland. His main fields of interest are public economics and public finance, public administration reforms, health care policy, economics and management and public procurement. In all these areas he delivers university lectures and seminars, realises research activities and provides consultancy and advisory services, connected dominantly with support to post-communist countries in the region. He has published as author, co-author or editor more than 250 books and professional articles in Slovak, Czech, English and other languages. He is editor in chief of the *NISPAcee Journal in Public Administration and Public Policy*, member of editorial boards of several other professional journals. Professor Nemec has published a number of books with the Network of Institutes and Schools of Public Administration in Central and Eastern Europe (NISPAcee), which have been translated into a number of regional languages and have been widely used for teaching and research purposes. He holds a master and doctoral degree from the School of Economics in Bratislava.

Ana Pavlovska-Daneva is an Assistant Professor of Administrative Law at the St Cyril and Methodius University of Skopje (Republic of Macedonia). She has authored and co-authored over fifteen publications, including four books. Dr Pavlovska-Daneva has participated in a number of working parties dealing with drafting various legislative acts in Macedonia, not exclusively in the field of Administrative Law. She has held visiting positions in Hungary and the US. Dr Pavlovska-Daneva holds LLB, LLM and PhD in Law degrees from the St Cyril and Methodius University of Skopje. She has completed a part of her undergraduate legal studies at the Lomonossov Moscow State University in Russia.

Gábor Péteri, Economist, PhD. He started his career at the City of Budapest, Planning and Economic Department. After working for decade at the Hungarian Institute of Public Administration, he went on to freelance consultant on several projects with the British Know How Fund, US AID and the World Bank in Hungary. From 1999 he held the research director position of the Local Government and Public Service Reform Initiative (LGI), of the Open Society Institute-Budapest. He presently works as a consultant, and is the director of development at the LGID Ltd a non-profit consulting company affiliated with the Open Society Network. He has published extensively on local government finances, financial management and policy formulation on local government reforms.

Juliana H. Pigey is a Senior Associate at the Urban Institute, a public policy research institute based in Washington, DC. Ms Pigey has worked on issues of local government finance and policy analysis and intergovernmental fiscal reform for the World Bank and for USAID in Albania, Bulgaria, Croatia, Georgia, Hungary, Kyrgyzstan, Latvia, Lithuania, Montenegro, Macedonia, Poland, Romania, Serbia and Tajikistan. Ms Pigey has prepared baseline studies of local government finance systems and assisted local governments with improving capital planning, budgeting and forecasting practices. She has also proposed reform programs to increase local fiscal autonomy, to develop municipal credit markets, and provided policy analysis and assistance in legislative developments. She has worked directly with local governments in France on fiscal and budgetary analysis, budget forecasting and debt management. Ms Pigey is co-author of the *Sourcebook for Policy Analysts and Trainers on Intergovernmental Fiscal Relations in Eastern Europe* (2005), published by the World Bank Institute. She holds an MA in international relations from l'Institut d'Etudes Politiques de Paris and a BA in political science and French from New York University.

Mudīte Priede is an Adviser on the Issues of Finance and Economy in the Latvian Association of Local and Regional Governments from 1997 and an Executive Director in the Jelgava District Council from 2001. Ms Priede graduated from the Latvia University of Agriculture, Faculty of Economics with a MA in Economics Science. She has published over five academic papers and co-authored five papers including 'Capital Investment Funding in Latvia', 'Local Government Borrowing', 'Regulation and competition in local utilities'. She has profound knowledge on the self-government system of Latvia and the EU; especially finance system, intergovernmental fiscal issues, EU funds, public-private partnership, public procurement, co-operation and relations between the state and local government sector, democratisation and decentralisation. She is Chairman of the State Examination Commission, Latvia University of Agriculture, Faculty of Social Sciences, a Member of the Committee of Self-Government Finance Stabilisation and a Member of Negotiation Commission of Latvia with the European Commission.

Clare T. Romanik, Senior Research Associate at the Urban Institute, presently directs the USAID Decentralization and Local Government Program in the Kyrgyz Republic. Previously, she served as Program Manager for the USAID Moldova Local Government Program. She has provided technical assistance to a dozen countries of Eastern Europe and Central Asia and holds a Masters in Public Affairs with a focus on Economics and Public Policy from the Woodrow Wilson School of Public and International Affairs at Princeton University.

Maria Salabuga serves as Policy Adviser to the Minster of Local Public Administration of the Republic of Moldova under the auspices of the United Nations Development Program (UNDP). Her prior experience includes a senior managerial position for the USAID Moldova Local Government Program, implemented by the Urban Institute. The program was aimed at increasing the autonomy, efficiency, responsiveness, accountability and transparency of more than 120 local governments. Ms Salabuga graduated with highest honours from the Moldovan Academy of Public Administration and is currently pursuing a doctorate degree at the Moldovan Academy of Economics.

Davor Savin is Professor of Economics at the University of Maribor (Slovenia) where he directs the Slovenian Institute of Banking and Finance. Prior to joining academia, Professor Savin served as the Chief Economic Adviser to the President of the Federal Assembly of the former Socialist Federative Republic of Yugoslavia, and Senior Adviser in the Federal Secretariat of Finance. He also held academic positions at the University of Dubrovnik in Croatia, University of Sarajevo in Bosnia and Herzegovina, University of Skopje in Macedonia, and Institute of Economic Sciences and Institute for Investment Research in Belgrade, Serbia. Professor Savin has authored over 300 bibliographical units and has advised a number of public and private clients on economic and financial issues. Professor Savin holds BSc(Econ) and LLB degrees from the University of Belgrade and an MSc(Econ) and PhD(Econ) also from the University of Belgrade. He has held a number of visiting positions in various counties of the former Yugoslavia, the UK, USA, Japan, amongst others.

Željko Šević is Professor of Accounting, Finance and Public Policy in the University of Greenwich Business School, where he also serves as the Director of Research, Outreach and European Affairs. He has been with the University since 1998. Professor Šević has been educated in the Netherlands, Scotland, Serbia and Sweden and has held visiting academic positions in Australia, Austria, Bulgaria, Croatia, Japan, Poland, Slovenia, the US and at the University for Peace established by the United Nations. Professor Šević is also a Honorary Distinguished Professor at the Zhytomyr Technological State University in Ukraine. Professor Šević's current research interests are in the public (sector) reform in Japan and Vietnam (on-going projects), and accounting reform in the public sector with the particular emphasis on the use of management accounting in public sector restructuring and the design of effective and efficient financial/fiscal information systems. In 2004 he was a Visiting Scholar at the Japanese Ministry of Finance, researching on and teaching policy evaluation methods (following his previous stay with the Ministry in 2002), and was a Visiting Fellow in the National Europe Centre (NEC) at the Australian National University, researching on the phenomenon of (professional) delegation in the modern democratic (public) decision-making process.

Sergii Slukhai is Professor of Economics at the Economics Faculty, Kyiv National Taras Shevchenko University. Born in 1955, he graduated from Kyiv National Taras Shevchenko University in 1978 with a degree equivalent to MA in Political Economy. He obtained PhD (Kandidat Nauk) and DSc (Doktor Nauk) in Economics from Kyiv National Taras Shevchenko University. He is a fellow of the Financial Scientific Research Institute under the Ministry of Finance of Ukraine. As an expert, he took part in different international projects sponsored by TACIS, MATRA, Open Society Institute, and so on dedicated to public finance in Ukraine. He was a research fellow at Munich University (1994 and 1997) and Fulbright Senior Scholar at Bloomington Indiana University (2000–2001). He was a member of the Academic Board Social Capital and Academic Publications under International Renaissance Foundation Ukraine (2004–2007). Professor Slukhai has published over 160 academic papers in the field of public finance, several monographs (among other *Intergovernmental Transfers in the Post-Socialist Countries: From Theory to Reality*) and co-authored several textbooks in Microeconomics and Economics.

Paweł Swianiewicz is currently the Chair of the Department of Local Development and Policy at the University of Warsaw (Poland) where he teaches courses on comparative local government politics, local government finance and urban economics. Since 2005 he has been President of the European Urban Research Association (EURA). His research focuses on decentralisation, local politics and policy-making in local governments, with a special focus on comparative analysis of Central and East European countries. He has been extensively involved as a consultant of British DFID, Council of Europe, UNDP and Open Society Institute projects in several countries of Eastern Europe and Central Asia. He was a research fellow in the School of Advanced Urban Studies, University of Bristol (1990) and in the Norwegian Centre for Organization and Management, University of Bergen (1994). In 1993 he was a senior Fulbright scholar at University of Chicago. Between 1995–2001 he was a director of the British Know How Fund Local Government Assistance Programme in Poland. Professor Swianiewicz holds PhD degrees in Economics and Economic Geography from the University of Warsaw.

Jean Tesche is a Professor of Economics at Sarajevo Graduate School of Business in Bosnia and Herzegovina. Prior to returning to teaching in 2005, she worked for the US Treasury's Office of Technical Assistance in the Ministry of Finance in the Balkans for 10 years. She taught in the Economics Department at Emory University from 1988–1994. She graduated with a degree in Russian from the University of Oregon and received her MBA as well as her PhD in Economics from Columbia Graduate School of Business in New York. She has published more than 30 articles and book chapters mostly dealing with the economies of Central and Eastern Europe, including tax issues, banking, fiscal decentralisation and pension reform. She has used computable general equilibrium models among other research methods.

Sabina Ymeri has just completed a two-year tenure as the Decentralization Specialist of the USAID project Local Government and Decentralisation in Albania (LGDA), implemented by the Urban Institute. In this capacity, she was responsible for policy analysis, developing draft legislation and proposals in the areas of local borrowing, conditional and unconditional transfers, local budget policy framework. She also trained municipal staff and council members in local fiscal policy, budgeting, service delivery, planning, and so on. Prior to the LGDA project, she was a project manager and researcher for the Albanian Institute for International Studies. She has published several studies on Albania and the EU, including, *Albania and EU: Perceptions and Realities* (2005, AIIS), *Rethinking EU Integration* (2004, AIIS). Ms Ymeri holds an MA in Economics from a joint program of the University of Bamberg, Germany and the University of Tirana, Faculty of Economy. She received her BA in Business Administration from the Budapest University of Economics, Faculty of International Management and Business.

Gerda Žigienė is an Adjunct Professor at Vilnius University, Kaunas Faculty of Humanities, Department of Finance and Accounting (Lithuania). She is also financial director of the second largest pharmaceutical company in Lithuania. She holds a BA in Business Management (Kaunas University of Technology, Lithuania), an MSc in Finance and Accounting (Vilnius University, Lithuania), and a PhD in Municipal Finance (University of Management and Economics (ISM), Lithuania). Her research interests include management and analysis of corporate finance and decentralisation and municipal bond issuing models of public finance.

Preface and acknowledgements

This book reviews the state of local public finance in all the transitional countries in Central and Eastern Europe (CEE), surveying the developments over the last almost twenty years, since the Berlin Wall fell and those countries have embarked on the path that we have labelled in the theory 'transition'. Transition countries included in this book are at various stages of development of their new public finance system, ranging from those that have joined the European Union in the first enlargement drive in 2004 to those that are still to be labelled as slow learners and fairly much at the beginning of the public finance transition process. In the book we have placed them in alphabetical order, without any prejudice, and it is up to a reader to judge their individual transitional performance.

The book is a result of collaboration of a number of scholars who have been members of the NISPAcee (The Network of Institutes and Schools of Public Administration in Central and Eastern Europe) Working Group on Public Sector Accounting and Finance. The Group has been very active since its inception in 2001, and has produced a number of thematic publications (Šević, 2005; 2006a; 2006b and 2007) in the last few years, dealing with a number of burning issues facing the transitional countries. In contrast to other titles produced, this book in fact provides a very authoritative and comprehensive picture of the current state of local public finance in each of the twenty countries included in the book. Authors have presented a broad institutional framework for local government in general and local government finance in particular and provided often rare insights in the development of local government finance model in a respective country. Therefore, we hope that the publication will be more than welcomed by both processionals and academics alike, who will find an interesting read, regardless of their angle of primary interest.

As with all the edited books, it took time to put the final version together, as it appeared to be a mastery to coordinate over 25 authors hailing from a similar number of countries. However, each author who contributed to this book was bound by a research protocol that was initially developed to ensure the comparability of country studies and facilitate comparative reading of the chapters. To a large extent authors have succeeded in adhering to the protocol, although in a few instances they had to depart from it, as the local specifics commanded that course of action. However, we hope that the reader will consider this 'departure' as in fact strength and zest of individualism on the part of the individual authors.

As the book took some time to complete we have had a chance to work with a number of people in Edward Elgar. At the very outset Dymphna Evans, at the time Senior Commissioning Editor provided full support for the book and commissioned the work. As Dymphna has left the Edward Elgar Publishing for some greener pastures, Alex Minton (now Alex O'Connell) took over as a contact editor. Finally, the work was handled by Suzanne Mursell, Elgar's Deputy Managing Editor, who took the project over when it was getting close to completion. It was a real pleasure to work with all of them and as in the past, the Elgar office has shown not only a very high level of professionalism, but they have also demonstrated a very high level of understanding for somewhat loose academics and their sense of time. All authors presented in this book would willingly join me in thanking the editorial team at Elgar's for their good results.

As English is not the first language for most of the authors, their contribution had to be spellchecked and professionally tightened up, after the initial assessment by the editor. Jane Finlay, a Scot in Paris, has done a superb job in improving, linguistically, the text of the book, as well as Gillian R. Haxell of the University of Greenwich Business School. Without their commitment this book would have been of a different quality and presentability. Both authors and the editor are very grateful to both of them for their support and good work.

Thanks must go to all in-country referees who critically reviewed various drafts of the chapters that make this book and pointed out the areas where there is clear room for improvement, as well as for those colleagues who worked as anonymous referees for Edward Elgar, assessing the suitability of the topic and the quality of initially submitted work. Although they are anonymous and their names cannot be listed here, they should be mentioned as those who unreservedly supported the publication and make this book happen as well. As with all collective works, the credit should be equally shared, whilst the editor should take the blame for any remaining errors. We have done our best not to have any errors in the main text, and we hope that our efforts will prove successful and that all errors have been corrected. However, the ultimate responsibility for those shortcomings rests with the editor.

We have done our share in presenting the developments in Central and Eastern European Countries (CEECs), with respect to public finance. However, we do hope that some other scholars and/or practitioners will set off, where we have stopped.

BIBLIOGRAPHY

Šević, Ž. (2005), *Financial Decentralization and Grant Transfers: A Critical Perspective*, Bratislava: NISPAcee.
Šević, Ž. (2006a), *Local Government Non-Tax Revenue Sources in Transition Countries: User Fees and Charges*, Bratislava: NISPAcee.
Šević, Ž. (2006b), *Local Government Financial Capacity Building in Transition Countries: Selected Country Studies*, Bratislava: NISPAcee.
Šević, Ž. (2007), *Debt Management in Transition Countries: Experience and Perspectives*, Bratislava: NISPAcee.

1. Local government finance in Central and Eastern Europe: whither way?

Željko Šević

INTRODUCTION

Modern political governance assumes some, in fact fairly high, level of decentralisation and substantial powers of the local government bodies. Traditionally, defence, national security (often fairly widely defined), foreign affairs and finance are to be controlled centrally, whilst all other public services (functions) may be to a varying degree delegated to the sub-national government bodies. Depending on the size of the country, its history and traditions, the layers of government will be defined. However, even the most centralist states will have local governments to some degree, at least as a token of local democratic empowerment. Over time the nature of the relationship between central (national, federal) and sub-national government (regional and local) may have been changing, but the very perimeters of the relationship usually remain fairly unchallenged. In times of crisis and other challenges the central governments are inclined to centralise more than in times of prosperity and development. In cases of emergency and conflict, usually indirect measures introduced by the central government limit to a large extent the independence and *de facto* powers of local government, without much legalistic intervention.

Central government takes care of those activities that, *stricto sensu*, can be defined as being extended from the very notion of sovereignty. Those activities are undertaken in an authoritative manner, so if challenged the government can generally resort to different enforcement measures that would include, as a last resort, different coercive measures. Local governments usually undertake welfare-related activities, and although they may have strong enforcement powers, they usually cannot use force and other coercive measures. In order to enforce the local government's decision, it may often be necessary to seek the assistance of centralised bodies. In European tradition even if the local police force is established, it would usually not be allowed to carry firearms and other qualified coercive tools. Therefore, often the internal affairs may be regarded as affairs of the state although the models of organisation may not be so straightforward. For instance, the police force may be regional, but then there will be highly sophisticated supervisory and control mechanisms that would ensure the professional uniformity and high level of collaboration nationally, as is shown in the example of the UK.

Positive practice shows that there is not a unique prescription as how to decentralise and what to decentralise. Every decentralisation to a large extent has a rather unique national flavour. As we have said, the uniqueness of that particular national decentralisation model can be due to national history, cultural traditions, international pressures (like impending membership of the EU, for instance), change in the political climate, national/nationalistic tensions in multiethnic counties, a failing current (political) governance model, and so on. The list of possible factors that triggered decentralisation is a long and practically non-exhaustive one. This is why a comparative study of a national decentralisation model may be useful, but by no mean enough for the design and implementation of a decentralisation model in another country.

Decentralisation has been a very popular trend in the 1990s and the re-examination of the central–local relationship has attracted the attention of scholars and professionals alike. This may have been mainly due to the dismantling of the socialist/communist systems in Central and Eastern European countries and the former Soviet Union, and also due to the search for a better (and cheaper) governance model in the West. The period from the 1980s on has been marked by the constant search for a more accountable and equally less resource-intensive model for delivering public services in the West. Although the focus was initially on the central government (see Saint-Martin, 2000), the sub-national government could not avoid the edge of public scrutiny. In order to downsize the government, politicians were easily 'sold' the model of necessary decentralisation, local community empowerment and a *subsidiarity* principle was easily endorsed. People (voters) should be provided with public services as close to them as possible, giving them a voice on how, when, and at what price (if any) the services will be rendered.

Decentralisation in Central and Eastern European countries (CEECs) has been endorsed as a tool for dismantling the socialist state, which according to the pervading theory was highly centralised. In order to facilitate transition to a democratic, market-orientated society, it was necessary to dismantle the old, omnipotent socialist state. However, the very issue of the state as a cohesive societal factor was largely neglected and often there was a vacuum left after the reform moves had been undertaken. This problem has only recently been documented in the political science literature (see Ganev, 2007), and there is still a need to assess this issue in economics and political economy literature, going beyond the classical assessment analysis of whether it was better to opt for a gradualist or big-bang approach to economic transition. It is widely known that the Chinese gradualist approach has worked well, but then that some Eastern European countries have done well themselves although a more big-bang-like approach has been adopted (for instance, Estonia). Decentralisation in CEECs has been strongly promoted by international financial institutions (foremost the World Bank) and national governmental donor agencies (American USAID, British DFID-Know How Fund, Swedish SIDA, and so on). To some extent it has been perceived as an unavoidable part of the public sector reform package, a prerequisite for the World Bank and/or foreign donor financing of reform attempts. Hence, a student of decentralisation efforts at the very beginning of the transitional process should not have been surprised at the high level of uniformity between decentralisation agendas in various, transitional countries.

Decentralisation initially usually meant deconcentration of central government bodies physically – establishing regional offices of government ministries, which was followed by the delegation of powers to regional and local governments, with clearly established reporting responsibilities and robust inspection/control systems in place. The real devolution or simply giving the original rights to local governments followed in the later stages of the transition process. Today in most, if not really all, countries in Central and Eastern Europe local governments have their own, original powers, as outlined in the constitution and other basic (systemic) laws. However, it is and should be possible to spread the powers of local government, empowering them to serve their residents to the best of their abilities. Often the central government did not mind transferring power to local government bodies in full, but unfortunately either money did not follow or the transfer of financial resources was significantly delayed. So, often in the early phases local governments failed to meet the expectations of citizens, as the central government simply obstructed them. It may be more visible in CEECs, but it is certainly not a 'CEE only' disease.

However, in the process of decentralisation in CEECs a phenomenon has emerged (especially in Poland) that some local governments were not really keen to get more power, as they perceived they would be more pressurised by the residents, who would continue to be dissatisfied with the service. In fact, blaming the central government as a pre-emptive strategy may have generally worked in some cases (see Bury and Swianiewitz, 2005; Bury, 2006). An additional problem that local governments still encounter in transitional countries is the relatively low level of civil engagement and civic activism. It is still relatively rare to have informal pressure groups formed or have a high level of citizens' involvement. Somehow it is still 'delegated' to the elected representatives and other professional politicians. Despite the efforts to strengthen civil society, it is still questionable to what extent the civil society structures are fully operational, although formally they may be there and intertwining with all the different strata of the society. The creation of a network of civil organisations at the national level generally improves the overall capacity of the society, although it does not guarantee that the organisations will be able to exercise the influence at the level normally expected from their Western counterparts.

Non-governmental organisations (NGOs) are still indirectly financed by the government, although they are covered by the veil of programme funding, as they formally apply with proposals of importance for the wider community and then the local government bodies fund them. However, the relatively lower level of economic development in transitional countries in general prevents philanthropy and investment in good causes by those who have accumulated sizable wealth. Similarly, although the very concept of the community may be alive and well, it is not really a priority of societal development, as more classical institutional issues are addressed. As money follows the decentralisation, it is expected that in the future local governments in CEECs will increasingly take into consideration the view of residents and their formal organisation and informal groups, in the attempt to strengthen the community and various strata of that community.

This book generally focuses on the finance (and financing) of the transitional local governments in CEECs. Transition has taken almost two decades by now, and many prominent scholars, who earned their reputation researching and writing on transition in former Eastern bloc countries, are posing the question as to whether it is over. Some countries, especially those that joined the European Union (EU) in May 2004, are now by some criteria developed countries, which have been admitted into the membership of the OECD, which generally shows that they have graduated from the group of transitional countries. However, the reform still faces the countries of the Balkans (albeit they are moving ahead well) and countries of the former Soviet Union (fSU). The process in the former is slow, and many of those countries are largely at the stage in which CEECs were in the very early 1990s. Amongst Eastern European countries covered in this book (Belarus, Moldova and Ukraine) we have recorded amazing differences. Whilst Belarus and Moldova are lagging somewhat, Ukraine is steaming ahead relatively well, especially following the Orange revolution. But, there are still many, both in the East and West, who may question whether decentralisation really delivers.

DECENTRALISATION: FASHION OR NEED?

Decentralisation has attracted a lot of attention in various fields of social sciences. It can be studied from the political science/public policy, economics, finance and financial management, organisation science, sociological, and so on point of view. All those approaches are equally legitimate and useful in understanding both the underlying logic and technicalities of decentralisation in various jurisdictions. In a very narrow sense decentralisation usually is reduced to empowering the local government at the expense of central government. In the case of a federal country, decentralisation is even more complicated, as often people question how the federations were built (from the top down or from the bottom up, see Šević, 2002). Sometimes the federal unit may in fact be the bearers of sovereignty and the federation is only powerful to the extent the federal units want it to be (for instance, the case of the former Yugoslav federation), so there is a presumption that historically the federal units have surrendered their right to the federal state and the federal state bears the sovereignty on behalf of the nation. This current parlance is certainly in line with the still dominant concept of the nation state, developed in the 19th century. How the future developments of social networking will influence this concept is still to be seen and tested. Certainly, the issues of international collaboration of the states and voluntary surrender of sovereignty because of mutually reaped benefits opens the question of the sustainability of the current nation state sovereignty concept (see Colombatto and Macey, 1996).

As we have already said, there is no unique and prescribed model of decentralisation. Often international and national donor agencies promote a particular model that has worked in some countries and on some continents, believing that it would survive the test of a new environment and new time. Often it may work in the short run, but the neglect of locally induced differences in the long run creates an unstable system. The very process of decentralisation is perceived as the transfer of the central state (national government) responsibilities to sub-national levels of government and their agencies, or even other entities (including more recently private interests). The classical theory would consider only the transfer of functions from the central to sub-national government (regional, local) as decentralisation, whilst more recently we would consider any relinquishing of the functions by the central government as a sign of decentralisation. Also, modern approaches to decentralisation would emphasise the transfer ultimately to citizens (citizenry) or to the bodies close to them (or at least closer than the central government, itself).

Decentralisation may take a number of forms. We still consider deconcentration, delegation and devolution as the main forms of governance decentralisation.

Deconcentration is in fact administrative decentralisation as the central bureaucracy is simply moved from the centre and the discharge of the functions is done through regional centres and/or branches of central government bodies (ministries, department, agencies, and so on). The decision-making process is still both initiated and completed at the central level, only the delivery is somewhat decentralised – physically. Delegation entails a higher level of decentralisation than deconcentration, as the functions of central government, that is, central government bodies, are willingly transferred to sub-national governments, their bodies, or even non-governmental organisations (NGOs), private companies and other private interests (citizens' associations, for instance). Delegation can even work at the central government level, when for instance some powers are given to semi-dependent government agencies, with clear targets to meet. Political delegation (empowerment of professionals by politicians) is increasingly a very favoured option as this generally allows those agencies to be free from daily political pressures on one hand and on the other allows the politicians the latitude of stating that the professionals have made a mistake, and they were there only to do an ultimate check-up (see Strøm et al., 2003). Finally, decentralisation may take the form of devolution. In this case the decentralisation is more or less complete and both administrative and decision-making powers are given to an organisation outside the central government. The sub-national government that has enjoyed the benefits of devolution will have the full rights to make decisions on the service, with or without some central government guidance. Devolution assumes, in financial terms, precisely defined fiscal authority and the capacity of the sub-national government to raise the funds to support the jurisdiction that has been acquired.

Decentralisation usually delivers because the point of service is closer to the citizens (ultimate users). Often local government is regarded as being the epitome of devolution, as usually the narrow portfolio of local government rights and duties is more or less exclusive. However, it may not be the case in reality. The classical model of looking at the central–peripheral (national vs. local government level) endorses fully the neo-classical principal–agent theory. Sub-national governments are agents of central government and it is the feature that dominates the relationship. This may be a very mechanistic and efficient model of the relationship, but it does not depict the reality at all. In fact, central government may (and should) have certain supervisory powers, but in many instances these supervisory powers would entitle the central government to lead by example and ensure cross-national consistency on various issues. The modern decentralised model of the relationship between the central (national) government and local governments would be that of partnership, rather than classical hierarchy. Different levels of government may find it beneficial to pool their resources and tackle the common problem in a co-operative manner. *Coterminosity* allows the 'partners' to define their mutual priorities, pool resources and deploy them in a manner that would ensure the best return on the investment, with a full consideration for various priorities that face both sides.

Central government may have some supervisory power, as we have pointed out, but sub-national government should not and is not to be seen as an extension of the central government and to be fully dependent on the central government's grace and favour behaviour. In fact, sub-national, that is primary local government, is usually a constitutional category and therefore the basic rights of local governments are established in the constitution (basic law) and cannot be, under normal conditions, affected by any action of the central government that is motivated by the political opportunism and expediency of the political needs of the day. However, through the fine-tuning mechanisms of coordination and supervision the central government often can influence the behaviour of the local governments. For instance, in the UK *a priori* targeting and performance expectations and *a posteriori* audit will largely invoke complacent behaviour by local governments, as they would not be red-circled as underperformers (see Šević, 2007).

The main problem with decentralisation is the still prevalent thought that local government is largely a result of decentralisation and not a layer of government in its own right and with its own focus, that usually should not affect the abilities of the central government to lead the country (effectively, if we may add). Often the arguments of macroeconomic stability, that is, the threat of macroeconomic imbalances due to the lack of local governments' own fiscal capacity, are put forward whenever the local governments are to be given more powers. This argument may hold, mainly in remote, borderline and far remote municipalities in the transitional economies, but then the question arises as to why the central government has not done enough to increase the capacity and self-sustainability of those local governments. If sustainability cannot arise locally, then through the grant transfers and equalisation measures (active government redistribution, financial policy) can this aim be relatively easily and cheaply achieved? And, many central governments are uneasy to be asked this question, let alone to be in a position to answer it satisfactorily.

However, this is just one side of the problem. In our view, the major problem is really to work on the creation of a true civic society, which proactively engages in the full range of the political processes. With the development of the full range of NGOs and societal/pressure groups, processes that promote transparency and allow citizens to be heard and influence the quality of life at the local level, one may expect that the local governance as such will be more engaging and the bodies of local government be in a position to clearly demonstrate the full ability to engage with citizens and through innovative partnerships and collaborations ensure that the local affairs are managed effectively and to the prevalent satisfaction of all sides concerned: local communities, citizenry, central government and the local government itself. Initial development of the civil society in CEECs has been triggered primarily by the international organisations and donor agencies, although there were some actions taken originally by the various alternative social groupings. With the development of think tanks and a full range of NGOs, the initial preconditions for an effective civil society have been met. In the last, almost two decades, the civil society has developed significantly, but there are still differences between the countries in the region. As a rule, the more advanced the country, with better results in both political and economic transition, the better developed is the third sector and the civil society as a whole.

With further development of all the range of civil society activities and engagements and the methods that will ensure rationality in the size, and promote the efficiency and effectiveness of the local government; the more local governments will be equipped to act as a layer of government on their own, not just an extension of the central government and closely tutored by the latter. In the condition of clearly marked turfs one may only talk about the fiscal abilities and fiscal capacities of local governments and financial management of local finance (revenues and expenditures) may make sense. Deconcentration and delegation that does not underline the fiscal capacity and abilities of local governments can only be an intermittent phase in the modern government's policies and practices.

SOURCES OF LOCAL FINANCE (REVENUES)

Local governments generally have limited fiscal capacity as the imposition and collection of taxes, in the final instance, is still a prerogative of the national, that is central, government. Even if the local government may impose taxes, this is within the limits set out by the law, enacted by the national parliament. Even if the local community may decide on a referendum to impose local contributions for a major capital project, in many countries, especially in the Balkans, these revenues are considered revenues of the budget and, even more, are rarely earmarked for the project. The total amount collected may be spent on a capital project (water or sewage system building and/or improvement, for instance), but it may not necessarily mean that the revenues as such will be earmarked. In the literature these voluntarily imposed contributions may often be called 'betterment levies' (see Council of Europe, 1997), but the process of imposing these two is different. In the former case the local referendum is usually held and the majority decision imposed, whilst in the latter case the local government itself imposes the levy, which will be used for the improvement of a publicly supplied service (infrastructure improvement).

The sources of local government finance are local taxes, transfer grants, user charges and fees, loans (borrowed finance) and other sources (privatisation, revenue from property ownership, ownership of enterprises, and so on). In Western Europe local taxes have played an important role (see Boorsma, 2006), in contrast to the North American experience where user charges and fees are in much wider use and their relative importance for local government budgets is higher (see Amborski, 2006). In CEECs the government transfers are still the dominant source of finance and the other sources are still to be explored in more depth.

In defining the fiscal relationship between the central government and sub-national governments one should take into consideration a set of principles, such as: *autonomy*, where the sub-national governments enjoy full independence and flexibility in setting their own priorities; *revenue adequacy*, where sub-national governments should be given all the necessary revenues to delivery their duties; *equity*, where funds should vary directly with fiscal need and inversely with the taxable capacity of each sub-national government unit; *predictability*, where grant formulae/mechanism should be known to all sub-national governments, so that they can plan their grant income with a high level of confidence; *efficiency*, where grant design should be neutral with respect to the choices of resource allocation by the sub-national/local government; *simplicity*, where the sub-national government's allocation should be based on objective factors and not political expediency; *underlined by an incentive system*, where sub-national governments should be provided with an incentive to practice sound financial management and inefficient practices are widely discouraged, and finally it is necessary to *safeguard a grantor's objectives* – meaning that the system design should ensure that well-defined principle values and objectives of the grantor are communicated down effectively to the grant recipients (see Shah, 1994). A well-designed grant transfer system has to reduce regional disparities (through fiscal equalisation programmes), compensate for benefit spillovers, set national minimum standards (benchmarks) and influence local priorities in areas of high national but generally low local importance/priority. Finally it should not have a destabilising influence on the national economy, through, for instance limiting the use of capital grants and encouraging private sector participation – public–private partnership (PPP). It should offer clear political guidance, a sound legal framework and good risk management backup to sub-national (local) governments (see World Bank, 1997).

Grants generally fit into two groups: specific and general grants. Specific grants are earmarked for special purposes or projects, whilst the general grants support the sub-national government without any conditions imposed. Specific grants can also be fairly wide or narrow, depending on the extent of the conditionality imposed. The wider specific grant may still leave some latitude to the sub-national government in spending it. The European Charter of Local Self-Government (Art. 9) recommends the use of general grants whenever it is possible. General grants give more freedom to the sub-national governments and also force them to be more proactive and to account for spending to both the general public (voters) and also central audit bodies (usually through a national public audit institution or another similar body). Specific grants are given in situations where sub-national (local) government acts primarily as an agent for the central authority, or where central government would like a local government to provide some services to non-residents or simply when local (sub-national) government has to achieve and attain the minimum level of service as set out by the central government (nationally). Generally, in all situations, the central government (as a grantor) generally expects some kind of desired behaviour demonstrated by a sub-national government. In order to achieve that, some conditions are attached to the use of resources transferred from the centre.

In the situations where specific grants are used, the central government may decide to use a light touch in controlling the use of resources. It could, for instance, assume that the local governments interested in attaining a high level of efficiency and effectiveness when using the earmarked central government resources. In fact, if a sub-national government unit is effective and efficient anyway, it will demonstrate the same level of care when acting as an agent on behalf of the central government. Often central governments in CEECs will opt for special purpose grants, claiming that they are easier to monitor and that the local governments are more responsible with the resources given to them under special conditions. However, this may be a somewhat false claim. We see this more as a lack of capacity on the part of local governments and failure by the central government to promote good practices (if not the best practices) nationally. Increasingly the central/national governments will consider the introduction of matching grants, where some (usually initial) funding will be provided (earmarked) by the central government and the rest will have to be provided by the sub-national (local) government. This practice is generally very good, as it increases interest in the success of the project by the local governments. The only problem is that this model may be just a show-off, if the local (sub-national) governments are not financially sound and do not have other sources of revenues which allow them to participate in the matching grant exercise. When the conditional grants are used, the grantor imposes the minimum standards upon the grantee, and it is widely used practice in CEECs. The minimum levels have to be enforced, but quite often the central government does not have any other alternative than to offer the service directly, at much higher prices. So, the issue of value-for-money certainly pops up. Minimum standards (of service) are there to ensure the same level of service nationally, allow people to be mobile and enjoy the level of service wherever they may go, and finally to ensure that the minorities are protected, especially when economic reasons would induce the local government to stop offering the service. However, often guidelines (instructions) issued linked with (national) benchmarking exercises may be more effective. The local governments would be asked to meet certain conditions in providing a service, which generally should immediately put them above the minimum threshold. Usually, targeting the minimum, or ensuring that the minimum is surpassed, may lead to undershooting and the failure to meet minimum standards (see Šević, 2003). However, if the service is crucial for the welfare of the population, stating publicly what the minimum standards are may be not only desired, but also required. Supervision and control in the case of special grants is, as a rule, robust. Nevertheless, CEE has shown that the central government does not often have enough instruments to interfere if the delivery of service has not ceased totally.

General grants are used more often in European countries, both in the East and in the West. General or block grants allow the central government to address the issues of imbalances (both horizontal and vertical). Vertical imbalances appear when the local government realises that with the current revenues they cannot provide the desired (or generally expected) level of services. Horizontal imbalances appear between two bodies of sub-national government at the same level. Namely, they may realise that the provision of the service as the same level may require, in fact, the application of different tax rates. Central government may react in the latter case and decide to subsidise the local government more in areas where there is a problem to raise enough local revenues to offer the (reasonably) expected level of (public) service. The latter option involving the central government is somehow (and not surprisingly) favoured in CEECs. The equalisation grants generally create a lot of problems, as the methodologies are often challenged by the local governments that are usually dissatisfied with the models offered, and require more funding to meet all the expectations in terms of the volume and quality of services to be rendered. The validity of the models offered (and they differ widely between various CEECs) can be challenged, but the most important feature is stability, which enables the sub-national level governments to plan, more or less confidently, revenues from grant transfers.

User fees and charges are another source of local government finance. This class of local public revenues is still relatively negligible, as up to 5 per cent of the local budgets may come from this source and, despite the topicality of the problem, their relative importance remains stable. Charges and fees have their particular appeal to politicians as they can replace taxes and citizens (voters) are ostensibly happier to pay for a defined service whose benefits (to them) they can immediately feel/see. Theory distinguishes between 'real charges' and 'quasi-charges'. When one enjoys the former he or she can see the benefits to him/her, whilst in the case of quasi-charges an individual will make a payment based on a particular formula which is not directly linked to the perceived benefits that he/she has enjoyed. From an economic point of view charges are attractive as they clearly eliminate the fee-on-margin concept that often is associated with general tax funded provision of public services. It also increases the discipline and rationality of the users. User charges also address the problem of false equality. The heavy users will have to pay more, while the lighter users will pay less, according to their usage levels. If the users belong to the group that is particularly vulnerable, there is always an option for price discrimination and support through social transfers. However, the move to quasi-charges to address the problem of dis-privileged groups maybe a gross error. Namely, quasi-charges may stimulate even further inefficient behaviour as the charge is defined in a rather generalist manner that does not link the charge and the usage level (for instance, electricity rate based on the size of the building, and so on).

A problem with the charges can be that they are attractive in principle, but then that they may under-deliver when linked with the monopolistic situation, which is often the case with the provision of public services. Charges that are linked with the real (full economic) cost are welcome here, but often the price is between marginal and average costs. Also, if the service is provided by a private entity or independent/semi-dependent company it is more than fair to cover the losses experienced and ensure that the company has not sunk due to the fact that it provided a service under unfavourable conditions. Regardless of who provides the service (local government itself, local government owned company, private contractor, joint owned company, and so on) the level of charges is to be controlled by the external body, and any change in charges should secure prior approval from the local government and/or other regulatory body overseeing the provision of particular services (postal regulator, gas regulator, electricity regulator, and so on).

Although some services are not suitable for user charges (defence, foreign affairs, public safety, and so on), there may be enough space to look at the provision problem more innovatively. For instance, the organisers of public events may want higher police presence, and if this was the case, they would have been obliged to pay a particular fee for the qualified and tailor-made security arrangement surrounding a big public event. Often football clubs pay additional fees to the police force to increase their presence at sport events. Similarly, one may consider the introduction of charges for the use of very popular and hence overcrowded roads, as London has done with the congestion charge for entering central London with a vehicle on work days, and so on. CEE experience with user charges is still limited, but growing. Currently in all the countries charges are used for the issuance of civic documents (birth, marriages, travel documents, personal identity documents, and so on), and for the services provided by the local authorities. In many cases the charges imposed centrally will remain in the budgets of the municipalities. But, overall, charges are still a negligible source of income for both central and local governments in all the countries. Certainly both Eastern and Western Europe can learn from North America how to utilise more the user charges and fees in securing sustainable public revenues for local governments. Interestingly, it seems that user charges and fees are often regarded as genuine local government income, so very rarely will the central government interfere, even under the pretence of securing the macroeconomic stability of the country (as they may do when the local taxes are imposed, or the local government applies for a permit to raise the funds in open market).

Local taxes have traditionally been favoured as a continental European mode of funding local government (see, for instance, Boorsma, 2006). It is of utmost importance to ensure that there is a good balance between taxes and grants, as the extensive use of grants can easily stifle initiative at the local level. The basic rule is to use the local taxes for financing locally provided services, and not to fund services that should be provided by the central government. As a rule, local politicians and local servants are more careful with funds that they have raised and feel accountable for directly to the electorate. In contrast, grants come from the central budget and the accountability relationship is different.

Local governments, as a rule, should be given the powers to change tax rates. Some limits may be imposed by the national legislator, but the final say within the band should be given by the local government. Equally, if the tax rates are centrally imposed the local governments may not really see those taxes as their own revenue, but rather an implicit transfer from the central government and it can, further, adversely affect their behaviour and ultimately the quality of service they provide to the local population. Genuinely determined local taxes also influence positively the behaviour of the local governments when it comes to collection. Practice has shown that, usually, the collection rates are comparatively higher if the local tax rates are determined locally.

Beside local taxes, there is a possibility to develop a tax sharing model, where the percentage of (usually) centrally collected taxes in a given territory is given to the local government. A tax sharing model can be devised for all levels of sub-national government where a certain percentage is retained by the central government, a similar or smaller percentage given to the regional/state government and finally the smallest percentage given to the local government. However, to be precise, this model of sharing revenues between three different levels of government usually works rather well with federal states, whilst often regional governments (if they exist) are the result, in CEECs, of either deconcentration or collaboration of local governments.

In the tax sharing model the local governments do not have a say about the rates. Also, it may favour the local governments that are in urban areas and have a significant presence of industry (especially headquarters of nationally and internationally renowned companies). In contrast the local governments in remote and least developed parts of the country may still depend largely upon the grant transfers and equalisation policies pursued by the central government. When the legislator considers allowing the local taxes and setting the framework for rates (directly or indirectly) it may consider a few features of a good local taxation model/policy. First of all, the high yield taxes should be considered when deciding on local taxes. Secondly, the local taxes should exercise even more than central taxes the qualities of low administration and compliance costs. Thirdly, the local taxes should demonstrate fairly low distortions and consequently should not lead to the eventual 'tax-flights'. Interestingly, in CEECs probably still due to the fact that the central government has a strong say when it comes to local tax rates, there is very little local tax competition. In fact, in some countries (notably Serbia) there is less local tax competition nowadays, than 20 years ago in the socialist times. As the former Yugoslavia was a highly decentralised federation, local governments have enjoyed unprecedented powers that some authors have been fairly surprised to discover (see, for instance, Meekel, 2004). Finally, the local taxes should promote efficient spending levels (see Council of Europe, 1997).

The range of local taxes is fairly limited. Local governments are usually allowed to levy taxes on property (real estate) and local income, although in the latter case it is often a shared tax model. Tax on trade, household taxes and company taxes may feature in some countries, but fairly rarely in CEECs, expect Hungary. Compared to other CEECs Hungary has used the fullest range of locally imposed taxes. And, it has worked rather well (see Davey and Peteri, 2006).

Revenues of local governments are in the best shape when they are balanced. Usually local taxes and grants will be most widely represented. However, one should not overlook the income from other sources. In CEECs both the central and local governments have enjoyed significant revenues from privatisation of state-owned assets, and in most countries these revenues were earmarked for capital/infrastructure investment. Also, some local governments may have sizeable stakes in commercial companies, and not necessarily only those delivering local public or quasi-public services. In those cases, the revenues may be considerable. Equally, other revenues from property may be a reasonible portion of revenues. It is important for a local government to ensure that the stream of revenues is ongoing in order to guarantee financial viability and uninterrupted provision of local services. To achieve this it is not only necessary to have an effective revenue model, but also to balance revenues with expenditures and ensure effective financial management.

LOCAL GOVERNMENT EXPENDITURES

Public finance theory generally is more concerned with the revenue side of the financial balance rather than with the expenditures (see, for instance, Foster, Jackman and Perlman, 1980). This is particularly the case with capital expenditure, understood generally as expenditure that yields a stream of future benefits. In CEECs capital expenditures have traditionally been linked with the characteristics of physical assets, although it may be argued that expenditure in education, for instance, may generate future benefits (see Musgrave, 1959; Jones and Pendlebury, 1996). Local government expenditures are driven by the legislative framework at least equally if not more than local revenues. Formally, local governments have fairly significant latitude when it comes to spending and setting the priorities, but *de facto*, they are driven in their decision making by the environment in which they are to operate. Central government is still there and may decide to inspect the efficiency and effectiveness of the use of allocated resources.

The structure of local government expenditures has changed over time, and changed significantly. It has been duly noted that the composition of services provided by local government has changed markedly over the last 30–35 years, and local government is 'increasingly providing human services (social welfare-type services) at the expense of its traditional property-based services (particularly roads)' (Australian Government, 2002, p. 102). Expenditure may also be linked with the particular revenue. For instance, specific grants are quite often earmarked for a particular infrastructure building project and, therefore, will be reported as capital expenditure. General grants as such are usually given to match operating/current expenditures. The general rule is that often the revenues of local governments are primarily used to finance current expenditures.

Allocation of expenditures will be correspondent with the legal powers and duties of local government. Some of the local services may be entirely in the jurisdiction of the local government, whilst in other cases local government may have shared jurisdiction with the central government. In a number of countries there is shared financial responsibility for, for instance, primary education. The central government will cover the costs of personnel (salaries, pensions and related costs), whilst the local government will take care of maintaining the building and ensuring that the costs of school operations are met. However, again, the central government in these models usually decides to set the threshold criteria and defines clearly what level of attainment local governments are expected to demonstrate in order to be deemed successful (meeting national standards). The range of services and practices varies largely from country to country. In some countries, local governments will be responsible for local safety (so-called 'city police'), whilst in others public safety will be linked with the sovereignty and consequently be in the exclusive powers of the central government. Increasingly, decentralisation literature argues that health should also be decentralised to the local level and in many transitional countries this has been the case, or they are in the process of change with an aim to decentralise the health services. Although the *subsidiarity principle* may be used to argue in favour of health decentralisation, the equality argument may still be used to justify a centralised approach to health. In general, every citizen should enjoy rights on health and, therefore, the quality of the health service should be unified throughout the country and should not be dependent on the region and/or municipality.

Local governments are usually charged with the provision of local communal services, some social, education, cultural and sport services, and a range of administrative services that relate usually to the civil status of citizens. Usually communal service expenditures are at least partially covered by user charges and fees imposed upon the users. It may be the case that every separate service is billed separately, or simply there is a summary charge based on some indicators. In the vast majority of cases the local governments in CEECs would establish a publicly owned company to supply communal services and therefore the revenues from charges and expenditures for the provision of the services will not be planned in the budget and will not, consequently, be reported in the annual financial report. Social, educational, cultural and sport functions will usually be directly financed from the budget and the corresponding budget lines will be planned and they should appear in the annual financial report, as well.

Again, the models of financing differ from country to country. Pre-school (early childhood) education is usually entrusted to local governments, but then, in some Western countries, the duties can be shared between national, regional and local authorities (see Šević Andrek, 2007). With the decentralisation seen as devolution, more and more social sphere duties will be entrusted to the local government, assuming that the local government where the power distance between the government and citizens is smaller may be much better at delivering services of this kind. In the modern model of inter-government relationships where local government is perceived as another layer of government with its own rights, the partnership model is more appropriate and co-financing of activities may be envisaged. Therefore, one layer of government may resume responsibility for particular aspects of the service, whilst the other may be more operationally involved on behalf of both. Certainly, this is something that merits further exploration, as theory still lacks the full focus on this emerging model.

In modern times local governments are also increasingly asked to consider the partnership with the private sector. Sector-wide modernisation efforts that seek additional room for controlling expenditures and look for cost-rationalising options, push both central and local governments to seek solutions that would bring investments from the private sector and would at the same time benefit the public. In some countries, going private, however, did not materialise in much saving (Šević, 2005a). In fact, the local governments were forced to resume offering the service themselves at the higher cost. However, in the CEECs the public–private partnership is still in its relatively nascent phase, and the local governments directly manage the delivery of services. Therefore, it is most unlikely that we will see significant change on the expenditure side when it comes to local government finance.

MODERNISATION AND FINANCIAL MANAGEMENT IN LOCAL GOVERNMENT

The last decade (or two) of the 20th and the first decade of the 21st century have been marked by a constant search for efficiency and effectiveness at all levels of government. Government has grown in size and has taken a sizeable portion of the national GDP. In order not to stifle economic growth and affect economic development, governments had to look for alternatives and ensure that public spending is under control. Government had to be 'reinvented' and de-bureaucratised, cutting down on red tape whenever and wherever possible. In the West, New Public Management (NPM) has become something of a fashion, and it has simply rolled over to the East with the Western consultants engaged in the public sector restructuring in the early 1990s. Although it may be agreed that NPM has influenced thinking and practice in CEECs there is no final account of the implementation of NPM doctrine in the region, although in each and every country one may find a publication in the style of a manual on NPM and its reach in public sector redesign. One of the last was published in Serbia a year after the regime of Slobodan Milosevic was toppled in October 2000, following the 'Bulldozer Revolution' (see Gordy, 2000; Hood, 1991). There are no accounts that CEECs have tried to develop their own NPM model, as often in reviews of literature authors claim that NPM is very much a nationally coloured model (Hood, 1991).

The change that NPM brought to the 'old public administration' model was not only in the methodology applied, based upon 'borrowing' from the private sector, but also an introduction of strategic concepts and accountability models into public management. Decentralisation meant that each government unit would be led by a manager who would be accountable and, therefore, his or her performance would be reported on and he or she judged on that. Goals, aims and objectives were to be clearly stated and made quantifiable, so that the mission-driven government could be imposed and the separation of strategic planning and operational execution could be made. The public sector re-focused from a focus on 'the procedure' to 'the results' (management by results). The monolithic structure of the government was replaced by a decentralised organisation, based on the structure of holding. The delineation between 'core' and 'other' functions of the state opened the window of possibility to 'source out' some functions or 'source in', taking into consideration the market situation. The highly hierarchical, military-like structure was replaced by a business-like structure (salaries based on merit, replacing Senior Civil Servants with managers, and so on), which promoted a lean-management model. However, NPM has evolved today far beyond these common characteristics. In different countries around the world, the term NPM has fairly diverse meanings and definitions. Probably, the vast mimicking of business practices by and within the public sector remained as the main (if not the only) common denominator.

The NPM is heavily concerned with the constant decreasing in costs of a 'product' and getting 'the best value for money'. The underlying feature of an NPM model is room for the implementation of a performance measurement/management system. All seven mentioned principles of public management (Hood, 1991) are *performance centred*, and without the performance management it would have been very difficult to justify the major change in the public sector. The difficulties of NPM can be focused on from two conflicting perspectives; namely, the performance measurement systems can be a logical consequence of NPM being implemented or, in fact, NPM can be a result of 'obsession' with performance measurement. In our view, it is possible that both explanations work. In a highly hierarchical organisation there is resistance to change. A formal introduction of a new model is necessary to ignite the change. In our view this is the case with the continental European models of civil service, where the extent of the public sector is wide and the hierarchy is predominant. But, anyway, introducing performance measurement/management initiates further changes.

NPM doctrine has focused on more proactive financial management in the public sector. Although it has primarily targeted the central government it has rolled down to the local government as well (Šević, 2004). Local government has to ensure that it operates under a balanced budget. In CEECs this has been a challenging task, due to years of soft-budget constraint conditions, which led to a position of no or very little budget discipline. In theory, local government can always be bailed out by the central government. Lawyers will claim that theoretically the government cannot go bankrupt (as a sovereign power), whilst economists would claim that it may in fact be possible and that the government can easily go bankrupt. In practice the central government can force local government to be more fiscally responsible and observe nationally imposed limits. Financial management in new conditions involves active treasury management, as local governments may consider different options to fund different projects, appear on capital markets and raise funds through borrowing. Also, if surpluses are recorded then they can be invested in capital markets. In fact, local government bodies may act as ordinary business entities in maximising their current financial (cash) position. However, the organisation of financial management function can be an obstacle. It is possible for a local government to have its own finance department and do all the necessary accounting and financial operations for itself, or the function can be centralised, either in a detachment of the Ministry of Finance (MoF), or in a unit that has been created by a few local governments to pool resources. In both cases there is some level of centralisation and often some of the opportunities which may be seized if the local government had its own finance unit, would be missed.

Similarly, the problem appears with single treasury accounts. If there is a single treasury account and all the public bodies have to conduct business through the Treasury, then the innovativeness and proactiveness of the financial management function may be stifled. It has been a fact that the USAID advisers have very strongly pushed towards a single treasury account, and at least in the early stages of transition all the countries have endorsed that solution. It is interesting to notice that in the Balkans USAID has pushed for a single treasury account, at the same time that it was advising against Payment System Administration (a payment clearing house from the socialist time) on the account that it was a quasi-fiscal, controlling organisation. In our view, it is necessary to decentralise the financial function and ensure that it is done in-house whenever it is possible. In some CEECs where municipalities are fairly small (the Baltic states, some Balkan states) it may be not justifiable to have separate financial units, but in an average municipality this should not be a problem, just an issue of capacity building.

Active treasury management by the local governments assumes that they would look for alternative sources of funds, borrow, lend and seek other opportunities to employ the funds effectively. However, one should take into consideration that *over-businessation* of the local government may lead to highly risky exposures that may not be justifiable and acceptable for public sector bodies. Including risk analysis in the decision making in local governments is something that has to be emphasised in the conditions of proactive financial management practices. Basic rule of thumb requires that only capital projects are financed by borrowed funds, whilst operating expenses must be covered from the 'real' sources. Borrowed money should not and must not be used for financing the structural deficit and payment in arrears.

The introduction, existing or pending, of accrual accounting should generally deliver a better picture of the financial position ('health') of local government bodies. Developing a concept of '*whole government accounting*' (as in the UK) would certainly lead to a change in the existing financial practices and would result in more responsive and focused local government bodies, with clear bills of (financial) health. Central government still may influence the behaviour of sub-national (local) governments through performance targeting and/or later performance audit. Performance audit still does not operate in CEECs, but under the influence of international trends it is likely that the post-performance audits would take place in the foreseeable future.

Despite the capacity-building efforts at the local government level, it seems to us that more work is required in order to raise the abilities of local government units to be better financially managed and have the ability to take care of their financial health themselves. Instructions and guidelines from the MoF may help, but should not replace the latitude that decentralised financial decision making normally gives.

CONCLUSION AND ORGANISATION OF THIS VOLUME

Local government finance in CEECs has been still a fairly non-researched area, despite the efforts that have been made until now (see Horváth, 2000; Kandeva, 2001). The World Bank Group, Local Government and Public Services Initiative (LGI) at the Open Society Budapest have made significant efforts to develop awareness about decentralisation, including fiscal decentralisation. Their efforts as such cannot be omitted in any assessment of scholarly and professional work devoted to decentralisation in CEECs. Decentralisation has been a very fashionable trend since the first day of transition. First of all, one considered economic decentralisation (dismantling central planning bodies and communication links) and later the decentralisation rolled over into the public sector. Decentralisation was initially largely seen (through rather ideological eyes) as an instrument for weakening the (highly centralised) socialist state. But, after almost two decades of transition experience, one may really question this dominant paradigm. Was the socialist state really that much centralised, especially those that had federal or quasi-federal organisational arrangements in place? It seems to us that the centralist nature of a socialist state has been somewhat overplayed within the concept of the neo-classical paradigm (where institutions do not pay the role, at all).

Often decentralisation was not accompanied or followed immediately by fiscal decentralisation. Consequently, local governments have initially had problems delivering the services and meeting the expectations of the local electorate. Therefore, often scholars have recorded the indolent behaviour of local governments which really were not seeking more funds through decentralisation, but rather would like to have central government providing most of the services (like in the socialist times). However, this kind of behaviour can be found rarely nowadays, in advanced phases of transition. It seems to us that currently there is a good balance between the rights and duties of local governments, and that local governments may finally emerge as a genuine independent layer of government, and not a just local extension of the nationally sovereign central government. The governance models that promote the community and sense of *communitarianism* would certainly strengthen the case for more independent local government, where rights will fully match the duties.

Local governments have to be empowered to impose local taxes and ensure in that way the quality of service that their citizens expect. Practice in transitional countries has shown a specific phenomenon. Namely, it is difficult for the local population to expect a level of service if the system as such is failing, and in the early stages of transition this is what was in fact happening and still may be found in some of the Balkan countries. Grants are still the major source of revenues for local governments, clearly showing that the central government influence over the local governments is still omnipotent. A move towards local taxes and user charges and fees (above the current approximately 5 per cent) would strengthen the case for local government fiscal independence and would certainly change the way local government behaves. In our view, the future of local government in the times of increased (or ever-increasing) accountability, search for excellence and cheaper modes of delivery of public and/or quasi-public service is in proper devolution. The central government should and will, most likely, retain only its sovereign right, whilst most of the other duties will be moved to local (sub-national) government level. And, this trend cannot be reversed – the powers are to be given back to communities (see Tullock, 1991).

This volume comprises 19 chapters analysing local government finance in respective CEECs. Authors have followed the common research protocol and have tried to deal with the issues facing the particular country in a rather uniform way. Endorsing the research protocol enables a reader to compare solutions in various counties and to make comparative conclusions. Authors have tried not only to present the legislative framework for local government and local government finance, but also to give a fairly critical account of the current developments in those areas. In our view they have succeeded, splendidly. Authors are mainly members of the Working Group on Public Sector Finance and Accounting at the Network of Institutes and Schools of Public Administration in Central and Eastern Europe (NISPAcee) and they have worked jointly on a number of projects. The Group has produced a number of books, edited by the editor of this volume, which tackled various burning issues in public sector finance (see: Šević, 2005b; 2006a; 2006b; 2007a), but the Group has never produced a volume that would look at local government finance in CEECs in a more holistic way, bringing together all the issues concerning local finance. We do hope that the book will fill the detected gap in the existing literature and will certainly initiate others to continue researching the fascinating issues of sub-national finance in transitional countries. Central Europe has largely finished its transition, or is in the final phases. Eastern Europe is lagging behind, but one should be realistic and say that it is heading forward with big steps and certainly will introduce modern models fairly soon. This book modestly tries to assess the current situation and give a hint as to how future developments in local government finance in a particular country will eventually burn out.

BIBLIOGRAPHY

Amborski, D. (2006), Applications of Municipal User Charges in Canada: Experience and Implications for Other Jurisdictions, in Ž. Šević, ed., *Local Government Non-Tax Revenue Sources in Transition Countries: User Fees and Charges*, Bratislava: NISPAcee, pp. 29–45.

Australian Government (2002), *Local Government National Report 2000–2001 Report on the Operation of the Local Government (Financial Assistance) Act*, Canberra: Australian Government – Department of Transport and Regional Affairs.

Bahl, R. (2000), *Intergovernmental Transfers in Developing and Transition Countries: Principles and Practice*, Urban and Local Government Paper No. 21097, Washington. DC: The World Bank.

Bird, R.M. and M. Smart (2001), *Intergovernmental Fiscal Transfers: Some Lessons from International Experience*, paper prepared for Symposium on Intergovernmental Transfers in Asian Countries: Issues and Practices, Asian Tax and Public Policy Program, Hitosubashi University, Tokyo, February.

Boorsma, P. (2006), Local Taxes: Why?, in Ž. Šević, ed., *Local Government Non-Tax Revenue Sources in Transition Countries: User Fees and Charges*, Bratislava: NISPAcee, pp. 46–58.

Broadway, R. (1992), *The Constitutional Division of Powers: An Economic Perspective*, Ottawa: Economic Council of Canada.

Bury, P. (2006), Charges in Local Government Services and Budgets in Poland, in Ž. Šević, ed., *Local Government Non-Tax Revenue Sources in Transition Countries: User Fees and Charges*, Bratislava: NISPAcee, pp. 73–83.

Bury, P. and P. Swianiewitz (2005), Grant Transfers in Financing Local Governments in Poland, in Ž. Šević, ed., *Financial Decentralization and Grant Transfers: A Critical Perspective*, Bratislava: NISPAcee, pp. 98–118.

Colombatto, E. and J.R. Macey (1996), A Public Choice Model of International Economic Co-operation and the Decline of the Nation State, *Cardozo Law Review*, **18**(3), pp. 401–32.

Council of Europe (1997), *Local Finance in Europe Report of the Steering Committee on Local and Regional Authorities (CDLR) on Local Finance in Europe*, Strasbourg: Council of Europe Publishing.

Council of Europe (1998), *Limitations of Local Taxation, Financial Equalisation and Methods for Calculating General Grants Report by the Steering Committee on Local and Regional Democracy (CDLR)*, Strasbourg: Council of Europe Publishing.

Davey, K. and G. Peteri (2006), Taxes, Transfers and Transition – Adjusting Local Finances to New Structures and Institutions: The experience of the Czech Republic, Hungary and Slovakia, *Local Government Studies*, **32**(5), 585–98.

Ethisham, A. ed. (1997), *Financing Decentralized Expenditures: An International Comparison of Grants*, Cheltenham, UK and Lyme, USA: Edward Elgar.

Foster, C.D., R.A. Jackman and M. Perlman (1980), *Local Government Finance in a Unitary State*, London: Allen & Unwin.

Ganev, V.I. (2007), *Preying on the State: The Transformation of Bulgaria since 1989*, Ithaca, NY: Cornell University Press.

Gordy, E. (2000), Serbia's Bulldozer Revolution: Conditions and Prospects, *Southeast European Politics*, **1**(2), 78–89.

Hood, C. (1991), A Public Management for All Seasons?, *Public Administration*, **69**, 3–19.

Horváth, T. (2000), *Decentralization: Experiments and Reforms*, Budapest: Open Society Institute – LGI.

Jones, R.H. and M. Pendlebury (1996), *Public Sector Accounting*, 4th edition, London: Pitman.

Kandeva, E. ed. (2001), *Stabilisation of Local Government*, Budapest: Open Society Institute – LGI.

Litvack, J., J. Ahmad and R. Bird (1998), *Rethinking Decentralization in Developing Countries*, Washington, DC: The World Bank.

Meekel, T. (2004), Serbie: comment rebâtir la relation entre l'État et les collectivités locales? [Serbia: How to Rebuild the Relations between the State and the Local Communities?], *Revue des Études Comparatives Est-Ouest*, **35**(1–2), 297–327.

Musgrave, R.A. (1959), *The Theory of Public Finance*, New York: McGraw Hill.

Oates, W. (1972), *Fiscal Federalism*, New York: Harcourt Brace Jovanovich.

Oates, W. (1985), Searching for Leviathan: An Empirical Study, *American Economic Review*, **75**(4), 748–57.

Putnam, R. (1993), *Making Democracy Work: Civic Traditions in Modern Italy*, Princeton: Princeton University Press.

Saint-Martin, D. (2000), *Building the New Managerialist State Consultants and the Politics of Public Sector Reform in Comparative Perspective*, Oxford: Oxford University Press.

Šević Andrek, E. (2007), *Predškolsko obrazovanje u Srbiji i Japanu* [Preschool Education in Serbia and Japan], unpublished PhD thesis, Novi Sad: University of Novi Sad.

Šević, Ž. (2002), Reforming Socialist Federations: Can It Really Work?, in R. Baker (ed.), *Transition from Authoritarianism: The Role of Civil Service*, Greenwich, CT: Greenwood Press, 275–90.

Šević, Ž. ed. (2003), *Gauging Success: Performance Measurement in South Eastern Europe*, Budapest and New York Open Society Institute – LGI.

Šević, Ž. (2004), An Accounting Aspect of the 'New Public Management': Accrual Accounting in the Public Sector, *Journal of Finance and Management in the Public Services*, **4**(1), 51–66.

Šević, Ž. (2005a), Measuring Performance on a Local Government Level in a Transitional Country: The Case of Serbia, *International Journal of Public Sector Management*, **18**(7), 582–603.

Šević, Ž. ed. (2005b), *Financial Decentralization and Grant Transfers: A Critical Perspective*, Bratislava: NISPAcee.

Šević, Ž. ed. (2006a), *Local Government Non-Tax Revenue Sources in Transition Countries: User Fees and Charges*, Bratislava: NISPAcee.

Šević, Ž. ed. (2006b), *Local Government Financial Capacity Building in Transition Countries: Selected Country Studies*, Bratislava: NISPAcee.

Šević, Ž. ed. (2007a), *Debt Management in Transition Countries: Experience and Perspectives*, Bratislava: NISPAcee.

Šević, Ž. (2007b), *The Local Government in a Decentralising State: The Case of the UK*, work in progress.

Shah, A. (1994), *The Reform of Intergovernmental Fiscal Relations in Developing and Emerging Market Economics*, Washington, DC: World Bank.

Silva, J.F. (2001), *Local Finance Reform from a Regional Perspective*, San Francisco: Public Policy Institute of California.
Strøm, K., V. C. Müller, and T. Bergman, eds (2003), *Delegation and Accountability in Parliamentary Democracies*, New York: Oxford University Press.
Ter-Minassin, T. ed. (1997), *Fiscal Federalism in Theory and Practice*, Washington, DC: The International Monetary Fund.
Tullock, G. (1991), *Orgnizacija moderne federalne države* [The Organisation of a Modern Federal State], Belgrade: Economics Institute.
World Bank (1997), *World Development Report 1997: The State in a Changing World*, New York: Oxford University Press for the World Bank.

2. Albania: decentralization and local government finance – key successes and future challenges

Juliana H. Pigey, Artan Hoxha and Sabina Ymeri

INTRODUCTION

Albania, a country with around 3.1 million inhabitants[1] and a GDP of 899.7 billion lek in 2006 (USD8.4 billion total, USD2709 per capita) has recorded an average growth rate of 6 per cent per year in the last decade. The country has implemented several reforms in the area of market economy and governance and is currently implementing its Stabilization and Association Agreement with the European Union.

Albania's decentralization reforms, which have been ongoing since 1999, constitute one of the unheralded successes of the country's transition period. Formerly one of the most isolated countries of Central and Eastern Europe, and having had to undergo wrenching economic, social, legal and administrative changes, Albania's decentralization reform is notable for the specific process it has followed, based on a participatory dialogue and consensus-building approach and fact-based guidance documents to clearly lay out the various policy options and their implications. Decentralization has also constituted the main public policy area in Albania where a consensus of the two main political parties – the Socialist Party and the Democratic Party – has been sustained, although they are in extreme opposition on just about every other issue faced by the country.

This chapter briefly analyses some of the notable changes which have taken place for Albania's local governments since 1999, and particularly for the municipalities and communes which have been the main focus of the decentralization reforms. This analysis does not claim to be exhaustive and the authors have focused on the key issues and challenges. Following a general introduction on the evolution of the decentralization framework, this chapter briefly addresses how citizen participation and accountability have improved. The core results and achievements in fiscal decentralization are illustrated through analysis of the greater autonomy of own revenues, predictability and stability of the transfer system and increased investment capacity of municipalities and communes (M/C). There are still serious challenges to be addressed in the budget process, the transfer of water systems and the urban planning system. Yet the reforms have opened the way to establish creditworthy local governments and soon, a new framework for borrowing will pave the way for increased investment potential.

We would like to stress that the authors of this chapter have been directly and deeply involved in many of these reforms, and since at least 1998 for two of them. They have benefited from a considerable mine of primary and secondary information, much of it unpublished and which has not yet necessarily been introduced into the research and academic circuits.

THE DECENTRALIZATION FRAMEWORK IN ALBANIA

The years of 1991 to 1998 were dominated by central reforms, including the establishment of the basic structures of a democratic system, and the structures of a market economy. The initial legal framework for a local government sector did not clearly define local government functions or the rules for their financing. A basis for a decentralized system with clear areas of authority of regulation of local governments did not exist. Over 95 per cent of local government expenditures (and revenues) were fully conditional and determined in detail by respective line Ministries, down to budget article and chapter. Of the 5 per cent of LG revenues defined in their 'independent budget', they could be used only for operating expenditures or investments and any end of year surplus or unused funds were captured by the central government. A comparative analysis of the situation of Albanian local governments with the text of the European Charter of Local Self-government (ECLSG) concluded that Albania was then in compliance with seven (out of 30) articles, of which four (out of 20) were core articles (Banks and Pigey, 1998).

From 1998, decentralization reform was placed at the top of the Government's priorities. The new Constitution, adopted by referendum in 1998, included clear provisions regarding local government. Albania signed and ratified the ECLSG in 1999. An Inter-ministerial Committee and a Group of Experts for Decentralization (GED) were named to develop a national decentralization strategy. The GED included national, local and civil society officials which, through extensive discussions, on the basis of factual policy guidance, defined Albania's vision for decentralization. The resulting National Strategy for Decentralisation and Local Autonomy, adopted by the Council of Ministers in December 1999, has constituted Albania's road map for decentralization reform over the past 6–7 years.

A key milestone in the second phase of Albania's decentralization reform was the adoption by Parliament on 31 July 2000 of the Law on Organization and Functioning of Local Governments (henceforth referred to as the LG Law). Albanian local governments presently consist of municipalities (65), communes (308) and regions (12). The elected bodies of municipalities and communes (M/C) – the council and the mayor – are elected every four years.[2] The council of the M/C is elected based on a proportional system, while the mayor is elected based on a majority system. The council of the region is composed by mayors of each M/C of that region and from councillors of each M/C in a proportional number to the respective size of population. The council of the M/C has normative and legislative powers; whereas the mayors have executive powers.

National territorial structures include twelve Prefects, one in each Region, representing the authority of the central government in the territory, and territorial branches of some line Ministries. Prefects carry out legal compliance review of acts and regulations adopted by the municipalities, communes and regions – in case of question for legality and disagreement between the Prefect and the respective local council, the Prefect cannot impede implementation but must send the case to court.

The LG Law defines local government functions as own, shared and delegated. Own local government functions are those over which municipalities and communes enjoy full decision-making authority, defined in the law as full administrative, service, regulatory and investment authority; these areas include basic local public services, such as solid waste, roads, public areas and parks, public lighting, water/wastewater, local economic development, local culture and sports. The law included transitional provisions to guide the transfer of some of the key functions (particularly in the area of water and wastewater management). However the timeline has proven to be quite ambitious, and there remain some unresolved areas, further discussed below.

The shared functions are defined by the LG Law as pre-school and pre-university education; primary health care services and protection of public health; social assistance and poverty alleviation; public order and civil protection; and environmental protection. These are areas which require considerable sectoral reform; Albanian officials could not fully agree on what could be the specific role of the local governments (and among the LGs, the respective roles of the municipalities/communes and the regions) in these sectors. By 2007, the only shared function which has been fully implemented is in the sector of social assistance. According to the Law on Social Aid and Services of 2005, the administration of social services establishments (retirement homes, orphanages) was defined as a local government responsibility, with ownership of the buildings to be transferred to the respective local governments. Municipalities and communes identify the beneficiaries of these services. As of 2006, funds for economic assistance and community works programmes are distributed to local governments as a block grant. Incentives for the effective use of social assistance funds are provided to local governments, which in addition to the distribution of cash benefits to poor families can use such funds for community works, providing a temporary job to poor people and even saving part of the earmarked transfer (Conway and Ymeri, 2007). Other types of shared functions such as education, primary health care, environmental protection and so on, are still undergoing an overall reform process.

Delegated functions of local governments must be either mandated by law or negotiated with individual local governments. Civil registry was the first delegated function implemented in this manner (in 2002). Since 2003, the State budget law has included an annex that establishes the delegated functions of communes and municipalities in health and education including, as of 2006, responsibility for certain investments in health and education facilities.

A key missing element in order to ensure some compliance of delegated functions was in the area of the definition of national standards local governments were expected to meet (and for which sufficient funding should be made available). In order to address this issue, a working group of national and local officials recommended basic health and safety standards for school facilities. The working group also developed procedures that define clearly the respective role of the Ministry and of local governments. Together the standards and procedures would provide formal rules to guide the implementation of the delegated function in the area of maintenance of education facilities. During 2005 and 2006 the Ministry of Education conducted a pilot programme in two municipalities and one commune. Through an open process of discussions with local stakeholders, the participating local governments allocated more funding from their own resources for school maintenance and made efficient and effective use of the funds by targeting tangible improvements to meet the basic health and safety standards in local schools. The Ministry of Education may consider applying the standards and process nationally to all local governments and all pre-university education facilities starting in 2009, pending the outcome of additional pilot test sites.

The own functions of the regions include adoption and implementation of regional development policies. Other functions can be delegated to them by their constituent municipalities/communes, or by the central government. Although the LG Law clearly establishes the right of local governments to own property, the process is regulated by two special laws adopted in 2001: (i) law on state immovable properties and (ii) law on transferring immovable state properties to LGs. As a basic principle, any immovable property that serves for the execution of a local own function will be transferred to LGs with full property rights. Immovable properties such local administrative buildings, roads, parks and other local public areas, water systems, landfills, cemeteries, schools, local forests, and so on will become the property of LGs.

The deadlines established by the law (two years) have proven to be too short. The process requires an initial inventory of the immovable properties (which previously had not been carried out). In 2002 a symbolic action was taken with the transferring of city halls. As of mid-2007, the Agency for Property Transfer has completed the State property inventory in the area of jurisdiction of 127 local governments. The Agency is understaffed, and there is poor coordination at the central government level. Local governments have not expressed any concern with the slow process over these years and have not lobbied the central government to accelerate it. Further, it is important to note, that unlike in Poland and Hungary, Albanian local governments will not receive surplus property (housing, commercial sites, land plots) from which they will generate property management revenue. They are receiving properties presently used to carry out basic local government functions, which are degraded and dilapidated, costly to maintain and require significant rehabilitation.

Despite some of the implementation delays overall, the LG Law had provided has provided a solid foundation and the authority for Albanian local governments to manage public affairs in their jurisdictions and improve the quality of services received by their citizens.

CITIZEN PARTICPATION AND LOCAL FINANCIAL ACCOUNTABILITY

As the relative weight of local government spending in total public expenditures has increased and the decision-making power of local authorities has expanded greatly, the focus of public attention on the impact of increased local autonomy on local communities has become stronger. The underlying assumption that decentralization based on subsidiarity will strengthen democracy and ensure the provision of more satisfactory public services is not easy to prove in objective quantitative terms. However, various research in the field and anecdotal cases indicate that the quality and accountability of local governance has improved in line with the expansion of local autonomy.

Albania lacks a coherent system of evaluation of services across local governments, and no national standards exist in the majority of public services. However, nationwide citizen perceptions on the quality of public services provided by their municipalities seem to have improved in 2006 compared to 2005 (Figure 2.1).

Figure 2.1 Measuring local services – citizens' opinion on services (good and very good)

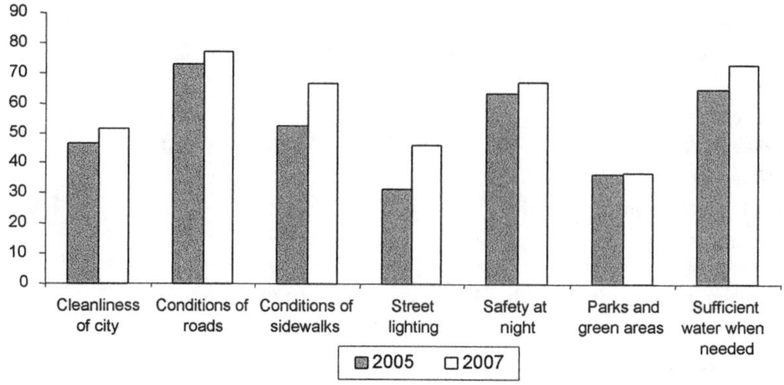

Source: 2007 USAID national survey of urban population.

Such improvements are not accidental, as increasingly more municipalities have introduced new modern methodologies in the planning and execution of their public functions, which include broad consultation with the communities on the identification of needs and priorities, costing of services, setting of output and outcome indicators and their evaluation and monitoring through the same participatory approach. The municipality of Erseka, a small town in southeastern Albania, is just one of the many Albanian cities that have applied such participatory performance management tools to considerable success in improving effectiveness and efficiency thanks to technical assistance by a USAID local government project and other donor support (Table 2.1).

Such new budgeting techniques, which rely on the participation and active involvement of the community in local governance, seem to have been successful in increasing the awareness of the community itself and increased their willingness to pay for the local services they receive. Thus, many municipalities and communes have increased local fees, in order to be able to cover the cost of services to respond to citizens' expectations in terms of quality and quantity. Other municipalities have chosen to decrease their tax rates and have experienced a dramatic increase in the tax base and overall tax revenues.

Table 2.1 Input, output and outcome analysis of Erseka Municipality Road Service

	Actual 2005	Target 2006	Actual 2006	Difference (2006 –2005)	Target 2007
Input (budgeted expenditures in lek)	32,310,000	13,168 ,000	13,078,000	- 19,232,000	11,435,180
A. Expenditures on road maintenance	2,610,000	1,530,000	1,470,000	- 1,140,000	1,960,000
B. Investment in roads	29,700,000	11,638,000	11,608,000	- 18,092,000	9,475,180
Output					
– Kilometres of maintained paved roads	4,641	5,311	5,271	+ 630	5,876
– Kilometres of asphalted roads in total	6,019	6,459	6,419	+ 0.4	7,024
– Kilometres of neighbourhood (secondary) paved roads	2,020	2,460	2,420	+0. 4	2,460
Outcome					
% of citizens, who are satisfied with primary roads	78	84	78.5	+ 0.5	82
% of citizens satisfied with secondary roads	25	30.4	30	+ 5	37.4

At the same time, the share of capital expenditures in overall expenditures has steadily increased from a mere 15 per cent in 1998 (almost fully financed by conditional central transfers) to 33 per cent in 2005 (largely financed by own local sources). Considering the high need for investments in local infrastructure these trends reinforce the sense of accountability and responsiveness of local governance to local needs.

Local governance seems to have improved both in terms of transparency and accountability. Local communities and citizens are becoming increasingly aware of the duties, responsibilities and rights of their local governments, and society is increasing its demand for better and more democratic local governance (Table 2.2).

Table 2.2 Accountability and responsiveness: 2007 USAID national survey of urban population

Accountability and responsiveness (% of sample)	2005	2007
My LG interested in what I think	35	45
Budget decisions reflect citizens priorities	33	41
I received good values for local taxes and fees	32	39
My LG applies taxes and fees fairly to all	33	44
My LG accomplishes what it says it will do	31	40
My LG solves local problems	51	55
LG manages funds well	42	54
My LG honours laws	52	61
Corruption is widespread	70	64
I know someone who paid a bribe	23	14

The results of the survey indicate a good start for the improvement of local governance. It seems that the rule of law is strengthening, local governments are increasingly responding to local needs and citizen priorities, and the perception of corruption is declining.

OWN LOCAL GOVERNMENT REVENUES KEY TO FINANCIAL AUTONOMY

The fiscal landscape of local governments has changed considerably since 2000, following a lengthy and deliberate process of reform to implement the key finance provisions of the LG Law. In December 2002 Parliament adopted the package of legislation that greatly expanded local authority over their own taxes and fees, consistent with the provisions of the LG Law:

- Municipalities and communes have full rate setting authority for fees. They also have full authority to decide on the manner of administration and collection of these fees.
- The property tax on buildings, the agriculture land tax (ALT)[3] and the local small business tax (Local SBT) are all defined as own local taxes. Municipalities and communes set the rates of these taxes, within a limit of +/– 30 per cent around the indicative tax rate, which is set in the laws. LGs define the means of administration and collection of the building tax

and the ALT. The local SBT continued to be collected by the General Tax Directorate until early 2007, when this was also fully transferred to M/C.

- Other own local taxes defined in the local taxes law and over which municipalities and communes may determine the rate are:
  - o Hotel tax: up to 5 per cent of the room price.
  - o Infrastructure impact tax: 1–3 per cent of investment value (2–4 per cent in Tirana).
  - o Tax on occupying public spaces, sign tax, temporary taxes: full LG autonomy to determine rates.
- Municipalities and communes received the full revenues of the simplified profit tax,[4] the vehicle registration tax and the immovable property transaction tax.[5] Single national rates are set in the laws, with no LG authority to change these rates.

There are still many areas where improvements in local tax administration and revenues can be made by the efforts of local councils and local tax offices:

- Most communes and some of the municipalities do not yet collect the property tax on buildings from residential taxpayers.
- Better and more complete registration of small businesses will also lead to improvements in the small business tax and the property tax on buildings.
- For many other local taxes, improvements in databases and tax administration systems will allow them to identify non-registered or non-paying taxpayers.
- Many communes in the plain and coastal area of Albania quickly introduced the ALT; it will take a longer period for the tax to be implemented in the more mountainous and poorer areas of Albania.

After three years of implementation, some weak points and necessary adjustments to the legislation are beginning to be identified. Among the most important are:

- The indicative rates for the property tax on buildings, the ALT and the SBT, are fixed in law and will lose their value over time due to the effects of inflation; they will need to be periodically adjusted via amendments to the law.
- The indicative rate for residential properties has been set very low, and even with an option to increase the rate by 30 per cent, this is still a low rate which limits future potential revenue.
- Differing indicative rates by geographic zone, with the highest rates for the municipalities of Tiranë and Durrës, and the lowest rates for communes in the northern regions of Albania, also limit potential revenues for most M/C.

The last point compounds the problem of fiscal concentration and fiscal inequality. In any country, higher tax potential exists in capital cities and in all regions of important economic activity. Regions with geographic handicaps (mountain areas, long distance from economic and business centres, poor road network) have lower tax bases. The Law on the Tax System, by setting different indicative tax rates by types of local governments and by regions, has further compounded this initial inequality and ensured that the poorer regions, as well as communes in economically dynamic areas, would continue to collect low own local tax revenues, on a per capita basis and in absolute value. Thus, 75 per cent of all local taxes and fees are concentrated in four districts of the country: Tiranë, Durrës, Vlorë and Fier, with Tiranë alone accounting for 43 per cent.

The equalization element of the unconditional transfer formula adjusts for the geographic differences in tax potential, for the local small business tax, simplified profit tax and vehicle registration tax – these three taxes account for over 40 per cent of local revenues from own taxes, shared taxes and fees. However, although the fiscal package did provide considerable discretion, there are always risks that modifications to central government fiscal policy may change in ways which negatively affect local governments. Indeed, in 2005, and consistent with the new Government's policy to decrease the overall tax burden on businesses, the Small Business Tax (SBT) rates were reduced by 50 per cent, including the local tax on the small business and the simplified profit tax (shared national tax). The reduction of these tax rates led a decline of LGs' SBT revenues from 3.6 billion leks in 2005 to 2.8 billion leks in 2006. Although funds were added to the unconditional transfer pool, the allocation via equalization formula did not fully compensate the municipalities most affected by the lowered rates (Tirana, Durrës, and so on). These two small businesses taxes were remerged into one tax and transformed into a purely local tax starting from January 2007, with the full responsibility for collection and administration also transferred to the municipalities and communes.

By the most common measures of the role of local governments, compared to GDP and to public expenditures, it would appear, as illustrated in Table 2.3, that the decentralization reforms have not made significant changes in the role and autonomy of Albania's municipalities and communes. LG total expenditures accounted for 3.8 per cent of GDP in 1998 and 4.3 per cent in 2006. However, by measures of M/C own expenditures and their local tax and fee revenues, considerable progress has been made: M/C taxes and fees now account for 1 per cent of GDP, compared to 0 in 1998.

Table 2.3 Evolution of LG expenditures and local tax and fee revenues to GDP 1998–2006

	1998	1999	2000	2001	2002	2003	2004	2005	2006
GDP (million lek)	412,326	474,291	530,906	587,717	624,717	682,670	766,379	836,833	899,693
State Budget Expenditures (million lek)	141,628	165,692	170,621	186,049	192,517	201,152	222,715	232,339	254,762
	1998	1999	2000	2001	2002	2003	2004	2005	2006
Total LG Expenditures (Thousand lek)	15,672,547	22,933,005	20,419,818	24,922,970	26,610,854	30,230,513	35,747,326	38,241,574	38,871,964
LG Own Expenditures	731,380	1,690,404	1,723,784	5,284,450	10,505,923	12,531,676	14,373,510	20,027,450	22,798,947
LG Local Tax and Fee Revenues	119,217	826,122	1,251,257	1,884,411	2,392,345	6,075,118	6,489,106	7,310,125	8,930,258
LG Expenditures/GDP (Percent)	3.8%	4.8%	3.8%	4.2%	4.3%	4.4%	4.7%	4.6%	4.3%
LG Own Expenditures/ GDP	0.2%	0.4%	0.3%	0.9%	1.7%	1.8%	1.9%	2.4%	2.5%
LG Local Tax and Fee Revenues/GDP	0.0%	0.2%	0.2%	0.3%	0.4%	0.9%	0.8%	0.9%	1.0%

Source: Statistical Office and Bank of Albania.

Table 2.4 Local government revenues by type – 2001–2006 (thousand lek/per cent)

	2001	2002	2003	2004	2005	2006
Total Local Government Revenues (Thousand lek)	25,464,738	26,680,899	30,716,760	36,491,428	37,584,168	38,232,390
Locally Generated Revenues Total Of which	2,341,110	2,979,304	8,414,610	10,056,648	11,380,657	12,359,373
Own Local Revenues, of which	1,995,837	2,597,048	6,265,801	6,687,454	8,066,052	9,824,735
Taxes	121,132	116,622	3,929,940	3,941,580	4,640,356	5,429,101
Fees	1,763,279	2,275,724	2,145,177	2,547,526	2,669,770	3,501,157
Non-tax Revenues	111,427	204,703	190,684	198,348	755,927	894,477
Shared Taxes	345,272	382,255	2,148,808	3,369,194	3,314,605	2,534,638
Revenues from National Sources Total Of which	23,123,628	23,701,595	22,302,150	26,434,781	26,203,510	25,873,017
General Transfers	5,658,853	9,276,082	6,554,081	6,611,177	7,300,000	9,800,000
Earmarked Conditional Transfers	17,464,775	14,425,514	15,748,069	19,823,604	18,903,510	16,073,017
Ratios % of total						
Locally Generated Revenues/Total Revenues	7.8%	9.7%	20.4%	18.3%	21.5%	25.7%
Local Taxes and Fees/Total Revenues	7.4%	9.0%	19.8%	17.8%	19.5%	23.4%
Revenues from National Sources/Total Revenues	90.8%	88.8%	72.6%	72.4%	69.7%	67.7%
General Transfers/Total Revenues	22.2%	34.8%	21.3%	18.1%	19.4%	25.6%
Earmarked Transfers/Total Revenues	68.6%	54.1%	51.3%	54.3%	50.3%	41.0%

Source: Statistical Office and Bank of Albania.

Table 2.4 illustrates the evolution of local government revenues by type for the period 2001–06. Reviewing the impact of the local fiscal reform, local taxes and fees now account for over 23 per cent of total revenue, more than three times their share in 2001 (7.4 per cent).

CENTRAL GOVERNMENT TRANSFERS: GREATER STABILITY AND TRANSPARENCY

Unconditional Transfers

Until the end of 2001, the block grant for operating purposes was distributed to municipalities and communes on an ad hoc basis. The unconditional transfer system was put into place in 2002. The determination of the total transfer pool is the outcome of the annual budget process of the Government. There have been some discussions to explore if the total pool could be determined based on a formula that provides a certain yield of some national taxes such as VAT, CIT and PIT. However, as the overall tax system in Albania is still in development, and tax revenue yield is among the lowest in the SEE region, compared to GDP, such a change may not be implemented before a few years.

The pool of unconditional transfers is allocated to the individual local governments (regions, municipalities and communes) according to a multiple-step formula that includes the use of some predefined criteria materialized by values of respective coefficients. From 2003, the formula also included criteria for horizontal equalization, linked to the implementation of the local fiscal reform. In 2006, funds were added to the pool to replace the prior conditional grants for roads, and they are now also distributed on a per capita basis, within the overall formula. Table 2.4 tracks the evolution of the general (unconditional) transfers since 2001.The formula and the resulting transfer for each LG unit individually are published in the annexes of the annual state budget law. Although the formula is not at present defined in permanent legislation, the key parameters have remained stable over the first years of implementation.

A notable aspect of the unconditional transfers from the State budget to local governments is their impact on horizontal equalization. Table 2.5 looks at the impact of the formula on local per capita revenues. The statistical measures in the columns labelled 'without' are for per capita revenues from the small business tax (SBT) and simplified profit tax (SPT). The columns labelled 'with' are for per capita revenues from SBT/SPT plus the unconditional grant. The value of the coefficient of variation declines steadily in each subsequent year, indicating that there is a progressive clustering of per capita revenues after applying equalization.

Table 2.5 Key statistical measures of revenues per capita for communes and municipalities – with and without the unconditional transfer, 2002–06

	Without	With	Without	With	Without	With	Without	With
	2003		2004		2005		2006	
Meen	580	2,639	519	2,728	528	3,281	337	2,959
Median	307	2,248	248	2,294	257	2,621	182	2,717
St. Dev	663	1,204	688	1,182	707	1,197	419	1,046
Minimum	155	1,501	0	1,751	0	2,501	0	1,901
Maximum	4,122	7,869	3,754	8,212	4,498	10,098	3,126	8,395
CV	114%	46%	133%	43%	134%	36%	124%	35%

Conditional Capital Investment Transfers

In 2003 and 2004, State subsidies in the form of conditional grants financed over two-thirds of capital investments (66 and 69 per cent respectively) in areas that are exclusively a local function by law. Line ministries continued to control the allocation and use of the investments through the end of 2005. In addition, the Government expanded the use of conditional grants in 2005 to include delegated responsibility for investments in pre-university education facilities and certain primary health facilities.

The funding of investments in own local functions through line ministries created a number of problems. In 2005 a joint national/local working group evaluated the conditional transfers for own local functions. Their main findings were that:

- The average urban road investment grant varies considerably year to year.
- Depending on the year, from 35 to 50 municipalities (out of a total of 65) received urban road investment subsidies for an average of 70 to 80 projects.
- Less than one-third of the communes receive subsidies for investments in rural roads in any given year (with the exception of 2004 – an electoral year).
- Funding levels have been insufficient for the extension of the road networks or for sustainable action to maintain the existing network.
- There is no apparent pattern or rationale for the allocation by individual local government or by regions.

As a result of the findings and recommendations of this working group, the Government implemented in the State budget for 2006 two important changes in the management of state investment subsidies in areas of own functions. For

Table 2.6 Evolution of net local discretion – 2001–06

	2001	**2002**	**2003**	**2004**	**2005**	**2006**
Total Local Government Revenues (Thousand lek)	25,464,738	26,680,899	30,716,760	36,491,428	37,584,168	38,232,390
Discretionary Reveneus	7,999,963	12,255,385	14,968,691	16,667,824	18,680,657	22,159,373
Of which						
Locally Generated Revenues	1,995,837	2,597,048	6,265,801	6,687,454	8,066,052	9,824,735
General Transfers	5,658,853	9,276,082	6,554,081	6,611,177	7,300,000	9,800,000
Shared Taxes	345,272	382,255	2,148,808	3,369,194	3,314,605	2,534,638
Ratio (percent)						
Discretionary Revenues/Total revenues[a]	31.4%	45.9%	48.7%	45.7%	49.7%	58.0%
Unfunded mandates[b]	2,178,981	1,680,827	1,772,069	1,609,473	1,520,318	1,739,751
As a percent of total revenues	8.6%	6.3%	5.8%	4.4%	4.0%	4.6%
Net local discretion (percent total local revenues)	22.9%	39.6%	43.0%	41.3%	45.7%	53.4%

Notes: a: Discretionary revenues are those sources which local governments autonomusly allocation and spending decisions.
b: Includes expenditures paid with local discretionay revenues for functions mandated or delegated by the central government.

the first time in 2006 each commune and municipality received a transfer that they must apply only to investments but at their own discretion as to sector or purpose. This transfer replaces 1.5 billion lek in investments in roads that were funded by conditional grants in 2005. Additional funding provided in 2006 from the State budget to local governments was managed through a conditional investment grant pool which amounted to 2.1 billion lek. Local governments competed for grants from this pool based on criteria that published as Annex 4 to the 2006 State budget law.

In Albania there has been measurable progress in fiscal decentralization as measured by 'net local discretion'. Table 2.6 shows that this measure increased from 23 per cent in 2001, to 41 per cent in 2003, to reach almost 54 per cent in 2006.[6] The big jump in net local discretion occurred in 2002 when Albania introduced the allocation by formula of unconditional transfers from the State budget to individual local governments. It has continued to grow steadily since as a result of further reforms to the system of transfers, tax sharing and local taxes and fees.

These reforms, combining increased stability, transparency and discretion, have enabled municipalities and communes to considerably increase the share of local expenditures which they allocate to investments.

LOCAL GOVERNMENT EXPENDITURE TRENDS: AUTONOMY PROMOTES CAPITAL EXPENDITURES

Budgeting and reporting of local government expenditures by sector has not yet fully caught up with the changes made in the legislative framework. In particular, recording of local government expenditures by the Treasury (where local governments must keep their accounts and which records all financial movements) does not yet reflect the changes in LG functions. Several analyses have demonstrated that expenditures recorded in the Treasury as 'administration' are reported by the local governments as service provision expenditures, such as for solid waste, roads maintenance, and so on.

Although analysis of sectoral expenditure allocation requires improved data collection, reliable data is available on the allocation of expenditures by economic classification. By the end of 2005, M/C investment expenditures exceeded 30 per cent of total expenditures, compared to less than 15 per cent in 1998 (Table 2.7). Thus, additional funding available to M/C through the fiscal decentralization reform has been largely allocated to investment rather than for increase of salaries.

Table 2.7 Share of capital expenditures in municipality and commune budgets

	1998	2000	2003	2005
Total Local Government Revenues (*Thousand lek*)	15,454,238	20,048,358	30,716,760	37,815,438
Capital Expenditures (*Thousand lek*)	2,319,346	4,567,293	7,217,498	12,362,935
Share of Capital Exp. in Total Budget	15%	22.8%	23.5%	33%

Source: Ministry of Finance.

LOCAL GOVERNMENT BUDGET PROCESS: THE CHALLENGE FOR TRANSPARENCY AND ACCOUNTABILITY

The Constitution of Albania establishes the local budget as distinct from the State budget. From 2001 to 2005 the actual practice and procedures continued to treat the local budget as part of the State budget. This reflects in part deficiencies in the legal framework. It also was the result of practices by the State Treasury in recording and reporting local revenues and expenditures. Despite these constraints, local governments have made progress in promoting greater citizen involvement in the budget process in those areas where they have discretionary authority over revenues and expenditures.

A dialogue on local budgeting, local finance and intergovernmental fiscal relations took place during July 2005 and July 2006. A working group of central and local government budget and finance specialists identified a series of practices that undermine and weaken the accountability of local elected officials for the allocation and use of public funds through the local budget. The main findings were that:

- No law specifies the date (deadline) for the adoption of the local budget.
- There is no clear legal provision that requires that the Treasury confirms before effecting a transaction involving local revenues and expenditures that it is included in the local budget.
- In practice, the details of the local budget process, including the deadline for adoption, derive from instructions issued annually by the Ministry of Finance, further expanded by additional instructions issued by the Ministry responsible for local governments.

- The weakness of the system of financial accounting and reporting means that it is difficult to track expenditures to ensure that local budgets are implemented as approved.
- Recorded details of budget plans for local governments are also relatively limited. Hence, it is difficult to undertake detailed analyses for individual local governments of implemented budgets against original budget plans. In particular, analyses of the variance between annual budget projections and actual out-turns are not undertaken systematically and regularly.

The Ministry of Finance addressed some of these recommendations in its 2006 and 2007 budget preparation and implementation instructions. They included measures related to the Treasury procedures for local fund management, the budget cycle for local governments and the consolidation of the local budget as a uniform budget, which had not been fully effected.

In 2006, a new working group on local budget and intergovernmental fiscal relations formulated a policy note on local budgeting and finance. That note served as the basis for the drafting of the sections dealing with local government in a comprehensive revision of the Law on the Budget Preparation, Execution and Monitoring in the Republic of Albania (Organic Budget Law). The Ministry of Finance disseminated a draft revision of the Organic Budget Law in July 2007. The MoF expected that Parliament would adopt the law before October 2007. The draft law has taken into consideration the majority of recommendations of the working group and is expected to bring about major improvements in local public financial management, assignment of tasks and transparency of local public finances.

LOCAL GOVERNMENT CREDITWORTHINESS AND THE POTENTIAL TO DEVELOP A LOCAL DEBT MARKET

The Law on Organization and Functioning of Local Governments allows in principle for the prospect of borrowing on the capital markets by local governments, and it indicates that the rules for local borrowing are to be defined in a specific law. To date, direct access by local governments to financial markets is not yet possible, in the absence of such specific law. The law that regulates local borrowing was expected to become effective by 1 January 2008.

At the time that the LG Law was adopted in 2000, no Albanian municipality or commune, not even the city of Tirana, could be considered creditworthy. From 2000 and as previously discussed, the expenditures of Albanian local governments have steadily increased, and they have growing responsibilities and functions. Although the relative weight of local expenditures to the GDP has not changed drastically during these years, local financial autonomy has dramatically increased, from less than 5 per cent in 1998, to reach almost 54 per cent in 2006. This significant qualitative change in the structure of local budgets has occurred due to the introduction of the unconditional fiscal transfers, accompanied by a steady increase in the weight of revenues from local taxes and fees, which in 2006 constituted more than 30 per cent of total local revenues.

The steady increasing trend of the share of own local revenues has been accompanied by the strengthening capacities in the execution of public investments by local governments. The national aggregate operational surplus of local governments in 2005 was 33 per cent.[7] The operational surplus is high not only for large local government units, due to their high tax potential, but also for smaller ones, due to the unconditional transfers. This operational surplus is largely dedicated to financing local infrastructure projects.

These positive fiscal developments and increasing capacities at the local level indicated that it is time to open up local access to more funding opportunities through the credit and capital markets. The Albanian government initiated in 2006 a broad process of consultations with relevant stakeholders on the drafting of the law for local borrowing. The draft law is currently at the last stage of the legislative process, expected to become effective for the 2008 fiscal year. The draft law defines a set of clear rules for prudent local borrowing in respect of local development policies, attempting to minimize risks for the macroeconomic stability of the country and providing sufficient guarantees for lenders and the necessary standards for a transparent local borrowing process.

The basic legal rules for local borrowing provided for in the draft law are as follows:

- *Purpose of borrowing*: Local debt is issued for public purposes. Local governments are entitled to borrow long term for financing capital improvement projects, and short term to finance temporary cash flow deficits.
- *Instruments of borrowing:* The forms of local debt range from bank loans, to securities, leasing, supplier's credit, and so on.
- *Domestic versus international markets:* Local government debt in domestic markets is subject to a legal review by the Ministry of Finance, to ensure compliance with the regulations in force and debt limitations. Prior approval by the Ministry of Finance is necessary for borrowing in international markets, given the obvious implications of international debt for the country as a whole. Such prior approval does not constitute an implicit sovereign guarantee for the local debt.

- *Local debt limitations:* The draft legal framework defines volume limits on the annual debt service only. Short-term debt service limits are set at the level of 10 per cent of total revenues from local taxes and fees of the previous fiscal year. Long-term debt limits are set at the level of 20 per cent of total local revenues from local taxes and fees and unconditional transfers of the previous fiscal year.
- *Debt security:* Local governments may incur general obligation debt, as well as pledge specific revenues as a security. In addition, other forms of security have been envisaged by the draft law, such as the opportunity for intercepting of funds in case of default, physical assets guarantee and so on.
- *Transparency:* All local governments must include a debt annex to their annual local budget, as well as maintain a special debt ledger with extensive information on their liabilities and financial position, accessible by the public. In addition, the Ministry of Finance is responsible for holding a Ledger of Local Debt, in a similar fashion as the ledger of central government debt and for ensuring compliance with local debt limitations.
- *Financial distress:* The draft law provides for a series of remedies in case of default on debt by the local governments. However, a specific law on local insolvency with more regulations on the matter is expected to become effective by 2010.

Based on the proposed debt limits of the draft law, the theoretical aggregate long-term annual debt service capacity based on the fiscal data for 2005 would amount to 6.5 billion lek or approximately USD65 million.

KEY ACHIEVEMENTS AND FUTURE CHALLENGES FOR ALBANIA'S LOCAL GOVERNMENTS

Although the implementation of the LG Law has taken longer than initially anticipated, Albania has ultimately benefited from a slower, more deliberate process, which provided adequate time to review potential policy options and their impacts. As of late 2007, there were a few key pending issues which have yet to be resolved. We focus in conclusion on two of these issues below.

Water Systems Transfer

There is still a period of transition under way in the transfer of responsibility in water/wastewater. The need to improve access to water as an important element of the National Strategy for Socio-Economic Development and the need to establish clear accountability for performance of this sector make it necessary to overcome the impasse that has stalled reforms in the water sector in Albania since 2003. Among the issues which need to be addressed in the approach the Government will finally take are:

- To develop a coherent definition of the roles and responsibilities of key players in the sector, including the national government, the Water Regulatory Agency, local governments and water operators that provides clear accountability for performance of the sector.
- A policy on operating subsidies to water operators that describes when and how this support will be phased out, except perhaps for certain high-cost rural water systems that may require some level of continuing subsidies. This policy also will have to consider the need for investment subsidies to address the immediate consequences of accumulated deferred maintenance in water systems.
- Measures to address accumulated liabilities of water companies, including contingent liabilities that may arise from legal claims related to property rights.
- Recognition of the need for social subsidies for households that cannot afford basic water consumption and implementation of means-tested, targeted subsidies with clear rules and procedures.
- A clear timetable for implementing the reforms in the water sector.

Urban Planning Issues

Reforms to the system of urban planning are an urgent, pending task. Accountability for managing urban growth is not clear. In a country where a large share of remittances is being invested in construction, local governments, although nominally responsible by law, in practice do not have the tools to regulate new construction, resolve conflicts among land uses and provide for orderly expansion of their community. This has an adverse impact on the efficiency of investments in basic infrastructure. It also contributes to a growing problem of unregulated and unplanned construction that will be costly and difficult to address.

The existing law and procedures are not suited to a process of urban growth that is driven largely by market forces, not Government fiat. Starting in the summer of 2006 the Government convened a dialogue of stakeholders in the central and local governments and in civil society to propose a new policy and eventually a new law on planning to address the shortcomings in the current legislation. The Government issued a policy statement in December 2006 and current efforts are focused on drafting a new planning law. The expectation was that Parliament would adopt the law during 2007.

Despite these pending challenges, in large measure, the success of the decentralization process to date in Albania reflects the positive impact of the continuing involvement of stakeholders from the national and local governments and from civil society, in the dialogue process on specific decentralization policy issues and options. From the fiscal point of view, Albanian local governments enjoy considerable discretion in the allocation of their funds, which, combined with greater local citizen participation, will help municipalities and communes meet the needs and expectations for improved public services in their communities.

NOTES

1. According to the 2001 national census, INSTAT (Institute of Statistics).
2. The mandate of four years is very recent based on a Constitutional amendment adopted in January 2007. Previously the mandate was three years.
3. Reintroduced after its suspension in 1996.
4. Defined as a national tax in the Law on Income Tax, but since 2007, re-merged with the Local Small Business Tax.
5. Both defined as local taxes in the Law on the System of Local Taxes.
6. Excluding pass-through transfers for education and health wages.
7. Operational surplus (deficit) calculated as the difference between total discretionary recurrent revenues with total discretionary operational expenditures.

BIBLIOGRAPHY

Legislation

Laws

- Law on the Preparation and Execution of the State Budget of the Republic of Albania, no. 8379, dated 29 July 1998
- Law on Organization and Functioning of Local Governments, no. 8652, dated 31 July 2000
- Law on the Territorial Administrative Division of the Local Government Units in the Republic of Albania, No 8653, dated 31 July 2000, amended by Law No. 9123, dated 29 July 2003.
- Law on Immovable State Property, no. 8743, dated 22 February 2001
- Law on Transfer of Immovable State Properties to Local Governments, no. 8744, dated 22 February 2001

- Law on the Prefect no. 8927, dated 25 July 2002
- Law on the System of Local Taxes, no. 8982, dated 12 December 2002, amended by Law No. 9456 dated 21 December 2005
- Law on the Local Small Business Tax, no. 8978, dated 12 December 2002
- Law on amendments to the Law on Personal Income Tax, no. 8979, dated 12 December 2002 (which establishes the Simplified Profits Tax, a national tax, the revenues of which are entirely transferred to municipalities and communes)
- Law on Small Business Tax, no. 9431, dated 13 October 2005

Council of Ministers decisions

- Strategy for Decentralization and Local Autonomy. CoM Decision, February 2000.
- Decision on Inventory of State Immovable Properties and Transfer to Local Governments, no. 500, dated 14 August 2001
- Policy Paper for the Water Sector Council of Ministers decision No. 550 dated 7 November 2002

Ministerial instructions

- Instruction No. 3 dated 27 January 2003 on the Simplified Profits Tax
- Instruction No. 4 dated 27 January 2003 on the Local Small Business Tax
- Instruction No. 5 dated 27 January 2003 on the Cooperation between central and local tax offices for the administration of the Local Small Business Tax and the Simplified Profits Tax
- Instruction No. 6 dated 04 February 2003 for Property Tax on Buildings
- Instruction No. 7 dated 04 February 2003 for Property Tax on Agriculture Land
- Instruction No. 8 dated 04 February 2003 for Tax on Immovable Property Transactions
- Instruction No. 9 dated 04 February 2003 for Tax on Vehicle Registration
- Instruction No. 10 dated 04 February 2003 for Local Taxes
- Instruction No. 12, dated 04 February 2003 for Delegated Functions in Health for 2003
- Instruction No. 13, dated 04 February 2003 for Delegated Functions in Education for 2003

Papers and Reports

Banks, C. and J. Pigey (1998), *Republic of Albania – Opportunities and Issues for Municipal Reform*, Project paper, Washington, DC: The Urban Institute.

Conway, F. and S. Ymeri (2007), *Albania Decentralization Status Report*. Local Government and Decentralization in Albania Program, Project review paper, Washington, DC: The Urban Institute.

Conway, F. et al. (2006), *Design of a Consistent Transfer System and Tax Sharing Mechanism – Final Report Task 4: New System of Local and National Interest Transfers and Tax Sharing*, Project paper, Washington, DC: The Urban Institute.

Hoxha, A. et al. (2002), *Albania Local Tax and Fee System – Policy Options and Recommendations for Reform*, Project paper, Washington, DC: The Urban Institute.

Hoxha, A. (2004), *Fiscal Decentralisation in SEE: The Case of Albania*, Paper presented at Stability Pact Conference, 8 September, Zagreb.

Hoxha, A. and J. Dhimitri (2006), *Fiscal Decentralisation in SEE: The Case of Albania*, Paper presented at Stability Pact Conference, 30 September, Skopje.

Hoxha, A. (2007), *Does Decentralization Support Good Government? Decentralization in Albania – A Top Down Perspective*, Conference paper, Tirana.

Pigey, J. and F. Conway (2006), *Delegation: A Strategy of Decentralization Avoidance or Enhancement? Albania Case Study: Control versus Rules-Based Delegation*, Paper presented at the European Group of Public Administration Annual Conference – Study Group 5 – Intergovernmental Relations, 7 September, Milan.

Pigey, J. and A. Hoxha (2001), *Unconditional Transfers for Local Government and Objective Formula for Distribution*, Project paper, Washington, DC: The Urban Institute.

Schroeder, L. (2000), *Republic of Albania Fiscal Decentralization Policy Study*, Project paper, Washington, DC: The Urban Institute.

Schroeder, L. (2004), *Albania Fiscal Decentralization Policy Study*, Project paper, Washington, DC: The Urban Institute.

World Bank (2004), *Albania: Decentralization in Transition*, Report No: 27885-ALB, Washington, DC: World Bank.

3. Local government finance in Belarus

Yuri Krivorotko

INTRODUCTION[1]

Since the disintegration of the Soviet Union, The Republic of Belarus has been engaged in economic reform and in reforming intergovernmental relations. During the first five years of the Republic's economic development, it became apparent that it would follow European models of local government, based on democratic principles and market economics. That direction is evident in the Law on Local Government and Self-Government adopted by the Belarus Parliament in February of 1991, which followed the requirements of the European Charter of Local Self-Government closely.

With the introduction of the Presidency in Belarus, however, the role and significance of this document have appreciably decreased. Since 1995, the initial document has undergone nine editions which have, step by step, eliminated the democratic spirit of this document and have replaced elements of decentralisation with elements of strict centralisation in intergovernmental relationships. Belarus is one of the post-socialist countries where local governments remain subject to State authority and State administration. Therefore, the local government system in Belarus is not an independent one. It remains a part of the national government system and is strictly subordinated to the centre.

It is no wonder that sub-national governments have no financial autonomy and are included in the Belarus State financial system. The reason for this is that a strong administrative and command tradition was inherited from the Soviet period. These traditions were firmly retained in the public consciousness as being positive. It is not by accident that Belarus has refused to liberalise its economy and decentralise its finance policy. Evidence of the socialist orientation of Belarus is seen in its development of 'hyper-centralisation' at all levels of governance and in the domination of State ownership in both the corporate and public sectors of the economy. Other patterns of ownership though, exist in the country legally, but they do not play a dominant role in management. Therefore, a distinct transition to a policy of financial decentralisation in local financial management will not be possible in the near future. Intergovernmental fiscal relations and local financial management in Belarus must yet be developed through a process of fiscal decentralisation. However, it will only be achieved by means of repeated economic experiments at the local level retaining some of the traditions of the Belarus economy.

BASIC LEGAL FRAMEWORK AND LOCAL GOVERNMENT FINANCE REGULATION

In Belarus, according to national legislation, there are two levels of government: the central or national government and the sub-national government. The local level consists of the region [*oblast*], the county [*rayon*], the city with region status, the city with rayon status, the urban settlement, the urban district, the rural settlement and the village.[2] Oblasts, rayons and cities with region status represent a higher level of local government and they have separate fiscal relations to state government. Other units represent lower levels of local government and their financial relations are subordinated to higher-level units. But, in fact, they do not have their own local budgets and function on the basis of cost-estimated financial plans [*smet*]. Their economic functions are virtually ignored. The practice of Belarus sub-national governments shows that the lower levels of local government cannot execute their full budgetary rights and depend on the budgetary decisions of the central government (as well as those of the oblast or rayon).

Actually, public administration in Belarus has a structure of four levels. On the first level is the central or national government; the second level includes six oblast governments (Brestskay, Vitebskaya, Gomelskaya, Grodnenskaya, Minskaya and Mogilevskaya) and the Minsk (capital of Belarus) city government. The third level comprises 118 rayons and 17 cities with oblast status and finally, the fourth level consists of 1,578 units, including cities with rayon status, as well as urban and rural settlements. Each territorial unit is guaranteed budgetary independence, although this clause of the Belarus Constitution is not effectively implemented. The rights of territorial governments at the regional and rayon levels to execute independent fiscal power is very limited, as executive power of locally elected bodies is increasingly delegated to local state administrations of oblast and rayon levels.

In Belarus the differentiation of expenditure assignments is similar to the practice of differentiation in the developed countries. The administrative expenditures of the central authorities, national defence, and environmental expenditures are financed from the central (Republican) budget. Hospital maintenance, garbage collection and other functions provided by the local level are funded from local budgets. Formally, the oblasts and rayons provide fixed subsidies to public utilities and to transport organisations for the maintenance of roads with regional status. They divide with the centre the responsibilities for the funding of rather amorphous joint expenditures, including those for education, public health services, social policy and grants to the economy.

As an analysis of revenue assignments reveals, there is no precise attachment of basic expenditure functions (for example, public health services, education, or national security) to some corresponding governmental tier. Legislative differentiation of expenditure assignments is reduced to a simple principle: each budget bears the responsibility for funding those organisations which are within its jurisdiction. Current legislation fixes expenditure assignments for the base budgets of rayons and cities of oblast status, without granting essential autonomy in determining the amount of funding (Table 3.1). As practical experience shows, the unfunded mandates are assigned to local budgets very frequently.

Legislation pertaining to local governments in Belarus provides for at least three finance regulators. The first is the Belarus Constitution in which one chapter is devoted to local government and self-government institutions. It determines the strategy of local government and self-government. However, local government and self-government in Belarus are strictly dependent on central government action. There is no clear or precise boundary between local and central authority. As is typical, the constitution does not clarify this relationship, but does so in subsequent editions. There are 119 Belarus constitutions which proclaim the appointment and dismissal of local executive and administrative heads by the decrees of the President of Belarus.

The Belarus Constitution provides for State intervention in local affairs in a manner that does not promote local governments or territorial communities as independent ('self') organisations [*samoorganizatsii*]. State intervention has also caused a division of representative and executive powers at the territorial level as stipulated in article 6 of the Belarus Constitution. This article declares that State power in Belarus is implemented on the basis of power division in legislative, judicial and executive branches. Thus, according to the Belarus Constitution there are two independent administrative bodies for territorial units – the local councils of deputies and an executive/administrative council of local governments, both of which are practically independent. By these structures of the Belarus Constitution, the State status of local councils is established. Arising from them is a unity of state and local functions, which to a certain degree contradicts the sense of article 4.4. of the European Charter of Local Self-Government. Thus, to achieve genuine autonomy for local government, it will be necessary to make certain changes in the legislative design of local self-government freed from the current system of State power.

Table 3.1 Financial responsibilities of governmental tiers in Belarus

Public services	Governmental tiers			
	Cities with rayon status and settlements	Rayons and cities with regional status	Oblasts (regions)	Central / State Government
Education				
• Pre-schools	x	x		
• Elementary schools	x	x	x	
• Secondary schools	x	x	x	
• Out-of-school education		x	x	x
• Secondary schools for children needed in social assistance		x	x	
• Technical education		x	x	x
• Universities				x
Water supply and sewerage	x	x	x	
Electricity, heating and gas supply	x	x	x	
National defence				x
Public safety			x	x
Environment protection				x
Health care			x	x
Local economic development	x	x	x	
Public light	x	x	x	
Fire protection		x	x	x
Civil defence		x	x	x
Public transport	x	x	x	

Source: Author's list produced from the Law on Local Government and Self-Government.

The second regulator is the Law on Local Government and Self-Government, initiated in 1991 and in force to the present after having undergone the revisions of nine editions. The last edition of the Law (16 May 2001) firmly fixed the right of the Belarus President to appoint and dismiss the Chairman of Executive Power of Local Government. The heads of local administrations are also appointed and dismissed by the President of Belarus. So the functional power division of the institutions discussed above are duplicative and unclear. And there is another contradiction in the Law pertaining to the election of the local councils in oblasts, rayons, cities and settlements. These elected councils appear to be of lesser authority than the executive power appointed by the President. As a result, executive committees are closely connected to the central line ministries (with their power to deliver resources) and consequently have more power over the local councils. Executive committees and local administrations directly execute the functions of Councils, so that representatives of the President at the local level and the elected Councils of Local Government often experience direct conflicts of interest.

The third legal regulating system of local government is the Budget Law of Belarus, which is accepted by the Belarus Parliament each financial year. The structure of local budgets, local budgetary parameters, indicators and aggregates, the structure of the own and fixed local taxes, the shared taxes in local budgets, the structure of revenues and expenditures of the consolidated local budget are all a part of this document. The Budget Law, which represents a central adjustment of the financial powers of local governments, links local budgets to the State budget. It reflects the absence of local government budget autonomy, regulating both their revenues and expenditures each fiscal year. As a matter of fact, this part of the regulatory system has assigned to the centre a primary power of taxation over the local budget process.

Further evolution of intergovernmental fiscal relations and local financial management in Belarus will demand the introduction of the Budget Code into the legislative base of local government and special laws regulating the financial activities of local authorities.

DEMOCRATIC LEGITIMACY AND FINANCIAL REPORTING

In the last five years the share of local budgets in the combined budget of Belarus has increased considerably, reaching more than 50 per cent. As in other European countries, the sub-national government budgets of Belarus provide for communal services, public health, culture and education, and they are subject to the influence of macroeconomic factors. Table 3.2 provides information on sub-national government budget expenditures as a share of budget expenditures and of the GDP.

Table 3.2 The shares of central (Republican) and sub-national budgets in the combined budget and in GDP of Belarus, 1998–2005 (in percentages)

Budgets	2000	2001	2002	2003	2004	2005
Central (Republican) budget	50.14	50.14	44.81	47.76	49.92*	51.8*
Sub-national governments budgets	49.86	49.86	50.19	52.24	50.08	48.2
Belarus combined budget	100.0	100.0	100.0	100.0	100.0*	100.0*
Share of sub-national budget expenditures in GDP	15.41	16.6	19.4	20.4	18.5	19.0
Share of Central (Republican) budget expenditures in GDP	18.9	19.2	14.6	18.65	18.45*	20.7*
Share of combined budget in GDP (sub-national budgets + central budget)	35.5	35.6	34.0	39.05	36.96*	40.0*

Note: * Without taking into account a social defence of population fund.
Source: Author's own calculations based on the Ministry of Finance reports.

As the table shows, the ratio of sub-national government budgets to GDP in Belarus is quite comparable to the ratio in developed countries. In comparison with some Central European and Baltic countries, the ratio of local budget expenditures to GDP is higher in Belarus (Horvath, 2000, p. 34).

Belarus legislation stipulates that local councils should have an independent fiscal base. The decentralisation effort has increased the share of local budget expenditures in the consolidated budget, but has not secured adequate fiscal autonomy for local governments. A significant share of expenditures, including their size and structure, remains the object of rigid regulation from the centre. They are impacted by various legislative and statutory acts established at the central level. As a result, local authorities have no opportunity to manage their own budgets independently. Under these systemic conditions there are no incentives optimally to implement local budgetary policy, to increase budgeting transparency and objectivity, to provide quality budgetary services and to monitor expenditures efficiently.

The absence of an independent local fiscal base in Belarus is also explained by the weakness of most local governments, especially of the rural communities. They are unable to execute their full budgetary rights and must depend on budgetary decisions of higher levels of government (oblast or rayon). The size of these local governments in terms of population (and, correspondingly, of their revenue base) is insufficient to generate enough revenue even to cover their administrative expenditures. There is one more common explanation of the absence of an independent local fiscal base. The formation of national policy in the field of local government depends on the degree of democratisation of society. Belarus is a country with a low level of democratisation and highly centralised traditions and its central government is not yet ready to offer real financial autonomy to local government units or to grant them real decision-making discretion in their own jurisdictions.

INDEPENDENT LOCAL GOVERNMENT REVENUES SOURCES

In Belarus local government financial sources consist of local budget revenues and local targeted and non-budget funds [*mestnye tselevye i vnebudzhetnye fondy*]. The local budget revenues represent an essential part of total local financial sources – about 85 per cent. The main local budget revenues include own and fixed taxes, shared taxes and central government transfers and grants (donations, subsidies and subventions[3]). Another part of local financial sources – targeted and non-budget funds – represents approximately 15 per cent and includes mainly non-tax [*nenalogovyh*] financial sources. They are additional revenues and saved financial resources, voluntary fees and user fees, revenues from local debt issues, securities and auctions, penalties for environmental pollution and other non-budget financial resources. However, targeted and non-budget funds and financial sources created by non-tax sources are included in the structure of local budgets by the Budget Law. The structure of local financial sources is shown in Table 3.3.

In recent years there has been a tendency on the part of the central government to reduce transfers and grants (donation and subsidies) and the stability of the 'own' tax base of local budgets. It may be explained by the stabilizing factors in the national economy of Belarus, economic growth and the reduction of the inflation rate and the improvement of other macroeconomic parameters. It is worth mentioning that there was a reduction of State transfers and grants, due to an experiment in local financial management in the Mogilev oblast from 2002 to 2004. In that experiment, the oblast declined transfers from the central government intended to cover social-cultural [*neproizvodstvennoy sfery*] expenditures. However, the local budget of the Mogilev oblast consists strictly of

Table 3.3 The structure of local financial sources in Belarus, 2000–05 (as a percentage of total local budget revenues)

		2000	2001	2002	2003	2004	2005
Local financial sources (total local budget revenues)	Per cent	100.0	100.0	100.0	100.0	100.0	100.0
Local budget revenues	Per cent	84.1	85.3	84.7	84.9	90.6	89.5
Own and fixed taxes	Per cent	37	38.23	45.44	46.8	49.5	43.8
	In national currency (bn. Belarus roubles)	760.3	1,433.10	2,166.10	3,405.5	4,643.7	5277.1
	Equivalent in USD (mil. USD)	644.3	907.0	1,128.2	1,579.5	2,140.0	2,452.2
Shared taxes	Per cent	32	30.4	25.53	23.04	24.4	24.8
	In national currency (bn. Belarus roubles)	485.7	871.5	1,217.10	1,680.43	2,286.6	2,983.76
	Equivalent in USD (mil. USD)	411.5	551.3	633.9	779.4	1,053.7	1386.5
State transfers and grants (donations, subsidies, subventions) from the central budget	Per cent	15.15	16.71	13.73	15.11	16.7	20.9
	In national currency (bn. Belarus roubles)	273.9	560.9	654.7	1,101.8	1,562.3	2,517.74
	Equivalent in USD (mil. USD)	231.8	354.9	341.0	511.0	720.0	1,169.95
Targeted and non-budget funds	Per cent	15.9	14.7	15.3	15.15	9.4	10.5
	In national currency (bn. Belarus roubles)	288.1	492.0	728.6	1105.1	888.8	1270.7
	Equivalent in USD (mil. USD)	244.2	311.4	379.5	512.6	409.6	590.5

Source: Author's own calculations based on the Ministry of Finance reports.

so-called national shared taxes. In other words, Mogilev oblast's budget retains 100 per cent of the profit tax and 100 per cent of the value added tax collected on its territory. The rates of shared taxes indicated above are planned so as to perform an expenditure assignment completely, that is to finance expenditures from taxes and fees collected in a given jurisdiction.

In Belarus, the function of collecting taxes, fees and charges is performed by the special central government body, the Ministry of Taxes and Tax Collection of the Republic of Belarus. The Ministry has a complete network of tax administration units located in the oblasts, rayons and cities with oblast status. Their function is to collect all taxes within the territory of their jurisdiction, both for the central budget and for local ones. These tax administrations are totally subordinated to the central government and managed by them. In the Belarus system of local budgets all local government revenues (taxes, fees, charges and transfers) including local taxes are determined beforehand by the centre as stipulated in the annual Budget Law of the Republic of Belarus. Local authorities can levy only those taxes, fees and charges determined by the Budget Law. In Belarus, the own revenue base consists of own taxes, fees, charges and fixed [*zakreplennyh*] taxes and fees.[4] They are also annually determined by the Budget Law of the Republic of Belarus and according to the structure displayed in Table 3.4.

Over the past five years, the centre has delegated some powers of taxation to local authorities in the field of financial administration. Local authorities have the right, for example, to increase or reduce tax rates, to provide exemptions and privileges for certain taxpayers, to establish and change the terms of payment for the land tax, the real estate tax, and for an ecological tax on resources extracted from the natural environment. The right has also been delegated for local authorities to give exemptions from personal income tax for individual taxpayers, for individual businessmen and for other individuals. Local authorities also have the right to regulate real estate tax rates. The following local taxes, fees and duties can also be regulated by the local authorities: parking fees; sales taxes in a retail network; duty for the services of hotels, restaurants, campsites, motels, bars and cafes; the advertisement tax; charges for individuals crossing the national borders and charges for trade preparation of mushrooms and plants. The local authorities can determine the tax rates, the tax base and terms of payments, objects of taxation and exemptions. In 2002 this measure has allowed an increase of the revenue base in the local budgets of some of the regions of Belarus.

Delegation of some of the powers of taxation to local authorities has not led to local government revenue autonomy. As mentioned above, local budgets in Belarus are not separated from the State budget system, so sub-national government budgets are components of the State budget. Its revenue parts are regulated by Budget Laws each fiscal year. In 2002 the local budget share of own revenue was 45.4 per cent of total revenues and the portion of shared taxes and transfers from the central budget was 39.3 per cent. On the other hand, the extent of the taxation power of local governments was at the rate of 8 per cent, that is, local authorities' levied taxes and collected revenues in their territory which amounted to 8 per cent of all revenues in their local budgets. By contrast, the degree of taxing power of the centre in respect to local budgets was defined at a rate of 92 per cent. So the centre almost exclusively retains the right to define the structure of taxes, to establish tax bases, tax rates and the regulation of taxes (Krivorotko, 2004b, pp. 132 –3).

Table 3.4 Structure of the own revenue base of local budgets of Belarus, fiscal year 2006

Fixed [*zakreplennye*] taxes and fees of the local authority by the Budget Law	Own taxes, fees, duties and charges
• Personal income tax	• Sale tax in retail trade
• Land tax	• Tax on services
• Real estate tax	• User duty
• Ecological tax for oil refining and mineral oil	• Targeted charges
• Tax on small business	• Resort duty
• Uniform tax from individual businessmen and other individuals	• Supplier duty
• Excises on wines and wine drinks	
• Gambling business tax	
• Advertisement fee	
• Fees for special usage of national resources	
• Bank deposit interests received by the local governments	
• Budget loans interests received by the local governments	
• Uniform tax for manufacturers of agricultural production	
• Tax on resources extracted from the natural environment	
• Financial sources from sale of property in abeyance	
• Rent for the lands received by the local authorities	
75%–78 % of own tax base	22%–25 % of own tax base

Source: Author's own calculations based on the Ministry of Finance reports.

Clearly, the development of independent local financial sources should be an important part of the implementation of fiscal decentralisation. Budget systems should be divided into two parts – the central and local budget systems – creating local financial autonomy by adopting special laws on local finance and budgets.

GRANT TRANSFERS

The grant and transfer system in Belarus is designed to equalise financial conditions for local governments and to fund public sector capital investments. In other words, it is designed to balance local budget revenues and expenditures. The full set of transfers and grants used in the local government financial system of Belarus is presented in Table 3.5.

Table 3.5 Central grants and transfers system in Belarus, fiscal year 2006: transfers and grants as a share of net excess expenditures (exceeding local budget revenues)

Item of transfers and grants	Share in per cent
Transfers (donations) to social-cultural sphere [*neproizvodstvennyu sferu*]	65.8
Grants (subventions) for housing construction	10.0
Grants (subventions) for funding of Minsk expenditures as a capital of Belarus	1.7
Grants (subventions) for construction of Minsk subway	0.2
Transfers (subventions) for financing of agricultural production expenditures	8.1
Transfers (subventions) for overcoming of consequence of Chernobyl catastrophe	14.2
Total:	100.00

Source: Author's own calculations based on the Ministry of Finance reports.

All central government transfers and grants are strictly programmed as established in the annual Budget Law adopted by the Belarus parliament. It is worth mentioning that the grants and transfers of the medium level (oblasts) governments are not applied. Instead, the method of shared taxation is used. The shared and ceded taxes – including the value added tax, profit tax, excise taxes, the shared portion of the personal income tax and the real estate tax – are equalised ('balanced') in the budgets of the rayons, cities with oblast status, cities with rayon status and the urban and rural settlements.

The most important central government transfers targeted at the social-cultural [*neproizvodstvennyh*] branches include expenditures for education, public health, culture, social care, payments of communal services and purchases of stock and equipment. Such transfers may be granted in the event of shortfalls of own and fixed [*zakreplennyh*] taxes, shared taxes, and of local taxes, fees and duties which lead to the inability to meet planned expenditures. These transfers are implemented from the special fund for financial support of administrative-territorial units in the central (Republican) budget. The equalisation of local government budgets is made on the expenditure side of local budgets through the simple method of vertical equalisation.

In Belarus the equalisation scheme is based on the grants formula, which includes the following components: a normative of per capita budgetary security as specified in the annual Budget Law; the number of inhabitants in the oblast or city; a correction coefficient taking into account the non-uniformity of social-cultural [*neproizvodstvennyh*] organisations and units located in the regions (Sorokina, 2000a, pp. 139–40). They are established for each social-cultural area. For example, in the capital, Minsk city, and in regional cities it is higher than in the countryside. By multiplying these components, the size of expenditures on social-cultural [*neproizvodstvennye*] programmes are determined. If revenue shortages occur with respect to the size of expenditures calculated, the central government is to draw from the fund for financial support of the administrative-territorial units for that purpose. Since 2002, the Belarus Ministry of Finance has introduced some corrective elements into the equalisation procedure which are now incorporated into the Budget Laws. Now, two separate normatives are to be used: the normative of budgetary security for explicit budget users (except for public health organisations) and the normative for public health organisations per habitant. The minimal normative is differentiated only for oblast budgets and the Minsk city budget.

Local budgets are balanced after the equalisation procedure is finished with grants (subventions and subsidies) provided from the central budget for housing construction, construction of municipal properties, maintenance of social sphere objects transmitted to local authorities, financing of school lunches, technical training colleges and schools located in polluted territories (mainly the Chernobyl catastrophe).

It should be mentioned that in practice the methods of equalising and balancing local budgets create unequal conditions for rayons and cities which use their own revenues to help fund their own needs and those which do not, but which receive significant grants from the central budget. It should be apparent that this allocation of central budget funds does not motivate sub-national governments to perform the necessary tasks to increase their own financial sources and reserves (Sorokina, 2000c, pp. 70–71). The main failing is that the bulk of grants allocated do not take into account the tax efforts of local authorities. As a result, the tax efforts of local authorities do not correlate with the level of social and economic development of their communities. The following principle of transfer allocations should, therefore, be realised: more effective local tax efforts should result in greater financial support from the centre.

To improve the grant and transfer system in Belarus local finance, it is necessary, first, to fix in legislation the system of financial equalisation, specifying effective equalisation conditions and methods of calculation so as to assure an incentive compatible distribution of grants and transfers. Second, it will be important for centre and local authorities to develop equalisation tools that do not infringe upon the interests of the most financially secure municipalities, but that also do not deprive subsidised authorities of incentives to improve their activities. Third, the system must create transparent procedure for the allocation of transfers which would tend to equalise the fiscal potentials and needs of municipalities and include the idea of revenue searching, instead of redistribution of central budget funds. Fourth, it is necessary to coordinate grants and transfers with the tax efforts of local authority. Finally, the grants and transfer system should not function as an instrument of political influence of the centre on sub-national governments.

LOCAL GOVERNMENT EXPENDITURES

Belarus local budget expenditures represent about 70 per cent of public sector expenses. The remaining 30 per cent of public sector expenditures are those of the central budget (see Table 3.6). Therefore, each local budget rouble used for welfare purposes has greater effect than a central budget rouble used for the same purpose. On the other hand, a rather large share of central budget expenditures continues to be used for public sector expenses which should be the prerogative of local governments. And although public sector expenditures from the central budget tend to decrease, their share of the total continues to be significant.

In recent years, local budget expenditures have been affected by the dynamics of development: rates of economic growth, the expansion of local sector needs and the development of social and industrial infrastructure (see Table 3.7).

Table 3.6 Funding of public sector expenditures (in percentages)

Public sector expenses (welfare sphere)	1997	1998	1999	2000	2001	2002	2003	2004	2005
Covered by the central budget	29.0	29.2	26.9	29.0	27.3	31.3	30.1	28.2*	31.3*
Covered by the local budgets	71.0	70.8	73.1	71.0	72.7	68.7	69.9	71.8	68.7
Total	100.0	100.0	100.0	100.0	100.0	100.0	100.0	100.0	100.0

Note: * Without taking into account a social defence of population fund.

Source: Author's own calculations based on the Ministry of Finance reports.

Table 3.7 The dynamics of local budget expenditures

	Expenditures	2000	2001	2002	2003	2004	2005
Local Budget Expenditures	In national currency (bn. Belarus roubles)	1,786.9	3,350.9	4,947.6	7,331.7	9,153.7	12,263.3
	Growth in per cent	302.3	187.5	147.6	148.2	124.8	134.0
	In equivalent USD (mil. USD)	1,514.3	2,120.8	2,576.9	3,400.6	4,218.3	5,698.7
	Growth in percent	82.0	140.1	121.5	132.0	124.0	135.1
Surplus (+), Deficit(-)	In per cent (to expenditures)	1.16	0.18	-3.66	-0.53	+2.48	-1.74
	In national currency (bn. Belarus roubles)	+20.7	+6.0	-181.0	-38.96	+227.6	-213.96
	In equivalent USD (mil USD)	+17.5	+3.8	-94.3	-17.7	+104.9	-99.4

Source: Author's own calculations based on the Ministry of Finance reports.

Over the last decade, the expenditure structure of local budgets has remained relatively constant. As a matter of fact, local budgets have not undergone substantive changes since the Soviet era. Therefore, expenditures have retained their traditional patterns for the social-cultural [*neproizvodstvenny*] sphere, including maintenance of educational organisations, public health, culture and payments of communal services. The same can be said of the funding of economic branches in the regions (transport and highways, public utilities, agriculture, industrial building materials, transport communication, trade), capital investment, State and local government administration and other expenditures.

Table 3.8 shows that a significant part of local budget expenditures is used on the neproizvodstvenny sphere in the rayons and cities, demonstrating the performance of local budgets with respect to their basic criteria. The invariance of the structure of local budget expenditures in the post-socialist period is a consequence of the absence of reforms at the local level, especially reforms in municipal management and finance and in privatisation. Many public utilities are subordinated to the centre. For example, the Ministry of Housing and Communal Services has centralised 11 public utilities, which could have been privatised. It is widely recognised that the privatisation of public utilities and municipal services can have considerable influence on the structure of expenditures, increasing the share of investments in the sphere of municipal services and in other enterprises in the regions. The structure of expenditures can also be changed through real local budget autonomy.

Table 3.8 Structure of local budget expenditures (in percentages)

Types of local budget expenditures	2000	2001	2002	2003	2004	2005
Expenditures on the social-cultural [*neproizvodstvenny*] sphere (education, public health, culture, fitness, mass media, social care)	48.9	51.0	55.0	50.0	51.3	54.2
Expenditures for financing of productivity branches in rayons and cities of oblast significance (industry, energy sector, construction, agriculture, transport, communications, road maintenance, market infrastructure, public utilities)	23.72	22.15	21.3	22.3	20.6	25.7
Expenditures for capital investments	5.96	5.77	2.85	5.0	5.2	2.6
Expenditures for State and local governance, national defence, national safety, science	3.95	4.02	3.85	4.4	4.7	3.0
Expenditures on other purposes (environment protection, purchases of equipment and stock)	1.64	2.9	2.5	4.6	4.9	4.2
Expenditures on target funds and non-budget funds (road fund, fund for nature protection, targeted housing loan, housing and investment fund, local fund for economic stabilisation, manufactures of agricultural production and other non-budget funds)	15.82	14.16	14.5	13.7	11.5	10.3
Total	100.0	100.0	100.0	100.0	100.0	100.0

Source: Author's own calculations based on the Ministry of Finance reports.

ACCOUNTING RULES, REGULATIONS AND LOCAL GOVERNMENT BUDGETING: PROCESS, SUPERVISION AND CONTROL

In Belarus, there are no specific rules of book-keeping for sub-national governments. Local authorities use the common rules of accounting applied in all government tiers and in all branches of the economy. Local authorities do not draw up and publish accounting balances (reports) by these standards. As a result, it is very difficult for regions and municipalities to make economic plans and calculations with a view to attracting investments. A prominent feature of the budget process in local financial administration is that the formation of local budgets occurs within the framework of a uniform State budget process. It imposes a certain specificity in the formation of local budgeting. According to the Budget Law of Belarus, the process of drawing up local budgets is automatically put in motion by the completion of the State budget.

Originally, the process of local budgeting began with the local governments. The main part of local budgeting is implemented by the rayon and the city with oblast status. The financial departments of local financial bodies, the rayons and cities, define opportunities to collect own revenues to supplement shared taxes. The expenditure side of local budgets is also simultaneously defined. The planned revenues and expenditures are submitted to the higher financial body, the oblast financial department. At this stage the opportunity to cover any local budget deficit from oblast and central budgets is determined. In the next stage of local budgeting macroeconomic aggregates are taken into account. Local budgets should be corrected on the basis of the macroeconomic parameters of the economy of Belarus as indicated by the Ministry of Economy and the Ministry of Finance. It is at this stage that the size of the consolidated budget, the amounts of central transfers and grants (subventions and subsidies) for local budgets, and the clarification and updating of total local budget revenues in the oblasts, rayons and cities with oblast status are achieved. After that the central and sub-national budgets are considered by the national government and the President of Belarus in the preparation of the State budget.

The next procedure consists of parliamentary hearings for the State budget in the Lower Chamber of the Belarus Parliament. Later, the budget is presented to the Upper Chamber for approval. After these parliamentary procedures the State budget is submitted to the President of the Republic of Belarus for signing, which gives it the force of law. The process's final stage is the adoption of local budgets in oblasts, rayons and cities by the Councils of Deputies.

In evaluating the above budget procedures, it should be noted that local budgeting has presented a lot of problems that need to be resolved. First, the process of planning and adopting the finalised local budgets is based entirely on the decisions of the central government. Second, the adoption of local budgets occurs only after the adoption of the State budget. Local councils have no opportunity to adopt their budgets before the beginning of a new fiscal year. Usually, this happens in January or February of the current fiscal year. Therefore, local authorities begin the new fiscal year without an adopted budget. Third, local budgets are not set up with separate operational and capital budgets. This vitiates the system of target controls over funding, both with respect to operational purposes and capital investment purposes. Fourth, forward planning and forecasting of local revenues and expenditures are not implemented. Fifth, the common standards and forms for budgeting in advanced countries and in some transition countries are not utilised.

The supervision and control systems over the activity of sub-national governments are basically implemented by external and internal control bodies. The external control bodies are implemented by the Committee of State control bodies, the Ministry of Finance's control bodies, the tax administrations of all levels, and the Committee of Economic Control in the regions. The basic internal body for controlling and supervising local government is the commission on budget and finance of the local council, which oversees the implementation of the local budget for a fiscal year. Independent audit organisations are not admitted to the process of control and supervision of the financial activities of local governments. Because State power is omnipresent in local governments, external State control is dominant in the Belarus system of local financial management. Supervision and balance in monitoring could be improved by introducing a public control chamber at the local level.

FURTHER DEVELOPMENT AND ACCESS TO FINANCIAL MARKETS

Serious reservations about the development of local government finance in Belarus are appropriate for the ways and means of accessing financial markets. According to the Law on Local Government and Self-Government, Belarus local governments can accumulate financial resources through borrowing. In practice, however, local governments do not have the full access to financial markets that would make borrowing possible. On the one hand, Belarus banks are not ready to grant credits to local government for investment purposes, because they do not yet have long-term financial resources in the face of rather high inflation rates. Moreover, the banks must accept huge credit risks to lend to local governments. On the other hand, sub-national governments are not yet ready to make loans due to the absence of legislatively defined borrowing procedures. Currently, many local councils have no current banking accounts and perform their functions through the banking accounts of local executive committees. This generates serious difficulties in the attempt to access financial markets and local governments fail to secure serious loans for current and capital purposes.

Despite these difficulties, however, the first steps in municipal borrowing are currently being taken in Belarus. A significant feature of municipal borrowing is a strict investment orientation in the housing sector, which is beginning to function on the basis of issues of municipal securities. Municipal securities occupy an insignificant place in the securities market in Belarus, but they provide housing construction loans in cities with oblast status through municipal bonds. The share of housing bonds in the Belarus security market structure of 1 January 2001 was about 1 per cent (Krivorotko and Radkov, 2001, p. 29). The first municipal loan in Belarus was in March 1993. At that time, bonds were issued to finance housing construction and were to be repaid in one year. The loan consisted of 2,250 bonds of different face value (with a return of 30 per cent per bond) with a total sum of 1 billion Belarus roubles (equivalent to 1,250,000 USD). The subsequent evolution of municipal borrowings is shown in Table 3.9.

Table 3.9 Borrowing in the housing sector (housing bonds in Belarus)

Borrowings	Duration	Number of issues	Amounts of the issues (mil. Belarus roubles)
The first Minsk targeted housing loan (one tranche)	1.11.96–30.06.99	1	500
The second Minsk targeted housing loan (one tranche)	22.11.96–22.11.02	1	3,900
The first Brest targeted housing loan (two tranches)	22.11.96–22.11.02; 06.07.99–10.07.01	2	1,500
The first Grodno targeted housing loan (one tranche)	15.10.99–15.09.02	1	400
The first Gomel targeted housing loan (one tranche)	14.06.0014.10.03	1	2,000

Source: Author's own calculations based on the State Committee of Securities reports.

As the figures in the table show, municipal borrowings are limited to housing construction, which is explained by the cautious position of local authorities in points of guarantees of loans repayment and by making the payments. One of the existing restrictions in the municipal borrowing sphere is the prohibition of purchasing bonds by individuals [*fizicheskimi litsami*]. The main weakness of municipal borrowings is the absence of regulations on municipal loans, including established restrictions on borrowing, authorised regulatory bodies, a legislative base for borrowing and special rules by which sub-national governments can access financial markets. Today, real maintenance of investment loans is achieved through the guarantees of reliable banks, which permit both the insuring of municipal loans against failure and the creation of confidence for investors to participate in regional projects and programmes. Another weakness of the borrowing system is the absence of a system to convert municipal securities into other reliable financial instruments, such as State short-term and long-term bonds, commercial paper and Central Bank bonds.

CONCLUSION

As has been shown, Belarus is far from achieving successful financial decentralisation. Despite the local budget independence proclaimed by the Constitution of Belarus, the budget system remains linked in a position of dependence to the State budget system. Local budgets are perceived by the public as vertical components of the state budget system and local budgets are strongly subordinated to the central budget. The degree of decentralisation, therefore, in local financial management is very low. A low level of taxing power, absence of local budgetary autonomy, chronic shortages of local government own revenues with respect to local expenditures are consequences of the hyper-centralised policy at the local level.

The further evolution of intergovernmental fiscal relations and local financial management will certainly require a deepening and improvement of the legislative base of local finance management in Belarus. First, the existing legislative base should be reconsidered and reformed. Clearly, it would be better to reject the Budget Law as a regulator of inter-budgetary fiscal relations and local financial management. In actual fact, the Budget Law strengthens the uniform budgetary process and the system of central control over the regions and sub-national governments. The amelioration of local financial legislation urgently demands the introduction of new, special laws regulating the financial activity of local authorities. In the view of the present author, Laws on Local Finance, Taxation and Budgets should be put into effect. To improve the coordination between the Budget Law and Laws on Local Finance, Taxation and Budgets, it is necessary to pass the Law on Conformity of Local Budgets to the State Budget. Additionally, it is necessary to introduce the Budget Code, which must incorporate a concept 'expenditure assignment', clarifying the rights and duties of local budget expenditures, of maintaining financial resources and of realising public services funding. Simultaneously, general principles of the distribution of the powers of taxation between authorities of different levels (central, regional and local) should be determined.

NOTES

1. The author would especially like to thank Robert Ebel, Adrian Ionescu and Joseph Hegedus for all the assistance in early stages of this research. Author's gratitude also goes to Tamara Sorokina and Dzmitry Sokal who provided insight into the Belarus local finance.
2. The Republic of Belarus is divided into provinces or oblasti without autonomous subunits. In turn, the oblast is divided into districts or so-called rayons. At the very bottom of the scale are cities with region status, cities with rayon status, urban settlements, urban districts and rural settlements and villages with only minor powers.
3. The terms 'donation', 'subvention' and 'subsidy' mean the specific transfers and grants from the central budget. A donation is the sum allocated from the budget of a higher level if the own and shared revenues for formation of the local budget are not sufficient. Donations are the no-purpose sums allocated for the local budgets' equalisation. Subvention is a grant or transfer allocated to local municipal units on specific goals and for a certain term from higher budgets. The subventions should be returned to the higher budgets if they are not used on a non-special purpose designation by the municipal unit. The order of subventions granting is established by the legislation. In this sphere, the central government performs legal and professional supervision. The relations in the subvention sphere are the financial toolkit by means of the regional centre's influence on the direction of municipal units' expenditures, especially on a municipal investment policy. A subsidy is a grant from the higher budget to the local budgets in case of participation in share financing of targeted expenditures.
4. Own taxes and fees may be introduced by the local authority. However, the content of own taxes, their tax base and limitations on tax rates are regulated by the Budget Law. According to the legislation, fixed [*zakreplennye*] taxes, fees and charges are assigned to local governments for an extended period.

BIBLIOGRAPHY

Bahl, R. (1991), *Fiscal Decentralisation, A report prepared for the Local Management Study*, Washington DC: US Agency for International Development.

Bahl, R. and J.F. Linn (1992), *Urban Finance in Developing Countries,* New York: Oxford University Press.

Bird, R., R. Ebel and C.I. Wallich eds (1995), *Decentralisation of the Socialist State,* Washington, DC: The World Bank.

Council of Europe (1985), *European Charter of Local Self-Government,* Strasburg: Council of Europe.

Davey, K. ed. (2002), *Fiscal Autonomy and Efficiency. Reforms in the Former Soviet Union,* Budapest: Local Government and Public Services Reform Initiative.

Dunn, J. and D. Wetzel (2000), *Fiscal Decentralisation in Former Socialist Economies: Progress and Prospects*, Washington, DC: The World Bank.

Ebel, R. (1999), *Fiscal Decentralisation and Intergovernmental Fiscal Relations, Distance Learning Modules*, Budapest: Open Society Institute

Horvath, T.M. ed. (2000), *Decentralisation: Experiments and Reforms*, Vol. 1, Budapest: Local Government and Public Services Reform Initiative.

Kandeva, E. ed. (2001), *Stabilisation of Local Governments*, Vol. 2, Budapest: Local Government and Public Services Reform Initiative.

Konstitutsia Respubliki Belarus 1994 goda (2004), s izmeneniami i dopolneniami. Prinaytna na respublikanskom referendume 24 Nojbraj 1996 [Constitution of Belarus of 1994 year (with changes and additions, it is accepted by a Republican referendum held on 24 November, 1996)], Minsk: Almafeya.

Krivorotko, Y. and V. Radkov (2001), Razvitie finansovyh instrumentov v munitsipalnom upravlenii [Evolution of financial tools in municipal management], *Munitsipalnay ekonomika* 7(3), 28–34.

Krivorotko, Y. (2002), Belorusskaj model mestnogo upravlenia: realnost i kritika [Belarus model of Local Government: reality and criticism], *Munitsipalnay ekonomika* **9**(1), 12–25.

Krivorotko, Y. (2003), Kontsepcia fiskalnoj detsentralizatsii: poidet li Belarus po puti ee realizatsii? [The concept of fiscal decentralisation: will Belarus go along with its realisation?], *Munitsipalnay ekonomika* **14**(2), 44–51.

Krivorotko, Y. (2004a), Munitsipalnye tsennye bumagi v sisteme denezhno-kreditnogo regulirovania Respubliki Belarus [Municipal securities in system of monetary and credit regulation of the Republic of Belarus], *Bankovski vestnik*, **258**(1), 19–20.

Krivorotko, Y. (2004b), *Belarus as the bordering country with the EU: New challenges for local finance development*, Sbornik prispevku z mezinarodni konference: Financni systemy kandidatskych zemi po vstupu do Evropske unie (31 May – 1 June 2004), Brno, Masarykova univerzita v Brne, pp. 130–35.

Lavrov A.J., M. Litvack and D. Sutherland (2000), *Fiscal Federalist Relations in Russian: A case for Sub-national Autonomy*, Working Papers, Paris: OECD.

Munteany, I. and V. Popa eds. (2001), *Developing New Rules in the Old Environment*, Vol. 3, Budapest: Local Government and Public Services Reform Initiative.

O Mestom upravlenii i samoupravlenii v Respublike Belarus (2000), [About Local Government and Self-Government in the Republic of Belarus], Zakon Respubliki Belarus 20 February 1991, Minsk: Natsionalny register zakonnyh aktov Respubliki Belarus.

Sidorchuk I. ed. (2007), *Mestnoe samoupravlenie v Belarusi*, [Local Government in Belarus], Minsk: Tonpick.

Sorokina, T. (2000a), *Budzhetny protsess v Belarusi* [Budget process in Belarus], Minsk: Belorusskij gosudarstvennyj ekonomicheskij universitet.

Sorokina, T. (2000b), Sovremennye tendentsii mezhbudzhetnyh otnoshenij [Modern tendencies of intergovernmental relations], *Vestnik Belorusskogo gosudarstvennogo economicheskogo universiteta*, **21**(4), 13–19.

Sorokina, T. (2000c), Regionalnye budzhety: formirovanie i ispolzovanie [Regional budgets: formation and utilisation], *Belorusskij economicheskij zhurnal* **12**(2), 65–72.

Wallich C.I., (1992), Local Finance and Intergovernmental Fiscal Relations in Developing and Transition Economies, A report prepared for the Economic Development Institute of the World Bank Urban Policy Seminar, Washington, DC: World Bank Institute.

World Bank (1999), *Credit Ratings and Bond Issuing at the Sub-national Level, Training Manual*, Washington, DC: The World Bank.

4. Local government finance in Bosnia and Herzegovina

Jean Tesche

INTRODUCTION

The current structure of Bosnia and Herzegovina was set up in December 1995 with the signing of the Dayton Peace Accords (US Department of State, 1995), which ended a devastating three-and-a-half year war. The Accords, which set up a decentralised state that was intended to be at least minimally acceptable to the warring parties, deal with the political, economic and monetary structures of the State of Bosnia and Herzegovina (Bosna i Hercegovina or BiH) in great detail, including the constitution, the military, the role of the international community and of neighbouring states, and internal borders. Since the Accords are crucial to understanding the structure of local government finance, and since BiH is unique among the Yugoslav successor states, they will be covered in some detail.

Bosnia and Herzegovina is a small country with slightly less than 4 million inhabitants (Agency for Statistics BiH, 2007). It is made up of two entities: the Federation of Bosnia and Herzegovina (hereafter called the Federation), and the Serb Republic (Republika Srpska, or RS). Around 70 per cent of the total population lives in the Federation, with approximately 30 per cent in the RS[1] (Federalni Zavod za Statistiku, 2003). The Federation is further divided into ten cantons, which was an attempt to give the two main ethnic groups some control at lower levels of government. Five of the cantons are majority Bosniak (Bosnian Muslim), three are majority Bosnian Croat and two are mixed.[2] In fact, all are mixed, but predominantly populated by one group or the other. Cantons vary by population and economic situation. Four have fewer than 100,000 inhabitants, three have between 200,000 and 300,000, and two have over 400,000 inhabitants (Federalni Zavod za Statistiku, 2003). Cantons are further divided into municipalities and two cities. The RS was overwhelmingly Bosnian Serb at the end of the war, but as more refugees have returned to their homes, it is again becoming more mixed. The RS is divided directly into municipalities and two cities with no intermediate level. The income disparity among municipalities in both entities varies greatly (World Bank, 2003). Yet another level of administration was added with the arbitration decision on Brčko District in March 1999 (Statute of the Brčko District of Bosnia and Herzegovina, 2000). Although it has only around 80,000 people, it was set up as an independent district, directly under the State with most of the institutions of an entity.

BiH was among the poorer republics before the war; per capita social product was only 68 per cent of the Yugoslav average in 1988 (Savezni Zavod za Statistiku, 1989). After the war, GDP was estimated at less than one fourth of the pre-war 12.8 billion DM (European Bank for Reconstruction and Development, 1999). GDP levels only reached 12 billion KM[3] again in 2003 (CBBH, 2003). The RS was less developed and lagged behind in post-war recovery. In 1995, the two entities were similar, with Federation GDP estimated at 2.9 billion DM and RS at 2 billion DM. By 2005, Federation GDP stood at 10.1 billion KM and RS GDP at 6.5 billion KM (Federalni Zavod za Statistiku, 2006; RS Institute of Statistics, 2007).

Together with the complex structure of government, another novelty in BiH is the role of the United Nations High Representative and European Union Special Representative, which is described in Annex 10 of the Dayton Accords (US Department of State, 1995). The Office of the High Representative (OHR) was set up to assist in implementation and serve as final arbiter of interpretation of the Accords. The Peace Implementation Council (PIC)[4] authorised the increased use of binding decisions at the High Representative's discretion in a number of areas at the Bonn PIC meeting in December 1998 (OHR, 1998). Although these powers were to be used as a last resort, their use has increased over time (OHR, 1997–2006). The High Representatives have been active in areas such as fiscal policy, legal reform and removing people from government positions.[5] The OHR was to have closed in 2007, but a new High Representative was appointed for one more year beginning in July 2007. Most of the imposed institutional changes have been in the direction of strengthening the State, partly because co-operation between and among governments in BiH is still a problem and partly in order to have a single interlocutor in the international arena. Additionally, a number of NATO troops and UN police have been stationed in BiH since the end of the war in 1995. The number of troops has declined over time and NATO's role was taken over by the European Union in December 2004, as was that of the UN's International Police Task Force (IPTF) mission in 2003 (EUPM, 2004).

Although some of the oversights or problems in the Accords have been highlighted in recent years, there has been no consensus on constitutional change.[6] BiH can still be considered to have only partial sovereignty, although it is a member of the United Nations and the Council of Europe. Many of the needed economic and administrative reforms have had to be pushed by the international community or imposed by the OHR. There are more than the usual problems in development assistance with local 'ownership' of reforms. Instead of the size and role of the state decreasing, as in most former socialist countries, the number of post-Dayton administration structures has proliferated. The international donors bear a substantial amount of the responsibility for this by continuing to deal with problems and obstructions with new layers of institutions. Twelve years after the wars, BiH is still a work in progress. It will take more time before its ultimate governing forms are decided.

THE BASIC LEGAL FRAMEWORK AND DEMOCRATIC LEGITIMACY

The Dayton Peace Accords (1995) contain most of the legal basis for the State of BiH, including the constitution. In them, the State has only a limited role. It is responsible for all foreign and international relations and customs, monetary policy, criminal law enforcement, and international communications and transport. The State has a two-house parliament, the House of Peoples and the House of Representatives, along with a rotating Presidency (among the three main ethnic groups) and a Council of Ministers, originally including only Foreign Trade, Foreign Affairs and Civil Affairs. This was augmented to six ministries in 2000 (OHR, 2000), and now to nine: Foreign Trade and Economic Relations, Foreign Affairs, Defence, Finance and Treasury, Civil Works, Human Rights and Refugees, Security, Justice and Communications and Transport (Council of Ministers, 2007). The OHR and donors have since pushed to increase the role of the State due to functional expediency as well as frustration with the lack of a meaningful State government with which to negotiate. Problems in negotiations to join NATO's Partnership for Peace and to reach agreement for the Stabilization and Association Agreement to start European Union (EU) accession discussions are examples of this. Either the State is not able to agree in order to make decisions or commit the entities, or the duplication of institutions such as the armies or police is a problem.

The Accords give entities all powers and functions not explicitly assigned to the State level. Each has its own fiscal system, social policies, police and army. The Federation has two houses of Parliament, the House of Representatives and the House of Peoples, while the RS has a single National Assembly. The Federation is divided into ten cantons and 79 municipalities (Federalni Zavod za Statistiku, 2007). The RS is divided directly into 63 municipalities (RS Institute for Statistics, 2007).[7] The Federation constitution is a product of the Washington Agreement that ended the fighting between Croats and Bosniaks in March 1994 (Constitution of FBiH, 1994). The Cantons in the Federation have their own consitutions and laws on local self-government (World Bank, 2003). The responsibilities assigned to local governments are similar to those in the Federation Consitution, including the imprecise language on the division of responsibilities (Jokay, 2001).

The Federation Constitution states that each municipality shall exercise self-rule on local matters. Each municipality has a statute, which is consistent with the Federation and Canton Constitutions. The RS Constitution (Constitution of the RS, 2001) was first published in 1992, but has been amended many times including by Decisions by the OHR. Municipalities in the RS have jurisdiction over specific needs at the local level such as education, health and social welfare.

Brčko District was set up as a single administrative unit of local self-government directly under the State of BiH, not the entities (Statute of the Brčko District of BiH, 2000). It includes the three municipal governments within the pre-war municipality. District authorities cannot delegate any governmental power not specifically assigned in the Statute to either entity. The Constitution of BiH, as well as the relevant laws and decisions of the institutions of BiH, apply in the District. Since the State still has only a limited role, in practice this has meant yet another complete set of institutions. Brčko has a parliament and complete judicial and fiscal systems.

In the current structure of BiH, local governments have little autonomy and virtually no place in central government priorities. Municipalities are essentially creatures of the entity, in the case of RS, or of the cantons in the Federation. In the Federation, cantons are the main unit of local government (Sakic, 2000). There is a great deal of frustration with the mismatch between expenditure responsibilities and revenues. There is no predictability in resource transfers and no mechanism for matching revenues with expenditure responsibilities. Almost at the same time that Dayton was signed, these problems with the fiscal structure were being pointed out (see for example: IMF, 1995; Fox and Wallich, 1997). However, in other areas, things worked out better than envisaged by the early reports. Tax harmonisation within the Federation did not turn out to be a major problem, Federation-wide tax laws and the law allocating those revenues (see the following section) were passed relatively easily in 1996. Inter-entity harmonisation of some tax laws and cooperation among tax administrations were and remain difficult issues. Just harmonising excise tax rates between the entities took years of negotiations and was accomplished only in 1999.

INDEPENDENT LOCAL GOVERNMENT REVENUE SOURCES

The revenue structures of the two entities are relatively similar. Most revenues sources of lower levels are assigned taxes or proportions of taxes collected by the entities. In spite of numerous donor reports and recommendations, there are still no formalised transfer mechanisms between levels of government in either entity (Fox and Wallich, 1997; Sakic, 2000; USAID, 2003, and World Bank, 2003). The only truly independent sources of revenues for cantons and municipalities are local taxes and fees. In both the Federation and RS, the entity level decides the revenue sources and sharing proportions. Tax revenues are mostly assigned to the jurisdictions where they are collected.

Until 2005, the State was entirely dependent on entity transfers and its own small revenues (consular fees, civil aviation and income from setting standards). Revenues transferred from the entities made up 60 per cent of the State budget in 1997, rising to more than 85 per cent of a growing total from 1998 (Table 4.1). Originally, two-thirds of these transfers were to come from the Federation and one-third from the RS to reflect the differences in the size of the two economies.

In December 2003, the State Indirect Taxation Authority (ITA) was created to deal with customs, excises and a value added tax (VAT), to be introduced in 2006, at the initiative of the High Representative and donors (World Bank, 2003; IMF, 2004b). The revenues collected by the ITA were to be allocated to the State external debt service, to replace entity transfers to the State, plus operating costs for the ITA. Only the remaining revenues were to be allocated to the entities and Brčko District (IMF, 2004b). The formula for the allocation of ITA revenues between the entities has yet to be determined, it is still being negotiated. It was thought that this would be a major loss of revenue for the cantons and municipalities, especially in the Federation, where they shared all of the sales tax revenues. In the RS, municipalities received nearly one third of sales tax revenues in 2002 and 2005 (Table 4.2). In fact, VAT revenues in the first year turned out to be quite robust, with increased indirect tax revenues going to the entities and Brčko, even after increased amounts went to the State. Although this new administration is seen as rationalising part of tax administration, in fact it adds another costly level of bureaucracy without addressing the existing problems of co-operation between the entities.

The fiscal structure in the Federation was set up with the 'Law on the Allocation of Public Revenue in the Federation of BiH' (1996, hereafter called the Allocation Law). All main tax revenues were regulated and collected by the Federation tax administration. Cantons regulate only the citizens' income tax (on non-wage income), property taxes and some fees and utilities. Cantons have their own revenue allocation laws. The main sources of Federation revenues were from customs, excises, administrative and Federal court fees and fines, and revenues from natural resources (see Table 4.2). With the introduction of the single Treasury account for customs and excise taxes in 2005 and the inclusion of VAT revenues in 2006, the Federation share of indirect taxes has remained by far the largest revenue source. Canton revenues are listed in the 'Law on the Federal Units' (1996). Municipal revenues are assigned by each canton. Municipal Councils only regulate municipal taxes such as fees for utilities and financial penalties.

As can be seen in Tables 4.2 and 4.3, most Federation taxes were allocated to either the Federation or the cantons; only the corporate tax was shared between them. All cantonal taxes are shared with municipalities. From 2006, indirect taxes are shared among all levels. All others, including indirect taxes (also for municipalities in 2006) are shared. The largest tax sources for cantons were sales and wage taxes. The major tax sources for municipalities were the shared sales and citizens taxes, together with fees. Now their share of indirect taxes is the largest single revenue source cantons have received more revenues than the Federation with the exception of 2002. However, by 2006, the canton share had increased to around two thirds more than the Federation. Municipal taxes have mostly stayed around one fourth of Cantonal Revenues (Table 4.2). Municipal revenues vary greatly by canton, but average around 20 per cent, increasing to 30 per cent in 2006 (Table 4.2).

In the RS, revenues from customs and excise taxes also belonged to the Entity (Table 4.2). Twenty-six per cent of revenues from income tax were allocated to the municipalities in the RS, while 30 per cent of sales taxes or 35 per cent for cities (Banja Luka and Srpsko Sarajevo) belongs to municipalities. All revenues from taxes on agriculture and forestry go to municipalities (Zakon o porezu na dohodak gradjana [Law on Citizen's Income Tax], 2001; Zakon o akcizama i porezu na promet [Law on Excise and Sales Tax], 2002, and World Bank, 2003). Total RS revenues were around one third the level in the Federation, not including canton revenue, in 1997, surpassing unconsolidated Federation revenue in 2006 (Table 4.1). Direct taxes play a much smaller role in revenues in the RS (Table 4.2). The RS introduced new direct tax laws in 2006, which came into effect in 2007. There is now a single 10 per cent rate for corporate profits and a two rate structure for personal income at 10 per cent and 15 per cent. Incomes from different sources are still calculated separately (Zakon o porezu na dobit, Zakon o porezu na dohodak, Official Gazette of the Republic of Srpska, 2006).

GRANT TRANSFERS AND LOCAL GOVERNMENT EXPENDITURES

Among the main problems with local government expenditure responsibilities is the lack of a clear division of responsibilities, and of a transparent, predictable method of allocating transfers. In addition, the administrative and technical abilities of municipalities to fulfil their obligations vary greatly (World Bank, 2003). In spite of the large differences in municipalities' abilities to raise revenues, equalising grants have not been seriously discussed, let alone implemented. This is the case within each entity, not even considering the possibility of inter-entity transfers. Indeed, as pointed out in Fox and Wallich (1997), redistribution policies were a problem among Yugoslav republics before 1990.

Expenditure responsibility in the Federation is laid out in the Constitution (1994) and the Allocation Law (1996). The Constitution states that the Federation shall have exclusive responsibility for economic, fiscal and energy policy, Federation finances and financial institutions, and financing government activities. The Federation and canton governments share responsibilities for health, communications and transport infrastructure, social welfare policy, tourism, and the use of natural resources. Cantons have all responsibilities not expressly granted to the Federation. Cantons may delegate functions and must delegate, for functions such as education, culture, radio and television, to a municipality where the majority of the population is different from that of the canton as a whole. In practice, cantons have given municipalites exclusive control over urban planning, utilities, pre-schools, school maintenance and transport, ambulances, health care supplies, culture, libraries and sport (World Bank, 2003).

In the RS, the Republic level is responsible for most areas including: defence, property relations, the banking and tax systems, the development of agriculture, public services, employment, health care, education, environmental protection and the public information system (Constitution of Republika Srpska, 2001). The main law that deals with local governments is the 'Law on Local Self-Governance of the Republika Srpska' (1999). Municipality responsibilities include development and urban planning, education, health and social welfare. In fact, in many areas, such as health, transportation, housing and many services, municipal responsibilities are similar in the two entities.

Table 4.1 State and entity revenues (not consolidated)

	1997	1998	1999	2000	2001	2002	2003	2003	2004	2005	2006
						million KM					
State									GFS**		
Own Revenue/ tax revenues*	20	20	31	32	38	41	51	7.0	9.0	252.4	422.8
Transfers from Entities	30	118	187	242	234	318	411	111.5	169.9	0	0
Other revenues	0	0	0	0	1	4	4	152.2	156.0	220.5	80.5
Total revenue	50	138	218	275	273	363	466	270.7	334.9	472.9	503.3
Federation of BiH											
Tax revenue	565	645	677	768	813	930	1,009	901	895	933	975
Other revenue	45	37	47	61	59	108	103	110	157	188	182
Total revenue	610	682	724	829	873	1,038	1,112	1,011	1,052	1,121	1,157
RS											
Tax revenue	197	295	561	632	687	778	794	776	807	891	1,050
Other revenue	12	62	93	96	94	151	133	225	174	143	161
Total revenue	209	357	654	728	780	929	927	1,002	981	1,034	1,211
Brčko District											
Tax revenue								141.0	140.4	124.7	108.0
Other revenue								58.9	65.7	54.0	33.0
Total revenue				23.1	98.1	138.7	206	200.0	206.1	178.7	202.0
						Per cent of total revenue					
State									GFS		
Own Revenue/ tax revenues *	40.0	14.5	14.4	11.8	13.8	11.3	10.9	2.6	2.7	53.4	84.0
Transfers from entities	60.0	85.5	85.6	88.2	85.7	87.6	88.3	41.2	50.7	0.0	0.0
Other revenues	0.0	0.0	0.0	0.0	0.5	1.1	0.8	56.2	46.6	46.6	16.0
Federation of BiH											
Tax revenue	92.6	94.6	93.5	92.7	93.2	89.6	90.8	89.1	85.1	83.2	84.3
Non tax revenue	7.4	5.4	6.5	7.3	6.8	10.4	9.2	10.9	14.9	16.8	15.7
RS											
Tax revenue	94.3	82.6	85.8	86.8	88.1	83.8	85.6	77.5	82.3	86.2	86.7
Non tax revenue	5.7	17.4	14.2	13.2	11.9	16.2	14.4	22.5	17.7	13.8	13.3

Notes: *Revenues from the Indirect Tax Authority via a single account after 2005.
**Figures restated from 2003 using Government Financial Statistics (GFS).

Sources: Central Bank of Bosnia and Herzegovina (CBBH) 2006b, 2004, 2005, and 2007a.

There are some differences as to the degree of co-financing, and secondary education is at the municipal level in the RS, but there are more similarities than differences (Sakic, 2000).

Cantons in the Federation have a fair amount of autonomy in setting their budget processes. All have their own budget laws. Cantons also administer the off-budget funds, pension, health and employment, in the Federation (World Bank, 2003). Municipalities in both entities, however, have much less autonomy or control over either resources or mandatory expenditures. Municipalities are dependent on transfers from higher levels, which averaged only 10 per cent of consolidated Federation (canton plus Federation) and 17 per cent of RS revenues in 2002 (Federation Ministry of Finance, 2003; Delegation of the European Union in BiH, 2003, and Table 4.2). Financing is mostly done at the canton level in the Federation (World Bank, 2003).

Prior to 2005, transfers from the entities went both upwards and downwards. As can be seen in Table 4.5, transfers upward to the State increased steadily from 1997 to 2003 (rising from 5 to 22 per cent in the Federation and from 12 to 15 per cent in the RS between 1998 and 2003). Until 2000, the only State expenses were for the smaller number of ministries and debt service. By 2003, there was a much larger budget for administration together with wages for the border service. The overall budget had grown from 110 million DM in 1997 to 509 million KM in 2003, and 453 million KM by 2006, excluding debt service in 2006 (Table 4.5).

The Federation budget (not including cantons or municipalities) has doubled from 600 million DM in 1997 to more than 1 billion KM since 2003. Restated using GFS methodology since 2003, this figure was slightly less than 1 billion in 2003 (Table 4.5). In 1997, the two largest areas of expenditure were military and transfers to households, at more than 35 per cent each, followed by transfers to the State. By 2006, the social benefits still accounted for 34 per cent, but wages and contributions fell to 14 per cent. As in the Federation, the largest expenditure in the RS budget in 1997 was the military (35 per cent), followed by other, unknown, expenses (23 per cent). Wages quickly increased to be the largest budget expenditure, remaining around 35 per cent, also followed by social benefits. The amounts transferred to lower levels of government are a very small part of the budget: consistently 1–2 per cent of Federation expenditures and less than 1 per cent in the RS (most is done through shared taxes, Tables 4.2 and 4.5). Transfers are negotiated annually. In spite of more than ten years of advice from various donors to produce a transparent sharing formula (Fox and Wallich, 1997; Sakic, 2000; USAID, 2003, for example), there has been little change in these processes. This means that municipalities cannot plan on a consistent revenue flow, and that some are unable to meet required

Table 4.2 Revenues by type of tax and level in both entities, 2002 and 2005

	2002 million KM				
	Federation	Canton	Municipality	RS	Municipality
Customs	516.2	0	0	146.7	0
Excises	450.7	0	0	58.5	0
Sales tax	0	718	67.3	113.9	51.9
Wage tax	0	112.8	23.6		
Profit tax	8.1	31	1	12.4	0.2
Citizen's tax	0	17.5	53	51.6	23.5
Other taxes	0	10.6	4		
Other fees and penalties	116.1	81.8	85.1		
User fees	3.7	32.3	7.3		
all other				69	17.9
Total	1094.8	1004	241.3	452.1	93.5
Percentage of Total					
Customs	100.0	0.0	0.0	100.0	0.0
Excises	100.0	0.0	0.0	100.0	0.0
Sales tax	0.0	91.4	8.6	68.7	31.3
Wage tax	0.0	82.7	17.3		
Profit tax	20.2	77.3	2.5	98.4	1.6
Citizen's tax	0.0	24.8	75.2	68.7	31.3
Other taxes	0.0	72.6	27.4		
Other fees and penalties	41.0	28.9	30.1		
User fees	8.5	74.6	16.9		
All other				79.4	20.6
Total	46.8	42.9	10.3	82.9	17.1

Notes: *2005 customs and excise revenues collected by the Indirect Tax Authority went into the single treasury account. From 2006 the single account included VAT.

Sources: Federation Ministry of Finance, 2003, Delegation of the EU in BiH, 2003, World Bank, 2003, CBBH Government Operations for FBIH and RS, 2007.

Table 4.2 (cont'd)

	2005 million KM Federation	Canton	Municipality	RS	Municipality
Single account	888	240	10	469	67
Goods, services	1	763	98	274	136
Payroll, workforce	0	143	29	105	35
Income, profit, capital gains	42	53	13	28	1
Property		6	52		34
Other tax	2	2	8	15	4
Total tax	933	1207	210	891	277
Single account	78.0	21.1	0.9	87.5	12.5
Goods, services	0.1	88.5	11.4	66.8	33.2
Payroll, workforce	0.0	83.1	16.9	75.0	25.0
Income, profit, capital gains	38.9	49.1	12.0	96.6	3.4
Property	0.0	10.3	89.7	0.0	100.0
Other tax	16.7	16.7	66.7	78.9	21.1
Total tax	39.7	51.4	8.9	76.3	23.7

Table 4.3 Federation revenues by level

	1999			2000			2002			2004			2006*		
							million KM								
	Fed.	Canton	Muni	Fed.	Canton	Muni	Fed.	Canton	Muni	Fed.	Canton	Muni	Fed.	Canton	Muni
Customs*	345.2			430.8	0	0	516.2	0	0	420.8	0	0	758.7	1252.7	147.6
Excises*	314.5			314.8	0	0	450.7	0	0	444.8	0	0			
Sales tax*		692.3	69.8	0	698.2	73.1	0	718	67.3	0	960.3	81.2	0	158.3	37.8
Wage tax				0	172.2	38.2	0	112.8	23.6	0	132.4	29	48.4	50.8	0.4
Profit tax				22.6	26.1	1.2	8.1	31	1	30.4	31.6	1.4	0	24.5	61.8
Citizen's tax				0	15.6	40.2	0	17.5	53	0	21.1	54.5	2.7	9.4	11.3
Other taxes							0	10.6	4	0	8.8	7.3	20.6	67.4	65
Other fees and penalties				52.7	137.2	31.5	116.1	81.8	85.1	20.9	69.5	54.8	5.9	38.0	25.5
User fees							3.7	32.3	7.3	5.3	27.3	23.9	165.5	103.3	74.9
All other	17.5	231.9	79.6							157.6	60.3	46.7	213.7	139.4	58.1
Total	677.2	924.2	149.4	820.9	1,049.3	1,84.2	1,094.8	1,004	241.3	1,079.8	1,311.3	298.8	1,001.8	1,704.4	424.3
Percentage of total															
Customs*	100.0	0.0	0.0	100.0	0.0	0.0	100.0	0.0	0.0	100.0	0.0	0.0	35.1	58.0	6.8
Excises*	100.0	0.0	0.0	100.0	0.0	0.0	100.0	0.0	0.0	100.0	0.0	0.0			
Sales tax*	0.0	90.8	9.2	0.0	90.5	9.5	0.0	91.4	8.6	0.0	92.2	7.8			
Wage tax				0.0	81.8	18.2	0.0	82.7	17.3	0.0	82.0	18.0	0.0	80.7	19.3
Profit tax				45.3	52.3	2.4	20.2	77.3	2.5	47.9	49.8	2.2	48.6	51.0	0.4
Citizen's tax				0.0	28.0	72.0	0.0	24.8	75.2	0.0	27.9	72.1	0.0	28.4	71.6
Other taxes							0.0	72.6	27.4	0.0	54.7	45.3	11.5	40.2	48.3
Other fees and penalties				23.8	62.0	14.2	41.0	28.9	30.1	14.4	47.9	37.7	13.5	44.1	42.5
User fees							8.5	74.6	16.9	9.4	48.3	42.3	8.5	54.8	36.7
All other	5.3	70.5	24.2							59.6	22.8	17.6	48.2	30.1	21.8
Total	38.7	52.8	8.5	40.0	51.1	9.0	46.8	42.9	10.3	40.1	48.7	11.1	32.0	54.4	13.6

Note: *All indirect taxes, including the new VAT, revenues from the Single Account in 2006. Some residual sales tax collections in 2006.

Sources: Federation Ministry of Finance, 2003; Delegation of the EU in BiH, 2003; World Bank, 2003; CBBH FBiH.

expenditures. They also receive a number of unfunded mandates (Sakic, 2000; USAID, 2003). The amounts transferred to households, which was mainly to the pension and health funds, dwarf the transfers: falling from 35 per cent of Federation expenditures in 1997, to 24 per cent in 2003 and increasing from 7 to 13 per cent of a much smaller budget over the same period in the RS (Table 4.5).

ACCOUNTING RULES, SUPERVISION AND CONTROL

The main focus of public finance reform has been on increasing accountability and control over management of public finance, especially the need for better expenditure management (World Bank, 2001). There has been a great deal of technical assistance in the accounting and control area in BiH. New budget classification systems have been introduced at all levels. The introduction of the Treasury general ledger system at the entity level January 2002 (OHR, 2002), and the State in June 2002 has helped, not least to make the process more transparent. Efforts to extend the Treasury system to canton and municipal levels are ongoing. International Accounting Standards (IAS) have been introduced in both entities, but are not consistently applied (World Bank, 2002).

Supreme Audit Institutions (SAIs) were set up at the State and entity levels in 2000. The State SAI based on the 'Law on Auditing of Financial Operations of the Institutions of Bosnia and Herzegovina' (1999) includes a Coordinating Board consisting of the three (State and two entities) Accountant Generals and Deputies. The SAIs have a broad mandate: the verification of public revenues, expenditures, assets and enterprises fully or partially owned or financed by the governments. BiH became a member of the International Organisation of Supreme Audit Institutions in 2001. So far, the SAIs have worked mainly on compliance audits, aimed at seeing that existing rules and laws are enforced (World Bank, 2002)

Internal audits were previously carried out through the Payment Bureau, a Yugoslav institution that administered and controlled all monetary transactions, including those of government budgets, enterprises, banks and taxpayers. When it was closed in January 2001, this function was replaced with inspection units in the Ministries of Finance and the Financial Police, neither of which was really prepared to perform this role. In 2001–02, a series of decisions from the High Representative set up special auditors for the Federation, the cantons and the RS (OHR, 2001b, 2002). The auditors examined public funds at all levels. The report submitted to OHR in June 2001 listed systematic irregularities in both entities. It stressed the need for funding and independence of the

Table 4.4 Federation: municipal revenue shares by canton

	2000				2002				2004				2006			
	Mil. KM		per cent		Mil. KM		per cent		Mil. KM		per cent		Mil. KM		per cent	
	Canton	Muni	Canton	Muni	Canton	Muni	Canton	Muni	Canton	Muni	Canton	Muni	Canton	Muni	Canton	Muni
1. Una-Sana	96.6	29.0	76.9	23.1	88.7	24.8	78.1	21.9	117.6	29	80.2	19.8	149.6	47.9	75.7	32.7
2. Posavina	18.4	3.4	84.4	15.6	15.7	3.6	81.3	18.7	20.4	5.8	77.9	22.1	28.4	6.9	80.5	26.3
3. Tuzla	172.6	39.1	81.5	18.5	157.1	45.9	77.4	22.6	219	59.2	78.7	21.3	287.9	89.2	76.3	32.1
4. Zenica–Doboj	115.4	29.9	79.4	20.6	114.7	29.4	79.6	20.4	152.9	38.8	79.8	20.2	215.7	59.6	78.4	31.1
5. Bosnia—Podrina	9.0	1.9	82.5	17.5	8.7	2.1	80.6	19.4	19	2.6	88.0	12.0	27.7	4.9	85.0	22.7
6. Central Bosnia	100.7	21.4	82.5	17.5	72.8	17.9	80.3	19.7	99.4	21.3	82.4	17.6	120.0	31.6	79.2	26.2
7. Herzeg–Neretva	114.1	28.4	80.1	19.9	82.4	30.5	73.0	27.0	108.9	46.5	70.1	29.9	141.2	69.4	67.0	44.7
8. West Herzegovina	40.0	11.4	77.8	22.2	33.6	11.2	75.0	25.0	45.9	15.8	74.4	25.6	61.8	21.7	74.0	35.2
9. Sarajevo	363.0	12.0	96.8	3.2	366.5	19.5	94.9	5.1	475.3	48.7	90.7	9.3	634.5	82.3	88.5	15.7
10. Canton No. 10	19.5	7.7	71.7	28.3	21.3	7.0	75.3	24.7	25.6	7.2	78.0	22.0	37.5	10.8	77.6	32.9
Total	1,049.3	184.2			961.5	191.9			1,284.0	2,74.9			1,704.3	424.3		
Average			81.4	18.6			79.6	20.4			80.0	20.0			78.2	29.9

Sources: World Bank, 2003; Ministry of Finance, Federation of Bosnia and Herzegovina, 2007.

audit function (OHR, 2001a). The 2001 Report on the Presidency identified a number of weaknesses in the management control systems in budget execution and lack of procedures on spending (Report on the Audit of the Presidency, 2002). By 2006, audits were performed on most institutions. The 2006 Report on the Presidency lists similar deficiencies as in the first report (Audit Office of the Institutions of Bosnia and Herzegovina, 2007).

Despite start-up problems, the establishment of an external audit function, together with the introduction of Treasury systems, are important steps towards better, more transparent, control of public finances. As with many economic reforms, the impetus for more accountability and transparency in public finance came from donors, not from the various BiH governments.

FURTHER DEVELOPMENTS: LOCAL GOVERNMENT AND FINANCIAL MARKETS

The external debt situation went from disastrous to manageable fairly quickly after the signing of the Dayton Accords at the end of 1995. BiH concluded agreements rescheduling debt with the London and Paris Clubs in December 1997 and October 1998, respectively. As a result of this, external debt dropped from 4 billion DM in 1997 to 3 billion in 1998. It has stabilised at around 4 billion KM since 2000 (CBBH, 2006b). External debt fell from over 130 per cent of GDP in 1996 to 65 per cent in 1998 and to less than 25 per cent by 2006, partly due to increasing GDP (IMF, 2001, 2002, 2004a, 2004b, 2006). Debt service as a percentage of exports also dropped dramatically, falling from 118 per cent of exports in 1995 to 53 per cent in 1996. It fell to less than 10 per cent in 1999, and to 5 per cent by 2006 (CBBH, 2006b). In 2006, the World Bank continued to be the largest debtor, accounting for more than 2 billion out of the total debt of nearly 4 billion KM, followed by the Paris club debt at less than 1 billion KM (or 25 per cent of total debt). Private debt to the London Club members is around 200 million KM, the same level as EBRD debt (CBBH, 2006b). One worrying aspect of new borrowing since 1998 is that about one half has consistently been used on current budget expenditures, leaving only half for financing infrastructure and investment (IMF, 2004a).

Internal debt is a bigger problem. This debt stems from three main sources: frozen foreign currency accounts, war damage claims and government arrears. The Federation has additional debt from voucher privatisation. The IMF (2004b) estimated total internal debt claims to be around 204 per cent of GDP for BiH as a whole. Of that, the Federation total was around 230 per cent and the RS around 164 per cent of their respective GDPs in 2001. In both entities,

Table 4.5 BiH expenditures: state, entities, Brčko District (unconsolidated)

								GFS			
						million KM					
	1997	1998	1999	2000	2001	2002	2003	2003	2004	2005	2006
State of BiH											
Wages and contributions					22	37.3	48	100.8	140.7	197.9	249
Border service (GFS: goods, svcs.) svcs.GFS)	0	0	0	6	30.8	50.7	54	50	64.1	85.6	100
Institutions (GFS: Social Benefits)	0	0	0	0	5.5	7.4	8.5	3.1	0.8	15.3	10
Ministries (GFS: Subsidies)	35	51	57.8	70.1	80	106.8	122.4	0.7	0.1	1.9	6
Debt service (GFS: Interest)	75	87	158.7	197.8	178.1	232.2	324.4	91.4	79.3	88.1	0
Other								8.5	10.6	10.7	88
TOTAL	110	138	216.5	273.9	294.4	397.1	509.3	254.5	295.6	399.5	453
Federation of BiH											
Wages and contributions	70	77	92	103	108.2	131.2	133.7	361	301	252	156
Goods and services	21	37	32	29.8	32.3	43.1	67	101	78	78	43
Military	254	276	291	309.6	290.2	386.7	270				
Reconstruction	17	43	26	47.2	46.6	53.5	70.5				
Subsidies (GFS: subsides and grants)	3	20	14	14	11.2	20	20	118	158	138	164
Other transfers to hshlds. (soc.benefits)	227	258	216	255	278.6	322.2	295.5	319	338	338	380
Transfers to the state	30	65	84	153	167.8	191.4	262.3				
Transfers to cantons and municipalities	4	7	16	25.1	10	14.5	13				
Net lending	0	0	0	-7	0	0	0	-7	22	188	267
Other	32	21	28	46.2	52.7	71.6	85.4	92	114	106	103
TOTAL	658	804	799	975.9	997.6	1234.2	1217.4	984	1011	1100	1113
RS											
Wages and contributions	25	155	209	346	346.3	356.7	354	336	359	344	362
Goods and services	31	50	162	85.8	113.4	81.9	104.7	158	92	66	121
Military	73	70	89	70							
Subsidies (GFS: subsidies and grants)	0	0	12	18.7	17.8	38.4	18	107	236	269	336
Transfers to funds	6	0	28	16	20.2	115.3	91				
Transfers to households (soc.benefits)	15	79	94	141.6	147.2	105.5	128.1	153	152	152	166
Transfers to municipalities	1	1	2	2.5	3	2	2				
Transfers to the state	0	55	92	101	135.4	129	149.1				
Clearance of arrears	0	0	0	34.8	24.5	63.2	25.8				
Capital expenditure	9	12	42	73	57.1	57.3	68.9				
Net lending								65	41	66	155
Other	49	25	32	18.5	25.2	78.5	38.1	149	83	81	64
TOTAL	209	447	762	907.9	890.1	1027.8	979.7	968	963	978	1204
Brčko District											
Wages and contributions								57.2	63	58.1	47.4
Goods and services								75.5	67.2	70.7	43.9
Social Benefits								20.9	20.1	27	
Subsidies								5	4.1		22
Interest											0
Other								3.2	2.9	6.7	0
TOTAL				23.1	98.1	138.7	113.3	161.8	157.3	162.5	113.3

Table 4.5 (cont'd)

	million KM							GFS			
	1997	1998	1999	2000	2001	2002	2003	2003	2004	2005	2006
Expenditure as a per cent of total											
State of BiH											
Wages and contributions					7.5	9.4	9.4	39.6	47.6	49.5	55.0
Wages and contributions				2.2	10.5	12.8	10.6	19.6	21.7	21.4	22.1
Border service (GFS: goods, svcs.) svcs.GFS)				0.0	1.9	1.9	1.7	1.2	0.3	3.8	2.2
Institutions (GFS: Social Benefits)	31.8	37.0	26.7	25.6	27.2	26.9	24.0	0.3	0.0	0.5	1.3
Ministries (GFS: Subsidies)	68.2	63.0	73.3	72.2	60.5	58.5	63.7	35.9	26.8	22.1	0.0
Other								3.3	3.6	2.7	19.4
TOTAL	100.0	100.0	100.0	100.0	100.0	100.0	100.0	100.0	100.0	100.0	100.0
Federation of BiH											
Wages and contributions	10.6	9.6	11.5	10.6	10.8	10.6	11.0	36.7	29.8	22.9	14.0
Goods and services	3.2	4.6	4.0	3.1	3.2	3.5	5.5	10.3	7.7	7.1	3.9
Military	38.6	34.3	36.4	31.7	29.1	31.3	22.2				
Reconstruction	2.6	5.3	3.3	4.8	4.7	4.3	5.8				
Subsidies (GFS: subsides and grants)	0.5	2.5	1.8	1.4	1.1	1.6	1.6	12.0	15.6	12.5	14.7
Other transfers to hshlds. (soc.benefits)	34.5	32.1	27.0	26.1	27.9	26.1	24.3	32.4	33.4	30.7	34.1
Transfers to the state	4.6	8.1	10.5	15.7	16.8	15.5	21.5				
Transfers to cantons and municipalities	0.6	0.9	2.0	2.6	1.0	1.2	1.1	0.0	0.0	0.0	0.0
Net lending	0.0	0.0	0.0	-0.7	0.0	0.0	0.0	-0.7	2.2	17.1	24.0
Other	4.9	2.6	3.5	4.7	5.3	5.8	7.0	9.3	11.3	9.6	9.3
TOTAL	100.0	100.0	100.0	100.0	100.0	100.0	100.0	100.0	100.0	100.0	100.0
RS											
Wages and contributions	12.0	34.7	27.4	38.1	38.9	34.7	36.1	37.2	38.9	37.7	34.5
Goods and services	14.8	11.2	21.3	9.5	12.7	8.0	10.7	17.5	10.0	7.2	11.5
Military	34.9	15.7	11.7	7.7	0.0	0.0	0.0				
Subsidies (GFS: subsidies and grants)	0.0	0.0	1.6	2.1	2.0	3.7	1.8	11.8	25.6	29.5	32.0
Transfers to funds	2.9	0.0	3.7	1.8	2.3	11.2	9.3	16.9	16.5	16.7	15.8
Transfers to households (soc. Benefits)	7.2	17.7	12.3	15.6	16.5	10.3	13.1				
Transfers to municipalities	0.5	0.2	0.3	0.3	0.3	0.2	0.2				
Transfers to the state	0.0	12.3	12.1	11.1	15.2	12.6	15.2				
Clearance of arrears	0.0	0.0	0.0	3.8	2.8	6.1	2.6				
Capital expenditure	4.3	2.7	5.5	8.0	6.4	5.6	7.0				
Net lending								7.2	4.4	7.2	14.8
Other	23.4	5.6	4.2	2.0	2.8	7.6	3.9	16.5	9.0	8.9	6.1
TOTAL	100.0	100.0	100.0	100.0	100.0	100.0	100.0	100.0	100.0	100.0	100.0
Brčko District											
Wages and contributions								35.4	40.1	35.8	41.8
Goods and services								46.7	42.7	43.5	38.7
Social Benefits								12.9	12.8	16.6	0.0
Subsidies								3.1	2.6	0.0	19.4
Interest								0.0	0.0	0.0	0.0
Other								2.0	1.8	4.1	0.0
TOTAL								100.0	100.0	100.0	100.0

Sources: IMF; CBBH 2004; 2005, 2006a; Government Operations BH, FBiH, RS, 2007.

war claims are by far the largest item, estimated at 139 per cent of GDP in the Federation, and 126 per cent in the RS, followed by vouchers from privatisation in the Federation (71 per cent of GDP) and frozen deposits in the RS (89 per cent of GDP). Arrears are estimated at 'only' 6 per cent of GDP in the Federation, and 9 per cent in the RS (IMF, 2004b).

The debt from frozen foreign currency accounts arose at the start of hostilities in Croatia and Slovenia in 1991. Virtually all foreign currency deposits in Yugoslavia were held by the National Bank of Yugoslavia in Belgrade, regardless of where the deposit was made. The original amounts were used long ago by the Yugoslav government, but all of the post-Yugoslav states are making efforts to repay domestic depositors. A second set of internal claims on the government is for war damages. In 2001, courts in RS ruled that citizens could sue their government for war damages (IMF, 2004b). In the Federation, there was no clear court ruling, but there have been a number of cases initiated. Both governments intend to convert part of this debt to long-term bonds and discounted cash. The final source of internal debt is government arrears in payments. These arrears include both late or non-payment of wages or pensions and late payments to suppliers.

The legal framework for sub-entity borrowing in the Federation is in the budget system laws and the 'Law on the Basis for Local Self-Governance of the Federation of BiH' (1995). Borrowing is authorised, but the policies are not spelled out. In the last few years, the annual budget execution laws have forbidden commercial borrowing below the Federation level. In the RS, short-term deficits can only be funded from the Republic level (IMF, 2004b). Sub-entity debt appears to be small. Borrowing at lower levels is allowed only for investment and up to a limit of 20 per cent of budget revenues in both entities (World Bank 2001). In 1999, interest and debt payments were less than 0.1 per cent and 0.4 per cent of canton expenditures, respectively. Canton lending to municipalities was less than 3 per cent of canton budgets, on average, in 1999 (World Bank, 2003). Municipal debt seems to be mostly from banks to cover short-term shortfalls. There is no legislation dealing with domestic borrowing guarantees (World Bank, 2001). Arrears and contingent liabilities are not included in debt calculations, however, and these items may be large.

CONCLUSIONS

A number of the problems with intergovernmental fiscal relations in BiH are due to the Dayton Peace Accords themselves. Although they are quite detailed in assigning fiscal responsibilities to different levels, they are not always consistent. The Accords were completed in a very short time as a compromise intended to stop the war, and therefore not every issue was thought through. A number of problems in local government finance became evident early on and are still unresolved. These include the imprecision of expenditure allocation rules between levels of government and the mismatch between revenue raising capacity and expenditures. A transparent formula for transfers and mechanisms for equalising resources is still missing. The method of financing of the State when all taxing authority lies with the entities was another problem that has now been addressed with the creation of the ITA and State level indirect taxes, but only due to pressure from the international community, rather than by the entities themselves.

Along with the Dayton structures, another part of the responsibility for continuing problems rests with the international community. There has been a kind of creeping colonialism. First it was hoped that the three ethnic groups and two entities would make the kinds of decisions that the international community wanted them to. When this didn't happen, it was followed by more and more frequent imposition of laws and institutions as international frustration with the lack of progress increased. It has become a vicious cycle where there is no need for BiH leaders to take responsibility or to co-operate since someone else will always make the difficult decisions. It may be time to let, or force, politicians to be held accountable for their decisions, which is admittedly difficult when they are still subject to dismissal by an outside authority.[8] Ultimately, the international community needs to back its way out of running the show and the citizens of BiH need to take responsibility for their destiny, with some safeguards.

On the positive side, the State is now functioning with a level of acceptance that was unimaginable in the early post-war years (although still not always good). BiH is still not a fully sovereign state. It needs to continue market-oriented and institutional reform, particularly to finish the SAA agreement for EU accession. Serious discussion of the issues brought up in this chapter, among others, by all levels of BiH governments, not by international donors, is needed. True fiscal decentralisation with clear powers and responsibilities has yet to be implemented. There is still little evidence that sub-State level politicians and institutions are ready to make decisions that will allow the country to function and prosper.

NOTES

1. Population figures have varied depending on the source. The BiH Agency for Statistics (2003) gives a figure of 3.8 million. The Federation Statistics Agency (2007) gives the Federation pop-

ulation at 2.8 million, but notes that 500,000 do not reside in the Federation. The RS Institute of Statistics (2004a) gives a figure of 1.4 million. More realistic estimates of the RS population are no more than 1 million (Delegation of the European Union in BiH, 2003, ESI, 2004a). Therefore, the ratio of Federation to RS population can vary from 61:39 to 74:26. No BiH-wide census has been taken since 1991.

2. The five Bosniak (Bosnian Muslim) cantons are: Una-Sana, Tuzla, Bosna-Podrina(Goražde), Zenica-Doboj, and Neretva-Herzegovina. The three majority Croat are: Posavina, West Herzegovina and Canton 10. The two mixed cantons are Central Bosnia and Sarajevo.
3. Convertible mark (konvertibilna marka, KM) banknotes were introduced in June 1998. The KM was pegged one to one with the Deutsche Mark, and from 2002 at 1.95583 to the Euro (CBBH, 2002). The use of DM or KM in the text depends on timing only, they are equivalent.
4. The Peace Implementation Council (PIC) was set up in December 1995. It is made up of 55 countries and agencies that support the peace process (OHR, 2004b).
5. Examples of the use of OHR's authority include removing senior managers of the RS electric company (OHR, Press Releases: 26 February 2003), and the Head of the Education Department in Brčko (23 September 2004), appointing the 16 members of the State level High Judicial Prosecutorial Council (4 June 2004), sanctions on the Serb Democratic Party (SDS) for non-cooperation with the International Criminal Tribunal of Yugoslavia (26 March 2004), or suspending budget payments to the Croatian Democratic Union (HDZ) of BiH for non-cooperation in educational policy, submitting draft legislation on the intelligence services to the State parliament (17 December 2003) and setting up a new State Indirect Tax Policy Commission (12 February 2003). Knaus and Martin (2003) strongly criticise the lack of transparency or checks on these OHR powers.
6. An interesting alternative raised in an ESI report (2004b) proposing the abolition of the Federation, leaving 12 sub-national units under the State including the ten cantons, Brčko District and the RS. Also see Tesche (2000) for a more thorough discussion of the various political and economic issues confronting BiH after the war.
7. Sources differ as to the number of municipalities in both entities. There have been some divisions and mergers of municipalities, but even recent sources vary, from 79 to 87 in the Federation and from 53 to 63 in the RS (Federalni zavod za statistiku, 2003, 2007; IMF 2004b; RS Institute of Statistics, 2007, World Bank, 2003).
8. As happened in December, 2004, when the High Representative removed nine people from various security or police positions, enacted eight legal amendments and ordered the RS General Auditor to perform special audits (OHR, 2004a). After a year of discussions on ending the role of the OHR in 2006–07, the new High Representative almost immediately removed a number of police officers from the RS policy in July 2007.

BIBLIOGRAPHY

Agency for Statistics Bosnia and Herzegovina (2003), *Statistical Bulletin 2*, Sarajevo: Agency for Statistics.

Audit Office of the Institutions of Bosnia and Herzegovina (2007), Izvestaj o reviziju Predsjednistva Bosne i Hercegovine [Audit report on the Presidency of Bosnia and Herzegovina], April, Sarajevo: Audit Office of the Institutions of Bosnia and Herzegovina

Central Bank of Bosnia and Herzegovina (CBBH) (2002), *Annual Report, 2002*, Sarajevo: CBBH.

Central Bank of Bosnia and Herzegovina (2003), *Annual Report, 2003*, Sarajevo: CBBH.

Central Bank of Bosnia and Herzegovina (2004), *Bilten 4, December*, Sarajevo: CBBH.

Central Bank of Bosnia and Herzegovina (2005), *Bilten 1, March*, Sarajevo: CBBH.
Central Bank of Bosnia and Herzegovina (2006a), *Bilten 1, March*, Sarajevo: CBBH.
Central Bank of Bosnia and Herzegovina (2006b), *Annual Report, 2006*, Sarajevo: CBBH.
Central Bank of Bosnia and Herzegovina (2007a), *Bilten 1, March*, Sarajevo: CBBH.
Central Bank of Bosnia and Herzegovina (2007b), *Government Operations for BH, FBIH and RS*, www.CBBH.ba.
Constitution of the Federation of Bosnia and Herzegovina (1994), January, Amended No. 13 (1997), No. 16 (2002), No. 22 (2002), No. 52 (2002), No. 60 (2002), No. 18 (2003), No. 63 (2003), Sarajevo: Official Gazette of the Federation of BiH.
Constitution of Republika Srpska (2001), September 26, Sarajevo: OHR. (Original: Official Gazette of the RS (1992), Amendments No. 150 (2002), No. 162 (2002), No. 131 (2003), No. 9 (2003).
Council of Ministers (2007), www.vijeceministera.gov.ba.
Delegation of the European Union in BiH (2003), *Studija o potencijalnim izvorima prihoda za Institutcije Bosne i Hercegovine* [Study on Potential Revenue Sources for the Institutions of Bosnia and Herzegovina], Sarajevo: Delegation of the EU in BiH.
European Bank for Reconstruction and Development (1999), *Transition Report, 1999: Ten Years of Transition*, London: EBRD.
European Stability Initiative (ESI) (2004a), *Governance and Democracy in Bosnia and Herzegovina: Post-industrial Society and the Authoritarian Temptation*, Berlin and Sarajevo: ESI.
European Stability Initiative (2004b), *Making Federalism Work: A Radical Proposal for Practical Reform*, Berlin and Sarajevo: ESI.
European Union Police Mission (EUPM) (2004), *Important Activities*, www.eupm.org/activities/Activities20031.htm.
Federalni Zavod za Statistiku [Federation Statistics Agency] (2003), *Kantoni u Brojkama, 2003* [Cantons in Numbers, 2003], Sarajevo: FZS.
Federalni Zavod za Statistiku [Federation Statistics Agency] (2006), *Kantoni u Brojkama, 2006* [Cantons in Numbers, 2006], Sarajevo: FZS.
Federalni Zavod za Statistiku [Federation Statistics Agency] (2007), *Kantoni u Brojkama, 2007* [Cantons in Numbers, 2006], Sarajevo: FZS.
Federation Ministry of Finance (2003), *Tabelarni Pregled* [Overview in Tables], Sarajevo: Federation Ministry of Finance.
Federation Ministry of Finance (2003–2006), *Tabelarni pregled* [Overview in Tables], Sarajevo: Federation Ministry of Finance.
Fox, W. and C. Wallich (1997), *Fiscal Federalism in Bosnia-Herzegovina: The Dayton Challenge*, The World Bank Policy Research Working Paper No. 1714, Washington, DC: The World Bank.
IMF (1995), *Fiscal Federalism, Taxation, and Expenditure in Bosnia and Herzegovina: Policy and Administrative Development for Nation-Building*, 14 December, Washington, DC: IMF.
IMF (2001), *Bosnia and Herzegovina: Fourth and Fifth Reviews Under the Standby Arrangement and Requests for Extension and Rephasing of the Arrangement. Staff Report and Press Release of the Executive Board Discussions*, Country Report No. 01/08, Washington, DC: IMF.
IMF (2002), *Statistical Appendix, No. 02/60*, Washington, DC: IMF.
IMF (2003), *Article 4 Consultations*, Country Report 04/67, Washington, DC: IMF.

IMF (2004a), *Bosnia and Herzegovina: Poverty Reduction Strategy, Mid-Term Development Strategy*, Country Report No. 04/114, Washington, DC: IMF.
IMF (2004b), *Selected Economic Issues,* BiH Country Report No. 04/54, IMF, Washington, DC.
IMF (2004c), *Statistical Appendix*, Country Report No. 04/76, Washington, DC: IMF.
Jokay, C. (2001), Local Government in Bosnia and Herzegovina, in E. Kandeva ed., *Local Governments in Central and Eastern Europe*, Budapest: LGI Books, pp. 89–140.
Knaus, G. and F. Martin (2003), Lessons from Bosnia and Herzegovina, Travails of the European Raj, *Journal of Democracy,* **14**(3), 60-74.
Law on Auditing of Financial Operations of the Institutions of Bosnia and Herzegovina (1999) No. 17, Sarajevo: Official Gazette of Bosnia and Herzegovina (BiH).
Law on Federal Units (1996), No. 9, Sarajevo: Official Gazette of the Federation of BiH.
*Law on Local Self-Governance of the Republic of Srpska Decembe*r (1999), Banja Luka: Official Gazette of the Republic of Srpska.
Law on the Basis for Local Self-Governance of the Federation of BiH (1995), No. 6/95, Sarajevo: Official Gazette of the Federation of BiH.
Law on the Allocation of Public Revenues in the Federation of Bosnia and Herzegovina and Funding of the Federation of Bosnia and Herzegovina (1996), No. 26, 30 December. Amendments No. 32 (1998), No. 54 (2001), Sarajevo: Official Gazette of the Federation of BiH.
OHR (1997–2006), *Press Releases,* http://www/ohr.int
OHR (1998), *PIC Bonn Conclusions*, http://ohr.int
OHR (2000), *Chronology 2000*, http://www/ohr.int
OHR (2001a), *Chronology 2001*, http://www/ohr.int
OHR (2001b), *HR's Decisions*, http://www/ohr.int, 5 February.
OHR (2002), *HR's Decisions*, http://www/ohr.int, 2 August, 21 October.
OHR (2004a), *HR's Decisions*, http://www/ohr.int, 17 December.
OHR (2004b), *Economic Newsletter*, Vol. 7, No. 1.
OHR (2004c), *General Information*, http://www/ohr.int
Report on the Audit of the Presidency of Bosnia and Herzegovina, Year 2001 (2002) www.revizija.gov.ba, No. 01-400-332/MB/02.
Report on the Audit of the Presidency of Bosnia and Herzegovina, Year 2006 (2007) www.revizija.gov.ba, April.
Republika Srpska Institute of Statistics (RSIS) (2004a), *Demographic Statistics, No. 7*, Banja Luka, RSIS.
Republika Srpska Institute of Statistics (2004b), *Quarterly Statistical Review, No. 1*, Banja Luka, RSIS.
Republika Srpska Institute of Statistics (2007), Website, www.rzs.ba
Sakic, M. (2000), *Analysis on Local Governance, Legal Jurisdiction and Practice in Bosnia and Herzegovina*, 28 August, Sarajevo: USAID.
Savezni zavod za statistiku [SZS, Federal Statistical Office] (1989), *Statisticki Godisnjak Jugoslavije 1989* [Statistical Yearbook Yugoslavia 1989], Belgrade: SZS.
School of Economics, University of Sarajevo (1999), Fiscal Decentralisation in Bosnia and Herzegovina, in *Fiscal Decentralisation Initiative for Central and Eastern Europe*, June, Sarajevo: School of Economics.
Statute of the Brčko District of Bosnia and Herzegovina (2000), August, Banja Luka: Official Gazette of the Republic of Srpska, and September Sarajevo: Official Gazette of Bosnia and Herzegovina (BiH).

Tesche, J. (2000), Bosnia and Herzegovina: Five Years after Dayton, *Post-Soviet Geography and Economics*, **41**(6), 376-90.
USAID (2003), *Local Government Assessment and Policy Recommendations*, November, Sarajevo: USAID.
US Department of State (1995), *Dayton Peace Accords: General Framework Agreement for Peace in Bosnia and Herzegovina*, December, Washington, DC: US Dept. of State, Office of Public Communication, Bureau of Public Affairs.
World Bank (2001), *Bosnia and Herzegovina, Towards Financial Sustainability and Credit Worthiness*, 22 October, Washington, DC: World Bank.
World Bank (2002), *Bosnia and Herzegovina, From Aid Dependency to Fiscal Self-Reliance: A Public Expenditure and Institutional Review*, Report No. 24297-BiH, Washington, DC: World Bank.
World Bank (2003), *Bosnia and Herzegovina, Creating an Efficient Decentralized Fiscal System*, June, Washington, DC: World Bank.
Zakon o porezu na dohodak gradjana [Law on Citizen's Income Tax] (2001) No. 01-107/01, Banja Luka: Official Gazette of the Republic of Srpska.
Zakon o akcizama i porezu na promet [Law on Excise and Sales Taxes] (2002) No. 01-020-356/02, Banja Luka: Official Gazette of the Republic of Srpska.
Zakon o porezu na dohodak [Law on Income Tax] (2006) No. 91/06, September, Banja Luka: Official Gazette of the Republic of Srpska.
Zakon o porezu na dobit [Law on Profit Tax] (2006) No. 91/06, September, Banja Luka: Official Gazette of the Republic of Srpska.

5. Strengthening local government finance: the case of Bulgaria

Svetlana Alexandrova

INTRODUCTION

Bulgaria has carried out a comprehensive decentralisation reform since the inception of transition. Decentralisation is a focal point where we examine social and economic problems at the sub-national level. In Bulgaria, the redistribution of authority and the responsibilities for the provision of public services by different levels of government is gradually being achieved, but gaps in the legislation on overlapping responsibilities and revenue autonomy remain. Despite progress in the area of administrative and fiscal decentralisation, local finance management also remains highly centralised. Ongoing decentralisation reform must be accompanied by better municipal management and decision making.

The purpose of this survey is to review Bulgarian experience in local finance management, in the organisation of administrative and territorial structures, in the division of responsibilities and duties of central, regional and local governments. The emerging new role of regional and local bodies is derived from EU regional and structural policy priorities and goals. The devolution of power from central to local authorities is regulated by a package of laws that has been harmonised with EU legislation.

Local governance and financial reform began in 1992 and has proved to be an extended process. The goals of local administrative and financial reform were: (1) to restructure and develop the territorial, functional and institutional organisation of local self-government and to improve its co-operation with the system of state management; (2) to establish and develop democratic procedures and mechanisms for the functioning of local self-government; (3) to enhance and widen the scope of the centralisation process; and (4) to integrate and join the nation's local and regional structures to the corresponding European structures.

The local government programme began with the adoption of legislation related to self-management and local finance. A new mechanism for the delegation of responsibilities to local authorities consists of measures promoting greater public participation and improving links between the central and the local governments; improving the institutional relationships ensuring competition among the regions, while promoting collaboration and the creation of productive and financial conditions encouraging economic growth and, finally, improving horizontal coordination. The principal focus of the survey is the capacity of the municipalities to provide public services and the degree of financial independence they enjoy. The divergence in their economic and social development will be seen as a consequence of their divergent economic potential and of the inefficient intergovernmental transfer system.

BASIC LEGAL FRAMEWORK AND LOCAL GOVERNMENT FINANCE REGULATIONS

The decentralisation of government decision making involves the delegation of increased powers to local authorities. In the literature there are different definitions for 'decentralisation'. One which is frequently used emphasises the transfer of authority and responsibility for public functions from the central government to sub-governments. Basic principles of good decentralisation relate to revenue autonomy, transparency, sound accountability and strong local institutional capacity.

Resources allocated are determined by the extent of power delegation for the delivery of public services. Bulgaria faces the problem of delegating responsibilities and building the capacity of lower levels to correspond with resource transfers. The framework of local self-government and fiscal decentralisation was developed after 1993. The essential acts regulating local government and local administration include the Law on Local Self-Government (1991), amended in 1998; the Municipal Property Act (1996); the Law on Local Taxes and Charges (1996); the Law on Administrative and Territorial Structure and Internal Division of Cities (1996); the Law on Regional Development (1998); the Municipal Budgets Act (1998); and the Structure Budget Act (1998). Decentralisation in Bulgaria was mandated by the new democratic constitution of 1990. The Constitution of the Republic of Bulgaria protects the autonomy of local self-government (Article 136 defines local self-government as follows: 'the municipality is the main administrative unit, which carries out local self-government'). In Bulgaria, the Constitution establishes public administration in territorial administrative units, based on local autonomy and decentralisation of public services. It mandated regular elections for mayors and municipal councils.

The Law on Local Self-Government and Local Administration (LLSGLA) establishes the municipality as a self-governing body with its own budget and the right to own property. Enacted in 1991, it defines the operations, rights and authority of local self-government, with municipalities generally having at least 6,000 inhabitants. The Local Government Act significantly increase the responsibilities and resources of sub-national governments

Functions of local governments specified in the above-mentioned laws include the following:

- managing municipal property, municipal enterprises, municipal finances, taxes and fees, and other administrative tasks;
- developing strategy activities and financial projections for them;
- financing local education (pre-school, primary and secondary);
- financing local health care (outpatient, policlinic and hospital care, preventive care, community care, and municipal sanitation);
- financing local cultural programmes: community centres, libraries and museums, etc.;
- financing public works and utilities (water, sewage, electric power, central heating, telephone line installation);
- maintaining streets and squares, parks, gardens, street lighting, landscaping, etc.;
- financing social welfare programmes (social care and welfare benefits, provision of subsidised housing and other social programmes);
- implementing local and national environmental protection programmes;
- maintaining historical, cultural and architectural monuments;
- financing sport and recreation centres.

Because the municipalities are generally not in a position to accomplish all these tasks, the government of Bulgaria has demonstrated its commitment to fiscal decentralisation by the Council of Minister's approval in May 2002 of the proposed Fiscal Decentralisation Concept and Program, and its implementation started 2003. Once approved by the National Assembly, the reforms to the Municipal Budget Act, the Local Taxes and Fees Act, and other laws on intergovernmental relations created a policy framework that increases local government revenue sources, clarifies expenditure responsibilities, and imposes greater fiscal discipline.

Changes in the legal framework of local finance have made it necessary to develop sound financial management at the local level. Thus, changes have been made to the State Budget Act (2003), to the Local Tax and Fees Act and to the Municipal Budgets Act. The Parliament accepted (2004) a new Regional Development Act which had been elaborated according to the requirements of EU regional policy development. Generally, the division of the tasks between the central government and local authority is regulated by the State Budget Act and the Municipality Budgets Act. The central and local government bodies jointly elaborated a decentralisation programme. The legislated amendments sought to facilitate the effective functioning of local governments.

Changes in the State Budget Act (2003) stressed the funding of responsibilities delegated to municipalities. The act declared that local taxes, fees, grants and subsidies are the main sources for financing local activities. Shared taxes are to finance the responsibilities delegated to municipalities. The government will provide continuous monitoring of financial decentralisation. The municipalities are responsible for mobilising and collecting revenues. Any deficits accrued in delegated assignments will be covered by the Ministry of Finance. The municipality's council decides and defines the local tax, fees and penalties. The usual practice is that the State budget announces the specific intergovernmental revenue flows (the revenue flows are determined by the line ministries) each year.

Municipalities apply two types of levies: fees and public service prices in compliance with the Local Taxes and Fees Act. Under the law the municipalities are empowered to determine the specific fees and prices. Municipalities have been empowered to provide public services funded by the revenues generated from them. They have the right to determine garbage collection and other fees, managing both the public services and the cash flows.

Local governments receive two thirds of their revenues as transfers from the central government. These transfers comprise four types:

- Conceded income tax revenues – these are conceded by the central government to the local authorities in order to fund the so-called 'delegated from the state activities'. The conceded amount from the income tax revenues depends on the expenditures for delegated activities for the respective municipality.
- General supplementary subsidy – if all the income tax revenues from one municipality are conceded to the municipality and the amount is not enough to fund the delegated activities, the government grants an additional amount of money to cover the difference (the cost of delegated activities is determined by the government).
- Equalisation subsidy – if the revenues from local taxes are lower (on a per capita basis) in some municipalities than the average national level, these municipalities receive the difference from the government.
- Subsidy for capital expenditures.

According to the Municipal Budget Act, intergovernmental transfers include shared taxes (conceded income tax revenues), general subsidies, supplementary subsidies and equalisation subsidies. The target subsidies are to finance capital costs for exceptional national and international projects within national investment programmes. The shared taxes and supplemental subsidies finance the municipality's delegated responsibilities. The supplemental subsidy covers the difference between budget credits for state activities and shared taxes revenues. The capital investments are financed by target subsidies which are relevant to needs. Municipal councils accept the budget, but the indicators for financing delegated activities are determined strictly by the Ministry of Finance. Target grants (national and EU programmes) for capital projects are not funded according to the anticipated economic and social returns of those projects. Limits on municipal debt have been established by legislation. Under the act, the cost of servicing budget debt, as well as debt amortisation, cannot exceed 25 per cent of the revenues generated internally by the municipality. Municipal debt cannot be based on mortgage collateral. The Municipal Debt Act (2005) facilitates the execution of the public project and contributes to the development of the public services.

DEMOCRATIC LEGITIMACY AND FINANCIAL REPORTING

The current system of financial management is based on transfers from the state to local governments. Exercising local self-management functions, municipalities participate in social and economic development planning through the municipal budget, property management, investment activities to meet the needs of inhabitants, and encouragement of economic activities. The economic development initiatives of local governments are placed in a development plan. Regional development policy aims at sustainable, balanced, regional development, reduction of interregional disparities, and establishment of regional cross-border co-operation that facilitates the EU-integration process. Regional plans are programming documents consisting of the priorities and goals of the territorial-administrative units.

With the amendment of the Administrative-Territorial Structure of Bulgaria Law of December 1998, 28 districts or counties were established. Bulgaria's administrative structure is currently comprised of 264 municipalities, which are included in 28 districts or oblasts. Responding to the need for regional programming, six regions were formed: the Northwest Region, the North Central Region, Northeast Region, the Southeast Region, the South Central Region and the Southwest Region. The efficient use of EU funding requires well-prepared regional plans, transparency of information and accountability. In the last two years an attempt has been made to initiate intergovernmental planning among the levels of government. The role of the regional level, developed in anticipation of EU accession, is defined by the newly accepted Regional Development Act. For the implementation of good local government policy it is critical that as administrative and territorial reform evolves, the specific functions of the local authorities in regional development policy be defined, communicated, understood and implemented. The Regional Development Act corresponds with EU criteria for regional development, programming and planning. The law states that the rules concerning effective interaction between municipalities and districts (such as the procedure for preparing and updating the regional development plans) must be adhered to. The Regional Development Act has established rules concerning effective interaction between municipalities and districts in the regional planning process. The districts are responsible for drawing up their own development strategy.

The role of the regions, districts and municipalities is defined in compliance with the principle of programming EU structural funds. The county or oblast is an executive body responsible for the coordination of regional planning activities. The counties (districts) are responsible for state policy execution and for the coordination of national and local interests. The districts or oblasts are administrative units whose regional governor is appointed by the central authority, the Council of Ministers.

The district strategy is elaborated by district or oblast authorities. The oblast strategy consists of the economic and social development analyses of the municipalities, the short- and long-term goals for developing businesses and promoting their competitiveness. The district strategy is approved by the district council, consisting of the mayors. On the basis of the Regional Development Act, the District Office represents the state in developing district strategy that acknowledges the general priorities and goals of the municipalities and prepares discussions on district social and economic development.

There are six regional offices to coordinate economic, social and regional programming tasks yet to be established. A Referendums Act (1996) regulates the citizens' participation in the political process. Taking into consideration that the local authority is close to the people, the assumption is that the decisions of the local authorities reflect the interests of the citizens. They do not participate very actively, however, in the discussion of the local bodies' decisions, and are passive with respect to municipal expenditure for public utilities.

Despite the Referendum Act, there is no tradition of holding referenda on significant municipal economic and social issues. In recent years, with NGO support, initiatives have been undertaken to organize civil forums on the crucial issues of municipal development. The government entrusts the following duties to the municipalities for their economic and technical development: the municipal budget, municipal property management, investment in business activities, supporting of economic activities, issuing binding regulations on investment, use of local resources and entrepreneurial activities and territorial land planning. Municipal bodies do not have the capacity to perform some of these functions, especially making appropriate investments and effectively using local financial resources.

NGOs have successfully developed decentralisation concepts. They provided opinions and expertise on legislation and evaluated current local management capacity. The NGOs, especially the Regional Associations of municipalities, organised training and forums to promote citizens' activities in designing strategic plans and the conception of municipal economic and social development.

The UNDP assessment of the absorption of EU funding at local levels underlined the need for proper development of municipal strategy plans, as well as the coordination of resource mobilisation at the local and regional levels. Citizens participate in government through elected bodies. The municipal council is one of these, elected by the population for a four-year term; it is a representative of the executive power and acts as a central body of local government. It determines municipal policy, adopts and audits the municipal budget, and directly sets the level of a certain number of local fees. The responsibilities of the municipal council include monitoring the regulation of local finance. Municipal councils are elected by a proportional vote for a period of four years. The number of members of the municipal council is defined by the total population and varies from 11 to 61 people.

Strategic plans are the basis for funding concrete measures of the pre-accession programmes and for perspective plans, structural funds are used. The municipal development plan consists of an in-depth analysis of economic and social development issues, priorities and goals and capital investment projects. The municipal plan is approved by the municipal council. There is no referendum or public discussion on the priorities, goals and measures of economic and social development. The role of the municipality in regional programming and development is designated in the Regional Development Act. Under article 14(1) the municipality's development plan is a basis for identifying the municipality's priorities, strategic objectives and financial needs.

The mayor is elected for a four-year term and also has executive power. The mayors' duties include the management, co-ordination, implementation and representation of the municipality's affairs and they are responsible for municipal administration. The municipal budget is proposed by the mayor and approved by the Ministry of Finance, which determines on the basis of natural indicators transfer and grants. The representative of the municipalities (mayors), usually negotiate responsibilities and expenditure assignments with the Ministry of Finance.

The transfer or devolution of power to local governments is the crucial element of decentralisation reform. Municipalities are faced with a growing demand for services that they are not enabled to finance adequately. The hard budget constraint and centralised decision-making of budget expenditures is the reason for weak local government bodies in policy formulation. As a result, the central government's decisions directly affect the lives of the citizens at the local level. In spite of the most recent amendments to the legislation, Bulgarian municipalities remain without significant revenue-raising power and the degree of devolution is low. The efficient management of scarce resources becomes extraordinarily important for local governments.

MANAGEMENT OF LOCAL FINANCE

The intergovernmental fiscal system includes shared taxes, subsidies and transfers, which conform to the objectives of the economic and social development of the municipalities. Fiscal decentralisation implies financial responsibilities for the municipalities. The main goal of fiscal decentralisation is to move governance closer to the people, and it requires strengthening local government finances. The idea is to give local governments some power to tax and responsibility for expenditures, with some autonomy to make independent financial decisions. The theoretical rationale for decentralisation is to achieve efficient allocation of local public goods (Musgrave and Musgrave 1984; Oates 1972). In Bulgaria around 70 per cent of sub-national governments' revenues come from shared taxes and grant transfers. The central government sets the rate and base of shared taxes and determines how the revenues will be divided. In Bulgaria, purely local revenues constitute an average of from 15 to 20 per cent of total municipal budget revenues (see Table 5.1).[1]

In Bulgaria, the financing of municipalities is centralised. The Ministry of Finance draws up and implements the state budget by dividing public service provision into municipal and central government mandates. The state thus assures both the richer and poorer municipalities of a minimum level of public services. Funding is based on state standards for mandates to finance education, health care, social care and culture (dividing public service organisation and provision into municipal and central government mandates). The

Ministry of Finance co-ordinates the process of drafting municipal budgets and oversees their implementation. It revises, where necessary, budget relations between the municipalities and the state budget. The Ministry also prepares an initial and an agreed plan for budget relations between the municipalities and the state. It maintains a database on municipal budgets with the related government and municipal mandates pursuant to the State Budget of the Republic of Bulgaria Act and the Local Self-Government and Local Administration Act within the calendar year. It makes analytic forecasts on municipal non-tax revenues. It collects, summarises and analyses information on municipal deficits and debt with a view to observing financial discipline. It develops reports and draft laws concerning municipal budgeting. Within the yearly budget procedure the Ministry of Finance, together with the National Association of Municipalities, develops a mechanism for assessment of the municipalities' investment needs and of the allocation of targeted subsidies for capital expenditures on the basis of the national investment strategy. Based on approved methods (mechanisms) the Ministry of Finance provides methodological instructions to the municipalities so that local expenditures comply with the law. The Ministry of Finance co-ordinates the policies and activities related to financial decentralisation. It participates in the development of legislative concepts, programmes and drafts aimed at implementing the financial decentralisation process.

Table 5.1 Main public finance indicators in Bulgaria

Indicators	1998	1999	2000	2001	2002	2003	2004	2005
GDP (mn. BGL)	21,577	22,776	26,752	29,617	32,606	34,546	38,275	41,948
Consolidated state budget (mn. BGL)	8,689	9,913	11,343	12,096	12,663	14,069	15,199	16,678
Local expenditures (mn. BGL)	1,736	2,022	2,178	2,114	2,388	2,197	2,335	2,648
Share of local expenditure to GDP (%)	8.0	8.8	8.1	7.1	7.3	6.5	6.1	6.4
Share of local expenditure to CSB (%)	19.9	20.4	19.2	17.4	18.8	15.5	15.4	16.2
Net revenue deficits as % of total revenues	8.7	8.9	7.2	4.5	2.6	1.8	1.6	1.5

Source: Ministry of Finance, National Statistical Institute, LGI, USAID.

Local government own revenues come from local fees, sales, concessions and procurement act transactions. The municipality defines a range of fees including those for garbage collection; for the use of market places; for holding auctions in public places or squares; for the use of kindergartens; for day schools; for vacation centres; for hostels; for social care centres and other forms of social service; for lodging or medical treatment at a resort; for the extraction of aggregates; for technical services; for administrative services; for dog licenses; for the purchase of grave plots and for safeguarding and protecting agriculture plots. For all the above-mentioned fees, the municipal council determines a base. Regarding the pricing of services, Bulgarian municipalities have the power to determine the types and amounts of user charges, so that they should ideally cover the cost of services supplied. The fees are the main component of the municipality's own revenues. Exercising full authority over fees and user charges constitutes a test of the Bulgarian municipality's competence and a precondition for gathering essential experience prior to obtaining the power of taxation.

At present, local governments collect directly about 3 per cent of the tax revenues presented in the consolidated state budget. Municipal revenues are derived from local taxes and fees and intergovernmental transfers. The municipal budget includes the following taxes: a real property tax, an inheritance tax, a gift tax, a property transfer tax and a tax on transport vehicles.

The property tax is the most appropriate source of local government revenue, and it is a core source of revenues in Bulgaria. It is suitable for local-level governments because local government services tend to benefit property owners and occupants. It is a tax on wealth and is highly visible in the local area. Potentially, the property tax can be a major revenue producer, but it rarely produces significant revenue in Bulgaria. A major problem associated with the implementation of the property tax is the evaluation of property values. It is a difficult tax to administer effectively, particularly in some areas of the country with only nascent real estate markets. The revenue from the specific local taxes (such as from dog licences or the vehicle tax) is relatively low and may not even exceed the administrative cost of collecting them. Property taxes accounted for 10.4 per cent of tax revenues in Bulgaria in 2002, against almost 40 per cent in Poland, 21 per cent in Latvia and 33 per cent in OECD member-states.

The share of tax revenue to GDP characterises the autonomy and capacity of local authorities to mobilise resources. The revenues from shared taxes and subsidies are the lion's share of local finance sources. Funding from the state budget is huge, but since 2003 the tendency has been to decrease funding as a result of implementation of the fiscal decentralisation programme. The state budget provides approximately 70 per cent of municipal revenues. So local finance has gradually decreased its dependency upon state funding, but its own revenues are not enough to fulfil delegated local responsibilities. The share of own revenues in total local revenues reached 23.7 per cent in 2002 and 32.5 per cent in 2005.

The rising trend of own revenues is due to increased revenues from garbage collection and income from municipal business activities and sales of municipal property. The contribution of own revenues is also changing; the share of the local tax was 6.9 per cent in 2002 and it reached 9.1 per cent in 2003 and 8.5 per cent in 2005. The revenue from the local tax slumped slightly because of the replacement of the road tax with direct payment to the Ministry of Transport for a vignette. The share of the components of own revenues increased as follows: local fees increased from 9.2 per cent in 2002 to 12 per cent in 2003 and 14.2 per cent in 2005, non-tax revenues accounted for 7.6 per cent in 2002 and reached 15 per cent in 2005. The average growth rate of the revenue was approximately 7 per cent in the last two years (2004–06). The proportion of own revenues and state budget transfer was 60:40 (2005). It indicated the positive changes in the revenue management and the decrease in the financial dependence on the budget. The non-tax revenues (sales, rent, procurement law transactions, concessions) contributed to the growth of the local own revenue (see Table 5.2).

Table 5.2 The share of extra subsidies to total state subsidies (mn. BGL)

Indicator	1998	1999	2000	2001	2002	2003	2004	2005
Share of extra subsidies to total budget subsidies	29.2	26.5	47	20.2	39.8	38.7	37.2	36.8

Source: Ministry of Finance.

Some public service responsibilities such as health care and land development are not under local government jurisdiction. Thus public health expenditure mandates have been cancelled reducing budget transfers (including shared tax and subsidies) to 56.2 per cent in 2005, having been 76.9 per cent in 2002. The amount of state transfer decreased from 63.3 per cent in 2004 to 55.3 per cent in 2006 (see Table 5.3). The expenditures of municipal budgets decreased because social benefits are now covered directly by the state budget.

Finally, municipal net revenue deficits have declined by a significant amount – from 7.2 per cent in 2000 to 1.8 per cent in 2003. The municipalities have succeeded in maintaining low levels of indebtedness – the average net revenue debt has been approximately 1.5 per cent for the last two years. As a whole intergovernmental transfers decreased relatively, because some service provision mandates were eliminated. Instability and uncertainty are also an element of tax sharing arrangements. One source of uncertainty for budget revenues is the unpredictable annual revision of sharing rates. The allocation of most shared taxes is based on where the taxes were collected – systems funded primarily by shared taxes can discover that revenue disparities are substantial. Those localities that have the weakest revenue base will be the worst off and other forms of redistribution will need to come into play. The traditional way to support weak municipalities is through shared taxes. Under the State Aid Act (adopted in 2002), poor municipalities receive special aid from the state in order to reduce interregional economic and social disparities and to ensure approximately equal opportunities to all municipalities. A State Aid Act promotes employability and a national micro-credit programme has contributed to micro business start-ups in lagging areas of the country.

Table 5.3 Dynamics of local revenues (%)

Revenues	1998	1999	2000	2001	2002	2003	2004	2005
Intergovernmental transfers as % of total revenues	84.2	84	83.5	82	76.9	66.2	64.7	56.8
Shared taxes	46.5	41.7	40.5	40.1	39.7	32.1	31.2	30.5
Subsidies	38.3	39.6	42.6	39.5	30.9	27.9	26.8	25.7
Own revenues	15.9	13.3	12.9	15.0	23.7	32.2	30.5	32.5
Local tax	7.7	4.8	4.5	6.0	6.9	9.1	8.9	8.5
Local fees	8.6	8.5	8.2	8.7	9.2	12.0	13.8	14.2

Source: Ministry of Finance.

Revenue autonomy is limited, affecting efforts to improve service delivery through decentralisation. Limited autonomy at the local level is perhaps the most significant signal that local finance management has not really been decentralised. The weak financial capacity of local governments is an obstacle to further fiscal decentralisation, and it may take many years before local entities can be given the responsibility for raising their own revenues. Clearly, the problem of providing and funding local government services needs to be resolved.

The problem includes the insufficient revenues and the unsteady and unpredictable municipal financial system, largely the result of frequent changes in the percentage of the municipal share of taxes. The sale of municipal property as a source of income has largely been completed. Local government revenue increased because of municipal property sales and charges for some services on concessions. Revenues from privatisation and property sales will henceforth remain at a low level. Bulgaria has made some progress in contracting out services and in identifying the required fees for managing those services. There may still be difficulties concerning the appropriate method for price determination and the ability to pay the required fees, and this may require special assistance. The regulatory framework does not yet provide the necessary information for the effective pricing of such services.

The imbalance in local budgets is an important issue arising from the lack of an efficient equalisation policy. Some municipalities, usually the large and industrially developed ones, have achieved budget surpluses, while other small and medium-sized ones have accumulated deficits (the number of these is 170, which is around 50 per cent of all Bulgarian municipalities). The disadvantages of revenue management have become apparent: bad financial planning, central subsidies transferred subjectively and a lack of effective vertical and horizontal financial equalisation policies.

Transfers include grants for the financing of current and investment expenditures. Intergovernmental grants are further classified by purpose (general or specific). For expenditure purposes, general-purpose grants can be used like own revenues, but their allocation is based on objective criteria and is at the central government's discretion. Specific grants are earmarked for certain purposes, and the allocation may or may not be conditional across sub-national governments. The subsidy is a tool to guarantee the balance between revenue and expenditure assignments. The delegated responsibilities are financed by general and additional (extra) subsidies. The total amount of subsidies (state transfer) in local revenues amounted to 25.9 per cent in 2006. A downward trend for subsidies is observed after 2000 (see Table 5.4). The subsidies for capital investment are small, but their use is determined by the municipality, which is also true of some general and additional subsidies.

Although the revenue from local taxes and fees and revenues from their own activities has been increasing, the municipalities continue to rely primarily on subsidies. The assessment criteria for determining the share of extra (additional) subsidies has not changed significantly. The dynamics of the shares of additional (extra) subsidies have been very changeable. They have been granted on the basis of local government targets. The share of the extra subsidies was highest in 2000 when they accounted for 47 per cent of total local revenues. They have since declined but continue to account for around 39 per cent. The share of the extra subsidies was reduced to around 20.2 per cent in 2001. The data demonstrate that this share is still relatively high. The small municipalities continue to rely on extra subsidies for the execution of delegated revenue assignments. For example, Bulgaria has created a formula for allocating resources, but typically, towards the end of the year it provides an extra, unplanned transfer to localities to finance unpaid bills. The average amount of unpaid bills for 2005 was around 7.7 per cent in terms of total local revenues. The average deficit per capita is 25BGL or 12.8 EUR. The large municipalities accumulated higher debts than the small ones. The size of distributed general subsidies to municipalities is identified by several quantitative indicators such as the total amount of responsibilities assigned, local tax revenue, the municipality's population, and the amount of equalisation subsidies.

Table 5.4 Average revenues per capita in EUR (2005)

Type of revenue	Average revenue per capita in EUR
Shared tax	31.7
Subsidies	27.5
Local tax	8.5
Local fees	14.4
Local own revenues	15.8
Other grant transfers	8.7
Total revenue	135.4

Source: National Statistical Institute.

Fiscal decentralisation in Bulgaria started gradually. Since 2003 local authorities have been permitted to determine the fees on services they provide. The policy of conditional current grants has not changed significantly. Such grants usually take the form of earmarked transfers for particular purposes, such as education, health or social assistance. In the past, allocations for these current expenditures were focused on inputs and the funding required to keep existing programmes functional. Although the amounts of conditional capital grants are small, the central government provides some grants to lower level governments for investment. The allocation of these grants has not been systematic – a subjective approach predominated. The practice has been that line ministries receive a particular amount of resources to allocate to lower levels of government in the areas of education, energy, transport, and so on.

Intergovernmental Transfers

Grant transfers will continue to play a role for financing local government units. The grant transfer is usually used for salaries and social security of the staff working in the local unit such as education or culture. The delegated expenditure assignments are covered by grants, a small part also coming from the municipality's own revenues.

Transfers constitute the principal means by which countries achieve 'vertical fiscal balance', ensuring that the revenues and expenditures of each level of government are approximately equal. The 'fiscal gaps' may of course be closed in following ways: by transferring revenue-raising power to local governments, by transferring responsibility for expenditures to the central government, or by reducing local expenditures or raising local revenues. In Bulgaria, however, there remains a sufficient mismatch in the revenues and expenditures assigned to different levels of government that some balancing role must be assigned to intergovernmental fiscal transfers, which need to be more objective and to be combined with the public's need for services.

Fiscal gaps still remain for all poorer local governments, but such 'gaps' are better considered in relation to the problem of achieving horizontal fiscal balance. Subsidies are used to equalise revenue and expenditure assignments. General subsidies are use to cover revenue shortage in health care, culture, security and defence. The procedure for defining the amount of delegated expenditures includes estimation of the current municipal expenditures, decisions of the municipality council, and agreements between municipal and central administration. Usually all municipalities receive equalised subsidies to cover the revenues gap, mainly for unpaid salaries and utilities costs (gas and energy). Subsidies for capital investments are very changeable. The share of capital investments are in delegated local activities (such as for education and culture). The sources for capital investments are target subsidies, sales and own municipal revenues.

The municipalities with economic potential succeed in covering delegated responsibilities with their own revenue. All the subsidies cover approximately 48 per cent of capital investments at the local level. The local authorities desire greater fiscal autonomy, but institutional and administrative capacity in revenue management is currently low and central control is extensive. The municipalities are unable to execute greater control over local taxation or assume greater local expenditure responsibilities. The practice of developed countries shows that fiscal discipline should increase in parallel with the increase of local autonomy. Balancing the budget is an important element of strengthening fiscal discipline. At present, municipalities are obliged to balance their budgets, but most of them continue to operate with deficit-financing supplemental appropriations during the year. Central government intervention is targeted at reducing municipal budget deficits, but is undertaken in a manner that does not encourage the municipalities. The difficulty in balancing their budgets stems from the funding of current activities through deficit-financing supplemental appropriations or long-term debt (especially for small- and medium-sized municipalities). Even where the legal and administrative capacity exists, local governments face a lack of appropriate financial incentives to mobilise their own revenues.

There is considerable divergence in the economic and social development of the municipalities. Only the largest towns with an industrial sector have not suffered from inadequate financial sources and capital investments. Some municipalities are in economic decline and suffer with a high rate of unemployment. The principles of distribution are based on the State Budget Act. The system of financial equalisation does not cover the disparities in the socio-economic situations of the municipalities very effectively. The system of financial equalisation does not react effectively to the deepening disparities in the socioeconomic situations of the municipalities (see Table 5.5).

Table 5.5 Average expenditure per capita in EUR (2005)

Expenditure Assignments	Average expenditure per capita in EUR
Administration	11.2
Defence and security	1.4
Education	42.5
Health services	10.9
Social care	23.5
Economic activities	9.1
Culture	3.9
Salaries and social insurance	45.4
Social transfers	20.7
Total	134.5

Source: National Statistical Institute.

The administrative expenditures for small cities constitute 17 per cent of total expenditures, while they average only 9 per cent for all cities. Social assistance expenditures in small cities are considerably higher, reaching 28 per cent of all expenditures, in comparison with the average social assistance expenditures for all cities, which are 18 per cent of total expenditures. There are also differences in revenues distributed to small cities. While shared taxes average 49 per cent of total revenues, the amount of shared tax revenue was scarcely 17 per cent of the total revenues in small cities in 2002. As a rule, the larger Bulgarian municipalities have better administrative and fiscal capabilities to provide public services and raise local revenues than the smaller ones have. A small city is officially defined as having a population of less than 10,000 people, based on the latest population census.[2] The low amount of the shared taxes in small municipalities is compensated by a larger amount of grant transfers (subsidies).

For that reason the distribution of state subsidies is unequal across municipalities. A larger share of such subsides is directed to the smaller cities than to the larger, middle-sized cities. State subsidies, representing approximately 60 per cent of total local revenues in small cities, are higher than the average level, which is 26 per cent. Own revenues amount to 22 per cent on average, but are scarcely 11 per cent for small cities. The general subsidies are used to cover revenue shortages in health care, culture, security and defence, especially for small municipalities. Total state transfers vary as a share of total local revenues, but are approximately 75 per cent annually.

It is anticipated that the sum of all transfers from the higher-level to lower-level governments will help to close the fiscal gap. Generally, vertical equalisation provides for the possibility of balancing revenues and expenditures at the local level. Subsidies are the instrument for vertical equalisation. Horizontal equalisation is intended to reduce fiscal divergence across municipalities. It is targeted to equalise the potential of municipalities for delivering quantitative public services. Vertical fiscal balance could be achieved in an accounting sense for the more affluent local governments. Expenditures and revenues (including governmental transfers) could be balanced according to the local authorities' capacity to raise resources. Fiscal gaps will still remain for all poorer local governments, but such 'gaps' are better considered in relation to the problem of achieving horizontal fiscal balance (within the local government sector).

There are different ways to measure horizontal fiscal disparities. The most immediate approach is simply to compare per capita revenues and expenditures across municipalities. However, both actual per capita revenues and expenditures may be misleading indicators of true fiscal disparities. In Bulgaria, per capita revenues are higher in rich regions because of economic growth and greater collection of tax revenues. Similarly, comparisons of actual per capita expenditures may be misleading. They are higher in poorer regions because of social benefits for vulnerable groups (unemployment benefits for the young, retired persons and the long-term unemployed).

In reality, the measurement of horizontal fiscal imbalances or disparities based on fiscal capacity and expenditure needs, as opposed to actual revenues and expenditures, is often complicated by the lack of available data. In practice, a useful approach to the measurement of horizontal fiscal imbalances is the comparison of actual per capita revenues and expenditures. The indicators utilised for revenues are income per capita or regional gross domestic product per capita and for expenditure needs, local costs per capita.

At present, the degree of equalisation is negotiated by municipals and state institutions. The degree of vertical and horizontal equalisation reflects a national consensus on solidarity – how much to take from relatively richer regions and from national or federal government budgets to support disadvantaged regions. In Bulgaria, some significant differences in fiscal capacity and expenditure needs appear across regions and local governments in terms of gross regional product per capita, unemployment rates and tax collections per capita. The practice of vertical equalisation is that it employs two approaches based on shared taxes and centralised redistributed subsidies. Many small local governments receive grants in addition from the state, in the absence of horizontal equalisation (in which the wealthy municipalities transfer financial resources to the poorer ones).

Local Government Expenditures

Municipal budgets occupy a significant place in the Bulgarian public finance sector: they represent 18 per cent of the consolidated state budget. The delegated expenditure assignments are for defence and safety, education, health services, social care, recreation and culture centres and road repair. The municipal budget covers 45 per cent of education expenditures, 12 per cent of health care expenditures, 24 per cent of social assistance and benefits expenditures, 26 per cent of culture expenditures, and 64 per cent of public works expenditures.[3] Traditionally, the most important components of local expenditures are education, the social sector, culture and recreation.

One of the tasks of grant transfers is to ignore the difference in revenue and expenditure assignment among municipalities. A municipality with economic potential would deliver different quantities of services in comparison with smaller, less affluent municipalities. Grant transfers are determined by the capacity to collect taxes and generate own revenues. This approach is not very efficient because it favours large municipalities, those with greater potential to collect tax revenues. The subsidies are distributed by the formulas based on quantitative indicators. The practice in Bulgaria shows that subsidies are used to fill the shortfall in salaries of the administrative staff in education and culture.

The ratio of total local government expenditures to GDP is an indicator of the degree of decentralisation. Total expenditures decrease as a result of eliminating some municipal responsibilities (for example, health care, social benefits). Public services and goods represent a commitment by the state. Expenditure for education, local administration and health care are relatively high in comparison with other expenditures. Those expenditures represent a substantial share of local own revenues. The following conclusions are offered regarding local expenditures: the financial discrepancy among municipalities has increased; subsidies have not proved an efficient tool for equalisation; municipalities generally cover budget deficits by sales of public properties or by imposing fees. All municipalities receive subsidies or grant transfers to cover the shortfalls in funding delegated responsibilities. The economic growth impacts on the mobilisation of the investments at the local level. The investment increased significantly – the data share of the investment was 17.9 per cent of the total expenditures in 2006 in comparison with 11.5 per cent in 2004 (see Table 5.6).

Table 5.6 The share of investments in local budgets

Indicators	1998	1999	2000	2001	2002	2003
Investments (mn. BGL)	211.2	172.5	158.0	121.2	196.0	240.0
The ratio of investments to budget expenditures (%)	12.7	9.3	7.9	6.5	8.6	11.0

Source: Ministry of Finance.

The capital investments were directed to public projects. Local governments in Bulgaria can cover on average only about one-third of their expenditures from local revenues (taxes and non-tax revenues). Municipalities can use some of their local revenues at their discretion, but there are some mandates that are compulsory – for example, garbage fee revenues must be used only for garbage collection and cleaning. As the garbage fee constitutes more than 50 per cent of local revenues of the municipalities, only about 15 per cent of the remaining expenditures are decided by the local authorities. We can also include debt financing and privatisation revenues that add additional sources of local revenues that can be used by local discretion. Therefore, we can maintain that about 20 per cent of the expenditures are freely decided by the local authorities and another 15 per cent are decided by them, but constrained in some way.

Accounting Rules, Regulations and the Local Government Budgeting Process

Local government reform in Bulgaria has two main characteristics. First, legislative and territorial administrative regulations have changed the quality of local management. Second, the role of civil society in the decision-making process has been developing very slowly. Decentralisation has to be accompanied by mechanisms which engage the participation of different types of entities in the process of policy decision-making. Decentralisation could improve efficiency by fostering accountability, reducing corruption and increasing cost-effectiveness in the government. Local authorities and citizens have not perceived that decentralisation has not only an administrative value, but also a civic dimension. Therefore, citizens have not taken the opportunity to become involved in public affairs; doing so would help them become accustomed to using freedom and exercising their civil rights. Civil society structures understand that decentralisation is a fundamental part of the environment and that it can help to improve the performance of the public sector, to assist in combating corruption and to assist local authorities in reducing poverty.

According to this view, when local governments are closer to the people, citizens will be more aware of sub-national governments' actions than they are of the actions of the central government. The assessment of local capacity development in Bulgaria shows some progress in terms of accountability. In large-scale municipalities NGOs play a role in establishing a partnership between local actors (for example, businesses, NGOs and social partners). Gradually, NGOs have taken part in policy-making processes at the local level. Direct participants in the implementation of regional development policy at the local level are mayors of municipalities and teams of experts from businesses and NGOs, who are involved in local economic and social development, investment policy, municipal property management and the funding of municipal operations. Their involvement is oriented mainly towards the formulation of specific municipal initiatives and the development of project ideas based on priorities, and the formulation of regional development plans. This partnership is the most recent trend in decentralisation, which has begun to establish itself as the new deal in rural and local development.

This approach recognises that public institutions with their new functions are complemented by other local actors as well. Thus, professional or representative organisations, the private sector, or other NGOs begin to be included in decision-making processes and also assume accountability. There is a range of municipal associations which express the interests of citizens. These local associations are organised for joint service delivery such as for social assistance, transport services, and so on. Also, lobby associations are active in transport, construction, tourism and culture.

In Bulgaria the central government sets policy, regulations and standards, while lower levels of government are responsible for much of the actual service delivery. Determining which public service competencies (expenditure responsibilities) are appropriate for which levels of government is the first step toward a more fiscally decentralised system of government. In Bulgarian practice the expenditure responsibilities are not clearly defined, which does not enhance accountability at local levels. The perception of accountability by the citizens and local partners is a long and comprehensive process. Accountability constitutes the trust citizens have in state and local administration institutions. Accountability forces local governments to explain or justify what they have done or failed to do. Local elections are the most common and powerful instrument of accountability, but other mechanisms such as citizen councils can also have some influence.

The Act on Local Self Government provides for local referendums which can be initiated by the municipal council. The practice of holding local referendums is not a popular one. In some municipalities where civil society is well organised and NGOs are strong the citizens participate in decision making. The local councils, with the assistance of NGOs, have organised public hearings at which citizens may express their opinions, ask questions and make proposals on matters of public interest. Improved information about local needs and preferences is one of the theoretical advantages of decentralisation, but there is no guarantee that leaders will actually act on these preferences unless they feel some sort of accountability to the citizenry. At present the Bulgarian approach to local governance shows that local authorities cannot perceive accountability as the validation of participation. In some municipalities, where attempts to increase participation prove successful, people can participate in holding a local government responsible for its actions. In Bulgarian regional policy, two issues stand out in considering the degree to which sub-national levels are politically accountable. The regulations and management principles are not oriented to promote accountability at the intermediate (district) level. The activities undertaken at that level remain centralised and responsibilities are not delegated to the same extent as at the local level.

Although accountability is limited in scope, political decentralisation in Bulgaria permits people at the local level of government to be choose the kind of government they want, but they do not yet participate actively in governance at that level. Bulgaria has made a start on the creation of electronic government (e-government), which is designed to enhance access to decision making and legislation in the areas of economic affairs and social policy. The accountability in Bulgaria is not highly developed, in part due to the yet insignificant role of the organisations of civil society in local governance. Resource allocation decisions in Bulgaria have not been made in a transparent manner and with accountability. The reason for this is that budget and control procedures are not yet comprehensive, comparable, suitable for checking, and available to the public.

CONCLUSION

Regulations specifying the procedures for transferring appropriations and subsidies from the state budget to municipal budgets have changed continuously during recent years. It has been very difficult, therefore, for local authorities to plan their budgets with a long-term perspective. Local own revenues are only a small portion of municipal budgets and local authorities depend mainly on the decisions of the central authorities.

Municipal expenditure responsibilities regularly exceed municipal revenues. They are not sustainable in the long run, and the overly detailed central regulations unnecessarily dilute municipal management control. Moreover, the municipal revenue base must expand with the growing demand for more and better local public services. The rather random relationship between revenue assignments and expenditure responsibilities does not discourage fiscal deficits and municipal revenue-raising efforts. Tax sharing has not reflected local revenue generation capacities. Nor has it been a good fit with the overall intergovernmental fiscal system. Although there has been some progress in fiscal decentralisation, Bulgarian state institutions are still largely responsible for financing local public services, especially education and culture.

The assessment of the execution of the concept of fiscal decentralisation pointed out that the financial statements and financial self-management of the Bulgarian municipalities were improved. The implementation of the decentralisation programme contributed to achieving significant changes in local finance management:

- there was a unified mechanism for equalising subsidies;
- the Municipal Debt Act was adopted and as a consequence the number of municipalities issuing municipal bonds increased;
- the municipalities were able to manage local revenue and administrate the local taxes and fees;
- the restriction on the allocation of capital subsidies was removed; and
- the local revenue structure was improved which contributed to the growth of the own revenue.

Despite this progress the municipalities are not empowered to plan their expenditure according to their priorities. The problem of the municipal debt has not yet been solved. It is essential that financial resource management be improved in accordance with the following principles. There must be:

- correspondence between the benefits of the activities and the finance costs;
- an expansion of the participation of civil society and local authorities in the budget process, as well as in the participation of citizens and their organisations in determining the financial and investment policy of municipalities;
- a balance between the legally regulated revenues and the legally entrusted expenditure responsibilities of municipalities;
- an expansion of the powers of municipalities to manage budget revenues and expenditures;
- a permanent legal framework for state transfers to municipalities; and
- an allocation of subsidies for municipalities through clear, understandable and permanent criteria.

NOTES

1. This average level relates to the period 1999–2003. In other words, the central government directly determines the general size of the municipal budgets, while being in no way accountable to local constituencies for public services provided.
2. Using this definition, 98 of Bulgaria's 264 municipalities are small cities.
3. Reported data for 2003 by the Ministry of Finance

BIBLIOGRAPHY

Bahl, R. (1999), Fiscal Decentralisation as Development Policy, *Public Budgeting and Finance*, 19(2), 59–75.

Bird, R.M. (1999a), *Sub-national Revenues: Realities and Prospects*, Toronto: University of Toronto.

Bird, R.M. (1999b), *Transfers and Incentives in Intergovernmental Fiscal Relations*, Toronto: University of Toronto.

Commission of the European Communities (2004), *EU Commission Regular Report on Bulgaria's Progress towards to Accession 2004*, Brussels: European Union.

Deangelis, M., R.W. Johnson, and C.Z. Kaczmarski (2002), *Building the Municipal Credit Market for Infrastructure Finance: the Legal Framework the Local Government Initiative*, Sofia: USAID.

Faguet, J.P. (2002), Decentralisation and Local Government, mimeo, London: London School of Economics.

International Monetary Fund (2003), *Government Finance Statistics*, Washington, DC: IMF.

IRIS Center (2002), A Synthesis of Research Finding, Conditions for Effective Decentralised Governance, College Park: University of Maryland – IRIS Center.

Litvack, J., J. Ahmad and R. Bird (1998), Rethink the Decentralisation in Developing Countries, Occasional paper 2149, Washington, DC: World Bank.

Local Government Forum (2001), *Fiscal Decentralization, A Survey*, Sofia: USAID – The Local Government Initiative.

Local Government Initiative and National Association of Municipalities of the Republic of Bulgaria (2003), *Small Cities Capacity Building Strategy*, Sofia: National Association of Municipalities of the Republic of Bulgaria.

Ministry of Finance (2006), *Statistics*, Sofia: Ministry of Finance of the Republic of Bulgaria.

Musgrave, R.A. (1961), Approaches to a Fiscal Theory of Political Federalism, in: NBER, *Public Finances: Needs, Sources, and Utilization: A Report of the National Bureau of Economic Research*, Princeton: Princeton University Press, pp. 97–122.

Musgrave, R.A. and P. B. Musgrave (1984), *Public Finance in Theory and Practice*, New York: McGraw-Hill.

National Statistical Institute (2003), *Local Finance*, Sofia: National Statistical Institute.

Oates, W. (1972), *Fiscal Federalism*, New York: Harcourt Brace Jovanovich.

OECD (2002), *Fiscal Decentralization in EU Applicant States and Selected EU Member States*, Paris: OECD.

Rodinelli D. (1981), Government Decentralisation in Comparative Perspective Theory and Practice in Developing Countries, *International Review of Administrative Services*, 47, 113–49.

Shah, A. (1994), *The Reform of Intergovernmental Fiscal Relations in Developing and Emerging Market Economies*, Policy and Research Series No. 23, Washington, DC: World Bank.

6. Local government finance in Croatia

Anto Bajo and Ivana Jakir-Bajo

INTRODUCTION

As a result of the proclamation of the Constitution of 1990 and the winning of independence, from 1991 to 1995 Croatia established its institutional and legislative framework for the development of local self-government. In the new legal environment, the counties were established, which carried out the functions of both government and self-government, as well as the municipalities and cities, which had self-governing functions, and a new model for the financing of local government units (LGUs) was laid down. In 1995, because of the consequences of the war, areas of special national concern (ASNC) were defined, which the central government endeavoured to help in their development, also encouraging the return of the displaced population. From 1995 to 2001, Croatia was a largely centralised state in which, in spite of there being local self-government, the bodies of central government were nevertheless dominant. This was a period marked by the reconstruction of the war-torn areas and the foundation of the new LGUs. In parallel with the foundation of the new LGUs up to 2000, the process of establishing what their assets were and the value of their assets went on. Although it has not yet resolved the problems of a clear division of fiscal authorities, since 2001, through the process of fiscal decentralisation, the government has transferred authority for the financing of education, health care and welfare to the LGUs. At the same time as transferring authority, the central government has provided LGUs with additional means through the allocation of grants and through an increase in the share of the joint tax revenues.

Accordingly, the fundamental objective of this chapter is to show the basic characteristics of the financing of LGUs in Croatia between 1990 and 2005, to highlight the processes of fiscal decentralisation and the processes with which Croatia is confronted in the reform and financing of LGUs.

THE LEGAL FRAMEWORK AND LOCAL GOVERNMENT FINANCE REGULATIONS

With the passing of the Constitution (1990) and the proclamation of independence (1991), the units of local self-government and administration were defined. The counties have a dual character, being units of local self-government and of local administration. The Constitution states that municipalities and cities are units of local self-government. The basic legal framework on sub-national government is structured around Chapter VI (Art. 132–137) of the Constitution and the Law on Local and Regional Self-Government (2001),[1] including: the Law on Financing of Local Self-Government and Administration Units (1993); the Law on the Areas of Counties, Cities, and Municipalities (1993); the Law on the City of Zagreb (1997); the Law on Communal Services (including utilities, 2003); and the amendments on the Sector Laws (education, health care, social assistance). Also affecting sub-national public management is the Budget Law (1994, revised in June 2003), and a set of ordinary laws and regulations, including the annual State budget laws, Decisions, Decrees and Instructions from line ministries and the Ministry of Finance on the chart of accounts, budgeting (including criteria on financial standards), reporting, monitoring and audit systems.

Areas of special national concern have been laid down in the Areas of Special National Concern Law (OG 44/96) for the sake of obviating the consequences of the war, the more rapid return of refugees and displaced persons, demographic and economic progress and the achievement of the maximum possible degree of evenness in regional growth. Since 2001, the Government and Ministry of Finance (MoF) have set the criteria for grant allocation stated in the annual law on budget execution instead of in the budget law or in the local government units financing law. The Local Government Financing Law (*Official Gazette*[2] 117/93 revised in 2001 and 2003) set up the current system for the financing of the LGUs. This encompasses the counties, cities and municipalities and the city of Zagreb, which has a special status in the financing system. Although both the LSG and the Budget Law allow for sub-national government to access borrowing, conflicting instructions have been passed, mainly through annual State budget laws.

The Main Characteristics of the LGU System

Croatia is a small unitary country (4.4 million people), with a decentralised administrative structure formed by central, regional and local governments. The central government administration itself is *de-concentrated*, with the Central

Office of State Administration representatives seated in each of the 20 counties, besides ministry representation and autonomous central agencies distributed throughout the territory. The 21 counties (including the 780,000-inhabitant city of Zagreb, which has county status) constitute the second/intermediate level of sub-national government, that is *regional self-government*. Cities (124, mainly urban, altogether housing 3 million people) and municipalities (426, mainly rural, housing 1.4 million people) represent the first level of sub-national government, that is *local self-government* (Figure 6.1).

Figure 6.1 Central and local government administration

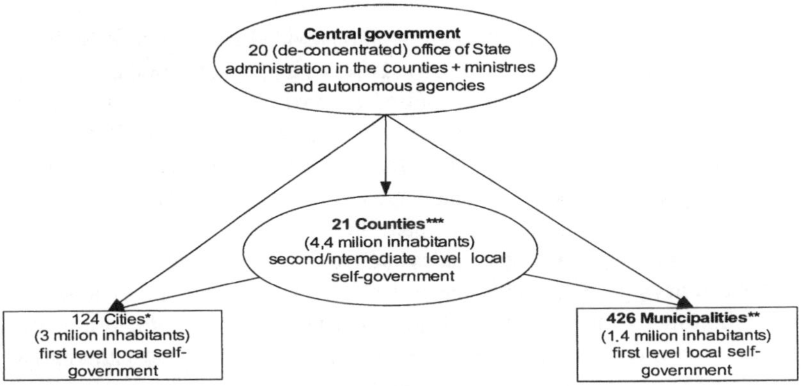

Notes:
* Urban communities, in general more than 10,000 inhabitants
** Communities of less than 10,000 inhabitants (most rural)
*** Including the City of Zagreb, 780,000 inhabitants

Source: Central Bureau of Statistics, 2007.

The situation with a number of LGUs has been aggravated by the creation of ASNC in response to the damage caused by the war. These areas were set up for the sake of more rapid development and they have a privileged status in financing. Through many tax exemptions, the government is attempting to jump-start the economic development of these regions. Out of the total, there are 111 LGUs in areas of ASNC with 482 thousand inhabitants. Until 2003, any decision concerning, or the approval of the foundation of, LGUs had to be taken by the Ministry of Justice, Administration and Local Self-Government and after that by the (newly-founded) Central Office of State Administration. This makes its decision according to opinions from line ministries (for example, the Ministry of Finance), counties, and other LGUs and competent institutions.

It should be stressed that both levels of sub-national administrative units (county and local) are governed by a Representative Body (the County Council and the Local Council, respectively), whose members are directly elected by residents, and by an Executive Body (headed by the City Mayor or the County and Municipality Prefect, respectively). The latter is appointed by the respective Councils, from among their members.

DIVISION OF RESPONSIBILITIES AND DEMOCRATIC LEGITIMACY

The Croatian system of LGU financing can be divided into two periods; the first from 1994 to 2001, and the second from 2001 on. In the first period the system of local government financing was centralised and the LGUs' autonomy in collecting revenue and allocating their expenditure was restricted. This period is marked by the passing of legal solutions in which the authorities for financing were settled, as was the distribution between central and local government of fiscal and administrative spheres of competence. In Croatia there were then three levels of government: central government, the counties and the LGUs (municipalities and cities). As well as having the status of units of local self-government, the counties were also administrative units of the central government. Since 2001, administrative and self-government functions can be carried out by all LGUs, and the authorities and competence of LGUs are more clearly defined.

A good indicator of the dynamics of change in these two periods is represented by the size of the LGUs, that is, the expenditure of the LGUs as a percentage of GDP and of the total expenditure of general government (Table 6.1).

Table 6.1 The budgets of LGUs as percentage of the general government budget and of GDP from 1997 to 2005

	1997	1998	1999	2000	2001	2002	2003	2004	2005
1. The revenue/expenditure of LGUs as % of the revenue/expenditure of general government									
Revenue	11.6	10.8	11.2	12.6	12.9	15.1	16.1	16.3	16.9
Expenditure	12.3	12.0	11.1	11.8	12.6	14.3	15.2	16.8	17.6
2. Revenue/expenditure of LGUs as % of GDP									
Revenue	6.1	6.3	5.9	6.2	6.0	7.0	7.5	7.3	7.5
Expenditure	6.0	6.3	6.1	6.4	6.2	7.0	7.5	7.4	7.7
3. General government expenditure as % of GDP	48.6	52.8	54.8	54.0	49.1	48.8	49.4	49.7	48.6

Source: Ministry of Finance of the Republic of Croatia and EBRD, 2007.

The size of the LGUs, that is the expenditure of LGUs as a percentage of GDP, right up to 2001 was not changed. From 2001, when decentralisation began, this percentage became larger. The size of revenue follows the same trend.

Deconcentration of Responsibilities

As we emphasised, Croatia has a political system with three tiers of government – central government, counties, and municipalities and cities. The counties, cities and municipalities regulate their own internal organisation and structure and the way they work in their statutes.

The county carries out matters of regional significance, particularly matters related to: education, health care, physical and town planning, economic development, traffic and the transportation infrastructure, and the planning and development of the network of educational, healthcare, welfare and cultural establishments. A county is at the same time a unit of local administration and one of local self-government. This dual role affects the work of the counties' bodies, which also have a certain dualism. These are present in the financing of its functions. Expenditure that relates to the administrative functions of the county carried out by the county office qua body of the national civil service (above all the pay of senior and junior civil servants and material costs) is financed from the national budget.

Cities and municipalities in their self-governing area of competence carry out matters of local importance through which the needs of citizens are met directly and which are not by the Constitution or law assigned to bodies of central government. Here they carry out the following assignments: housing, physical and town planning, communal economy matters, child care, welfare, primary health care, pre-school and elementary school education, culture, physical culture and sport, protection and improvement of the environment and civilian protection and fire protection.

All municipalities and cities may also carry out matters from the self-government jurisdiction of the county in their own area, if they provide funds for the financing of them. Even in spite of the many laws, there is no clear delimitation of function between the levels of government. As can be seen in Table 6.2 almost all the functions are financed from both central and local government levels.

From 2001, in the fiscal decentralisation programme, the central government transferred responsibility for financing education, health care, welfare and fire departments to the LGUs. Central government transferred authorities for financing only a part of the costs of health care and education (that is, for the material costs and expenditure for the procurement on non-financial assets) and full costs (with salaries) to the LGUs that took responsibilities for financing welfare (welfare responsibilities include payment of financial benefits and provision of services, that is, homes for the elderly, child protection, and so on) and fire departments. Financing of the decentralised functions was taken on by the LGUs with the greatest fiscal capacities. Of the 570 LGUs, 53 of them (20 counties, the city of Zagreb and 32 cities) assumed the obligation of financing the decentralised functions. In addition, from 2002 the financing of the fire departments was taken on by 83 LGUs (municipalities and cities).

Table 6.2 Distribution of functions according to levels of government

		Central government	Municipalities	Cities	Counties
1.	General public services	x	x	x	x
2.	Defence	x			
3.	Public order and security	x	x	x	
4.	Education	x	x	x	x
4.1.	Preschool		x	x	
4.2.	Elementary	x	x	x	x
4.3.	Secondary	x			x
4.4.	Tertiary	x			
5.	Health care	x			x
6.	Social security and welfare	x	x	x	x
7.	Housing and communal economy matters and services		x	x	
8.	Recreation, culture and religion		x	x	
9.	Agriculture, forestry, hunting, fishing	x			x
10.	Mining, industry, construction	x	x	x	x
11.	Traffic and communications	x	x	x	x
11.1.	Road transport	x	x	x	x
11.2.	Rail transport	x			
11.3.	Air transport	x			
12.	Other economic matters and services	x	x	x	x

Notes: Housing and communal economy services: drinking water supply, drainage and treatment of sewage, gas and heat supply, public transport, cleaning, deposition of waste, maintenance of public areas, maintaining of roads, retail markets, cemetery and crematorium maintenance, chimney sweeping, street lighting (management, maintenance of facilities and devices). Welfare responsibilities include payment of financial benefits and provision of services (that is, homes for the elderly, child protection, and so on).

Source: Ott and Bajo, 2001.

LGUs and Democratic Legitimacy

Communication between the LGUs and citizens is insufficient. Rare are the examples of LGUs which supply their citizens with brochures in which it is explained, in a simple way, what has been done within a year and how, and what is planned to be done. There is no example of asking citizens about possible changes in setting up some new programmes. Another very important party in the budget process is the non-governmental sector. The role of the NGOs regarding budget monitoring in Croatia is still very passive. The extent of activity of all interested parties (NGOs, media, citizens, and so on) is best indicated by the fact that from the year the 2001 financial statements of LGUs (summarised data for counties, towns and municipalities) have not been published, concerning which no one raised any question. The public does not participate in the budgetary process, and especially not in budget adoption. This is a completely closed process, where the budget becomes available to the public after it has been adopted and published in the local official gazette.

INDEPENDENT LOCAL GOVERNMENT REVENUE SOURCES

The fiscal autonomy of LGUs in collecting their own revenue is relatively low. The most productive tax revenue is shared with central government, which at the same time determines the tax base and the rates of these taxes. The LGUs obtain the least amount of revenue from their own taxes. LGUs have autonomy in the use of non-tax revenue and just a small part of their own tax revenue. The most important non-tax revenue (municipal economy charges and contributions) must be used for the financing of the utility or communal economy infrastructure.

Fiscal autonomy means the capacity of LGUs independently to fix the bases and rates of taxation as well as non-taxation revenue. LGUs in Croatia are not autonomous in the determination of base and rates of tax revenue. This can be seen from Table 6.3.

To a relatively small extent, the LGUs can set the rates of local tax revenue. The rates of shared taxes (which are divided between municipality, city, county and central government) and of county taxes are completely determined by central government. The rates of municipal and city taxes are, on the whole, determined by the municipal or city authority, but within the framework of the limits set by central government. LGUs autonomously determine the rates of surtax on income tax within the framework of a limit (the maximum possible rate of surtax) set by the central government.

Table 6.3 Division of authorities for setting rates of individual taxes

	Central government	Local government autonomously	Local government restrictedly
Shared taxes			
Income tax	x		
Profit tax	x		
Real estate sales tax	x		
County taxes			
Tax on gifts and inheritances	x		
Tax on road motor vehicles	x		
Tax on vessels	x		
Tax on coin operated machines for amusement	x		
Municipal and city taxes			
Consumption tax			x
Second home tax			x
Use of public land tax		x	
Tax on uncultivated but cultivable agricultural land			x
Tax on unused entrepreneurial real estate			x
Tax on undeveloped building land			x
Tax on trade name or corporate name			x
Surtax on income tax			x

Source: Ott and Bajo, 2001.

Tax revenue sharing. The system for the financing of local units is very largely based on the tax sharing (particularly personal income tax) between central government and the local units. From 1993 on The Financing of Units of Local and Regional Self-Government Law (which governs the tax sharing) has changed 11 times, and in the 2001–07 period alone it was altered six times. Such frequent alterations of the Law and of the manner of personal income tax sharing create confusion from the point of view of the role and fiscal effects of the tax on the financial positions of the local units.

From 1994 to 2001 central government ceded to the counties, municipalities and cities some of the tax revenues raised in their areas (Table 6.4).

Table 6.4 Tax revenue sharing between central government and LGUs from 1994 to 2001, in per cent

Tax on:	Central government	Counties	Municipalities and cities	Zagreb
Income	60	8	32	–
Income (in City of Zagreb)	50	5		45
Profit	70	10	20	
Profit (in City of Zagreb)	70	–	–	30
Real estate sales	40	–	60	–

Source: The Law on Financing of Local and Regional Self-Government.

Local units that take on the financing of decentralised functions have been given by central government a larger share in the personal income tax since 2001 (Table 6.5).

Table 6.5 Tax revenue sharing between central and LGUs from 2001 to 2006, in per cent

Tax on:	Central government	Counties	Municipalities and cities	Decentralised functions	Equalisation Fund
Income	25,6	10	34	10,4	21
Profit	70	10	20	–	–
Real estate sales	40	–	60	–	–

Source: The Law on Financing of Local and Regional Self-Government.

Apart from that, if they cannot finance the decentralised functions (up to the level of the established minimum financial standard) with the revenue obtained from personal income tax, the local units will receive additional resources from the equalisation fund. This fund is actually part of the personal income tax revenue that central government cedes to local government units for the funding of the decentralised functions. Only 345 local units take part in filling this fund. The remaining 225 local units are exempted for they are in a special position in the financing system (areas of special national concern and hill and mountain areas).

In 2007 the Government and the Finance Ministry changed the percentage share of the local government units in the tax sharing (Table 6.6).

Central government has taken all the profit tax and retained the same share of real estate transfer tax as in the previous year. Thus profit tax is now paid entirely into the central government budget.

Table 6.6 Tax revenue sharing between central and LGUs from 2007, in per cent

Tax on:	Central government	Counties	Municipalities and cities	Decentralised functions	Equalisation Fund
income	-	15	52	12	21
profit	100	0	0	–	–
real estate sales	40	–	60	–	–

Source: The Law on Financing of Local and Regional Self-Government.

Non-tax revenue is the autonomous revenue of LGUs, the purpose of which is set in advance. LGUs independently set the rates of non-tax revenue and independently carry out the collection of this revenue.

Capital revenue is obtained by LGUs by the sale of assets and the privatisation of the local utility firms.

Autonomy in Setting Revenue

The revenue of LGUs increased significantly from 2001, thanks to the beginnings of fiscal decentralisation or the increased share of LGUs in income tax.

With the beginning of the fiscal decentralisation process in 2001, the central government to a greater extent ceded part of the revenue to LGUs through income tax and at the same time raised the level of grants. For this reason, revenue increased from 2001 to 2005. The structure of this is dominated by tax revenue, the share of which increased from 53 per cent in 1997 to 59 per cent of the entire revenue of LGUs in 2005. At the same time the proportion of non-tax revenues in the budgets of LGUs decreased from 33 to 28 per cent in 2005, and central government budget grants comprised 7 per cent of the revenue of LGUs.

Non-tax revenue has become the second most important revenue component of Croatian aggregate local budgets (Table 6.7). However, in Croatia the local non-tax revenues are formed by a myriad of fees, charges, and 'contributions' levied by councils and utility companies, which have hardly been transparent or properly associated with specific rights or services acquired.

Let us see the structure of the tax revenue in Table 6.8.

It is mainly the taxes LGUs share with the central government according to set percentages that dominate the structure of tax revenue. Primarily this means income tax, profit tax and real estate sales tax. Income tax and profit tax increased from 1997 to 2005. Most of this increase is the result of a larger share of income tax revenue for LGUs that took on the obligation to finance the decentralised functions. On the other hand a large number of LGUs took advantage of the possibility of introducing surtax, which additionally increased their total budgetary revenue.

SYSTEM OF FISCAL EQUALISATION

The system of fiscal equalisation through which the central government endeavours to even up the development of inadequately developed regions in Croatia is based upon two main mechanisms: (1) vertical – revenue sharing; and (2) horizontal – current and capital grants.

Vertical Fiscal Equalisation

Current special purpose grants – equalisation grants for decentralised functions. From 2001, central government provided an additional share in income tax for the 53 LGUs that had taken on the obligation to finance the decentralised functions (see Tables 6.5 and 6.6). Thus LGUs that assumed the financing of all the decentralised functions were able to increase their share in income tax by 10.4 per cent from 2001 to 2006 and 12 per cent from 2007. If they took on the financing of only some of the functions, then this share was fixed as shown in Table 6.7.

The distributions of the equalisation fund adjust disparities in the value of the additional income tax share. The total of the two sources were added up to the expenditure norms (minimal financial standards) set for the decentralised functions.

Table 6.7 Local government units' additional share in income tax for decentralised functions, in per cent

Decentralised functions	Elementary education	Secondary education	Health care	Welfare	Fire departments	Total
2001–06	2.9	2.0	2.5	2.0	1	10.4
2007–	3.1	2.3	3.2	2.2	1.3	12.0

Source: Ministry of Finance of the Republic of Croatia, 2004.

The distribution of resources from the equalisation fund and the establishment of the total liabilities (expenditure) that need to be provided for an individual LGU for the financing of the decentralised functions assumed are determined pursuant to certain minimum financial standards. At the recommendation of the competent ministry, the Government and MoF each year set the minimum

Table 6.8 The structure of total revenue of local government units from 1997 to 2006, in million Kuna and in per cent

In million Kuna	1997	1998	1999	2000	2001	2002	2003	2004	2005	2006
Tax revenue	3,994	4,838	4,624	4,995	5,273	7,066	8,380	9,656	10,335	11,589
Grants	582	839	644	698	961	1,237	1,504	963	1,165	2,142
Non-tax revenue	2,524	2,530	2,555	2,980	3,043	3,484	3,890	4,256	4,872	5,267
Capital revenue	473	443	555	736	684	704	710	851	908	1,470
Total revenue	7,573	8,650	8,378	9,409	9,961	12,491	14,484	15,727	17,397	20,605
Revenue as % of total revenue										
Tax revenue	53	56	55	53	53	57	58	61	59	56
Grants	8	10	8	7	10	10	10	6	7	10
Non-tax revenue	33	29	30	32	31	28	27	27	28	26
Capital revenue	6	5	7	8	7	6	5	6	6	8
Total revenue	100	100	100	100	100	100	100	100	100	100

Source: Ministry of Finance of the Republic of Croatia.

Table 6.9 Structure of tax revenue from 1997 to 2006 in million Kuna

	1997	1998	1999	2000	2001	2002	2003	2004	2005	2006
Income tax and surtax	2,612	3,136	2,967	3,177	3,625	5,068	6,119	7,190	7,478	8,371
of which: surtax on income tax	n/a	n/a	-	-	-	712	783	-	1,040	-
Profit tax	719	1,016	975	1,095	892	1,171	1,400	1,457	1,788	2,047
Real estate sales tax	505	539	513	540	592	524	527	630	666	740
Goods and services tax	146	145	158	174	162	289	333	377	402	428
Other taxes	13	1	11	9	1	15	1	4	1	2
Total	3,995	4,837	4,624	4,995	5,273	7,066	8,381	9,656	10,335	11,589
Tax revenues as % of total tax revenue										
Income tax and surtax	65	65	64	64	69	72	73	74	72	72
of which: surtax on income tax	n/a	n/a				10	9		10	
Profit tax	18	21	21	22	17	17	17	15	17	18
Real estate sales tax	13	11	11	11	11	7	6	7	6	6
Goods and services tax	4	3	3	3	3	4	4	4	4	4
Other taxes	0	0	0	0	0	0	0	0	0	0
Total	100	100	100	100	100	100	100	100	100	100

Source: Ministry of Finance of the Republic of Croatia.

financial standards or the cost of performing some activity. In defining minimum financial standards, the competent ministries take into consideration the differing needs for public resources of the LGUs.

Horizontal Fiscal Equalisation

Current grants. Central government allocates current grants to financially worse-off LGUs with a below-average fiscal capacity. Between 1994 and 2001 current general grants from the national budget were allocated to counties in the area of which the revenue of all the LGUs (cities and municipalities), not including the city of Zagreb, was less than 75 per cent of the national per capita revenue. The grant was provided from the national budget, the amount being the difference between the per capita revenue realised in the county and the 75 per cent republic average per capita revenue. This assumes that all LGUs have the average tax burden. Grants cannot be allocated to counties in the area of which the rate of surtax is less than 1 per cent and the rates of taxation and the amounts of taxation are lower than the highest rates regulated by law, or the amount of the tax collected locally. In a similar way, the counties allotted grants to the cities and municipalities in their area. Unfortunately, although defined by law, these criteria were never actually used in the real calculation and definition of the criteria for the allocation of central government grants to LGUs.

From 2001 central government in the annual budget execution laws set new criteria for the allocation of current general grants. Central government allocated such grants only to counties in the area of which there are LGUs (cities and municipalities) that form part of the group of LGUs that belong to the ASNC. Counties must allocate at least 50 per cent of the current general grants that they obtain from central government to cities and municipalities that do belong to ASNC. The other 50 per cent of the resources can be allocated by the county according to its own criteria to the other cities and municipalities.

Capital grants via the competent ministries and Regional Development Fund. Capital grants are allocated to cities and municipalities that suffered war damage or natural disasters, or for some given matters. These are usually grants for capital projects that last longer than one year. LGUs send applications for financing to the authorised ministries (for example, the Ministry of the Sea, Tourism, Transport and Development). Apart from via the different ministries, capital grants are also allocated via the Regional Development Fund. This fund was founded in 2001 to encourage even regional development of areas that have a GDP lower than 65 per cent of the Croatian mean GDP.

This fund is financed from the national budget, with revenue from privatisation, bonds, loans, donations and other sources.

LOCAL GOVERNMENT EXPENDITURES

Until 2001, local government expenditures were reported according to the cash flow principle (only after the payment was made). In 2002, the modified accrual principle was introduced, in which expenditures were recognised at the moment when the liability was incurred. At the same time, a new classification of expenditures was introduced; as a result, it is impossible to compare all types of expenditures in detail until 2001 with the expenditures in subsequent years. Two years' practice in the implementation of the new system of fiscal and financial reporting (according to IMF GFS 2001) has helped the MoF and government to get an overview of the real financial position of all LGUs. The MoF does the consolidated financial statement (statement on cash flow, balance sheet, statement on changes of assets and liabilities) of all LGUs. Thanks to this, for the first time, information on a cash flow and accrual base can be obtained.

Autonomy in Setting Expenditure

LGUs have restricted autonomy in determining the purpose of resources. This is shown by the structure of budgetary expenditure of LGUs in which goods and services and labour expenses are dominant (Table 6.10).

Faster growth of current expenditures was mostly a result of the decentralisation process, whereby commitments for financing the major part of current operations in education, social welfare, health and fire fighting were transferred to LGUs (Table 6.11). The growth of capital expenditure from 2003 was financed not only from capital revenues, but also from the outturn of current revenues, transferred unutilised funds from the previous year and receipts from borrowing.

Most of the expenditure of LGUs according to functions is related to housing and communal amenities, and then come general public (administrative) services, and education. We should mention that expenditure for public order and security is related to the financing of the fire departments.

Table 6.10 Expenditure of LGUs from 1997 to 2006, in million Kuna

	1997	1998	1999	2000	2001	2002	2003	2004	2005	2006
1. Current expenditure	4,942	5,801	6,064	6,769	8,237	9,366	10,875	11,800	13,268	14,748
1.1. for labour	1,320	1,556	1,705	1,874	1,356	2,029	2,257	2,771	2,982	3,336
1.2. for goods and services	2,027	2,360	2,247	2,538	2,475	3,703	4,244	4,826	5,227	5,959
1.3. financial expenditures	48	79	134	143	203	232	172	173	242	210
1.4. Subsidies and other current transfers	1,548	1,814	1,978	2,214	4,203	3,402	4,184	4,031	4,725	5,243
2. Capital expenditure	2,473	2,930	2,647	2,939	2,017	2,358	3,540	4,067	4,464	6,775
Total (1+2)	7,415	8,731	8,711	9,708	10,254	11,724	14,415	15,867	17,732	21,523
Individual expenditure as % of total expenditures										
1. Current expenditure	67	66	70	70	80	80	75	74	75	69
1.1. for labour	18	18	20	19	13	17	16	17	17	15
1.2. for goods and services	27	27	26	26	24	32	29	30	29	28
1.3. financial expenditures	1	1	2	1	2	2	1	1	1	1
1.4. Subsidies and other current transfers	21	21	23	23	41	29	29	25	27	24
2. Capital expenditure	33	34	30	30	20	20	25	26	25	31
Total (1+2)	100	100	100	100	100	100	100	100	100	100

Source: Ministry of Finance of the Republic of Croatia.

Table 6.11 Expenditure according to the functions of LGUs 1999–2005, in million Kuna and in per cent

	1999	%	2000	%	2001	%	2002	%	2003	%	2004	%	2005	%
General public services	1,985	23	2,104	25	2,363	23	2,271	20	2,672	18	2,697	17	3,063	17
Defence*		0		0		0	1	0	2	0	2	0	1	0
Public order and safety**	41	0	68	1	97	1	338	3	490	3	453	3	499	3
Economic affairs	1,824	21	1,760	21	2,179	22	1,898	16	2,364	16	2,751	17	2,927	16
Environmental protection		0		0		0	436	4	562	4	648	4	700	4
Housing and community amenities	2,023	24	2,048	24	2,648	26	2,211	19	3,111	21	3,337	21	3,660	21
Health	94	1	75	1	105	1	485	4	575	4	530	3	606	3
Recreation, culture and religion	1,391	16	1,223	14	1,302	13	1,321	11	1,600	11	1,962	12	2,204	12
Education	977	11	1,017	12	1,087	11	1,997	17	2,539	17	2,713	17	3,034	17
Social protection	266	3	256	3	312	3	573	5	671	5	784	5	1,087	6
Total	8,601	100	8,551	100	10,093	100	11,531	100	14,586	100	15,877	100	17,783	100

Notes: *Expenditure for civilian protection. **This expenditure relates to financing the fire departments.

Source: Ministry of Finance of the Republic of Croatia and IMF.

ACCOUNTING RULES, REGULATIONS AND LOCAL GOVERNMENT BUDGETING PROCESS

The local and regional government system has changed significantly since 2001. The accounting system reform and the transfer from the cash flow principle to a modified accrual principle opened up a new perspective for the budget and finance operations of local and regional governments. A number of other reforms have been launched and the new Budget Act (OG 96/03) added a new dynamic to the budgetary processes, to the way budgets are created, to budgetary classification with an accent on introducing programme classification and to other elements. These reforms will influence not only the methodological changes in planning, creating and executing budgets, but also changes in the perception of the purpose of the budget. Thus, the main objective will no longer be only to track the deviations of the actual in comparison with the planned, but also, through a more informative and transparent budget document and budgetary systems, to improve the quality, efficiency and effectiveness of providing public services and goods to citizens.

Unfortunately, the principle of monitoring public sector functions in terms of measurement criteria and the quality of the goods and services has not yet been completely adopted. The basic reasons for this can be found in the overlapping of authorities for financing, in the various sources from which public functions are financed, the small number of programmes that have clearly defined objectives and, ultimately, the lack of understanding of the needs for and importance of introducing a system of performance measurement. The results of the survey carried out (Jakir-Bajo, 2003) show that it is not at all possible to say whether the quality of services in these functions has actually been increased, because performance indicators for programmes in the school, healthcare and welfare systems have not been developed to any extent. Performance indicators are used partially only in housing and communal affairs, sport and recreation, culture and economic affairs.

The section below provides an overview of the steps and requirements of the LGUs' budgetary process.

Economic and fiscal policy guidelines. In April, the MoF issues the economic and fiscal policy report for the current year, the plan for the next year and an estimate of development for the next two years. By the end of April, economic and fiscal policy guidelines for the three-year period have been prepared. The Government decides about the proposed guidelines, sets fiscal policy for the following year and approves the estimated public spending amount (maximum amount of expenditures by main groups).

Adopting the budget. The MoF submits guidelines and instructions for budget preparation to LGUs by the end of May. After the receipt of the guidelines and instructions for state budget preparation, the department responsible for the budget provides instructions for the preparation of LGUs' budgets to budgetary and extra-budgetary institutions. Based on these instructions, the institutions prepare their financial plans, which they submit as proposals to the budget department. Each LGU sets deadlines for the preparation of financial plans in the instructions, but it is important to allow enough time for discussion and preparation of a draft budget by 15 October – the date by which the budget department should submit a draft budget and draft consolidated budget to the board. The board draws up a budget proposal and submits it to the representative body for adoption by 15 November.

Budget execution. The budget execution is based on the adopted annual budget, that is, the established annual plan of revenues and expenditures, receipts and expenses. Monthly allotments are determined (based on monthly financial plans) by budgetary institutions. On the one hand, monthly allotments are determined according to the financial plan of the institution ('plan of wishes'), and on the other hand, according to budgetary possibilities (with regard to flow of revenues) and according to the framework of the set annual budget. Monthly spending of departments and their budgetary institutions should be within the limits of the allotted resources. Budgets may allocate funds to budgetary institutions on a monthly, weekly or daily basis, depending on how well developed their financial and information system is, and depending on how well they are connected with budgetary institutions. Funds transferred to budgetary institutions should be recorded in the budget by the type of expenditure for which the funds are transferred. Expenditures that budgetary institutions incurred and financed from the transferred funds should correspond to the expenditures recorded in the budget.

In the process of execution, most LGUs transfer funds in a lump sum directly to budgetary institutions' accounts (most frequently determined according to the monthly financial plan). At the end of the period for which funds have been received, the institution reports its spending to the LGU in order to record the same expenditures in the budget. In systems in which money is transferred to budgetary institutions, records in the budget and monitoring of the institutions are based on cash flow, and not on accrual, which is the basis of budgetary institutions' accounting records. Another weakness is the lack of information on the maturity of liabilities, as a result of which greater amounts of cash than are immediately necessary are often transferred to the institutions' accounts. Money sits in the accounts of specific institutions, while the local administration simultaneously borrows due to the need to settle the matured liabilities of other institutions. A solution that would ensure efficiency in budget execution requires connecting institutions and the main budget into a single information system in which the accrued expenditures of the institution would be immediately entered both as liabilities and budget expenditures. In this case, the budget would pay the institution's liabilities against maturity, that is, funds would still be transferred, but this transfer from the budget would mean the closing of liabilities (by type of expenditure), while records of settled liabilities would be harmonised against feedback information from the institution.

SUPERVISION AND CONTROL: INTERNAL CONTROL AND THE STATE AUDIT

Budgetary and internal supervision. An LGU is obliged to set up some form of internal control (*Official Gazette* 92/96). Internal control has to be carried out to check on the regularity of the use of budgetary resources and the application of laws and regulations. Yet, in most LGUs, there is no organised internal control. The basic reason for this is the lack of well-qualified staff.

The National Audit Office (NAO) audits the local government unit's budget each year. All 571 LGUs fall under the competence of the NAO. Apart from the Central Audit Office, there are 20 branch offices located in the county centres. Auditing of the budgets of LGUs implies two kinds of audit, an audit of regularity and an audit of effectiveness. For the moment it is mainly regularity audits that are carried out, although each of them also contains elements of effectiveness auditing.

LGUs draw up reports about the execution of the budget. Fundamental financial reports are also given to the Auditing Office, twice a year. Half-yearly reports are delivered by 15 July, and annual reports are given in by the end of February for the preceding year. After receiving the report and pursuant to the audit of the budget and the operations of the LGU being carried out, the national auditors draw up a report about the audit. This is sent to the representative body of the LGU. Once a year, reports about audits of LGUs that have been carried out are submitted to Parliament. For the moment, no prior auditing is carried out in the LGUs, only post hoc audits. The possibility of taking on commercial auditors is not provided for by the law. The auditing of companies in which an LGU is the major or a partial shareholder is carried out by the NAO. Audits depend on the programme of work of the NAO. However, these companies are also subject to commercial auditing, like other privately owned companies.

It can be said that the NAO has carried out its business correctly, however the question is to what extent the findings of the national auditing are really used and applied in correcting the irregularities in the operations of the budgets of the LGUs.

LGUs AND FINANCIAL MARKETS

All LGUs (municipalities, cities and counties) can take on long-term debt by taking out loans on the money and capital market and contract debts to their contractors, exclusively for a capital investment project, for reconstruction and development, financed from their budgets. They can take on debt pursuant to the decision of the representative body of the LGU with the prior consent of the Government of the Republic of Croatia. In 2003, the provision about contracting debts with contractors of works was rescinded. Short-term borrowing of LGUs is possible for the financing of the regular activities of the body and the spending agencies of their budgets, only when the revenue of the budget does not come in evenly throughout the year.

All LGUs, the current revenues of which are greater than current expenditure, or whose operating revenues are greater than operating expenditures, meet the criteria for being able to borrow. The following are excluded from operating receipts: (1) from domestic and foreign grants, subsidies and transfers from the central government budget and the budgets of other LGUs; and (2) from special contracts about citizen co-financing and voluntary levies.

From 1996 to 1998 LGUs were able to borrow on the domestic and foreign capital markets up to 30 per cent of the budgetary expenditures incurred in the previous year. From 1998 to 2007 the MoF and the Government established a lower borrowing ceiling and total annual liabilities (annuities) of an LGU were not to exceed 20 per cent of the budgetary revenue realised in the preceding year (Table 6.12). The amount of the average annuities on loans, including guarantees issued, was included in the amount of the total annual liabilities, as well as the amount of outstanding liabilities carried over from the previous years. The Government and the MOF introduced an additional restriction in 2003 and 2007, and LGUs can now take on debt up to at most 3 then 2 and 2.3 per cent respectively, of the totally realised operating revenue of all LGUs. By laying down an additional limit, the Government and the MoF have tightened the conditions for borrowing and indirectly stimulated competition among LGUs for gaining authorisation for their borrowing.

Table 6.12 Conditions for LGU borrowing for capital investment (reconstruction and development) 1996–2007

Year	Annual borrowing limit (annual liability)		Additional limit
1996			
1997	30% of budgetary expenditure		None
1998			None
1999			
2000		Included is the amount of the average annual annuities on loans, guarantees given from the previous years, and short-term outstanding liabilities	
2001			
2002	20% of realised revenue		
2003			3% of the total revenue of all LGUs
2004			
2005			2% of the total revenue of all LGUs
2006			2% of the total revenue of all LGUs
2007			2.3% of the total revenue of all LGUs

Source: *Official Gazette.*

CONCLUSION

Croatia is a small country with too many LGUs. This causes the accumulation of oversized administrative machinery at several tiers of government and an inadequate division of functions and responsibilities. The situation has been aggravated by the creation of areas of special national concern in response to damage caused by the war.

For the central government, the task remains to check the first effects of the process of fiscal decentralisation, to control much more effectively the purposes for which grants are used, and to define more appropriately the criteria for the allocation of intergovernmental grants and revenue sharing with LGUs. Nevertheless, further progress in reform will to a great extent depend on the capacity and knowledge of individuals at the central government level and also in the LGUs who have to carry out the ideas of the initiators of the reform on the ground.

Reform of the financing of LGUs in Croatia should be carried out in several phases. For that to be done, additional concrete research into the financial position of the LGUs still needs to be carried out especially in the areas of: fiscal capacity indicators (focus on criteria for vertical and horizontal equalisations); LGU borrowing and indebtedness (the regulation and role of the central government); efficiency of the revenue and expenditure, and administrative and compliance costs of revenue collection and benefits arising from the expenditure. The main problem in the reform of LGU financing is the excessive politicisation that might attend any new initiative.

NOTES

1. Which replaced the Local Self-Government and Administration Law (1992).
2. *Official Gazette* (OG), in Croatian *Narodne novıne* (NN).

BIBLIOGRAPHY

Bajo, A. (2004), *Local government units borrowing in Croatia; opportunities and constraints*, Newsletter of Institute of Public Finance No.15, Zagreb: Institute of Public Finance, Available from: http://www.ijf.hr/eng/newsletter/news15.pdf.

Bajo, A. and M. Bronić (2007), Assessments of the Effectiveness of the Croatian Fiscal Equalisation Model, *Financial Theory and Practice*, **31**(1), 1–26. Available from: http://www.ijf.hr/eng/FTP/2007/1/bajo-bronic.pdf

Croatian Central Bureau of Statistics (various years), *Statistical Yearbook*, Zagreb: Central Bureau of Statistics.

Jakir-Bajo, I. (2003), The System of Performance Measurement in the Croatian Public Sector, in Ž. Šević ed., *Gauging Success: Performance Measurement in South Eastern Europe*, Budapest: Open Society Institute, pp. 61–80.

Ministry of Finance (various years), *Monthly Statistical Review,* Zagreb: Ministry of Finance RC.

Naputak o postupku zaduživanja i davanja jamstava jedinica lokalne i područne (regionalne) samouprave [Decree on borrowing procedures and guarantees issued of Local and Regional Government Self-government], NN 32/02 and 49/03, Zagreb: Narodne novine.

Ott, K. and A. Bajo (2001), Lokalne financije i lokalni proračuni [Local Government Finance and Budgeting], *Financijska teorija i praksa*, **23**(3), 311–449.

Ustav Republike Hrvatske [The Constitution of the Republic of Croatia], NN 56/90, 135/97, and 113/00, Zagreb: Narodne novine.

Zakon o brdsko-planinskim područjima [The Law on Mountainous and Hilly Areas], NN 12/02, Zagreb: Narodne novine.

Zakon o financiranju jedinica lokalne i područne regionalne samouprave [The law on Financing of Local and Regional Self-government], NN 117/93, 69/97, 33/00, 127/00, 59/01, 107/01, 117/01 and 150/02, Zagreb: Narodne novine.

Zakon o fondu za regionalni razvoj Republike Hrvatske [The Law on Regional Development Fund of the Republic of Croatia], NN 107/01, Zagreb: Narodne novine.

Zakon o gradu Zagrebu [The Law on the City of Zagreb], NN 62/01, Zagreb: Narodne novine.
Zakoni o izvršavanju državnog proračuna od 1999. do 2007. godine [The Laws on Budget Execution from 1999 to 2007], Zagreb: Narodne novine.
Zakon o javnoj nabavi [The Law on Public Procurement], NN 117/01, Zagreb: Narodne novine.
Zakon o komunalnom gospodarstvu [The Law on Local Public Utilities], NN 26/03, Zagreb: Narodne novine.
Zakon o otocima [The Law on Islands], NN 34/99, Zagreb: Narodne novine.
Zakon o područjima posebne državne skrbi [The Law on Area of Special National Concern], NN 44/96, 57/96, 124/97, 78/99, 73/00, 127/00, 88/02, 42/05 and 90/05, Zagreb: Narodne novine.
Zakon o proračunu [The Budget Law], NN 96/03, Zagreb: Narodne novine.
Zakon o sustavu državne uprave [The Law on the System of Public Administration], NN 75/93, 48/99, 15/00, 127/00, 59/01 and 199/03), Zagreb: Narodne novine.
Zakon o vatrogastvu [The Law on fire-fighting], NN 58/93 and 196/99, Zagreb: Narodne novine.

7. Fiscal decentralisation in the Czech Republic: problems and prospects

Phillip J. Bryson and Gary C. Cornia

INTRODUCTION: HISTORICAL BACKGROUND

The transition of the Czech economy to market orientation and the pursuit of decentralisation of the public sector to achieve local self-government (*samospráva*) have been the two pillars of post-communist development. Their effects were adjudged by the European Union as sufficient to justify membership under criteria demanding democracy and market economies in member countries.

It is our objective to review the process of decentralisation since the Velvet Revolution and the end of central planning in Czechoslovakia. We will note the fiscal changes which began before the Velvet Divorce of the two countries in 1993 and have continued to the present. We will evaluate the effort to achieve fiscal decentralisation by reviewing the process from both organisational and budgetary perspectives, and we will document our finding that the process has failed to generate complete or genuine local self-government. The collapse of central planning in Czechoslovakia came two decades after the Prague Spring of 1968, which had culminated in the Warsaw Pact invasion of Prague. There was rejoicing in the hope of *samospráva* in Czechoslovakia because the former regime had retained all power centrally.

Independence and Growing Numbers of Municipalities

Czech governmental and administrative systems, including the fiscal organization, were composed until recently of only two tiers, the national centre and the municipalities. At the present moment, there are 6,249 independent municipalities in the Czech Republic, which is substantially more than were extant in 1989. Many towns and villages that had been forced into larger, more convenient administrative units during the communist period were permitted to reclaim their independence after 1989 and they did so with an enthusiasm that reflected a keen local demand for political autonomy.

The problem with this large number of small municipalities is providing competent administration for them. Resource and personnel limitations are the common stumbling blocks (Houerou and Rutkowski, 1996). In the Czech Republic, this challenge seems to recommend either the administrative union of small groups of villages, and/or the establishment of an intermediate governmental tier to assist the municipalities with their administrative challenges. Over the past few years 11 new regional administrative units, the *Kraje*, have been established. The new regions will in fact assume some of the administrative functions of the centre and some of those of the municipalities, but the municipalities are not vertically subordinated to the regions and they still report directly to the centre. The regions have not received a mandate to assist small municipalities lacking the resources to manage their administrative functions independently. But there has been a tendency for the smaller municipalities to begin to look for alliances with neighbouring towns or villages to specialize and divide the labour of social, educational and other public service functions.

Early Transition Fiscal Reform

Between 1990 and 1993 a number of common institutions, including a more Western-style tax system, were introduced in Czechoslovakia. Then, pursuing long-latent, nationalist aspirations, the Slovaks got their accommodating neighbours to dismantle the federation in the 'Velvet Divorce' of 1993. Much had already been accomplished since Soviet troops had withdrawn from the region, but reformers still faced many serious problems. The majority of retail trade was conducted in state-controlled stores. The ubiquitous, publicly-owned and subsidised housing was in poor repair. Large, inefficient agricultural collectives had not disappeared from the rural areas. There were no functioning markets to establish scarcity prices or to indicate the value of homes, farms and businesses. After embarking on the path of transformation, economic change was commendable; the Czech Republic had relatively low inflation and unemployment. Significant budget deficits were avoided. Strong economic performance and effective macroeconomic policies were generally maintained after 1989's Velvet Revolution; prices were liberalised early, a far-ranging privatisation effort was implemented with fair success, and Czech export endeavours were reoriented toward the European Union.

Importantly, the legal foundations of decentralization were established in Czech legislation. Laws on the municipality and, more recently, on the new regions were supplemented by many other acts that provide the basis for local autonomy and also for a more recent, extensive effort to reform public administration in a country being admitted to the European Union. But even after 15 years of transformation efforts, there remains much to accomplish. For a time, political forces sought to avoid transformation agonies through more gradual transition measures, intending to shield non-competitive firms from market shock. The Ministry of Finance and the banking system were not quick learners in a market environment that attaches importance to creditworthiness for loans. The finance ministry permitted the large, state-owned banks to keep less than profitable firms in business. This ultimately damaged the Czech reputation for transformation success in late 1997 when Vaclav Klaus was ousted as Prime Minister in a campaign finance scandal.

The Czech government and its Finance Ministry had tended to ignore pressure to move ahead with the privatisation of the large banks. Since that time, progress has been steady if not rapid. The banking sector, important because it will remain the primary source of investment funds in Eastern Europe for some time to come, has been successfully privatised. The state of the banking sector has important implications for the development of the real estate market. Because scarce investment funds are vital for investment processes promoting development, relatively little money has been available for a home mortgage market.

CZECH LOCAL FINANCE AND REVENUE SOURCES

Early Reform and the Legacy of Centralism

Another fundamental fiscal issue is how centralised the taxation system should be. In spite of the Czech Republic's post-revolutionary willingness to achieve greater municipal independence, the Czech system has not yet completely emerged from the centralist era. The transition to markets required a more robust tax system than that of pre-revolutionary Czechoslovakia. The ineffective, command-oriented fiscal systems required thorough revamping (Holzman, 1992). Preparations for a comprehensive tax reform were undertaken before the 1993 division of Czechoslovakia into two republics. Being modelled after the fiscal systems of Western Europe, the new fiscal system incorporated important elements of decentralisation. Although a clear improvement, the results were sometimes complex and distorted. It was apparently somewhat defective in considering carefully the size of revenue flows required to satisfy national and local needs.

Czech local revenue sources: corporate and personal income tax

In designing its fiscal system, the Czech Republic sought to achieve an effective balance between indirect and direct taxation. This is a challenge because of the non-transparent nature of taxation under the previous, central planning regime, which completely hid taxation from the public view. Public officials in the post-communist period have had to move toward the abandonment of indirect and invisible tax sources, greatly increasing the sensitive citizenry's awareness of direct taxation's impacts. At the end of the first decade of post-communist taxation, indirect taxes were still generating about 54 per cent of the central government's revenues while direct taxes were producing only about 46 per cent. Personal income tax rates, since that tax was introduced in January 1993, have ranged from 15 per cent on an annual tax base up to Kč 84,000 up to 40 per cent on an annual base greater than Kč 756,000. The general corporate income tax rate is 39 per cent (Czech Taxation in 1997). Revenues derived from these tax sources will be considered in some detail below.

Czech personal and corporate income taxes are, of course, the most significant direct taxes. Since some important tax revisions were made in 1996, 20 per cent of the corporate income tax yield returns to the locality where it was collected. Unfortunately, this arrangement did not represent a net gain for the municipalities; the additional revenues had to replace 40 per cent of the wage tax yield the 1996 revisions transferred from cities and towns to the central budget. In any case, inter-jurisdictional revenue sharing is an established practice, as in other transitional countries. As observed above, directing corporate tax revenues back to the areas from which they were collected is based on the unusual assumption that shared tax revenues should belong to the area that permitted their generation.[1] The Czech road tax is also a direct tax.

In the early transition years the central government turned over a considerable share of the personal income tax revenues collected to local governments. In 1994 the local governments received 89 per cent of such revenues and in the following year 87.6 per cent of total personal income tax revenues. In 1996 the share dropped to 63 per cent and then remained at about that level. Corporate income tax followed a contrasting pattern, with the centre initially transferring only a small portion to the municipalities. In 1994 only two tenths of 1 per cent of corporate income taxes accrued to local budgets. Very soon, however, the amounts increased to the level of over 20 per cent. From 1996 to 1999 it increased only gradually to 26 per cent, reaching 31 per cent in 2000.

The VAT and sales taxes

The value added tax (VAT) is the most significant of the Czech Republic's indirect taxes. Currently, it has separate rates for basic necessities (which are taxed at 5 per cent) and other commodities and services (22 per cent). The higher rate was for some time, at least, the second-highest among countries in transition (Bird et al., 1995). Other indirect taxes are customs duties and the excise tax on gasoline, tobacco, and alcoholic beverages. These taxes are supplemented by a road tax, inheritance taxes, real estate transfer taxes, and others. These taxes yield, as we would expect, more modest revenues than those already addressed above.

Privatization revenues and local government debt

The total resources available to Czech municipalities include far more than just the transfer of tax revenues and grants from the central government. Since the transition began, considerable housing properties and many local enterprises have been transferred to the municipalities. It cannot, unfortunately, be expected that Czech municipalities will be able to fund a good portion of their financial needs through the privatisation of these properties and the one-time generation of sales revenues. Some privatisation has occurred, even of the housing properties, but the resulting aggregate revenues have represented only a small percentage, well under 10 per cent, of the total budget revenues of the municipalities.

Such revenues provided a temporary supplement to the fiscal effort of the early transition period, but the revenue system still had to bring revenue flows to local governments to a viable and sustained level. This effort is still an ongoing one and some municipalities have felt it necessary to generate additional revenues through debt. Most of the larger towns and cities have been quite responsible in leveraging expenditures, but the Czech Finance Ministry has been quite concerned about local governments doing so. While the finance ministry has wanted to limit the amount of local debt, the local governments were concerned about meagre budgets. Deficits grew rapidly for a number of the municipalities as the government in Prague considered various proposals regarding further modifications of the distribution of tax revenues.

Property tax

Because of the special role that the property tax plays in the municipal finances of a number of countries, we will take time to consider this fiscal instrument at greater length. The property tax has the potential to be the most significant tax for local governments, especially for small ones. It represents a revenue source that can secure autonomy for local governments in both design and implementation. In the Czech Republic the property tax has certainly not been developed to its potential. It has failed to provide adequate revenues, which it could do with minimal distortion of private allocation processes (Oates, 1996). Occasional proposals by the Czech Ministry of Finance to generate greater revenue yields have not resonated with the parliament.

Admittedly, the Czech 'real estate tax', even if it were increased substantially, would not produce revenue sufficient to meet all local needs. Other taxes would still have to contribute revenues to fund the backlog of badly needed municipal projects. The reason the property tax is so important is that it gives local governments more autonomous control over their own fiscal affairs, which is a hallmark of genuine self-government. The fiscal system of the Czech Republic can be described as one without local taxes, because all policy prerogatives, like all tax revenues, accrue to the national government (Kameníčková, 1998).

Potential and Actual Roles of the Property Tax in Fiscal Decentralisation

The fiscal institutions of a country will play a major role in determining the effectiveness of a property tax. Who establishes tax policy and who administers the tax are both very important questions. Policy issues include such things as the types of property included in the tax base, the rate applied, and the revenue importance of properties. Questions of administration include the valuation of the property, record keeping, and the actual tax collection. Central decision makers and national institutional traditions are responsible for each of these administrative and policy functions; municipal, district and regional governments merely function within the framework provided for them. Figure 7.1 provides a topology illustrative of the trade-offs countries face in establishing the participation of local governments with the nation.

In the United States property taxation has been decentralised with respect both to policy and administration. In other countries, like the United Kingdom, parts of the process are centralised while others are not. In the Czech Republic, obviously influenced by the previous regime's centralist inclinations and traditions, both functions have been centralised. Fiscal decentralisation has not been an event following the end of the central planning regime, but a process largely still waiting for rediscovery. A willingness to conform to Western, democratic conditions and the perceived benefits accruing to EU membership have served to change perspectives and motivations to the extent that has occurred.

Figure 7.1 Property tax policy and administration

Policy: determining types of property included in the tax base, the tax rate, and revenue importance of the property record keeping, tax, etc.

		Central Government	*Sub-National Government*
Administration: property valuation, collection, etc.	*Central Government*	Czech Republic France Sweden	Netherlands
	Sub-National Government	Germany United Kingdom	United States Japan

Source: Dillinger (1988). Embellishments by the authors.

The Czech Republic's Decentralization Initiatives

When municipalities set about to implement a property tax system, more than nominal problems must be overcome. Because this tax is highly visible and because Marxist–Leninist regimes were of limited credibility, it was retained at strictly nominal levels during that era. But in spite of this legacy and the natural tendency of any citizenry to oppose property taxes, there is much to recommend them. A tax on real property will 'make good sense as part of the tax system as a whole' because 'the property tax scores quite well in terms of both its efficiency and its equity aspects' (Kameníčková, 1998, p. 16).

If all revenues are delivered as transfers from the centre, will such transfers be available without the accompanying influence of the centre? Can one speak of genuine fiscal decentralisation if local governments enjoy only limited fiscal autonomy? Can independence be achieved if the sub-national governments do not gain access to independent revenues? It is our view that independent revenue sources are indispensable for the policy independence of municipalities so that cities and towns will not be left dependent on the state, even if transfers and grants provide funding sufficient for expenditures of the types that correspond to central preferences. Central and East Europe's countries in transition have perceived a fairly standard set of taxes and user fees to be well suited for their local governments. They have not generally felt the property tax should be increased from the current low, rather symbolic levels insufficient to fund municipal services or perform the necessary administrative tasks.

Self-government for the Czech regions and municipalities cannot be achieved so long as the centre maintains control over local fiscal policy matters. The tax system of the Czech Republic has been characterised as one in which 'there are no local taxes', since the significant characteristics of all the Czech taxes are determined by the central government or by the national parliament.[2] Reflecting the accession mandates of the EU, the Czech Republic has established administrative regions (*kraje*) and implemented a 'reform of public administration'. The Czech government intends to achieve organisational decentralisation and some positive changes are being discussed and implemented. But if municipalities currently wish to augment available revenues, they must seek opportunities from sources other than taxation. They may sell off public properties transferred to them by the central government or incur debt to offset revenue shortfalls. But these sources are not without potential peril, since the privatisation of property represents a revenue source that does not recur and cannot provide a sustainable cash flow; moreover, municipal loans must also be used with prudence.

Characteristics of the Czech Real Estate Tax

The tax yield of the Czech real estate tax is determined by the base and rate of the tax. Tax legislation includes both land and buildings in the property tax base and the valuation of each is undertaken separately. National law prescribes the process by which the actual value of property is to be determined. Basically, the tax base reflects the floor space of buildings and the area of land plots. Tax rates, also centrally determined, differ for buildings and for land.

The taxable value of land plots and buildings is primarily a function of their areas in square metres, that is, valuation is not based on market prices. This non-market value system is unavoidable, given the developmental state of the Czech fiscal system, the real estate market and the scarcity of professional property tax administrators.

Valuations of properties and buildings are adjusted by a coefficient for city size where they are located and city tax administrators can adjust their municipality's coefficient up one level or down two. The city of Prague has the option of applying a coefficient of 5 to certain, well-located properties. For buildings with multiple levels, the number of square metres of each additional level is multiplied by a factor of 0.75 and added to the value of the ground floor base. The tax rate and coefficient for each parcel of real estate reflect attributes of the land, that is, the location, the size of the parcel, and the use to which it is put.

They determine the amount of the real estate tax as assessed by the taxpayer. After calculating the tax due, the taxpayer files the return and the payment at the District Offices of the Finance Ministry. The Ministry then transfers the property tax revenues back to the municipality of the taxpayer.

Czech policymakers have attempted to encourage the construction of private residences by exempting new homes from property tax for their first 15 years. For older individuals who have had their properties restored through restitution but lack the income both to maintain them and pay taxes, there is a 15-year moratorium from the property tax. In parts of some larger cities, such exemptions represent a major share of the potential tax revenues. There are also other instances in the tax policies of transition countries where social welfare concerns have led to exemptions which might imperil tax revenue adequacy.[3]

The Property Tax Contribution to Czech Municipal Budgets

Although Czech municipal budgets are fairly well funded as compared to other transition countries, Czech cities and towns must live with the difficulties arising from inadequate funding from the centre. The aggregate of local budgets represented just 25 per cent of the national budget in 1993 (see Table 7.1). That share grew rather continually, although it stagnated at about 30 per cent from 1997 to 1999, reaching a high of 32.6 per cent in the year 2000. The Czechs have continually improved municipal funding through tax-sharing and grants since the end of the central planning era, gradually approaching a level of funding for the municipalities that corresponds to levels characteristic of Western economies.

Grants provided by the national government have been more variable, viewed as a share of the local budgets. Table 7.1 indicates that grants have ranged from percentages in the low twenties to over thirty. In the long run, they have been about 30 per cent of total local budget revenues. Other forms of revenue transfers have tended to increase while grants have become less significant.

What stands out in these data is the relative insignificance of the real estate tax in the Czech Republic, explained partly by the fact that the tax is subject to moral hazard problems (Bryson and Cornia, 2003). The state is clearly motivated to retain property tax at traditionally low levels. Nor are local leaders inclined to insist the national government make a more serious effort to identify properties and collect the tax. It is much easier to be satisfied with the revenue-sharing and grants the federal government provides. Because the state provides all the revenues for municipal investment projects, it alone determines which projects will be funded. Municipal political independence is obviously a corollary to the accessibility of independent financial sources.

Table 7.1 Czech local and national budgets, selected years, 1993–2005

Year	1993	1995	1996	1998	1999	2000	2004	2005
Local Budget as % of National Budget	25.45	29.34	33.5	30.8	30.9	32.6	29.13	28.78
State Grants to Local Budgets	27.03	33.28	59.44	37.39	41.43	46.05	24.96	31.6
Grants as % of Local Budgets	29.67	25.77	36.75	23.79	22.07	25.33	8.08	9.44
Total Local Revenues	101	129	162	162	188	181	309	335
Local Budget Expenditures	90.1	132.3	171.1	158	173	190	231	246
National Budget Tax Revenues	224.6	255.4	283	495	524	544	963	1060
Local Budget Tax Revenues	35.97	70.68	72.67	83.32	87.01	95.81	166.79	216.14
Real Estate Tax	3.021	3.799	4.018	4.108	4.248	4.437	4.919	4.966
RE Tax as % of Local Revs	2.99	2.95	2.48	2.53	2.26	2.44	1.59	1.48

Notes: Years 2004 and 2005 reflect new statistical protocols. Local budgets become sub-national budgets and include regional offices, municipalities and voluntary unions. Since 2000, grants declined substantially while transfers increased correspondingly.

Source: Czech Statistical Office and own calculations.

Only in 1994 (a year omitted from Table 7.1 to save space) did real estate tax provide in excess of 3 per cent of the total revenues available to local governments. In all the other years after 1993, as noted in Table 7.1, its share was between 2 and 3 per cent. After 2000 the declining proportion fell below 2 per cent. Other funds have been increasing in volume, while the real estate tax decreased.

Non-tax revenue sources: local users' fees

The Czech Finance Ministry has proposed reclassifying local fees (*Místní Poplatky*) as taxes, and there is strong interest in permitting the municipalities to use this revenue source to enhance sub-national revenues. To this point, local fees yield revenues of a magnitude similar to that of the property tax, but were actually larger in the last two years before the turn of the century.

Together, property tax and local fees amounted in 2001 and 2002 to only about 5.5–6 per cent of total local revenues (Table 7.2).

The small amount of revenues generated by local user fees is explained in part by the fact that user fees are not designed with the exclusive purpose of revenue generation. Sometimes they are administered for regulatory purposes, sometimes they are designed to ration scarce public space or other public resources among competing uses. Dog licences are issued for example, not only to raise funds, but also because the presence of pets in high-rise housing can have external effects. If municipalities were to pursue greater revenues through user fees, however, greater fiscal effort would certainly make that possible. Particularly if third degree price discrimination were used where appropriate, giving attention to differing demand elasticities stemming from segments of the population or different income groups, greater revenue generation would certainly be achievable. Where there are hardship cases, subsidies (substantially smaller than the revenue generated) could alleviate the hardship where appropriate.

Table 7.2 Users fees and property tax revenues, 2001 and 2002 (in mil. Kč)

Revenue Source	2001	2002
Property Tax	4,568	4,571
As % of Total Revenues	2.5%	2.2%
Users Fees	5,388	7,998
Users Fees plus Property Tax as % of Total Revenues	5.4%	6.0%
Non-tax Revenue	23,016	23,809

Source: Hospodaření územních samosprava, *Obec a Finance*, March, 2003. http://denik.obce.cz/go/clanek.asp?id=5521879.

The Czech system of inter-governmental grants

Revenue sharing and financial grants have been an increasingly important source of local funds. Table 7.3 provides data for an overview of these efforts. We begin by considering the aggregate of tax revenues accruing to the local governments as a percentage of the total of the Republic's consolidated government budgets. In 1994 local tax revenues were only 13.6 per cent of the consolidated budgets. Increasing to 15 per cent in 1995, the share then declined for three straight years, being lower at 12.8 per cent in 1997 than it had been in 1994. The next three years it increased again, reaching a high in 2000 of 15 per cent. By 2003 it had reached 18 per cent and it remained there through 2005.

The municipalities have relied heavily on grants from the federal government in providing public goods and services. Through the latter part of the 1990s, grants represented approximately a quarter of municipal revenues. Their increase after 2001 and through the current decade, under the positive influence of preparations for admission into the EU, has been very dramatic. Economic reforms and the addition of EU grants to those of the Czech Republic increased significantly the share of local budgets derived from grants in the current decade.

Table 7.3 Local and state tax revenue sharing (in mil. Kč)

	1994	1995	1996	1997	1998	1999	2000	2001	2002	2003	2004	2005
Tax Revenues, State	349,027	391,228	439,186	464,087	495,232	524,765	544,142	582,498	610,490	653,602	702,342	754,421
Tax Revenues, Local	54,428	68,167	70,000	76,091	83,319	87,011	95,807	88,840	109,718	118,890	128,707	168,519
Consolidated budgets, Total	401,503	457,022	506,202	592,474	575,836	608,585	636,618	727,227	716,435	767,584	826,004	917,719
Local Share in %	0.136	0.149	0.138	0.128	0.145	0.143	0.150	0.122	0.153	0.182	0.183	0.184
Local PI Tax Revenues	48,716	60,096	50,818	54,503	58,581	60,078	63,501	25,848	32,264	34,387	38,114	47,656
National PI Tax Revenues	5,804	8,491	29,726	33,378	36,339	35,224	34,771	78,547	82,140	88,631	95,212	94,775
Total PI Tax Revenues	54,520	68,587	80,544	87,881	94,920	95,302	98,272	104,395	114,404	123,018	133,329	142,431
Local as % of Total	0.894	0.876	0.631	0.620	0.617	0.630	0.646	0.248	0.282	0.280	0.286	0.335
Local CI Tax Revenues	128	3,145	14,139	13,361	16,232	18,773	23,470	23,187	28,823	31,635	34,287	44,528
State CI Tax Revenues	63,624	63,337	47,676	42,202	51,324	51,343	52,322	68,841	76,893	84,274	85,522	100,293
Total CI Tax Revenues	63,752	66,482	61,815	55,563	67,556	70,116	75,792	92,028	105,716	115,909	119,809	144,821
Local as % of Total	0.002	0.047	0.229	0.240	0.240	0.268	0.310	0.252	0.273	0.273	0.286	0.307
National Government Grants	30,980	34,803	61,504	35,839	37,355	41,374	45,939	67,210	87,074	138,433	137,432	119,859
Current	24,003	21,747	48,882	23,958	24,982	27,658	30,429	52,973	68,729	114,138	111,626	103,026
Capital	6,977	13,056	12,622	11,881	12,373	13,716	15,510	14,237	18,275	24,295	25,806	16,833
Local Rev & Grants Total	112,241	130,041	163,831	145,342	157,178	187,700	181,814	192,423	236,572	298,933	306,739	331,612
Consolidated Public Budgets	504,283	522,753	562,792	487,655	637,656	688,844	707,844	727,227	901,411	848,207	922,443	1,016,013
Local Share	0.223	0.249	0.291	0.298	0.246	0.272	0.257	0.265	0.262	0.352	0.333	0.326

Source: Government Financial Statistics: Fiscal Data for the Czech Republic, Ministry of Finance, Czech Republic, and authors' calculations. See the web site, http://www.mfcr.cz/cps/rde/xchg/mfcr/hs.xsl/vlad_fin_stat.html

The share of taxes transferred increased through the 1990s, but this paralleled a reduction in the volume of transfers to local governments. Transfers and shared taxes combined remained at about 70 per cent of total municipal receipts. Although local governments became less dependent on state budget transfers, a 'meaningful degree of tax autonomy for local authorities was still missing' (Oliveira and Martinez-Vazquez, 2001[4]). Unlike most other European countries, including those in transition, the Czech Republic has no system of equalisation grants at the district or municipal level. Nor did the 2000 reforms make any provision for such grants. Nevertheless, a complex system of conditional grants or subsidies transfers funds to municipalities. These are distributed for specific purposes and local governments have no discretion in their use. They must generally report on the specific expenditures thus enabled (Oliveira and Martinez-Vazquez, 2001). The flows of funds in the form of earmarked subsidies, however, have been in continuous decline. In 1999 earmarked subsidies represented no more than 24 per cent of all local government revenues.

Earmarked grants take the form of categorical grants and capital transfers and both types fund municipal current expenditures. Categorical grants finance those activities delegated by the central government and must be spent on specific, well-defined programmes. These transfers, which require no matching funds from local governments, are usually distributed on a per capita basis for social programmes – social benefits, hospital and assistance institutions, early education, fire brigades, and for other general government services (see Oliveira and Martinez-Vazquez, 2001).

Central governments use categorical transfers *inter alia* to redistribute fiscal resources, adjust for vertical imbalances, counter externalities, and promote local government expenditures in support of national programmes. If they were to rely, instead, on unconditional grants rather than categorical transfers, central authority would grant greater decision-making autonomy to local officials. The Czech Republic was criticised in this period for its nearly exclusive use of earmarked grants, which suggested that central authorities believed they had correctly identified local priorities and had better information on needs than local officials did. Recently, this criticism was renewed by the OECD (2006), in an economic review indicating that the 'broad thrust of policy' in the area of sub-national government financing, 'should be towards giving more flexibility, in particular by switching from earmarked grants to block grants or increased tax allocation ... for example through widening of the statutory limits on real-estate taxation'.

Capital transfers also represent significant grants both from the general budget and the State Environmental Fund. They are intended to accomplish a variety of purposes: fire protection, natural gas distribution, schools, public transport, and the development of industrial zones, hospitals, water and sewerage treatment plants and numerous other kinds of capital infrastructure projects. With these grants, matching funds are almost always required of the municipalities. Specific transfers of these types have provided negative incentives for revenue generation on the part of local governments, since the central government apparently makes a systematic reduction in such transfers as local governments increase their own revenues (see Oliveira and Martinez-Vazquez, 2001).

Oliveira and Martinez-Vazquez (2001) contend that the Czech Republic tends to be less efficient and fair by allocating grants conditionally and at the discretion of central authorities rather than through the use of objective formulas or well-publicised legislative procedures and criteria. They suggest as an alternative to a system of application for grants on a project-by-project basis that the central government develops a comprehensive expenditure plan for local governments which then transfers funds according to their availability.

IS THE CZECH GOVERNMENT'S RELATIVE LARGESSE A SUBSTITUTE FOR LOCAL AUTONOMY?

Many do not see the failure to implement a serious property tax as a problem for Czech local autonomy. Their view is that the municipalities have not needed independent revenues because the central government has in fact supplied adequate funds. Compared to a number of transition countries, the Czech Republic has indeed been relatively generous in supplying funds for the needs of the regions, districts and municipalities. The EU apparently saw this as evidence that the Czech Republic was developing satisfactorily as a modern democracy and was therefore prepared to become a full member of the EU. Reservations in this regard were addressed through the 'reform of public administration' in the early years of the current decade. This reform will be addressed momentarily.

It is our position that this view was too narrow. There are significant problems in the fiscal development of the Czech Republic's sub-national governments. The central government has been quite slow in developing fiscally independent municipalities and regions (Bryson and Cornia, 2000), maintaining offices at all political levels for what they term 'state administration' to perform under strictly central discretion many tasks routinely considered local tasks in Western countries. Even for the tasks rather arbitrarily designated by the centre as activities for 'self-government', the centre too often establishes the policies, allocates the funds, and directs the local officers how to spend the money.

There are many examples of policies and actions which demonstrate the centre's inclinations to oversee or even manage local activities. Local governments have had public housing (of poor quality and in need of major expenditures) turned over to them without the funds to maintain or repair them. Housing units may be privatised as a supplementary revenue source, but such activities are hardly the domain of local decision makers. Housing rents and tariffs on such public utilities as water and gas are still regulated by the central government, and they are held at levels below full cost recovery. Likewise, the salaries of local government employees are controlled by central government (Martinez-Vazquez and McNab, 1997, p. xv).

Under democratic traditions, municipalities have the responsibility for the development of their own capital infrastructure. In the Czech Republic, local governments are still dependent upon the central government for the financing of capital expenditures, which is provided in the form of earmarked grants and subsidised loans.

Regional governments, only recently established in the reform of public administration, are now being phased in. They have been funded in the transition period by transfers from the state budget. To begin with, they inherit some of the state's former responsibilities, for example secondary education, regional planning and inter-city transport (Martinez-Vazquez and McNab, 1997, p. 6).

Czech Centralisation and EU Accession

Because of the determination of the Czech Republic to join the EU, the latter could easily have pressured the Czechs to provide genuine autonomy for sub-national governments by mandating fiscal decentralisation. After all, the EU requires accession countries to develop democratic institutions and functioning market economies. Unfortunately, the Czech system has retained its centralised character. Local governments continue to perform little beyond 'state administration', that is to act as an agent of central administration of delegated tasks.

This is not to say, of course, that the Czech central government is not willing to provide an acceptable level of transfers of funds so that essential public services can be provided by sub-national governments. And the European Union found Czech intergovernmental fiscal performance acceptable for membership. This is in the context, however, of a continental tradition unconcerned about a rather high degree of centralisation. Although the EU insisted on a 'reform of public administration' before accession, those reforms failed to address the problem of local fiscal autonomy directly.

The EU has shown little concern about fiscal decentralisation of accession countries. In its monitoring of Czech progress, the EU was concerned only about the Supreme Audit Office created by the Czechs in 1993 and its system of internal financial controls (Agenda, 2000). In the 2000 Regular Report by the Commission on the Czech Republic's Progress towards Accession (EC, 2000), the Czech Republic was enjoined to strengthen its financial control functions at all levels and make other institutional preparations to interact financially with the EU. But the more serious, long-term problem of failure to provide for local autonomy was not mentioned as a subject of concern. The nature of financial transfers from the centre to local governments with strings and controls attached, and disinterest in the property tax as a means of independent financial leverage, are testimony to the failure to take the problem of local autonomy seriously.

Public Administration Reform as a Substitute for Fiscal Decentralisation

As observed above, the EU has shown little interest in promoting fiscal decentralisation, but it did pursue a related initiative, an organisational 'reform of public administration'. This section considers whether these reforms represent a legitimate alternative to fiscal decentralisation.

The reorganisation of the sub-national territories was the main thrust of organisational reform. The former districts (*okresy*) were eliminated and new regional governments (*kraje*) were established in the Czech Republic, which had previously been a two-tier system of government. The *kraje* were initially funded by transfers from the state budget and inherited some of the state's former responsibilities, for example secondary education, regional planning and inter-city transport (see Martinez-Vazquez and McNab, 1997).

By 2000, the Czech Republic was moving from two-level to four-level government. Regional government was established between the municipal and central levels. The new, fourth tier became the European Union in Brussels. The Czech Republic's joining the EU is not the subject of this chapter, but we wish to consider some of the implications of the organisational reforms. The goal was to modernise central administration and provide 'territorial public administration'.

It was intended that the new regional governments 'bring state administration to the people' (*přiblížit státní správu občanům*) (Bártíková, 2003), that is, to achieve greater involvement of citizens in sub-national governance. This is an implicit admission that there had previously been too much centralisation in Czech governance. Having policy decisions about health-care centres, regional schools, land-use policies, and so on, moved closer to the citizens affected implies a healthy devolution of central powers. The question is whether an institutional reorganisation of the Czech Republic will obviate the need for fiscal decentralisation. Can the process of decentralising policy institutions be a substitute for granting Czech municipalities fiscal autonomy?

Before the reforms, the state implemented its policies not only indirectly through cooperation with self-governing municipalities, but directly as well. It implemented its policies through district offices regionally, and at the bottom level through its own offices and through the agency of municipalities authorized and compensated to perform 'state administration' (*přenesený působnost*). On 1 January, 2003, 73 Czech district offices (*Okresy*) were closed and their tasks were transferred to 205 newly designated 'cities with expanded functions' (*obcí s rozšířenou působností*) (Postránecký, 2003).

A large variety of activities was transferred to the cities with expanded functions. Specific tasks included such things as the issuing of permits, IDs and driver's licences, decisions concerning historical buildings, conscription duties, alimony payments, state social and unemployment support, and so on (see Bártíková, 2003). While the 205 towns carry out these new tasks of 'state administration' as agents for the central government, they retain their own tasks of 'public administration' or of self-government (*samosprava*). For state administration they receive compensation in part through user fees paid by citizen recipients of public services, but mostly from the central government, which also retains the responsibility for the quality of the services provided.

There is no question that the establishment of regional self-government with freely elected representatives moves government closer to the people. Nevertheless, if sub-national governments lack the capacity to respond to local choices in service provision, their freedom of action is severely constrained. A high-profile Czech government document suggests that the problem of local fiscal autonomy will not disappear. Bureš et al. (2002, p. 21) tell us on behalf of the Ministry of the Interior (*Ministerstvo Vnitra*) that municipal 'own revenues' so critical to fiscal decentralization are available only through local users' fees. This paltry source of revenue certainly cannot 'fit the actual needs' of local governments. The municipalities and regions have access to independent revenues only through the privatisation of their own properties and the centrally controlled and collected, nominal property tax. The fiscal problem is mentioned by these authors (Bureš et al., 2002) because they recognise that organisational reform can neither ignore nor compensate for the fiscal dimension of local governance. But the Czech Ministry of the Interior has no answer to the implicit but weighty questions regarding local finance. When mentioning that local governments are 'temporarily financed mostly by subsidies (grants)', it is asserted that the aim is to strengthen their own tax revenues. Presently, the rate of regional own revenues to subsidies is circa 1:6 (Bureš et al., 2002). But no more is said about how this is to be ameliorated. One notes that this statement is made by the Interior Ministry, not Finance. From time to time there have been discussions as to whether the parliament should make changes in the property tax suggested by the Finance Ministry, but proposals for strengthening the tax have consistently failed.

CONCLUSIONS

The Prague government has discussed a number of issues which have significant implications for the property tax, which remains the best possibility for financial autonomy for Czech municipalities. The Finance Ministry has suggested that the cities and towns could reclassify the user fees they charge for local public services as taxes, and expand their current range, assuring some increase in revenues. The central government has also tried to convince the municipalities that excessive debt levels are irresponsible and can be hazardous. In a small number of municipalities, debt has grown quite rapidly. Czech local finance is largely a story of the effort of the central government to generate sufficient resources for the municipalities. The municipalities have been given increasing service provision responsibilities and increasing resources (although not necessarily sufficient) with which to provide them.

At the local level, the tax initiative is both small and declining. Local revenues from users' fees generated by the provision of services and from local tax collection amounted to no more than 2.2 per cent of GDP from 1993 to 1996. Since then, it has fallen to 1.7 per cent. This compares poorly with member countries of the European Union such as Norway (12 per cent), Spain (5.9 per cent), Denmark and Sweden (17 per cent), France (4.4 per cent) and Hungary (3.8 per cent) (see Bryson, 2008).

The reformed fiscal system 'has neither provided municipalities with additional meaningful sources of revenues nor introduced the necessary reforms of the real estate tax'. Municipalities would have to be assisted in acquiring the ability to make market assessments of urban properties to make the tax a meaningful source of local revenues. Institutions blocking the incentives and prerogatives of local government to secure and expand property tax revenues would have to be modified. Reforming the property tax would improve the level of both the autonomy and accountability of sub-national governments (Oliveira and Martinez-Vazquez, 2001, p. 45). The reform of revenue assignments implemented in the year 2000 still leaves important, unresolved issues in the Czech Republic's system of intergovernmental fiscal relations. They offer no effective incentive mechanism to mobilise local tax effort and one must expect the dependence of local authorities on the centre and the tax-sharing revenues and transfers it provides to continue.

NOTES

1. Bird et al. (1995) write of a 'tendency for local governments to feel they have a primary claim on tax revenues generated within their jurisdiction', pointing out that such 'Source-based taxation (also known as derivation-based) is unusual at the sub-national level in market economies because of the inequities and inefficiencies that are likely to result from allowing sub-national governments to keep large shares of the taxes levied on firms producing for a national or world market' (see p. 37).
2. Kameníčková (1996) writes: 'As a result of this, a discord occurs in local budgets between the authority and competence of the municipality on the expense side which is rather high, and the competence on the income side which is very limited' (p. 16).
3. See Holzman (1992) which indicates that the Czech Republic also grants exemptions on the VAT for consumer goods 'with detrimental consequences for tax revenue' (p. 242).
4. Much data is available in this excellent source and we are indebted to it for much of this section.

BIBLIOGRAPHY

Agenda 2000 – Commission Opinion on the Czech Republic's Application for Membership of the European Union, (1997) DOC/97/17, Brussels, 15 July.

Bártíková, G. (2002), Změny v územní veřejné správě od 1. 1. 2003, *Deník Veřejné Správy* http://denik.obce.cz/go/clanek.asp?id=5279535, Prague.

Bártíková, G. (2003), Informační servis k reformě veřejné správy, Praha: Ministerstvo vnitra http://www.mvcr.cz/aktualit/sdeleni/2003/reforma.html.

Bird, R.M., Robert D.E. and C.I. Wallich (1995), *Decentralization of the Socialist State: Intergovernmental Finance in Transition Economies*, Washington, DC: World Bank.

Bryson, P.J. and G.C. Cornia (2000), Fiscal Decentralisation in Economic Transformation: The Czech and Slovak Cases, *Europe-Asia Studies*, **52**(3), 507–22.

Bryson, P.J. and G.C. Cornia (2001), Taxes on Real Property in the Czech Republic, in *The Development of Property Taxation in Economies in Transition: Case Studies from Central and Eastern Europe*. Washington, DC: World Bank, pp. 39–50.

Bryson, P.J. and G.C. Cornia (2003), Moral Hazard in Property Tax Administration: A Comparative Analysis of the Czech and Slovak Republic, *Comparative Economics Studies*, **45**(1), 44-62.

Bryson, P. J. (2008), User Fees in Local Finance: Performance and Potential in the Czech Republic and Slovakia, *Eastern European Economics*, **46**(2), 5–27.

Bureš, P. et al. (2002), *Public Administration Reform in the Czech Republic*, Prague: mimeo

Czech Taxation in 1997 (1997), Prague: Trade Links

Dillinger, W. (1988), *Urban Property Taxation in Developing Countries*, Policy Research Working Paper Series No. 41, Washington, DC: World Bank.

EC (2000), *Regular Report From the Commission on The Czech Republic's Progress towards Accession*. http://www.europa.eu.int/comm/enlargement/report_11_00/pdf/en/cz_en.pdf, accessed January 2002.

Holzman, R. (1992), Tax Reform in Countries in Transition: Central Policy Issues, *Public Finance/Finances Publiques*, **47**(3), 233–55.

Houerou, P. and M. Rutkowski (1996), Federal Transfers in Russia: Their Impact on Regional Revenues and Incomes, *Comparative Economic Studies*, **38**(2/3), 21–44.

Kameníčková, V. (1996), Jak jsou na tom obce v České republice? Praha: Ministìrstvo financi, Czech Republic, November, p. 16.

Kameníčková, V. (1998), Možnosti a meze zmìn v rozpočtem určení daní, *Obec a Finance*, 5, 22–23.

Martinez-Vazquez, J. and Robert McNab (1997), *Tax Systems in Transition Economies*, International Studies Program, Working Paper 1–97, Georgia State University School, of Policy Studies.

Oates, W.E. (1996), Taxation in a Federal System: The Tax-Assignment Problem, *Public Economics Review*, **1**(1), 35–60.

OECD (2006), *Economic Survey of the Czech Republic, 2006, Policy Brief*, online at http://www.oecd.org/document/32/0,3343,en_33873108_33873293_36629536_1_1_1_1,00.html

Oliveira, J. and J. Martinez-Vazquez (2001), *Czech Republic: Intergovernmental Fiscal Relations in the Transition*, Washington, DC: World Bank.

Postránecký, J. (2003), Obce s rozšířenou působností (Soulad správních obvodů a standardizace veřejných služeb*), Deník Veřejné Správy,* http://denik.obce.cz/go/clanek.asp?id=5520002. Accessed 8 July, 2003.

8. Local government finance in Estonia

Kenneth A. Kriz

INTRODUCTION

In this chapter, we analyse the development of the public finance system in Estonia from transition to the present. We will see that while Estonia has delegated some semblance of local government responsibility and authority, in fact, Estonian local governments have little autonomy and are weak in relation to the central government. This situation is created by the presence of central government laws that assign most revenue sources to the central government, while delegating substantial expenditure responsibilities to local governments.

Estonia regained independence in 1991. Since then it has embarked on ambitious reforms of its economic and political system. Membership in the EU, effective May 2004, means a new phase of structural reforms will commence. An important area of structural reforms is the organisation of the public sector, including intergovernmental relations and the fiscal relationship between the central government and local governments.

Local self-governance allows for the recognition and aggregation of local preferences in the creation of a responsive governmental structure. Truly autonomous local governments are not possible without stable, robust revenue sources and healthy mechanisms for local expenditure decision-making and accountability. The study of local government finance is therefore of great importance for an overall assessment of the functioning of the local government sector.

BASIC LEGAL FRAMEWORK AND LOCAL GOVERNMENT FINANCE REGULATIONS

Independent local governments were re-established in Estonia at the end of the Communist period, but most of the legislation establishing and enabling local governments and their finances were written during the 1993–95 period. This legislation has been revisited several times, with major changes undertaken in the late 1990s and early 2000s. However, the territorial organisation has remained essentially unchanged since Estonia regained independence with the exception of a few municipalities merging. As of June 2004 there were 241 local government units in Estonia, 202 rural authorities and 39 towns. The size of the units varies widely, from approximately 70 inhabitants in the smallest to approximately 400,000 inhabitants in the largest. The majority of Estonian municipalities are small, with 70 per cent of municipalities having less than 3,000 inhabitants.

The Estonian Constitution establishes the right of local government in its Chapter XIV. Local governments are given the authority to resolve local issues in Section 154. The intent of the Constitution was codified in the Local Government Organisation Act (hereafter the LGOA – RT I 1993, 37, 558; consolidated text RT I 1999, 82, 755). A regional intermediate level of government (the *maakond* or county) is established in Chapter 6 of the Government of the Republic Act (RT I 1995, 94, 1628).

The Constitution and LGOA assign broad powers to local government. Certain local government functions are prescribed in the LGOA, including social services (including pre-primary through secondary schools, libraries, community centres, museums, sports facilities, shelters, care homes and health care institutions), housing, public infrastructure (for example, water, sewerage, and transportation) and physical planning, unless such functions are assigned by law to other persons (LGOA Chapter 1, Sections 6 (1) and (2)).

Independent representative councils (*volikogu*) are authorised to decide issues for the jurisdiction, including the provision of services beyond those specifically assigned in the LGOA. The *volikogu* and the executive of the local government are the sole elected representatives of a local jurisdiction and are the delegated decision-making authority at the local level. There are also restrictions in the LGOA on unfunded mandates from the central level – the central government cannot impose functions on municipalities without funding them from the state budget.

The relationship between the central and local governments in Estonia is one of central pre-emption. Local governments have the authority to deal with local issues, but supervisory control is exercised by the central government over not only the legality but also the purposefulness of the local government activities. In the exercise of supervisory control, the central government can peremptorily:

- Issue a precept for the elimination of deficiencies in a legal instrument or act;
- Suspend the performance of an act or the validity of a legal instrument; and
- Invalidate a legal instrument (LGOA Chapter 11, Section 661(2)).

Additionally, county governors exercise supervisory control over their local governments (LGOA Chapter 11, Sections 66 and 661). County governors are directly responsible to the central government, so this level of supervisory control further subordinates local governments to the central government. Although the LGOA grants local governments autonomy in name, in fact they are constrained to a great extent.

THE ROLE OF LOCAL GOVERNMENTS IN PROGRAMME DELIVERY

Local governments play a significant role in programme delivery in Estonia. Table 8.1 shows the share of local government spending in total government spending for the period 1993–2003. Local government spending fell in the immediate post-transition years, and then climbed gradually from 1994 to 1998, falling off in 1999 and 2000. In 2001, the central government transferred spending responsibilities for primary education to local governments. This is reflected in Table 8.1 as a large jump in local expenditure share. In 2002 local government spending started trending downward to its final level at around 25 per cent of total spending.

This share of total spending is comparable to OECD countries (Joumard and Kongsrud 2003, p. 164). However, these broad figures may hide the true situation of local governments, which may be significantly constrained in their ability to be truly autonomous. Some of the conditions which may limit local government autonomy are laws restricting the discretion of local governments, a tradition of specific funding of services by the central government, lack of revenue autonomy and lack of administrative capacity. We turn next to a more full examination of local government revenues and expenditures in Estonia.

Table 8.1 Government spending, 1993–2006

	1993	1994	1995	1996	1997	1998	1999
Local government (% of GDP)	11.4	6.9	7.7	8.0	7.8	8.2	8.6
General government (% of GDP)	36.2	37.0	39.1	39.9	37.4	38.1	40.3
Local government (% of General)	31.5	18.6	19.7	20.2	20.8	21.5	21.2

	2000	2001	2002	2003	2004	2005	2006
Local government (% of GDP)	7.3	9.0	9.4	9.1	9.0	8.3	8.2
General government (% of GDP)	35.3	33.5	34.2	35.3	34.2	33.2	33.2
Local government (% of General)	20.6	26.9	27.4	25.9	26.2	24.9	24.8

Source: Ministry of Finance.

LOCAL GOVERNMENT REVENUE SOURCES

Local governments in Estonia have few truly autonomous local government revenue sources. The primary revenue sources for local governments include shared taxes, own taxes, user fees and charges, income from the sale and use of property, and transfers from the central government. For most local governments truly autonomous revenue sources provide a very small proportion of local government income (Hoag and Kasoff 1999, p. 923 and Kungla 1999, p. 32).

As with the majority of laws governing local governments, the laws governing public finance in general were passed during the early phase of economic transition. The Rural Municipality and City Budgets Act (hereafter RMCBA – RT I 1993, 42, 615) was passed in June of 1993. The RMCBA gave authority as well as guidance to local governments in budget and finance matters. It was amended a few times until 2002, and then it was amended extensively over the next two years. The Local Taxes Act (RT1 I 1994, 68, 1169) was passed in September 1994 and remained largely intact in its original writing until 2000. It underwent extensive amendments twice in 2000 and then twice in 2002. The Local Taxes Act established the authority and procedural requirements for local governments to collect tax revenue. The Act allows local governments to levy eight types of local taxes: sales tax, boat tax, advertisement tax, road and street closure tax, motor vehicle tax, animal tax, entertainment tax, and parking charge. The sales tax rate is constrained to no more than 1 per cent of the taxable value of purchases. It is paid directly into the local government treasury.

With all other local taxes, local government councils can set rates without limit. There are exemptions in the Local Taxes Act for the advertising tax (political advertising and government notices) and the animal tax (police and defence forces along with those housing animals for no more than one month).

The structure of local revenue for the country as a whole is presented in Table 8.2. In order to standardise the figures, the revenue sources are presented first in per capita figures and then as percentages of gross domestic product (conversions to Euros were made at the fixed rate of 15.65 Estonian kroons per Euro). The basic structure of local government revenue is obvious. The personal income tax, land tax, grants from the central government and income from properties and property sales make up almost 90 per cent of local government revenue. It is apparent that while the Local Taxes Act assigns a large number of taxes to the local level, they are producing little in the way of revenue. Taxes which are truly local make up less than 1 per cent of revenue. Overall, the burden of local taxation is not great, consuming around 9 per cent of GDP, a figure similar to that of the US.

Table 8.2 Estonian local government revenue structure, 2006[1]

Revenue Source	Per Capita (Euros)	% of GDP	% of Total
Taxes			
Personal Income Tax	372.23	3.83	43.27
Land Tax	24.58	0.25	2.86
Local Taxes	6.27	0.06	0.73
State Fees	2.21	0.02	0.26
Operating Income	75.48	0.78	8.77
Property Sales	73.64	0.76	8.56
Revenue from Property	14.16	0.15	1.65
Grants	285.83	2.94	33.23
Other income	5.88	0.06	0.68
Total Revenue	860.28	8.85	100.00

Source: Ministry of Finance.

Another issue that emerges from Table 8.2 is that user charges and fee income are a very small proportion of local government budgets. Local governments collect State Fees on behalf of the central government, keeping a small portion of some fees. User charges (reported in Table 8.2 under 'Operating Income') are collected in five main areas: education, cultural and recreational activities, health services, social welfare, and utilities (including public transport). As shown in Kriz et al. (2005), user charge and fee use in Estonia is underdeveloped. Fees for services are largely assigned to the central government (even for some local public services) and user charges are not administered in order to match benefits and costs.

Table 8.3 Estonian local government revenue structure by region, 2006 (percentage of total revenues)

Revenue Source	North	Central	Northeast	West	South
Taxes					
Personal Income Tax	49.22	41.07	36.68	39.06	38.05
Land Tax	2.94	3.92	1.66	3.55	2.42
Local Taxes	1.41	0.01	0.11	0.30	0.24
State Fees	0.30	0.18	0.16	0.30	0.22
Local Fees	10.01	7.44	5.56	8.30	8.60
Property Sales	15.99	1.09	1.14	7.19	1.68
Revenue from					
Property	1.51	0.90	6.27	0.92	0.67
Grants	17.82	44.53	48.01	39.80	47.55
Other income	0.80	0.86	0.39	0.58	0.57

Note: The Government of the Republic Regulation No. 126 of 3 April 2001 defines the regions as follows: Central: Järva, Lääne-Viru and Rapla counties; Northeast: Ida-Viru county; South: Jõgeva, Põlva, Tartu, Valga, Viljandi and Võru counties; West: Hiiu, Lääne, Pärnu and Saare counties; North: Harju county.

Source: Ministry of Finance.

The revenue structure of local governments is not uniform throughout the country. Table 8.3 presents the revenue structure by region (as defined by the Estonia government). The more economically active North and West regions of the country produce more of their revenues through shared taxes and local taxes. In the economically challenged areas of the Northeast, Central and South, less than 10 per cent of revenues come from sustainable autonomous local revenue sources. The majority of revenues at the local level come from the central government in the form of transfers with the exception of the North region.

GRANT TRANSFERS

There are two main types of grant transfers to local governments in Estonia. The first is the major source of funds for most Estonian local governments, the 'Budget Equalisation Fund'. The basic framework authorising the Budget Equalisation Fund is established in the State Budget Act (RT I 1999, 55, 584; consolidated text RT I 2002, 67, 405). The Budget Equalisation Fund is a formula-driven, unconditional lump-sum grant given by the central government. The goal of the fund is to foster the provision of basic services across jurisdictions with different cost structures and abilities to pay for services. The size of the fund is determined annually through negotiations among the authorised representatives of local governments, local government associations and the central government. The parameters of the fund (size and distribution principles) are then set forth in the draft state budget. If agreement cannot be reached among the negotiators, the size of the fund and its distribution is decided by the central government, which is required to present the dissenting opinions of fund parameters to the Republic's legislative body (the *Riigikogu*) in an explanatory memorandum to the draft budget. Regardless of the nature of the decision, the size of the fund and the principles of the distribution are required to be published in the state budget.

The absolute size of the equalisation fund varies each year depending on the economic condition of the country and the revenue needs of the central government. However, the formula for determining the distribution of the fund has remained the same. There are two basic components to the formula. The first is a component capturing the difference between amounts allocated over the prior two years from the central government to a local government in shared taxes and mineral deposit user charges and the country-wide average for the same. This is multiplied by a standardisation coefficient (a constant representing the planned equalisation level – the higher the coefficient the greater the equalisation). Then the result is multiplied by 0.9 times the population of the local government unit (in essence, the standardisation coefficient is multiplied by 0.9) (Kungla 1999, p. 26, Pedastaar 2001, p. 8, Ainsoo et al. 2002, p. 291). One problem with the equalisation formula has been that the standardisation coefficient has changed each year. The amounts received under the fund can vary dramatically with the coefficient, so local governments would prefer a stable coefficient.

The second major source of transfers to local governments is through individual appropriations in the state budget. Obviously, these are conditional, specific purpose transfers. Table 8.4 shows specific transfers as a percentage of total transfers for Estonian local governments in 2003 (the most recent data available).

Table 8.4 Source of specific transfers, 2003 (percentage of total central government transfers)

Source	Operating Grants	Capital Grants (Public Investment Programme)
Ministry of Education and Research	1.46	4.05
Ministry of Defence	0.02	0.00
Ministry of the Environment	0.05	0.85
Ministry of Culture	1.18	1.95
Ministry of Economic Affairs and Communication	0.57	1.67
Ministry of Agriculture	0.33	0.01
Ministry of Finance	0.29	0.00
Ministry of Internal Affairs	1.53	0.00
Ministry of Social Affairs	0.42	0.07
County Governments	1.09	0.01
Riigikogu	0.23	0.00
Central Budget Reserves and Resources	2.45	0.40
Total	9.60	9.02

Source: Banks' annual reports.

By far the largest specific grant programme is through the Ministry of Education and Research. They provide grants to cover the costs of teachers' salaries and benefits for the primary grades as well as grants used to teach the Estonian language and to provide for youth programs (Ainsoo et al. 2002, p. 293). They also provide large capital grants through the Public Investment Programme to renovate and build new schools. The second largest specific grant programme is through the Ministry of Culture, providing operating and capital grants to support the development of arts and cultural programmes.

LOCAL GOVERNMENT EXPENDITURES

As we have seen, the LGOA allocates local governments the responsibility for delivery of many basic local public goods. We next turn to an analysis of expenditures made to deliver services mandated in the LGOA as well as those services decided locally. Local government expenditures classified according to function are shown in Table 8.5. Expenditures for primary and secondary education (as well as pre-primary education) are the predominant expenditure item for local governments, accounting for 40–45 per cent of total expenditures. The next largest functional area is the economy. This category covers expenses related to maintenance of streets and roads, public transport and provision of utilities. General government administrative expenditures consume another 10 per cent of total local government spending. The expenditure distribution of Estonian municipalities has remained relatively stable since the early 1990s. Administrative expenditures have fallen, replaced largely with expenditures on recreation, culture and social welfare. The falling administrative expenditures are likely due to increased efficiency at the local level as well as the sale of public assets to the private sector. Increased spending on amenity items such as culture and recreation is predictable given the increase in real per capita disposable incomes over the last few years. Spending in these areas is generally thought to be 'normal' in the sense of having positive income elasticity. Social welfare spending has been declining since 1998, marking the recent period of growth and stabilisation of the Estonian economy.

In terms of liquidity management, the major enabling legislation for local government is remarkably silent. For the central government, the State Budget Act is fairly detailed in prescribing the management of idle cash funds and budgetary reserves. It specifies rules for funding and use of funds, the policy for appointing an investment advisor, and the establishment of an advisory council for fund oversight. In contrast, the rules for local governments regarding use of reserves and investment of idle cash appear to be limited to two sections of the RMCBA. The only requirements of the Act are: first, that the local government must designate the amount of cash reserves at the time of budget passage and second, that the two permissible uses of cash reserves are to cover expenditures in the event of delay in receipt of revenue and to cover any revenue shortfalls during budget execution. In this case of delayed revenue receipt, local governments are required to restore the cash reserves in the same budget year 'in the amount specified by the council'. This seems to imply first that the local government council must be involved in the decision to restore the funds (which is good for budgetary accountability) and second, that the council could vote to restore less than or more than the amount of reserves used (which is questionable from the standpoint of accountability). In the case of revenue shortfall the council must approve the use of the reserves.

Table 8.5 Local government expenditures by sector, 1993–2006 (percentage of total expenditures)

Function	1993	1994	1995	1996	1997	1998	1999	2000	2001	2002	2003	2003	2004	2005	2006
Administration	11.1	15.5	15.1	12.3	11.8	11.3	10.8	11.2	9.1	8.6	9.0	9.3	9.3	8.8	8.7
Public order and security	3.0	0.7	0.6	0.6	0.5	0.4	0.3	0.3	1.0	0.9	0.9	0.9	0.9	0.3	0.4
Education and science	33.7	45.1	45.0	42.0	40.5	40.0	39.3	38.8	45.0	44.1	44.1	43.9	45.5	43.5	41.7
Recreation, culture, and religion	6.3	7.7	8.1	8.9	9.0	10.5	10.7	11.4	10.3	10.3	13.1	13.0	13.2	14.2	14.2
Public health	1.7	0.9	1.1	1.8	1.6	1.7	1.5	1.5	1.4	1.3	0.6	0.6	0.7	0.5	0.8
Social welfare	4.0	2.8	3.5	4.4	10.8	11.5	10.7	10.6	9.2	8.6	8.9	8.9	7.9	8.4	7.8
Economy	30.9	25.7	24.3	27.5	23.7	22.2	24.5	23.8	22.1	24.1	23.4	23.4	22.5	24.2	26.4
Other	0.0	0.0	0.0	0.5	0.2	0.3	0.1	0.1	0.2	0.5	0.0	0.0	0.0	0.0	0.0
Transfers	9.4	1.6	2.1	2.0	2.1	2.1	2.2	2.2	1.7	1.7	n/a	n/a	n/a	n/a	n/a
Total expenditures	100	100	100	100	100	100	100	100	100	100	100	100	100	100	100

Notes: n/a indicates missing value. Data for 2003 are preliminary as the Ministry of Finance introduced a new account methodology.

Sources: 1993–2002: Kriz et al.(2005). Original data sources used were: 1996–2002: calculations based on Ministry of Finance (1996–2003). GDP data for all years from Statistical Office of Estonia, Statistical Database. 2003–2006: Statistical Office of Estonia, Regional Development Database.

Table 8.6 shows data on local government spending by economic division for the period 1993–2003 (2003 was the last year of consistent data available). The striking point that arises from the data is the remarkable stability of the division between current and capital expenditure. Since 1997, capital expenditure has accounted for roughly 20 per cent of local government spending. There was a slight decrease in the ratio of capital to current spending in 2003, but data comparability issues limit a strong statement regarding the trend (the Ministry of Finance reclassified public accounts for). This stability is somewhat surprising. The post-transition condition of municipal capital stock was not good, and one might expect that municipalities would have increased capital investment. Offsetting factors such as poor budgetary conditions or inability to generate autonomous revenue may have led to the relative stability of capital spending over the period.

Table 8.6 Local government expenditures by economic definition, 1993–2003 (percentage of total expenditure unless noted)

	1993	1994	1995	1996	1997	1998	1999	2000	2001	2002	2003
Current expenditure	84.2	84.7	77.9	72.6	79.2	77.5	76.9	80.8	80.5	79.8	82.8
Goods and services	59.5	78.8	75.1	64.3	61.4	n/a	60.8	64.0	65.3	69.6	71.1
Wages and salaries	19.1	34.4	24.6	32.3	31.9	n/a	31.4	33.0	39.1	38.4	40.6
Other goods and services	40.4	44.4	50.5	32.0	29.5	n/a	29.4	31.0	26.3	31.2	30.5
Subsidies and transfers	24.7	5.8	1.9	7.4	16.2	n/a	14.0	14.3	13.8	8.9	11.8
Other	0.0	0.2	0.9	0.9	1.6	n/a	2.1	2.5	1.4	1.3	n/a
Capital expenditures	15.8	15.3	22.1	27.4	20.8	22.5	23.1	19.2	19.5	20.2	17.2
Total expenditures	100.0	100.0	100.0	100.0	100.0	100.0	100.0	100.0	100.0	100.0	100.0
Total expenditures, % of GDP	11.4	6.9	8.4	8.5	8.1	8.2	8.5	7.5	9.3	9.6	9.3

Notes: n/a indicates missing value. In 1998 the Statistical Office of Estonia did not collect data on expenditures. Therefore, IMF data was used. The data for expenditures collected by the IMF did not disaggregate spending by economic definition.

Sources: 1996–97: Statistical Office of Estonia (1996–97), 1999–2003: Statistical Office of Estonia, Statistical Database.

Because of the way that Estonian local governments use financing transactions, the assessment of the deficit or surplus position of governments is difficult. But one can get a broad feel for the operating position of the governments by looking at the net financing transactions necessary to 'zero out' the operating statements. Data comparing local governments and the central government for the period 1999–2006 is shown in Table 8.7. It appears from this that there is a divergence of fortunes of the central government and local governments during this period. The central government has recovered from a sharp deficit in the late 1990s to record four straight years of large surpluses. In contrast, local governments have seen stubborn persistent deficits in the range of 5 to 12 per cent of total revenues until last year, when they began to run surpluses as a whole.

Table 8.7 Financial position of Estonian governments, 1999–2006 (figures are surplus (deficit) as percentage of revenue)

Year	Central Government	Local Governments
1999	-13.32	-8.03
2000	-2.42	-5.36
2001	3.23	-10.41
2002	1.02	-11.88
2003	7.12	-7.12
2004	8.80	-4.52
2005	7.70	-0.58
2006	11.59	5.58

Note: 2006 data is preliminary.
Source: Ministry of Finance.

What are potential explanations for this divergence? Revenue from own sources could have been growing in both the central and local governments as GDP grew (GDP grew at an average annual rate of 6.6 per cent during this period) while local government expenditures grew faster than central government expenditures. Or local government revenues could have grown slower than central government revenues. The first explanation would suggest a problem with expenditure control at the local level while the second suggests constrained local governments unable to raise sufficient revenues to service growing expenditure needs. Tables 8.8 and 8.9 shed some light on this issue. Table 8.8 shows revenues before transfers for the central government and local governments during the 2000–2006 period as a percentage of GDP.[2] The striking thing about the revenue series is that it is flat for both the central and the local governments. There is some cyclical movement, but essentially central government revenues have consumed around 25 per cent of GDP and local government revenues about 5 per cent of GDP throughout the first seven years of the decade.

Table 8.8 Revenues of Estonian governments, 2000–2006 (figures are revenues as percentage of GDP)

Year	Central Government	Local Governments
2000	25.24	5.07
2001	24.45	4.94
2002	25.20	5.04
2003	25.71	4.92
2004	24.97	5.04
2005	24.44	4.84
2006	24.93	4.95

Note: 2006 data is preliminary.

Table 8.9 shows data for the same period on expenditures. Both series show decreasing expenditures over the period. There is a slight rise in expenditures in local governments in 2001, but this is due to the shifting of general education funding to local governments. So the overspending hypothesis is unlikely to explain the situation of persistent deficits.

Table 8.9 Expenditures of Estonian governments, 2000–2006 (figures are expenditures as percentage of GDP)

Year	Central Government	Local Governments
2000	27.86	8.55
2001	26.19	10.11
2002	27.13	9.69
2003	26.84	9.14
2004	25.58	8.97
2005	25.11	8.26
2006	25.44	8.23

Note: 2006 data is preliminary.

The data suggests a rather persistent level of imbalance in local government finance. It appears that the central government has shifted much expenditure responsibility to local governments without commensurate revenue raising capacity. This highlights an important point about incomplete fiscal decentralisation. Because the central government controls such a large portion of the revenue base either directly through transfers or indirectly through negotiating the sharing formula for the principal local government tax revenues, the central government can effectively force local governments into a deficit or surplus position and to a certain extent mask its own financial position through incomplete subsidisation of mandated services.

ACCOUNTING RULES, REGULATIONS AND LOCAL GOVERNMENT BUDGETING PROCESS

Estonia has, in recent years, made an effort to make its financial accounting rules conform to international accounting and financial reporting standards. This effort includes the public sector as well as the private sector. A longstanding goal of Estonian governments has been to enhance and develop foreign direct investment. A recognition was made early in the transition that if foreign investors were to feel comfortable investing in Estonian enterprises, they needed to have accurate and current information on the financial position of firms and of the government.

Although there were early attempts at standardisation of accounting rules, the passage of the Accounting Act (RT I 2002, 102, 600) was a watershed moment in Estonian accounting practice. In the Act, the explicit goal of conformance with international standards was formalised. In terms of its effects on governmental entities, the Act delegates the establishment of specific accounting rules for the central and local governments to the Ministry of Finance. However the Act further requires that the rules 'are based on and are in compliance with the accounting principles generally accepted in Estonia and the international public sector accounting standards [IPSAS – the standards approved by the Public Sector Committee of the International Federation of Accountants (IFAC)] and in accordance with which the state accounting entities are required to organise their accounting and financial reporting'. IPSAS requires a fundamentally business-like reporting model. Double entry, accrual basis accounting is to be used if possible. The entity, objective, conservative and other fundamental reporting goals are principally the same as applied by for-profit businesses.

Two major problems have been noted about the Estonian local government accounting system. The first problem is that until recently, the Ministry of Finance changed the accounting rules and account classification scheme frequently (Ainsoo et al. 2002, p. 313). This produced a situation where local government finance officials did not have the ability to view easily comparable financial statements and where accounting professionals required a lot of time and effort keeping current with changes. The other major problem with the practice of accounting in Estonia is a distinct lack of professional capacity, especially in less populated and more remote areas. Most of the major Western accounting firms have offices in Tallinn, but there is still a perceived problem that smaller municipalities have difficulty getting professional accounting services at an affordable rate. Therefore, the quality of financial reporting is spotty in non-urban areas.

The local government budget process in Estonia is governed by the RMCBA. This Act specifies several budget process and informational requirements. The budget year is defined in the Act to begin on 1 January and end on 31 December. A draft budget must be prepared and presented to the local government council not later than 1 December. It must include revenue and expenditure information for the preceding budgetary year (actual data), the current budgetary year (budget data), and the proposed revenue and expenditure for the coming budgetary year. Additionally data must be presented on capital spending commitments and obligations for coming budgetary years arising from borrowing. Local government councils are free to require that additional information be submitted with the draft budget, though in practice most do not. Before a draft budget is presented to the council, a local government must submit an application for any state aid amounts included in the budget to the central government's Minister of Finance. In terms of information requirements, draft budgets, passed budgets, amendments to budgets, supplementary budgets and annual reports must be published pursuant to a procedure provided for in the statutes of the rural municipality or city. Additionally, passed budgets must be presented to state authorities. Finally, the Act prescribes rules for continuances in the event that a budget cannot be passed and precludes local councils from acting on any legislation if a new budget is not passed within three months of the start of the budgetary year.

The Act also contains many provisions with respect to budget execution. If the need arises to reallocate an expenditure specified in the budget, a local government must draft a petition to the council. The budget must be amended using the same procedure as the original budget. A council may, during the budgetary year, pass a supplementary budget for additional expenditures. The government must submit to the council a supplementary budget with justification of the need for additional expenditure and its inevitability in the current budgetary year along with information on the use of appropriations for which supplementary funding is applied. Also information must be submitted on additional revenue and savings with which the additional expenditure will be covered. If the government receives additional allocations of specific purpose money from the central government budget during a budgetary year, it may add the revenue and the corresponding expenditures into the budget but must promptly notify the council of its actions. Supplementary budgets must be passed using the same procedure as the original budget. The emphasis in the Act with respect to budget execution is obviously to restrict bureaucratic discretion and emphasise council control.

Those are the required steps in the passage and amendment of budgets. In practice, the budget process varies widely. Ainsoo et al. present a 'typical' budget cycle for local governments. The preparation phase begins eight to nine months prior to passage of the budget, with the economic department preparing reports of expenditures and budget execution and forecasts of own-source revenues. Based on these items, a Budget and Economic Committee sets preliminary expenditure ceilings. The town council then acts on a draft decree for expenditure ceilings. During the next three months, preparation of and deliberation on the draft budget takes place. A final draft budget is prepared and deliberated on in December (Ainsoo et al. 2002, pp. 306–7).

SUPERVISION AND CONTROL: THE STATE AUDIT

Auditing in Estonian governments is relatively underdeveloped. Under the LGOA, the primary responsibility for auditing lies with an audit committee. The LGOA requires that the audit committee monitors:

- conformity of the activities of the government with regulations and resolutions of the council;
- accuracy of accounting of agencies and the purposeful use of funds;
- timely collection and registration of revenue and conformity of expenditure with the budget;
- performance of contracts entered into by the local government; and
- lawfulness and purposefulness of the activities of the local government and its agencies.

Each year the audit committee must present an audit report regarding these matters to the local council, which then has ten days to take a formal position on the report.

A major problem in many local governments is the lack of competence of its members. There is often a lack of systematic and regular control over local government organisations, agencies and enterprises. Membership on the committee is inherently political, with both the coalition and opposition parties represented on the committee. There is a tradition of electing the head of the audit committee from the opposition (Ainsoo et al. 2002, p. 316).

The audit committee is responsible for the internal control function. Another major impediment to effective internal control is the lack of a specific internal audit function. Only in the larger municipalities is there a specific internal auditor position. In terms of external audit, the LGOA requires an annual external audit and opinion of an auditor appointed by the local government council concerning the report on the implementation of the rural municipality or city budget. This opinion becomes part of the annual report on budget implementation that is approved by the local council.

In addition to the independent external audit, the State Audit Office is empowered to audit the activities of a local government with respect to its handling of funds transferred from the state budget. In practice, though, this is an infrequently used and incomplete control. The State Audit Office is relatively sparsely staffed and in 2003 carried out only two audits of implementation of state budget funds by local units (these were the Tallinn City Court and Harju County, which encompasses Tallinn, so in effect the State Audit sphere did not affect most of the country). There are plans to broaden the role of the State Audit Office, with a plan to perform one comprehensive audit of a local government in 2004 along with the state funds audits (Riigikontroll 2004).

FURTHER DEVELOPMENTS: LOCAL GOVERNMENT AND FINANCIAL MARKETS

Capital market access for Estonian local governments is regulated by the RMCBA. The Act allows local governments to take loans and leases, issue debt securities and assume other debt obligations subject to several conditions regarding the size, purpose and collateralisation of debt. The Act also lays out several procedural requirements for the issuance of debt.

With regard to size conditions, the total amount of debt outstanding along with any proposed debt cannot exceed 60 per cent of proposed budget revenue for that budgetary year, adjusted to exclude specific purpose allocations from the state budget. Further, the total amount of debt payments (for both principal and interest) may not exceed 20 per cent of the proposed adjusted budget revenue for the budgetary year during which the debt is taken. The purpose of the restriction is that debt can only be issued to carry out investments prescribed in the rural municipality or city development plan. This provides effectively for a debate on all projects to be funded through debt issuance since the development plan is debated annually. In terms of collateralisation, local governments are forbidden from pledging assets as security for loans. In terms of accountability, this is probably good, since governments cannot place the jurisdiction in a situation where assets may be seized to compensate debt holders. But this restriction may have the effect of raising the borrowing cost for local governments since uncollateralised debt usually carries higher interest rates due to having no back-up source of repayment. Additionally, the Act lays out that the following entities must be notified when a government borrows:

- County governor;
- Ministry of Finance; and
- the Financial Supervision Authority (which governs security issuance in Estonia).

The central government has the right to suspend making of payments from the budget equalisation fund to a local government if the loan or debt is not registered properly.

While in theory Estonian local governments have virtually unlimited access to capital markets, in practice most of the debt of local governments is taken in the form of loans. There are at least three broad problems with this situation. As pointed out by several authors, borrowing in public markets opens the borrower to market-based fiscal discipline (compare Peterson undated, p. 9 and Leigland 1997, p. 60). With greater public borrowing, municipalities would be open to greater levels of scrutiny and disclosure. A related issue is the problem of 'relationship' lending. Banks seek a relationship with a borrower. While this may be good in the short term, in the long run it can lead to problems of information monopolies, where a bank gathers so much information on the financial condition of the borrower that it can charge higher interest rates than would be obtained in a competitive situation (Rajan 1992, p. 1392). Another problem with bank loans is that they tend to have relatively short maturities. This is a problem for two reasons. First, in an economic sense the benefit of borrowing for capital investment is that it allows for temporal matching of costs and benefits. The benefit flow from capital investment is typically realised over long periods of time. If debt service payments are required quickly, the situation from an economic sense is hardly better than 'pay as you go' financing, and we would expect to see underinvestment problems. Second, in a financial sense short amortisation of existing debt may 'crowd-out' future investment unless significant tax increases are forthcoming. This is usually politically unpalatable. In this case, existing debt is usually refinanced and new investment is not possible.

Another issue in the general area of borrowing is the debt burden of local governments. The RMCBA requires debt to be no more than 60 per cent of revenues after adjusting out specific central government transfers. As shown in Table 8.10, around 2.5 per cent of local governments had debt burdens above the legal limit. Another 11 per cent of local governments had debt between 40 and 60 per cent of adjusted revenues. Debt burdens were greatest in the North and South portions of the country. The North includes the rapidly growing Tallinn area, so higher debt burdens may indicate greater demand for public investment. The South includes the second largest city, Tartu, which is also growing strongly, but it also contains some of the poorest areas.

Table 8.10 Measures of debt burden, 2006 (figures are percentages of municipalities exceeding debt service burden levels unless specified)

Debt Burden	Country	Central	North	Northeast	South	West
>10% of Adjusted Revenues	70.12	63.64	84.00	56.52	73.12	69.64
>20% of Adjusted Revenues	48.13	43.18	56.00	47.83	52.69	41.07
>30% of Adjusted Revenues	31.54	20.45	36.00	21.74	41.94	25.00
>40% of Adjusted Revenues	13.69	2.27	16.00	8.70	18.28	16.07
>50% of Adjusted Revenues	6.64	2.27	8.00	8.70	9.68	3.57
>60% of Adjusted Revenues	2.49	0.00	4.00	4.35	3.23	1.79
Maximum Burden	107.30	56.40	107.30	94.40	82.60	62.10
Average Burden	21.94	17.30	27.53	19.94	24.25	20.08

Source: Ministry of Finance.

It is important to note that debt service burdens have been improving over time. Table 8.11 shows the distribution of changes in debt burdens from 2000 to 2006. In almost all of the regions, the majority of changes were toward lower levels of debt. There was a deterioration noted in some municipalities, especially those in the North and South. Again, these regions contain fast-growing centres of population, so there may be more demand for public capital.

Table 8.11 Debt burden changes, 2000 –2006 (figures are percentages of municipalities with changes in debt burden within the range shown)

Change in debt burden	Country	Central	North	Northeast	South	West
Decrease more than 20%	24.07	27.27	8.00	13.04	22.58	35.71
Decrease 20% to 10%	15.77	18.18	28.00	17.39	12.90	12.50
Decrease less then 10%	12.03	9.09	16.00	13.04	13.98	8.93
Increase less than 10%	24.90	29.55	28.00	43.48	17.20	25.00
Increase 10% to 20%	11.20	9.09	4.00	8.70	13.98	12.50
Increase more than 20%	12.03	6.82	16.00	4.35	19.35	5.36

Source: Ministry of Finance.

CONCLUSION

In this chapter we have presented and analysed the system of local government finance in Estonia. The findings can be separated into three broad categories: findings on autonomy, findings on institutional structure and findings on the capacity of Estonian local governments to properly carry out the financing of public services.

In terms of autonomy, Estonian local governments are severely constrained in their ability to raise revenue independently. Most of the tax sources specifically assigned to local governments are not robust in terms of their ability to generate revenue. Shared taxes account for the vast majority of revenues. Local governments must negotiate with the central government for the shares as well as for the standardisation coefficient in the Budget Equalisation Fund. But one can ask whether this is a case of negotiation between equals as local governments are also not autonomous in legal terms. One recommendation would be to give local governments more autonomy over their revenue sources by granting them a specific tax base which is more robust. We understand that there are potential moral hazard issues with granting of more autonomy, but it is unclear both how pronounced these are as well as how having the central government involved so fundamentally in local resource allocation decisions helps the situation. As an alternative to this, local governments could be granted more autonomy in developing new sources of revenue. The pattern of autonomy also seems curious from a risk management perspective. In the area of borrowing, the area with potentially the direst consequences in terms of sustainability, local governments have relative freedom in determining terms, relationships and structure of transactions. This is one area where arguably there should be a stronger central government involvement. One suggestion would be to require competitive bidding on loans and offer incentives to governments that use public debt issuance. Another alternative might be the use of bond banks or some other scheme by which the central government intermediates between the market and borrowers.

We have also seen that Estonia has most of the institutional structures in place to carry out effective local government finance. The laws seem to be well developed in most areas. Curiously, though, the laws are extremely specific in some areas while rather vague in some areas. This is especially true in the area of auditing. Little mention is made regarding the qualification of auditors. Also, requirements for financial reporting need more than a passing mention in the Accounting Act. Control structures need improvement in most areas. There is little evidence of strong systems of local government accounting or auditing in most local governments. The development of professional accounting and auditing practices is vital to long-run financial stability.

This last point is important in the development of local government financial-administrative capacity. Training programmes are necessary for all professionals in local government, but also for elected officials. Since the audit committees are so intimately tied up in the accountability cycle, those elected to the committees need formal training in accounting and auditing practice as well as contracting, since they are ultimately responsible for contracting with external auditors. Elected officials responsible for budget formulation also require training on the economic and financial implications of budget decisions.

As Estonia enters the next phase of transition, these are the three areas that demand the most attention. The nation has made good choices in the early path to a fully functioning Western-style democracy. Now another set of choices will help shape how well Estonian local governments (and the nation as a whole) are able to face the next few years.

NOTES

1. Unless otherwise noted, the source of all data is the Estonian Ministry of Finance databases.
2. One may be tempted to call this own-source revenue. However, the bulk of non-transfer local government revenues come from shared taxes, over which the local government has only a modicum of control.

BIBLIOGRAPHY

Ainsoo, D., A. Jaansoo, T. Milt, E. Pedastsaar, G. Sootla, A. Surva, P. Tammert and T. Tüür (2002), Local government budgeting: Estonia, in: M. Hogye ed., *Local Government Budgeting*. Budapest: Local Government and Public Service Reform Initiative, Open Society Institute, 273–327.

Hoag, J. and M. Kasoff (1999), Estonia in transition, *Journal of Economic Issues*, **33**(4), 919–31.

Joumard, I. and P.M. Kongsrud (2003), Fiscal relations across government levels, *OECD Economic Studies*, **36**(1), 155-229.

Kriz, K.A., A. Paulus and K. Staehr (2005), Local government fees and user charges in Estonia, in: Ž. Šević, ed. *Working Group on Public Sector Finance and Accounting (Group V), the 12th NISPAcee Annual Conference, 13–15 May 2004 Vilnius*.

Kungla, T. (1999), *Fiscal decentralisation in Estonia*, Discussion Papers, No. 13, Budapest: Local Government and Public Service Reform Initiative, Open Society Institute.

Leigland, J. (1997), Accelerating municipal bond market development in emerging economies: An assessment of strategies and progress. *Public Budgeting & Finance*, **17**(2), 57–79.

Pedastaar, E. (2001), *Local government functions and their financing and local government borrowing in Estonia*, in: 9th NISPAcee Annual Conference, 10–12 May 2001 Riga. Available from: http://www.nispa.sk/news/conf2001.html [Accessed 1 April 2004].

Peterson, G.E. (Undated), *Banks or Bonds? Building a municipal credit market* [online]. Paris: Organisation for Economic Co-operation and Development. Available from: http://www.oecd.org/LongAbstract/0,2546,en_2649_37413_21559375_119808_1_13_37413,00.html [Accessed 24 November 2004].

Rajan, R. (1992), Insiders and outsiders: The choice between informed and arm's-length debt, *Journal of Finance*, **47**(4), 1367–1400.

Riigikontroll – The State Audit Office of Estonia (2004), *Annual Report 2003*, Tallinn: Riigikontroll.

9. Decentralisation under fiscal pressure: local government finances in Hungary

Gábor Péteri

INTRODUCTION

Public sector reforms comprise various forms of transformation: decentralisation is only one, but is a critical component in the wide range of political, administrative, financial and service management actions. Consequently, analysis of local governments and municipal finances would require constant reference to other elements of the public sector. Establishment of new municipal structures is strongly connected to changes in the political mechanism, devolution of power, redefinition of the state's role and modernisation of governance methods. So this chapter on the evolution of local government finances during the past two decades will provide only a fragmented description of recent fiscal decentralisation trends.

Decentralisation reform in Hungary might be regarded as a success, in terms of creating new institutions and mechanisms in a relatively short period. A particularity of the Hungarian decentralisation reform process was that it had a quick start followed by a relatively long process of adjustment and learning (Péteri, 2002). However, the seemingly fast launch of formulating the reform concepts was based on the policy design efforts of the late 1980s. This was the period when the constitutional principles of democratisation and decentralisation were developed. Way before the political conditions for decentralisation reforms were ripe, the basic concepts on the critical elements of devolution had already been designed. The territorial structure of local governments evolved during the 1980s; deregulation and transformation of the national administration were prepared for functional changes; new principles of civil service were under preparation and experimental changes began in the public service management. All the major political forces behind the transition agreed that decentralisation was one of the primary objectives of the transformation, formally started with the multi-party parliamentary elections in June 1990.

This consensus on decentralisation supported devolution and re-assignment of fiscal revenues to the local level and designing a modern system of intergovernmental fiscal relations. Therefore, in the early 1990s, Hungary had responded to the economic crises of transition countries with a firm decentralisation and privatisation policy. This was supported by effective political co-ordination and the government's reform management capacity, which was based on domestic and international professional expertise. Support from the general public was also critical for continuing the radical reforms.

The past one-and-a-half decades was not a linear development process of public sector reforms. In 1995–96 there was a turning point in economic policy. After this period, the harsh fiscal measures at the national level forced local governments to utilise all their available assets, own source revenues and options for increasing service efficiency. This painful adjustment process made it possible for local public services and municipal administration to be more or less compatible with other developed countries' systems by the time Hungary formally joined the European Union in May 2004.

LEGISLATION AND GOVERNANCE

Legislation on Local Governments

There is a two-level government structure in Hungary, with two basic forms of elected local governments: municipal and county local governments (plus the capital city of Budapest under a special regulation). Local governments are autonomous in managing local public affairs and they are free to define their organisational, management and financial structures. Only Parliament may define the statutory powers and responsibilities of local self-governments. Local decisions may be overruled by the Constitutional Court and the courts, but only if such decisions involve an infringement of the law. Various types of local governments (villages, cities, counties, capital city districts, and so on) are equal in their powers and an elected local government is not allowed to overrule the decisions of other localities.

Parallel to the establishment of a modern, decentralised system of local government, the legislative process on demolishing the powers of the centralised state was launched. Local governments independently manage mandatory and optional local functions, but at the same time they are responsible for those public administration functions delegated to them. Obviously, the local management of public services and administrative functions is implemented in a complex, regulatory and controlled environment. However, these rules and regulations are always set by laws and central government units have no discretionary powers over municipal decisions.

These principles, together with detailed regulations were set by the Act with constitutional power on local self-governments in 1990. However, the establishment of the complex system of public services in a decentralised environment took more than half a decade to legislate and to enforce (Kopányi et al., 2004; Péteri, 2004a). The basic issue was to establish the new structures and procedures of legal control over local governments. As one of the primary goals of decentralisation was to abolish the transmission functions of the Soviet-type county councils, the legal supervision was organised first at the regional level. Later, it was adjusted to the county administrative borders and transferred from the Presidential administration to the government, the Ministry of Interior.

The local government framework of public sector reform had been legislated earlier than the actual rules of public service delivery were redesigned. The new rules and supervisory institutions have been developed with some delay. This allowed the sectoral line ministries to adjust the professional requirements of effective and equitable service delivery to the highly autonomous local government system. This adjustment process was not smooth at all and conflicts occurred mainly in two areas.

First, the sectoral legislation on human and urban services had set high professional standards and performance criteria for local governments, working under diverse conditions. As national government units had very limited legal and administrative influence on localities, new forms of decentralised, internal mechanisms of quality control and self-assessment had to be established. It was the most successfully developed in the area of public education by creating independent professional support services. In the sphere of urban utility services, these mechanisms were supplemented by external forms of environmental control and supervision.

Second, financial requirements and funding schemes have also caused several conflicts. The system of intergovernmental finances was primarily based on the principles of general grants, allocated by objective criteria. However, both line ministries and municipalities questioned this model of fiscal transfers. The ministries wanted greater influence on spending at local level and the local governments were against the practice of 'unfounded mandates' that is re-assignment of new public functions to the local level, without providing the necessary means.

In the field of financial management, the regulatory, audit and information systems followed the new, decentralised practices of intergovernmental finances with some delay. The State Audit Office, established in 1989, had to be transferred into an efficient organisation, capable of dealing with the highly fragmented local governments. The intergovernmental transfers, designed for an amalgamated municipal system, required a new government information network and refined equalisation techniques, which were completed by the late 1990s. A new unified accounting system was introduced in 1991 and rules of municipal property registration were established, focusing on physical indicators of assets (1992). Budgeting rules and procedures had to be adjusted to the requirements of democratic institutions and participatory mechanisms. The fiscal problems in 1995–96 led to redesigning the operational rules of budgetary institutions (1996), the extensive use of certified local audit (since 1994) and adaptation of bankruptcy regulations for local governments (1996).

This legal and institutional framework was established over a relatively long period. The uniqueness of the Hungarian decentralisation process was that the constitutional rules of decentralisation and the fiscal regulations had been set up before the actual transformation of local public services was begun. This has created tension between central and municipal actors, and has also led to an evolutionary process of developing modern public services.

Fragmentation of Local Government Structure

Hungary has a fragmented settlement (urban) structure: the average population size of villages is 1,258; there are 24 large cities with an average population of 92,000 and Budapest, the capital city, 1.8 million (17 per cent of the country's total population). Due to geographical and economic factors there are two main types of regions: the mostly agrarian Great Hungarian Plain which is more scarcely populated, but has larger average size villages; while the Trans-Danubian and the Northern regions have smaller, but more numerous villages. In general, the western part of the country is richer than the east. Two regional development regions (NUTS II) of the country are among the ten poorest in the European Union.

The extensive political decentralisation in 1990 followed this urban structure by allowing autonomous local government status to each and every settlement. This was a political response on the forced amalgamation under the Soviet-type local government system. As a consequence, there are 3,177 democratically elected local governments in Hungary, with an average size of 3,210 inhabitants. Most of these local governments are villages and 54 per cent of them have a smaller than 1,000 population (Table 9.1).

Table 9.1 Number of local governments

	1991	1993	1996	2000	2002
Village municipalities by population size					
up to 199	295	301	312	322	315
200–499	682	718	697	711	706
500– 999	703	704	703	688	687
1,000– 4,999	1,119	1,107	1,125	1,115	1,110
5,000+	106	94	89	77	65
Urban local governments					
up to 9,999	45	60	76	95	117
10,000+	103	103	101	104	112
Cities with county right	20	20	22	22	22
Capital city and districts	23	23	24	24	24
County local governments	19	19	19	19	19
Total	3,115	3,149	3,168	3,177	3,177

Source: National Office of Statistics.

Legislation on local government co-operation tried to cope with this highly fragmented system of local governments. The Act on Local Governments, 1990, gave the possibility of voluntary co-operation for municipalities and set the basic rules and forms. Specific forms of co-operation are the district administrative offices, where municipalities do not establish their own 'city halls', but jointly provide administrative services. Forty-eight per cent of local governments operate their own offices and one-third of municipalities joined other municipal administrations. Without strong incentives these regulations did not have sufficient impact on municipal co-operation in other areas of service management, so the Act CXXXV of 1997 on Municipal Associations and Inter-Municipal Co-operation further specified and simplified the co-operation process.

Lately in 2004, the Act on Multi-purpose Municipal Associations at Sub-county Level has set a new institutional framework for co-operation. According to these rules, local governments, municipalities and county local governments are authorised to co-operate or to establish institutionalised forms of association on a strictly voluntary basis. Rules and procedures set by these laws protect the rights of the municipalities participating in the associations (for example, requiring a qualified majority for basic decisions, a minimum of 60 per cent of the population for creating a multi-purpose association). The association has a legal status. Local government competencies and functions can be transferred to the association, which might also be the subject of intergovernmental transfers. The new multi-purpose associations are more complex forms of co-operation. Boundaries of the potential, voluntary associations follow the sub-county regional development units (there are 166 statistical units) and if they manage educational, social, health care and regional development functions jointly, they are eligible for further grants from the national budget. These multi-purpose associations are authorised to provide almost any municipal services specified by the law (except the real local ones, such as housing, cemeteries and fire protection).

POLITICS OF LOCAL GOVERNMENTS

Local government elections are held every four years. The last local elections were held in the autumn of 2006. Rules for local elections are different depending on the type of local government. Municipalities with a population of up to 10,000 have one ward, where each candidate is on a shortlist. In larger cities (population over 10,000 and in the capital city districts) individual constituencies are mixed with party lists. Depending on the city size, the number of wards and councillors on the party list are defined. Party lists receive the residual votes. County and capital city local governments are elected on party lists. The number of councillors is proportionate to the size of the municipality (Table 9.2).

Table 9.2 Allocation of wards and seats on lists

Population	Number of individual wards	Seats by lists
up to100		3
101 – 600		5
601–1,300		7
1,301–3,000		9
3,001–5,000		11
5,001–10,000		13
10,000 –25,000	10	7
25,001–50,000	14	9
50,000–60,000	15	10
60,000–70,000	16	11
70,000	+ 1 ward/pop.10,000	+ 1 seat/pop.10,000
Capital city		66
County local governments		40–80

Source: National Office of Statistics.

Results of the last elections show that political parties are active mostly in cities and the county local governments. Directly elected local mayors in towns and villages are typically 'independent' candidates, which means that they are not members of political parties (but often supported by some of them). At the last municipal election 78 per cent of mayors are independent ones (http://www.valasztas.hu/). In large, urban municipalities the political parties are present, but local councils are still not dominated by them. According to a survey only 31 per cent of councillors belonged to a fraction (organised group) within the municipal representative body (Soós et al., 2002)

Where more than 30 per cent of local representatives are elected by the same minority group, they may form a local minority government (minimum three councillors). These minority local governments may have their own functions and budget assigned by the local council to them.

LOCAL EXPENDITURES AND SERVICE MANAGEMENT

Hungary has a decentralised public sector. Measured by local expenditures as a percentage of GDP, the relative share of local governments is around 13 per cent. This ratio slightly decreased since the early 1990s, but mostly due to economic growth and a higher gross domestic product. In this period the scope of local government functions was also changed slightly, by assigning new competencies (for example, fire protection) or by modifying the salary schemes for civil servants.

Table 9.3 Local government expenditures as percentage of GDP (1994–2003)

Year	Local expenditures as percentage of GDP
1994	17.2
1995	14.4
1996	13.2
1997	13.4
1998	13.4
1999	13.0
2000	12.5
2001	12.8
2002	13.7
2003	13.6
2004	13.2

Source: Ministry of Finance.

Local Government Functions and Competencies

The Act on Local Governments specifies the status of local governments and principles of the relationship between the national administration and the elected local governments. The most important conditions are that only laws can regulate local government basic matters and the Act on Local Governments has a constitutional right. Consequently, no ministerial or government actions can influence the important elements of local government operation.

The following tasks of municipal governments are specified by the Act on Local Governments: administration, kindergarten, primary education, library services, local sports, basic health care services, basic social/welfare services, maintenance of public cemeteries, communal waste management, public cleansing, municipal development, environmental protection, water supplies and sewerage treatment, maintenance of local roads, street lighting, municipal fire services, local tasks of civil defence and co-operation with national/ethnic minority governments. These local functions are divided into two groups: mandatory services and optional services. The mandatory municipal tasks are the provision of potable water, kindergarten and primary education, basic health and welfare services, public lighting, maintenance of local roads and cemeteries and protection of minority rights.

Mandatory services provided by the county local governments include those regional services, which should be made available for a wider group of customers. So, they are typically services with spillovers, such as secondary education and dormitories, library services, child care and family protection, special education and health care services, specialised social services and co-ordination of regional employment functions, and so on.

A peculiarity of the assignment of functions in Hungary is that competencies can be transferred between the two different types of local governments under specific rules. Urban local governments are authorised to take over the control of regional services organisations (for example, secondary schools), where the majority of users are local residents, for a period of four years. This transfer will not change the ownership of assets, but funding and human resource management decisions will be moved to the other local government for a minimum of three years, if it has been announced before the annual budgeting season (October). This flexible assignment of functions has increased local autonomy, but made the intergovernmental fiscal schemes more complicated. Local governments with highly varying own revenue-raising capacity manage services of similarly high costs.

Transfer of Assets

The basic principle behind property devolution was that all assets connected to functions assigned to local government should be transferred to those entities. When a local government became responsible for a specific service (education, utilities, and so on), then all the assets required for the delivery of that service had to be transferred to that level of government. The basic local government law has classified two types of assets: core property that could not be alienated, such as public spaces, streets and monuments; and properties outside this core group that were subject to other laws, such as civil codes, sectoral legislation, privatisation or concession laws.

The core property was divided into two categories. Non-negotiable core property (such as roads and city parks) was distinguished from a sub-group of core assets that could be alienated under specific conditions. In the latter case, locally elected bodies were authorised to regulate transactions on these assets (such as water networks and public buildings). This municipal discretion could be also limited by local referendum.

The actual transfer of property was implemented in two ways: (i) by virtue of law or (ii) through property transfer committees. These commissions had only administrative and management competencies and they were merely allowed to implement laws. As a first step, local governments became the owners of a significant part of former state-owned assets. Urban land, water flows, municipal roads, infrastructure, utility companies and the land value of privatised state-owned enterprises all became part of local ownership. Local governments had the right to transform their municipal companies into market-based ventures. Table 9.4 shows how the composition of local government's balance sheet has changed during the past decade.

As a first step, municipalities received tangible fixed assets (housing stock, equipment and buildings of public companies, and so on). By the mid-1990s social housing stock was sold and the utility companies were transformed to business entities where local governments became shareholders (consequently the share of their financial assets became significant). In the late 1990s, local government assets were transferred for operation to private sector entities and municipal shares were sold. At the same time, urban land and property were reassessed, so the value of tangible fixed assets dominated the municipal balance sheets yet again.

Local governments also benefited from the transformation of state-owned enterprises. Local governments received shares of the formerly state-owned companies and then had the right to acquire land and benefit from privatisation revenues. Only the former state-owned urban land with no structures became local assets. To minimise the risks, legislation on municipal business activities in Hungary only allows the participation of local governments in companies with limited liability (Péteri, 2003a).

Table 9.4 Composition of local government balance sheet (percentage of fixed assets)

	Tangible fixed assets	Financial investments	of this: shares	Assets transferred for operation	Total fixed assets
1991	97.1	2.8	1.9	0.0	100.0
1992	65.3	34.6	33.0	0.0	100.0
1993	57.6	34.9	33.0	7.4	100.0
1994	54.9	36.9	34.7	7.9	100.0
1995	55.5	36.6	34.0	7.8	100.0
1996	51.5	41.6	38.2	6.8	100.0
1997	54.1	36.7	32.2	7.6	100.0
1998	58.6	32.1	28.4	9.1	100.0
2001	63.7	19.7	16.3	16.4	100.0
2002	74.3	9.6	8.3	14.7	100.0
2003	78.9	6.5	5.7	14.5	100.0
2004	77.9	6.4	5.4	15.5	100.0
2005	77.9	6.0	5.1	15.9	100.0

Source: Local Government Fiscal Database (http://hoka.mki.gov.hu/hoka/index.html).

Service Management at the Local Level

Local governments are primarily responsible for human services. The single largest spending item is public education (including kindergartens, dormitories, day care services provided at schools, and so on) (Table 9.5). Municipalities also provide health care services: general practitioners, polyclinics and a set of hospitals are operated in locally owned buildings, but they are financed by the national health insurance fund. During the past decade, the share of social and welfare services has doubled.

The general administration is the other expenditure item, which showed a significant increase during this period. This expenditure category covers several different types of items, which are not always properly accounted for and also includes various capital investment expenses. So, beyond the higher administrative (mostly salary) costs, this might also explain the high share of administrative expenses.

Table 9.5 Local government expenditures by sector 1991, 2003[a] (in per cent)

Sectors	1991	Services	2003
Education	36.5	Education	31.2
Culture, sports	4.7	Culture, sports	5.1
Health care	23.0	Health care	16.7
Social services	6.1	Social services	12.3
Administration	6.5	Administration	16.2
Housing	1.9	Housing and communal services	7.3
Communal services	4.4		
Transportation	5.9	Transportation	3.1
Water management	2.6	Environmental services	3.8
Industry, commerce	4.6	Industry, agriculture	3.1
Others (transfers, loan repayment)	3.8	Miscellaneous	1.2
Total	100.0	Total	100.0

Note: (a) The functional categorisation of public services has been modified, so sectoral breakdown of expenditures is not comparable for all the services.

Source: Ministry of Finance.

Municipal budgets are mostly used for current expenditures (72 per cent) and transfers or subsidies (8 per cent) (Table 9.6). Wages, salaries, operational and maintenance costs have shown a stable increase over the past years. Capital expenditures are typically higher in the years prior to local election years (1998, 2002 and 2006). As wages and salaries are two-thirds of current expenditures and they are the subject of national regulations, any major changes in the government's policy will significantly modify the share of these expenses. In 2002 the new incoming Socialist-led coalition government increased teachers' salaries by 50 per cent, which has placed a high burden on local governments funding education services.

Due to the fragmented system of local governments, co-operation was always highly preferred and supported. Legal options for associations and joint service delivery have been provided by the evolving legislation. These were encouraged through fiscal incentives and the minimum levels of public services were specified by sectoral regulations. After a slow learning and adjustment process, local governments have built up various joint service delivery arrangements. The last wave of regulations on local government co-operation has introduced new incentives. Intergovernmental transfers have been connected to service performance indicators, so local governments with sub-standard services will not be eligible for grants after a transition period. In addition, specific national budget funds have been provided for the operational expenditures of the newly created multi-purpose associations (Table 9.7). Due to the financial incentives and informal government pressure, 95 per cent of the sub-county statistical units have established some forms of multi-purpose municipal associations. The majority of them are responsible for local government services, beyond the classical regional development functions.

Table 9.6 Local government current and capital expenditures (in per cent)

Expenditures	1995	1997	1999	2001	2003	2005
1. Current expenditures	71.2	67.0	70.4	68.4	73.8	71.6
Wages, salaries	42.5	39.6	41.4	41.5	49.2	46.9
O&M costs	28.7	27.4	29.0	26.9	24.7	24.7
2. Transfers, subsidies	8.0	7.6	8.6	8.8	7.2	8.0
3. Capital expenditures	16.5	18.0	17.1	19.8	16.5	18.7
4. Miscellaneous	4.3	7.4	3.8	3.0	2.5	1.7
5. Total expenditures	100.0	100.0	100.0	100.0	100.0	100.0

Source: Ministry of Finance.

Table 9.7 Multi-purpose municipal associations, 31 December 2004

Multi-purpose municipal associations	Number	Percentage
Multi-purpose association for all the functions	90	54
Multi-purpose association with limited functions	28	17
Multi-purpose association for regional development purposes only	39	24
Sub-county units without multi-purpose municipal associations	9	5
Total number of sub-county units	166	100

Source: Ministry of Interior.

However, this new model of co-operation is still faced with some structural problems. The standard boundaries of sub-county statistical units might not cover the real catchment areas of services (for example, water might be different from waste collection or education service areas). Secondly, mayors represent the member municipalities in the multi-purpose municipal associations, so their accountability is limited. Finally, there are no mechanisms for own source revenue raising at the association level, so these new forms of co-operation will be heavily dependent on intergovernmental transfers.

Transformation of public utilities

Public utilities and other communal services, including housing, were transformed in the first years of transition. Reorganisation was forced by the elimination of national budget subsidies. Price – rent-setting authorities were also transferred to local governments in 1991–92. Two exceptions of operational subsidies remained in the water sector: water and sewage charges above a certain level and collection of liquid waste from septic tanks are still subsidised.

Beyond this strong pressure to modernise communal services, local governments also received the assets (equipment, networks) of service companies. Water, sewage pipes and wells became local government core assets. The former state-owned and the county water companies were transferred to local governments, which became the owners of the networks. These local governments have created several new service organisations and operating companies. For example, the five national and 28 regional water and sewage companies were transformed to 400 local government service organisations in 1991–92 (leaving only five state-owned regional companies in operation). The municipal solid waste companies were similarly dissolved.

As a consequence of this 'stick and carrot' decentralisation policy, alternative forms of service delivery (contracting out, BOT, concessions) have evolved and private investors have entered this market. Water management services are more often provided by associations (20–25 per cent of local governments). Municipal solid waste services are organised around local governments with landfills. They are managed by large collection companies, which very often enter into contracts with 50–70 municipalities. Companies are typically joint stock or limited liability companies with municipal owners on their boards. The contracting procedures are regulated by public procurement rules. So, the market forces guide horizontal co-operation effectively. In Hungary, local governments had to specify the organisational setting of local utilities before 1996. They were presented with three options: (i) to manage the service from within the local administration, (ii) to establish a budgetary organisation or (iii) to establish an entity according to the Company Law. This forced municipalities to avoid unclear, mixed forms of 'public companies' and develop more efficient and acceptable forms of operation and management.

These changes forced local governments to develop new organisational and management forms in the field of public utilities. The concession law was one of the early regulations in this area, but later, local governments developed contractual relationships with service organisations. Our surveys in 1994 and

2006 showed the development of service arrangements (Table 9.8). In-house (budgetary) organisations were mostly used for housing management and public services financed by general budget revenues. External service providers or contract-based service management by in-house units were more frequently used at charge-based services.

Table 9.8 Methods of utility and communal service management, 1994, 2006[a] (in percent)

Urban services	Delivered by local governments, 1994	Delivered by own service institutions, 2006
Public cleansing	78	76.3
Park maintenance	77	73.3
Housing and rental unit mgmt	79	62.1
Maintenance of cemeteries		51.6
Waste water management	21	13.9
Water services	8	13.8
Municipal solid waste collection	28	11.4
Funeral services	20	11.1
Management of public bath	42	9.7
Municipal solid waste disposition	44	9.7
District heating	33	5.9
Production of heating energy	n.a.	4.5
Urban public transportation	4	1.7
Chimney sweeping	3	1.7

Note: (a) 1994 data are based on a survey at 400 municipalities . The question was: 'How is this service organised at your municipality?' (see Péteri, 1996). In 2006 a similar question was asked at sample of 406 municipalities Péteri (2007).

Involvement of third sector in service delivery

The emerging non-profit sector in Hungary also had an impact on local public service delivery. Local governments co-operate in several ways with NGOs of various types. Local non-profit organisations and community-based organisations provide human services and this way they supplement municipal functions. However, local governments and their service organisations also establish their own 'foundations'. These special forms of non-profit organisations carry out fundraising and supplement public funds available for schools, cultural and social institutions, and support special municipal tasks, such as urban rehabilitation and environmental protection.

Table 9.9 shows the increase in non-profit organisations in public education during the past decade. These non-public schools are more significant in secondary education, where they respond to the diverse needs of pupils. At this level of education (6/8–12 grades) the number of pupils in church and other non-profit schools has doubled (now 20 per cent). In the elementary schools their share increased by four times (to 2.1 per cent).

Table 9.9 Non-state service providers in public education in per cent

Level of education	Share of pupils	
	in church schools	in private or non-profit schools
Primary schools (1993)	1.9	0.2
Comprehensive secondary schools (gymnasium) (1995)	9.9	1.5
Primary schools (2003)	4.2	0.9
Comprehensive secondary schools (gymnasium) (2003)	16.4	3.5

Source: Ministry of Education.

LOCAL OWN SOURCE REVENUES

The present taxation system in Hungary was designed and legislated between 1988 and 1992. The first step was the introduction of the value added tax and the personal income tax in 1988. This was an early innovation, well before other transition countries and the political changes of 1990. PIT was used for funding municipal functions, under the old, input-based budgeting practices in a two-step allocation mechanism of intergovernmental transfers. The components of the modern local taxation were designed after the political transformation, by legislating various own source municipal revenues (taxes, user charges, capital revenues, and so on).

There are two types of local own source revenues, which are roughly one-third of total municipal budgets (Table 9.10). The own source current revenues are increasing and represent 26 per cent of total revenues. The capital revenues are declining as the assets and property of local governments are sold (9 per cent).

Table 9.10 Local government revenues, 1998, 2005

Revenues	Percentage	
	1998	2005
Operational revenues	8.6	9.2
Fees, dues	1.6	2.2
Local taxes	9.8	13.2
Other own revenues	2.8	1.8
Total own current revenues	22.7	26.4
PIT shared	14.0	14.6
Vehicle tax	0.7	1.6
Shared total	14.7	16.3
Capital own source revenues	10.3	9.0
General grants	21.5	22.5
Capital investment grants	3.6	3.4
Other grants	5.2	3.4
Grants total	31.3	29.3
Transfers	18.4	15.0
Loans	2.6	3.9
Total local government revenues	100.0	100.0

Source: Ministry of Finance.

Local taxes are optional: four different types of taxes can be levied by local governments. The national tax regulations set the tax base, specify the core set of exemptions and identify the techniques of tax levies and the maximum tax rate. This approach allows local governments to develop diverse tax policies. The system of intergovernmental transfers provides incentives to introduce local taxes: in 1992 only 47 per cent of local governments levied one form of local taxes, whereas now, 96 per cent of localities use them. Local taxes are more significant for larger, urban municipalities: they provide 15 per cent of cities' revenues and 23 per cent in Budapest.

The most often used and largest local tax revenue is the *business tax* (Table 9.11.). It is levied on the modified gross turnover of business entities, deducting the value of materials used for production, at a maximum rate of 2 per cent. Business tax gives the majority of local tax revenues (85 per cent) and is levied by three-quarters of municipalities. The business tax is highly concentrated in the capital city and several large, industrial urban centres. As the local business tax is the one which is preferred, it has now exceeded the amount collected from corporate income tax by the national budget. Because of the high tax burden on businesses, it is regarded as one of the major obstacles for the Hungarian economy's competitiveness.

Table 9.11 Local taxes, 1997, 2006

Local taxes	Local tax yield (%)	
	1997	2006
1. Property taxes	11.5	11.9
1.1 tax on buildings	10.0	10.3
1.2 tax on plots	1.5	1.6
2. Communal taxes	2.9	3.4
2.1 on enterprises	1.1	1.5
2.2 on private persons	1.8	1.9
3. Business tax	83.9	82.2
4. Tax on tourism	1.7	2.5
4.1 by days	1.2	1.9
4.2 by units	0.5	0.6
Total	100.0	100.0

Source: ÖNKORKÉP (1998).

SHARED REVENUES AND TRANSFERS

Local governments are connected to other parts of general government finances: they benefit from shared revenues and receive various types of grants. These centrally controlled revenues are allocated to local governments in many different ways. Most of them are general grants, so local governments have a large amount of discretion in spending the transfers and shared revenues. There are two major types of shared revenues: personal income tax and the motor vehicle tax. Forty per cent of nationally collected PIT is allocated to local governments in two different ways: one quarter of the total shared PIT remains at the place of origin and the remainder is transferred to municipalities through various grant formulae.

As the total amount of PIT increased during the past decade, both the sharing ratio and the local (origin based) part was changing. Since 1988, when the total PIT was used as municipal revenue, the sharing ratio declined to 35 per cent by the late 1990s. Out of this lower amount, only 5 per cent was left at the place of origin. These rules have changed slightly since 2002: the combined impact of growing national PIT revenues and modification of sharing regulations on local budgets are shown in Figure 9.1.

Figure 9.1 Shared PIT in percentage of local revenues

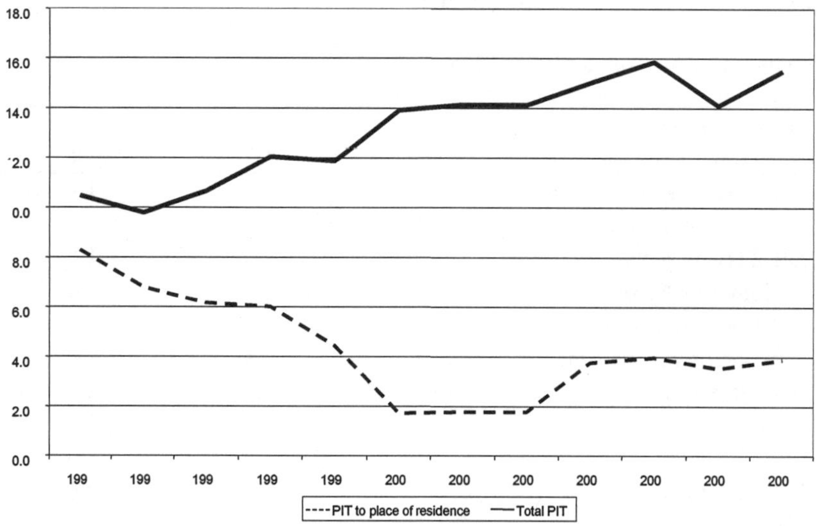

The transformation of sharing regulations is partly politically driven. PIT is a more significant revenue for large urban centres and the capital city. Differences in the political colour of the national government/parliament and the cities have influenced the sharing mechanisms: less PIT is shared and left at the place of origin when these cities are led by the opposition parties. This is an important fiscal regulatory technique, in a country where one-quarter of local expenditures are made in Budapest (plus 40 per cent in the other cities).

Intergovernmental transfers are equal to 45 per cent of local government revenues (Table 9.10). Two-thirds of these transfers are grants from the national budget, while the remaining portions are transfers from other public funds, such as the health insurance fund. This latter group of transfers is allocated according to sectoral rules (an adjusted form of DRG) and planning procedures. In the field of health care, the transfers are earmarked.

However, a major part of central grants is allocated as (i) general grants, (ii) equalisation grants and (iii) transfers for capital investment projects (Table 9.14). Since 1996 there have been several structural changes in the transfer system. First of all, the share of grants for equalisation purposes has increased. Because of bigger differences in own source revenues, more transfers were allocated for revenue equalisation purposes. The share of capital investment grants has declined. Within the group of general grants, the transfers allocated by the number of population – as an objective measure of needs – has also declined.

Table 9.12 Main types of local government transfers, 1996, 2005 (in per cent)

	2005	1996
General (normative) grants	80.6	85.6
• according to population	9.5	21.1
• mixed criteria	3.7	0.7
• by number of users	50.7	47.1
• central appropriations	6.8	13.7
• normative, earmarked	9.9	2.9
Equalisation grants	10.0	3.6
• deficit grant	1.8	0.8
• for revenue equalisation	8.2	2.8
Capital investment grants	6.2	10.8
Others	3.2	0.0
Total	100.0	100.0

Source: Republic of Hungary, Budget Laws of 1996 and 2005.

General grants are the largest item among the various transfers (81 per cent). Most of these funds are allocated to municipalities by the number of users or customers of services (number of pupils, users of homes for the elderly, and so on). On average, these transfers cover only two-thirds of total service expenses. Small portions of these general grants are allocated by objective criteria upon local demand for services, such as size of population. There are approximately 90 different basic indicators with different weights, which make the transfer system rather complex.

Equalisation grants are used mostly for compensating for differences in the municipal revenue base. Local governments below the average per capita local PIT and business tax revenues, receive grants up to the amount of the standardised level of these two types of revenues. The revenue equalisation grant allocation formula is based on the averages of PIT and business tax in municipalities of different size. This rough proxy measure of local 'revenue capacity' makes the equalisation more refined. However, this formula has also introduced a disincentive because revenues from municipalities with tax revenues way above the averages are 'taken' by the national budget (in the form of not allocating the planned amount of general grants to these municipalities).

There is another minor equalisation grant, which is only 1.8 per cent of total national transfers, but more than one-third of municipalities are eligible for this. It is calculated on the basis of the difference between accepted expenditures and estimated revenues of local revenues. Mostly small municipalities without any significant own source revenues receive this grant.

There are two types of *capital investment grants*: specific grants for large local capital investment projects (for example, hospitals) and grants for public services with spillovers (water, waste water treatment, municipal solid waste management). This latter group of transfers was a matching grant until 2004, when 40–60 per cent of (standardised) costs were covered by the national budget. The grant allocation schemes have been modified recently, as they did not provide sufficient incentives for an efficient use of public funds. So, from that year on, the logic of capital grants has been changed.

In the case of grants for building sewage collection networks, local governments receive transfers only if a set number of users are connected to the network (80 per cent of the planned units) and grants are allocated according to the number of connections on a per capita basis. This would force local governments to decrease the costs of the capital investments and to make the networks operation more efficient by reaching the minimum number of required users (and future customers who pay the connection fees and the user charges).

Assessment of the Transfer System

Beyond the reform of the intergovernmental transfer system in 1990, the most important development was the change in the logic of grant allocation (Table 9.13). One year prior to the establishment of politically autonomous local governments, new incentives were introduced by the simplified model of general grants. Earlier, the method of grant allocation was based on the calculation of the difference between the estimated level of municipal expenditures and the planned local revenues ($E_i - R_i = G_i$). Grants were budgeted in co-operation with sectoral ministries and allocated through the counties, as intermediary levels of government.

In 1990, this logic of detailed sectoral control over local budgets was abolished. Since then, local government spending has not been directly monitored, as total local expenditures are equal to the sum of own source revenues and grants made available for the locality ($R + G = E$). The general rules of grant allocation have been improved: there are five times more basic allocation criteria; the discretionary buffer fund for the first year has been eliminated and new equalisation techniques have been introduced. The most important impact of this grant allocation technique was that it has created new incentives for economising on total expenditures.

ence between standardised expenditures and revenues, calculated by average fiscal capacity and effort ($E_{estimated} - R_{required} = G_{calculated,}$). In Hungary, only the standard revenue-based equalisation grant allocation method has been applied. This was an important step in the institutional learning process for developing more advanced concepts of intergovernmental transfers.

Table 9.13 Development of grant allocation methods

Types of transfers	Expenditure	Revenue	Transfers
Earmarked, centralised (gap-filling)	Individual decision on appropriations ($EI_{estimate}$)	Individual revenue assessment ($RI_{planned}$)	Individual bargaining ($EI_{estimate} - RI_{planned}$)
General grants	Local decision on expenditure levels ($E = R + G$)	Local authority to generate revenues (R)	General grants (G)
Fiscal capacity based grants	Accepted expenditure levels based on objective measures of 'needs' ($E_{accepted}$)	Potential revenue at standardized revenue bases subject to national average tax rates and charges ($R_{required}$)	Calculated grant ($G_{calculated} = E_{accepted} - R_{required}$)

For the overall assessment of the Hungarian system of intergovernmental finances, the following questions should be answered (see Table 9.14):

a) Do the grants create incentives at local level for efficient management of municipal funds?
b) Do the transfers guarantee the minimum level services for local governments with different functions?
c) How is horizontal equalisation achieved on both sides of the budget?

The general grant system provides sufficient incentives for own source revenue-raising in municipalities, so this is an important innovation, introduced in 1990. However, the transfers allocated by capacity indicators of existing service organisations do not make the local governments interested in searching for the most efficient forms of service delivery. Joint service organisations, other forms of co-operation and contracting out might decrease the grants available for the local budgets, which are considered as a loss in 'power'.

The general (normative) grant is the best method for contributing to the different local functions: municipalities with various functions are treated similarly and it leaves a high level of local discretion for using the municipal budgets. However, the transfers allocated by units of service (number of customers) cannot deal with the problem of varying costs: local governments with different costs receive the same amount of national budget funds. On the revenue side of the budget the equalisation mechanisms are quite developed.

Table 9.14 Objectives of intergovernmental fiscal transfers

General fiscal goals	Objectives of intergovernmental fiscal transfers by expenditure	revenue side of the local budget
1. Providing local *incentives*	(i) Stimulating rational municipal spending (ii) Promoting efficiency in local service provision	Promoting own source revenue-raising (increase 'tax effort')
2. Guaranteeing minimum level of services for local governments in different positions	(i) Ensuring access to locally provided services (ii) Recognising objective differences in unit costs of municipal services	Equalising differences in local revenue-raising potential (tax base)
3. *Horizontal equalisation* between local governments of similar type and with comparable functions	Recognising the objectively measured variations in costs of local expenditure needs (scope and unit costs)	Compensating for the unequal distribution of revenue bases (tax capacity)

The purposes of horizontal equalisation can hardly be achieved by these techniques of intergovernmental transfers. Only some elements of the revenue equalisation help to decrease the differences between local governments with similar functions. This is why the regional inequalities are one of the biggest problems of the present system of municipal finances.

LOCAL GOVERNMENT BORROWING

In Hungary, the National Savings Bank (OTP) dominates the municipal market because 81 per cent of local governments have their accounts with this bank. This former state-owned bank inherited a monopolistic position with an extended network of local branches. Later, new actors entered this market and, for example, the Austrian Raiffeisen Bank controls 8 per cent of the municipal market. This concentrated character of municipal lending makes local government borrowing easier because the banks are familiar with the fiscal status of local governments and they can develop a trust-based relationship with their clients.

The fiscal incentives for municipal lending are less favourable. The most important condition for local borrowing – the stable local revenue flow – is missing. The frequent changes in the revenue-sharing system and permanent debates about the elimination of the local business tax do not help the predictability of municipal revenues in the long run. Local government revenues can be freely used for loan repayment, as there is no strict separation between current and capital budgets. Local governments are well equipped with own assets to provide collateral for loans and issued loan guarantees. Any property with full or limited negotiability may be used for securing loans, with the exception of 'core property', such as public spaces, municipal water flows and streets.

There are limits to local government borrowing, by defining the total municipal debt service (including guarantees issued, but not taking into consideration the short-term loans) in percentage of locally controlled current own source revenues. The limit set by the law is 70 per cent of these specific subgroups of own source revenues, so this ratio is approximately 17–18 per cent of the total budget revenues. This type of regulation clearly sends the message to municipalities that the central budget does not take any responsibility for loan repayment and grants or shared revenues are not part of the debt limitation formula.

Municipal borrowing is also encouraged by clear regulations on local bankruptcy. Hungary is the only country in Central Europe which legislated local government loan adjustment procedures in 1996. At the time of fiscal restriction, the law on municipal 'bankruptcy' regulated the liquidation procedures. Debtors who do not receive their money (for example, suppliers, contractors and banks) after 90 days have the right to initiate the liquidation procedure. If there is no agreement on debt rescheduling, the court appoints a debt manager who has the authority to control local government financial decisions. The minimum level of services, defined by law, has to be continuously provided. All payments and financial decisions are made by the appointed debt manager. Options for consolidation might bring about severe cutbacks in expenditures, an increase in own source revenues, a reorganisation of local services and the sale of municipal property, and so on.

In Hungary, the law on municipal bankruptcy had a preventive affect. During the past seven years, only 20 municipalities were subjects of debt management procedures. Experiences from the implementation show that – interestingly –

creditors have never initiated debt restructuring. (Jókay et al. 2004). This was always carried out by the local governments, which were typically small size municipalities (with a population of 300–5,000).

The primary cause of bankruptcies was large-scale capital investments in infrastructure, which are typically heavily subsidised projects. If any promised transfer did not reach the municipality on time, or there were unexpected changes in costs or in the planned revenue flow, then these municipalities had to announce the default. In other bankruptcy cases, local governments were involved in market activities (local economic development or tourism promotion, building hostels), which made them more vulnerable in the market. Thirdly, there were some criminal cases when, quite simply, public money was stolen.

The debt management procedures were usually completed in one or two years. Typically, local governments were able to come to an agreement with their debtors. Alternatively, local government property was used for repayment. Often, this has caused significant losses for local governments, because valuable assets were transferred to debtors at a low price. But in general, the local bankruptcy law has been successful and has fulfilled its mission.

CONCLUSIONS: LEARNING BY DOING

The past one-and-a-half decades of fiscal decentralisation in Hungary was characterised by a permanent learning process. The political and constitutional reforms of 1990 were important turning points, but they simply opened the door for a series of further refinements. Legislative changes and new political mechanisms introduced in that short period were also based on the relatively long learning process of the 1980s. The spirit of these market-oriented and democratic reforms was the basis for continuous development under the years of economic recovery until 1998.

The institutional framework established by the basic laws helped the local governments to benefit from decentralisation and to respond successfully to the harsh fiscal measures of the early 1990s. Wide assignment of public functions to local governments, relatively high municipal discretion in managing them and privatisation of public services created a favourable environment for local innovations.

A critical condition for decentralisation was the transformation of the ministries' role. Based on the sectoral legislation, by the mid-1990s, the new functions of the line ministries and agencies were formulated. The planning and regulatory tasks and the professional support services have gradually been developed. This has liberated local governments from the heavy hand of the central administration and changed the role of the intermediary level of government. Compared to other transition countries, the development of these new supervisory, control and audit functions was a key element of successful decentralisation.

By the end of this learning period, solutions were being found for the effective management of public services in fragmented municipal structures. The largest problem of the local government system in Hungary seems to be solved by not eliminating the democratic benefits of extensive decentralisation. New forms of multi-purpose co-operation were introduced from 2004 and market mechanisms forced integration in the area of urban services. This was the basis for an efficient public service management, without harming the political consensus, guaranteed by the constitutional laws of local governments.

The future regional development structures and the pressure to reform the taxation system will initiate changes in intergovernmental fiscal relations. Elimination of the local business tax for economic reasons and the establishment of elected regional governments will help towards the reforms in other areas. Two options for improving the local government revenue base are the wider use of property taxes or introducing local personal income tax. The latter would be another form of sharing mechanism, providing new conditions for accountability.

In the transfer mechanism, the predictability and stability of grants would create more favourable conditions for local governments. The complexity of intergovernmental transfers should be maintained, but the proportion of needs-based allocation criteria might be increased in comparison to actual service capacity-related grants.

BIBLIOGRAPHY

Baldersheim, H., M. Illner, A. Offerdal, L. Rose and P. Swianiewicz (eds) (1996), *Local Democracy and the Processes of Transformation in East-Central Europe*, Boulder, CO: Westview Press.

Bird, R., R. Ebel and C.I. Wallich (1995), *Decentralization of the Socialist State*, Washington, DC: World Bank.

Bird, R. and C. Wallich (1992), *Financing Local Governments in Hungary*, Policy Research Working Papers, WPS, 869, Washington, DC: World Bank.

Davey, K. and G. Péteri (1998), Local government finances: options for reforms, Nagykovácsi: Local Government Know-How Programme and Pontes Kft.

Davey, K., M.T. Horváth and G. Péteri (2000), A helyi önállóság és önkormányzati feladatok (Local Self-government and Tasks for Municipalities), *Közigazgatás-fejlesztési füzetek* (Local Administration Development Notes), 1. szám, Budapest: MEH.

Ebel, R. and G. Péteri (eds) (2007), *Kosovo Decentralization Briefing Book*, Priština: Forum 2015/KFOS/LGI.

Horváth, M.T. and G. Péteri (2004), Threats of Transformation Failures: Local Public Utility Sector in Central and Eastern Europe, *Society and Economy* **26**(2–3), 295–324.

Jókay, K., L. Osváth, G. Sóvágó and G. Szmetana (2004), *Az önkormányzati adósságrendezések oknyomozása 1996–2003* (Investigation of municipal debt management 1996–2003), ÁSZ FMI, manuscript.

Kopányi, M., D. Wetzel and S. El Daher (eds) (2004), *Intergovernmental Finance in Hungary*, Washington, DC: The World Bank

ÖNKORKÉP (1998), *Nagyító alatt – zárszámadás* (Analysis of the local governments' annual budget), March.

ÖNKORKÉP (2004), *Nagyító alatt – zárszámadás* (Analysis of the local governments' annual budget), September.

Péteri, G. (1996), Változások a szolgáltatásszervezésben (Changes in Management of Local Services), in: T.M. Horváth and J. Kiss (eds), *Aréna és otthon*, Budapest: PTI.

Péteri, G. (ed.) (2002), *Mastering Decentralisation and Public Administration Reforms in CEE*, Budapest: Open Society Institute Local Government and Public Service Reform Initiative.

Péteri, G. (ed.) (2003a), *From Usage to Ownership. Transfer of Public Property to Local Governments in Central Europe*, Budapest: Open Society Institute Local Government and Public Service Reform Initiative.

Péteri, G. (2003b), *A régió erőforrásai* (Resources of the regions), IDEA Programme, manuscript.

Péteri, G. (2004a), Strengthening local management capacity: institutional development in transition, in M. Kopányi et al. (eds), *Intergovernmental Finance in Hungary*, Budapest: The World Bank and Open Society Institute Local Government and Public Service Reform Initiative.

Péteri, G. (2004b), *Mechanisms for allocation of general equalisation grants, PHRD Grant for Preparation of the Second Programmatic Adjustment Loan,* Sofia: Club Ekonomika, manuscript.

Péteri, G. (2004c), *Municipal Debt Control: Experiences of Central-Eastern European Countries, PHRD Grant for Preparation of the Second Programmatic Adjustment Loan,* Sofia: Club Ekonomika, manuscript.

Péteri, G. (2007), *Greater Responsibilities, Transforming Functions, New Roles*, Budapest: Hungarian Institute of Public Administration.

Shah, A. (1994), *The Reform of Intergovernmental Fiscal Relations in Developing and Emerging Market Economies*, Washington, DC: The World Bank.

Shah, A. (1998), *Fiscal Federalism and Macroeconomic Governance: For Better or for Worse?*, Washington, DC: World Bank.

Soós, G., G. Tóka, and G. Wright (eds) (2002), *The State of Local Democracy in Central Europe*, Budapest: Open Society Institute Local Government and Public Service Reform Initiative.

Swianiewicz, P. (ed.) (2001), *Public Perception of Local Governments*, Budapest: Open Society Institute Local Government and Public Service Reform Initiative.

10. Local government finance in Latvia

Mudīte Priede and Solvita Klapare

INTRODUCTION

In 1991, Latvia regained independence and moved towards democracy and market economy. It soon became a member of the Organization for Security and Co-operation in Europe, the Council of Europe, the World Trade Organization and NATO. In 2004, Latvia became a member of the European Union. After regaining independence, the Latvian economy experienced a sharp decline as its economic links with the former USSR were lost. Real GDP fell by 50 per cent. As a response, the government began not only to impose fiscal discipline on itself, but also limit enterprise subsidies. Reform programmes involved important steps towards liberalisation and created a competitive and open economic environment. From 1996, the economy began to grow significantly, stagnating briefly in 1999 as a result of the financial crisis in Russia. Annual GDP growth since 1996 averaged 6 per cent, reaching 11.9 in 2006.

Until 1991, Latvia's budget was linked to the USSR budget with centralised distribution of funds. After regaining independence, the 1990 Law on the USSR State Budget lost its effect, although Latvia's budget still received instalments from the Soviet Union's state taxes and revenues. Over the last 15 years, local governments in Latvia have experienced fundamental changes that may be illustrated by several stages closely linked to the process of renewal of independent public administration in the country. While maintaining structural principles of socialistic local governments, newly elected municipal councils were established. Local government reform started in 1991 with the Supreme Council passing Laws on Rural, Town and Regional Governments.

BASIC LEGAL FRAMEWORK AND LG FINANCE REGULATIONS

Citizens of the Republic of Latvia (RoL) execute state public power through the highest decision-making institution, the democratically elected Parliament (*Saeima*), and through directly elected local governments and regional councils. According to the Constitution of the RoL, *Satversme*, the Parliament appoints the highest state executive power – the Cabinet of Ministers (CoM).

The highest normative act with legal power in respect to local governments is the European Charter of Local Governments, ratified by the Parliament of Latvia on 22 February 1996. Twenty-nine of the 30 paragraphs of the Charter are binding to Latvia as a member of the European Council (EC). This means that theoretically Latvia has accepted the principles of the Charter, however, as demonstrated further in the text, in practice it does not follow a number of provisions related to local government finance.

According to the Law on Local Governments (LG law),[1] there are two types of local governments: town and rural at the lowest level, and regional (district) governments. Town and rural governments serve as local executive authorities with elected councils. Councils' established institutions and entities ensure execution of functions assigned by legislation, tasks ascribed in the LG law, assigned by the CoM, and LG voluntary initiatives. Lowest level governments are divided into towns, villages (rural governments called '*pagasts*') and territories (governments amalgamated through administrative territorial reform, called '*novads*') – all have equal functions and rights. Functions of regional governments differ from those of the lowest level. Republican status cities (that is, seven largest cities and the capital, Riga, with more than one-third of Latvia's total 2.3 million population) perform functions of both the lowest level and regional governments.

Equal, direct, closed and proportional LG elections take place every four years. Since 1997, regional government decision-making bodies (councils) are no longer directly elected, but formed by the chairmen of each town, *novads* and *pagasts* of the region's territory. As of 1 January 2007, there are 553 local governments in Latvia: 432 *pagasts*, 35 *novads*, 53 towns, 7 Republican status cities and 26 regional governments.

While decentralisation is essential, it is not the only prerequisite for autonomous local governments. Based on the three theoretical models distinguished by Batley, Stoker and Wright, the model of Latvia's local governance is closest to the interaction model, characterised by influence and control from the central government, whilst retaining a high degree of independence by local authorities. The model of district governments, on the other hand, corresponds to the agency model, with no directly elected political body and tax revenue base (Vanags, 1997). Improvements in the legal framework are necessary to adjust Latvia's model to a relatively autonomous one. For example, the principle of local governance is not defined in the Constitution of Latvia. Moreover, one of the constraints in achieving a larger degree of autonomy lies in the provision of funding to perform newly delegated functions. After regaining independence, a process of delegating additional functions to LGs, as well as decentralisation of tasks was launched. Although the number of tasks to be carried out by local authorities was increased, the financial and technical capacity has not been adequately supported. Such capacity, however, existed within the central government ministries.

Latvia has established an effective system of intergovernmental negotiations. This is clearly illustrated by the budget adoption process. LGs may independently prepare and approve budgets and collect budget revenues in accordance with legislation in order to ensure macroeconomic stability corresponding to the revenue basis. Local budget preparation begins with determination of the share of local budgets in the general state budget, as well as financial requirements of the state budget and grants. The latter is based on the state budget funding ability and extent of functions performed by LGs. Based on the assessment, the CoM agrees with local governments on the total amount of state budget grants to be allocated in the upcoming economic year and its distribution among LGs, giving consideration to the equalisation of finances across LGs.

During the process of harmonisation, the CoM is represented by the Minister of Finance. LGs are represented by a public organisation established in accordance with the requirements of art. 96 of the LG law, the Latvian Association of Local and Regional Governments (LALRG). The protocol of negotiations reflecting consensus or disagreement is attached to the draft state budget, which is then submitted by the CoM to the Parliament.

DEMOCRATIC LEGITIMACY AND FINANCIAL REPORTING

According to the subsidiarity principle, the lowest local government level must perform as many tasks as possible. When defining the competencies of local authorities, the LG law states that one of the main objectives is to implement the principle of decentralisation of functions to the lowest level possible, and to provide adequate funding for execution of these functions. The competencies of LGs include territorial and district administration, socio-economic development and facilitation of culture and education; state administrative functions, the performance of which is transferred to the relevant local government; functions that are within the competence of other LGs, the performance of which has been transferred to the respective LG; one-time tasks, the performance of which has been assigned by the state administrative institutions; and voluntary initiatives (LG Law art. 6).

Permanent functions are the responsibility of local governments with funding provided in their local budgets, unless stated otherwise in the legislation. In transferring new permanent functions that involve increased expenditures, law that assigns the function must specify a source of revenue (LG Law art. 7). Unfortunately, this is not always the case. In the interest of the residents of the relevant administrative territory, LGs may voluntarily carry out initiatives with respect to any matter if it is not within competence of the Parliament, the CoM, particular ministries, other state administrative institutions, the courts or other LGs, and if such activities are not prohibited by the law (LG Law art. 12). LG law assigns 20 permanent functions to rural and amalgamated LGs and towns and only four permanent functions to the regional municipalities. Lowest level LGs are responsible for ensuring residential utility services; public services and facilities; education of residents; maintenance of cultural activities, preservation of traditional cultural values and development of creative folk activity; access to health care; social assistance to residents; and so on.

Regional LGs' functions include provision of civil defence; organisation of public transport services; and organisation of education for pedagogic staff and methodical educational work (LG Law art. 15). Although the number of regional functions is limited, most carry out various voluntary tasks and, to some extent, support weaker LGs in carrying out their tasks. Arrangement of permanent functions is the responsibility of the respective LG, although practical implementation often depends both on political views and local circumstances. According to the results of a World Bank study (2000), LGs in Latvia carry out almost the same range of functions as local authorities in the north European countries, whose revenue share reaches 25 per cent of GDP. In Latvia, LG revenue share is only approximately 10.5 per cent of GDP. In addition, the central government often delegates new functions without providing any supplementary funding. It is important that the costs of the existing functions are assessed, inconsistencies in the normative acts eliminated and delegation of unfunded mandates prevented.

Civil participation is important to be able to move towards well-functioning local autonomy, and efforts are being made by LGs to involve their residents in the process of decision making. LG law stipulates that meetings of councils and committees must be open. Also, the Law on the Management of Budget and Finances stipulates that local budgets must be publicly available. It is a common practice to hold meetings with residents prior to the adoption of the budget. Furthermore, to ensure improved information exchange, as of 2002, LGs are required to prepare an annual public report.

INDEPENDENT LG REVENUE SOURCES

One of the goals of the government of Latvia is to ensure the country's financial sustainability. Thus, it is essential to implement up-to-date and internationally recognised fiscal policy. One of the most important objectives of such policy is a limitation of fiscal deficit. Fulfilment of state fiscal policy directly affects local budget revenue. Paragraph 9 of the Charter suggests that the structure of LG funds is divided in two broader categories: own funds and funds managed at the discretion of local jurisdiction, and financial transfers.

Prior to 1995, the structure of local revenues has been changed every year. After regaining independence, LGs began to share revenue derived from various taxes, reaching agreement on exact distribution every year. Distribution of grants and earmarked grants, for example, has been notably inconsistent. At the same time, several monetary reforms have been implemented – from Soviet roubles to Latvian roubles, then to Latvian Lats (LVL). During this period inflation went up significantly. In 1992, due to high inflation, the budget had to be approved twice yearly. LGs received earmarked grants, as well as donations for the allowances to the poor, because of increased energy prices. In 1993, the proportion of shared state taxes (profit, personal income and turnover taxes) that LGs receive was changed.[2]

In 1994, equalisation of LG finances was introduced. The equalisation mechanism was changed every year until 1998, when a more permanent Law on Equalisation of Local Government Finances was passed. In 1994, LGs were assigned a share of the personal income tax (PIT) and grants from the equalisation fund, as well as earmarked grants for investments.[3] According to the Law on Taxes and Duties, the tax and fee system consists of state taxes, state fees and local fees. Each tax has its separate law, which must match the umbrella law. State taxes are paid in the state budget or distributed between the state and local budgets, based on the respective tax law. None of these taxes is stipulated as an LG tax. For example, since 1997, Republican cities receive 100 per cent of real estate tax (prior to 1998 the land and property tax[4]), 73 per cent of PIT[5], 25 per cent of the lottery and gambling tax[6], and 60 per cent of the natural resource tax (see Table 10.1).[7]

Table 10.1 The structure of LG revenues from taxes, 2005, LVL and EUR (million)

	LVL	EUR
Shared taxes	376.0	535.0
personal income tax	370.6	527.3
lottery and gambling tax	3.2	4.6
natural resource tax	2.2	3.1
Own taxes	61.6	87.6
real estate tax	61.6	87.6

Source: State Treasury.

The State Revenue Service carries out administration of the PIT, except in three LGs – Riga, Liepaja and Ventspils – which carry out individual tax administration. The tax revenue share transferred to local budgets within the calendar year is based on the share coefficient assigned to each LG of PIT collected in the state two years prior to the calendar year.[8] The situation in which LGs are not involved in the PIT administration does not provoke the interest of local authorities in the economic development of their territories. LGs have no access to information about PIT revenues that will actually be collected from their residents. That precludes them from making a timely response to economic changes. Paragraph 3 of the Charter states that at least part of the financial means of local governments must be obtained through local taxes and fees, and that LG must be allowed to stipulate specific tax rates within the limits established by the central law. Latvia has accepted this paragraph, but none of the taxes is defined as a local tax in Latvian legislation and local authorities have no authority to adjust tax rates. Until 1995, however, the LGs were allowed to introduce new local taxes. As far as the real estate tax is concerned, LGs may change the tax rate, but only by decreasing it.[9] In some LG chairmen's opinion, it is necessary for LGs to also be able to increase the tax rate.

Since 1997, district governments have no own tax revenue. Ninety per cent of the district government income consists of grants and earmarked grants. Since 1997, local budgets have been divided into the base budget (consisting of tax and non-tax payments and transfers) and special budgets. Until 1997, special budgets were considered additional budgets. Earmarked grants and general grants form around 26 per cent of LG revenue, of which only around 7 per cent are general grants.

According to the World Bank (2000), Latvia has been ahead of many other transition countries in making an optimal choice of revenue instruments for local governments. The choice of both the personal income and property tax as major sources of revenue is appropriate, because the tax bases of those tend to be relatively stable during business cycles of the economy; they are not easily exportable; and there tends to be a more identifiable linkage between payment of these taxes and benefits received by taxpayers from local public services. Non-tax revenues consist of local fees and user charges (that is, revenue from entrepreneurship and property, local duties, payments for paid services offered by budget institutions and other local revenue, and revenue from properties rented from the local government), penalties and sanctions and other non-tax income (revenue from apartment and municipal services). Non-tax revenues represent, on average, 25 per cent of the total revenue (see Table 10.2).

Table 10.2 The structure of revenues from non-tax sources, 2005, LVL and EUR (million)

	LVL	EUR
Revenue from entrepreneurship and property	0.9	1.3
State and local fees and payments	54.2	77.1
incl. local fees	2.3	3.3
state fees that are transferred to local budgets	1.3	1.8
revenue from paid services offered by budget institutions (user charges)	48.6	69.2
Penalties and sanctions	1.2	1.7
Other non-tax income	25.7	36.6
income from apartment and communal services	13.0	18.5

Source: State Treasury.

According to the Law on Taxes and Duties, local authorities may impose local fees in accordance with the procedures prescribed in the CoM Regulations on the Order in which LGs may impose local fees. Such fees may be charged for official documents prepared by the LG council; events of a recreational nature in public places; vacation and tourist accommodation; trade in public places; keeping all types of animals; using transport within special regime zones; placement of advertisements, posters and announcements in public places; keeping boats, motorboats and sailboats; use of LG insignia; and construction permits.

District councils may, in accordance with procedures prescribed in the CoM regulations, impose in their administrative territory a fee for issuing official documents (and for certified copies thereof) prepared by a regional council or for utilisation of the regional government's regalia.

The term 'user charge' is not defined in Latvian legislation, although it is used in laws and regulations. The form and size of the local service fee are defined by the council. The structure of revenues varies depending on the type of LG: the biggest share of revenue in Republican cities is formed by shared revenue, approximately 55 per cent. In contrast, 50 per cent of regional government revenues come from state grants and 48 per cent from subsidies of the equalisation fund. Lowest level governments receive 37 per cent from shared revenue.

GRANT TRANSFERS

The Law on Local Government Budgets stipulates that in order to strengthen the economic base of the regions and ensure the performance of state functions, the state budget may assign general and earmarked grants for the implementation of certain tasks. There are two sources of donations: the state budget and the equalisation fund, which is formed from state budget allocations and payments made by the most affluent LGs. There are no mixed earmarked grants that may be freely assigned either for operational costs or capital investments.

Based on the theory of fiscal decentralisation, income from the PIT is a transfer payment from the central government (rather than local own revenue), since this tax is administered by the central government except for the three biggest cities. In addition, both the tax rate and base are determined by the central government. Because the tax represents the biggest share of LG revenue, both local governments and finance specialists in Latvia and abroad consider it a local own revenue. Thus, official publications offer different definitions of the tax. OECD publications, for example, consider it a transfer payment or a shared tax, and Latvia is characterised as a centralised state. On the other hand, the EC in its official publications defines this revenue as own revenue and Latvia is ranked among highly decentralised countries.

The structure of earmarked grants has been relatively constant since 1997. The biggest share is formed by grants for teachers' salaries, representing around 90–95 per cent of total earmarked grants annually. Every year, the state budget allocates grants for investments in LGs within the Public Investment Program (PIP), and grants for preparation of the territorial plans and amalgamation projects. However, the share of these earmarked grants is inconsiderable.

General purpose grants are divided into three groups: grants for implementation of the Law on Administrative Territorial Reform, grants for regional development planning, and equalisation grants. The central government controls the use of grants through generally established procedures, that is, by the State Audit assessments of the appropriateness of the use of grants.

Earmarked grants may be broken up into three groups: for education activities (90 per cent of total), investments and other purposes. The major share of the grants for education is assigned to institutions of general secondary education, professional education and special education. These grants also provide for the partial payment of salaries of teachers of music, and art schools and mandatory state social protection instalments. Since 1995, earmarked grants for investments may be obtained through the PIP. The programme is prepared by the Ministry of Economy for the next three years, taking into account priorities, financial strategy and economic development prognoses. To prepare and submit a proposal, LG needs to follow the MoE issued methodology for preparing investment project proposals. Although the PIP is prepared every year for a three-year period, funding is approved only for the upcoming economic year. In recent years the state budget funds represented around one-fourth of the PIP, the remaining share consisting of loans, foreign grants and other funds (including a co-financing share provided by local governments). Unfortunately, for several years a practice of assigning earmarked investments continued in parallel with the PIP earmarked investments. When approving the annual budget, politicians designate their own 'political investments', that is funding for various state institutions and local governments, in many cases even without a proper project proposal.

The finance equalisation system plays an important role to ensure equal development opportunities of LGs. There are rich vicinities, whose wealth comes from their economic and geographical position, and there are territories unable to perform their functions using their own revenues. The equalisation system was introduced in Latvia in 1995 and consists of regulations on financial necessity (or expenditure need), and revenue equalisation. The system is partially based on inter-municipal financing (horizontal equalisation) and partially on general state grants (vertical equalisation). Equalisation of LG expenditures and revenues is done separately for the three levels of LGs – Republican cities, rural and regional governments.[10]

Equalisation is carried out in an integrated way by comparing the expenditure needs and revenue of each of the 553 LGs. Those with a revenue basis of 10 per cent higher than the calculated expenditure need contribute 45 per cent of the surplus to the equalisation system. Those with revenues below 100 per cent (for the regions), 95 per cent (for the Republican cities) and 90 per cent (for the towns/*pagasts*/*novads*) of the expenditure need, receive grants from the equalisation fund, which brings their budgets up to 100 per cent, 95 per cent and 90 per cent of their expenditure needs, respectively. Ceilings mean that LGs between 100 per cent, 95 per cent or 90 per cent (according to the type of the LG) and 110 per cent of the expenditure need covered by the revenues, neither contribute to nor receive grants from the system (a so-called 'neutral zone').

To achieve the equalisation of LG finances, the first step is to determine total financial need in the country. The LALRG and the Ministry of Finance (MoF) do not have a common view on the methodology. The MoF uses Paragraph 8 of the Law, which stipulates that 'total minimum financial necessity of local governments in the economic year must be calculated in the process of preparation of the annual state budget law and must be included in the annual negotiation protocol between the CoM and the LALRG. In doing so, the following factors must be taken into account: total LGs' financial necessity calculated during the budget preparation year; forecast of the state macroeconomic figures for the economic year; re-division of functions between LGs, as well as between LGs and government for the economic year; and priorities set for the economic year'. The experience from recent years shows that the MoF, in order to determine the total financial necessity of LGs for the economic year, applies the inflation index on the previous year's financial necessity. LALRG, however, when determining total financial necessity, follows Paragraph 13 of the Law, that is: 'total local government expenditures for carrying out the functions of local governments, defined by the LG law, and which are not financed by earmarked grants'. Despite the efficiency of the Equalisation Law, the parties have not achieved agreement on the calculation of total financial necessity. Problem may possibly be solved by issuing the CoM regulations that establish an acceptable methodology for calculating financial necessity.

The system of equalisation of expenditure needs is based on the following main criteria: LG type; number of residents; number of children up to the age of six; number of young residents in the age from seven to 18; number of residents above the working age; number of children in orphanages; and number of dwellers in guest-houses and centres for the elderly. The first five criteria are real ('objective') criteria, that is, those that LGs cannot influence, whereas criteria 6 and 7 are so-called 'quasi objective', as these are based on number of children and people in the centres for the elderly based on 1 January 1998 data (see Phare, 1999). The last two criteria have been developed to adjust for the fact that some local authorities take care of a larger number of orphanages and elderly people due to the special service centres founded under the previous, communist system.

The equalisation system is based on calculations of revenue from two taxes (personal income and real estate tax) prior to the start of the equalisation year. If tax revenue appears smaller or larger than planned, corrections of equalisation grant amounts are not made. It is interesting to note that payments into the fund are positively related to per capita gross regional product, a measure of fiscal capacity. This is what is intended by the equalisation formula. Payments from the Fund do not go to those LGs with lower fiscal capacity, but rather to those with higher expenditure needs, as proxied by the percentage of population below and above the working age. This result is also largely intended by the current equalisation formula. Payments into the Fund are mainly intended to equalise fiscal capacity, while payments from the Fund are more needs-based. The current mechanism provides a high degree of equalisation and it addresses what otherwise could be a significant problem, given the large fiscal disparities existing among LGs (World Bank, 2000). Whether or not such a high degree of equalisation is needed or whether it is excessive are difficult questions to answer. What degree of equalisation is desirable depends on the level of national solidarity and societal norms. The current degree of equalisation may be considered excessive, if wealthier communities are equalised below the average of poorer communities. Excessive equalisation may have the effect of reducing revenue mobilisation efforts by those communities that are brought up to a national average. It may also discourage revenue mobilisation by those LGs that have to contribute to the fund. An even harder question to answer is whether the high degree of equalisation may slow down national economic growth by diverting resources from areas with higher economic growth potential to areas with a lower potential.

LG EXPENDITURES

The purpose of LG revenue is to cover expenditures to enable implementing mandatory functions and voluntary initiatives stipulated by the LG law. Decisions on revenue use are made by LGs independently, except on the use of earmarked grants. As is the case with total revenue, Latvia's LG expenditures as a share of the GDP have remained relatively stable since 1997, at around 10 per cent. Comparing the LG expenditure share of GDP to that of other economies with a unitary intergovernmental system, Latvia is similar to other transition countries. This is well below the level prevailing in the neighbouring Nordic countries, often over 20 per cent of GDP. This higher rate is often cited as a model case for the reform of local governance in Latvia (World Bank, 2000). The share of capital expenditures has been gradually increasing since 1997 when it was at 12.1 per cent, reaching 21.5 per cent in 2002. The loan repayment share is not substantial – about 0.5 per cent. Based on the research of the authors, as a percentage of overall LG expenditure, the total expenditure of regions is approximately 9 per cent. Expenditures are primarily assigned for education (52.7 per cent in 2000), social care and administration. The expenditures of Republican cities are also primarily used for education (40.9 per cent in 2000), housing and community amenities (33.7 per cent), social care (8.4 per cent) and administration (8.3 per cent). As in the Republican cities, the expenditures of rural and town budgets also go primarily to education (49.8 per cent in 2000), housing and community services (23.9 per cent), administration (11.7 per cent) and sports and culture (6.4 per cent), less is assigned for social care (5.7 per cent).

As demonstrated by the preceding paragraphs, LG expenditure assignments still need to become more efficient, that is, through clarification of functions and their financing, and cost reduction. In Latvia, the annual budget expenditure cannot exceed revenue, which consists of the current year's planned budget revenue and the previous year's budget surplus, and loans. In the early and mid-1990s, several foreign finance companies issued loans to LGs with a state guarantee for improving district heating, water supply and wastewater treatment facilities. In many cases, the loans had favourable terms – no interest, deferred payments, and so on. But now some LGs have problems repaying those loans, and stabilisation has been launched for a number of them. Another fact that contributes to loan repayment difficulties is lack of experience in development of economically feasible business plans until the mid-1990s. Moreover, in some LGs, the number of utility users had decreased. Since 1999, 14 local governments have been stabilised and 13 stabilisation loans issued in the amount of LVL 3.97 million (EUR 5.65 million).

The Law on Stabilisation of Local Government Finance, Land Utilisation, and the Supervision of Financial Activities of Local Governments was passed in May 1998. Although the initial intention of the law was to use a broad range of financial and administrative measures to prevent a crisis, the law, in fact, envisages only one – a state stabilisation loan. LG finances must be stabilised if at least one of the following is observed:

- the LG's debt obligations with repayment scheduled for the current fiscal year plus debt incurred in the previous year exceed 20 per cent of the total local budget of the current fiscal year;
- the LG cannot or because of demonstrable conditions will not be able to settle its debt obligations;
- the LG's debt exceeds market value of its assets.

Local government financial stabilisation is implemented using LG financial sources; state budget (stabilisation loans); and donations, grants and other, including foreign, assistance. Thus, it may be concluded that LGs in Latvia cannot become bankrupt, as the mechanism of stabilisation does not allow this. Bad borrowing practices may be encouraged by provision of stabilisation loans. On the other hand, the LGs use stabilisation as a very last resort, as none of the LG chairmen wants to be seen as a chairman whose activities have brought the LG to a difficult financial situation requiring supervisory intervention from the political hierarchy.

ACCOUNTING RULES, REGULATIONS AND LG BUDGETING PROCESS

At the initial stage of the budget preparation, the government prepares a document that reflects fiscal and economic targets from a medium-term macroeconomic and fiscal perspective. Latvia's LGs are involved in the budget preparation from the very beginning. State budget preparation starts in February, when sector ministries submit 'base expenditure' calculations. During the budget preparation, the LALRG meets with the Minister of Finance every month to discuss LG revenue, including tax projections, amounts of earmarked grants, the size of state budget grants to be assigned to the equalisation fund, and the total limit of LG loans and guarantees. The most sensitive issue during the negotiations relates to the calculation of equalisation of LG finances. LALRG has monthly Finance and Economics Committee meetings, during which LGs are informed about the status of negotiations and introduced to the calculations. Budget projections are electronically transmitted to all LGs.

LGs prepare, approve and execute their budgets independently, in accordance with the legislation. Preparation and approval of the budget is the responsibility of the LG chairman. There is an established procedure for state budget formation, but local governments can choose their own approach. The most commonly used budgets include the functions budget, structural-units budget and programmes budget.

Accounting procedures in Latvia are defined by the Law on Accounting, which is harmonised in accordance with the EU directives. The law stipulates that accounting must be arranged so that a third party qualified in accounting is able to receive a clear view of the financial situation of the enterprise and its economic activities within a specified period of time, as well as being able to observe the start of each economic activity and follow its roadmap.

LGs submit to the State Treasury an annual report consisting of a balance sheet, cash flow statement, revenue and expenditure account, local government liabilities and material stock resources, and base operational indicators and explanations. The Law on Budget and Finance Management stipulates that the State Treasury at year-end closes all accounts opened within the current economic year. State base budget accounts are opened for state-financed budget institutions in the next economic year, based on the allocations assigned by the financing plans. It causes problems for LGs that have not used assigned investment funds within that year. The unused balance is not transferable to the next year. Authors believe that earmarked grants for investments should be transferable to the following year's budget.

SUPERVISION AND CONTROL: THE STATE AUDIT

Different terminology is used when talking about 'management control' and internal control'. However, these terms have the same meaning as 'audit' – a term used in normative acts, which, in fact, replaces the word 'control' in Latvia. Based on the management theory, the functions of a manager include planning, organising, controlling and motivating. The term 'management control' is often used to describe the third of these functions; the term 'internal control' is more related to the revision of finances (Urban Institute, 2000b).

Lack of internal control is the weakest point in Latvia's LG management system. Until 2001, LGs were required to appoint Audit Commissions, whereas now they can decide on the need of such commissions. Audit Commissions may be considered external control bodies, as they are elected proportionally to membership in each political party. If professional criteria are not considered when electing the Audit Commission, such a commission is not able to ensure the performance of duties assigned to it, and their audits are more formal and do not bring real benefits. This reality is the main reason why LGs may choose whether to appoint the commission.

With reference to external audits, Latvia's system is very strict. In 1993, an independent collegial institution, State Audit (SA), was established to assume responsibility for auditing the status of state and local property (including financial means) and related operations. The responsibility of the SA is to perform supervision so that collection and use, as well as operations related to the state and the LGs' base and special budgets, are lawful and useful. SA controls all state and local institutions, enterprises, business enterprises and physical persons possessing state or local properties financed by state or LG funds, or which carry out the state or local government (public) procurement.

LGs at least annually must invite an audit company or sworn auditor to perform an audit, and pay fees specially assigned in the budget for that purpose. After the receipt of an auditor's opinion, the LG submits it along with the annual report to the SA. The Director of the Local Governments Audit

Department of the SA, based on the sworn auditor's opinion, issues his assessment and submits it to the LG for submission to the State Treasury. The Local Governments Audit Department in accordance with the approved plan performs up to 50 financial audits annually, thus also testing the efficiency of sworn auditors. Control over LGs' activities is very strict. If one happened to break the law (used earmarked grants for other purposes than prescribed, for instance), SA may impose penalties.

From the above, it may be derived that the financial control system in Latvia is well established. In the authors' opinion the SA, however, must not control local activities from the viewpoint of usefulness, since the local authority makes its decisions independently.

FUTHER DEVELOPMENTS: LG AND FINANCIAL MARKETS

Even after regaining independence, funding for local investments was assigned in a centralised way. Starting from 1993, LGs started to borrow funds from local and foreign credit institutions independently. The first Law on Budget and Financial Management (passed in March 1994) did not set any limits on LG borrowings; it only stated that the MoF provides short-term loans with one-year repayment to the LGs for liquidity financing. According to the information of the LALRG, commercial bank lending to LGs without central government intervention has a relatively short history, that is, from 1995 to 1997. It was the time when banks had a wide network and felt comfortable lending to LGs outside the capital Riga, as local branches were in a good position to obtain necessary credit information. During this period the loan portfolio grew both as a percentage of total loans and in LVL terms. From 1995 to 1996, gross loans made by banks to all sectors grew by 12.9 per cent, of which the growth in LG loans accounted for 31 per cent.

During 1996 and early 1997, interest rates steadily declined and banks were able to lend to LGs for up to two years with fixed interest rates ranging from 9 to 20 per cent. There have been no reported cases of default related to loans issued by Latvian banks during the period of 1995–97. Problems emerged, however, with foreign loan repayments after 1997. The main reason for that was unrealistic business plans. For example, it was necessary to launch the stabilisation process in the township *Strenči*. In 1996, the municipality, using a UNIBANK of Denmark interest-free loan of USD 2.9 million, reconstructed its heating supply system and water treatment facilities and built a solid waste plant. The project initially was estimated to generate revenue and projected as a source of repayment revenues from increased tariffs. In reality, heat consumption decreased by 40 per cent of that estimated in the business plan. The local government appeared to be in a situation where nearly the entire budget would go on the credit repayment. As a result, the stabilisation process was initiated.[11]

Another reason for problems with loan repayment was related to the assessment of municipal creditworthiness. Until 1996, there was no separate institution assessing the financial capacity of the LGs, and the MoF was performing this function. Before implementing larger scale projects, credit institutions occasionally asked for an opinion from a sector ministry (most often the Ministry of Economy), as well as the MoF. In many cases international credit institutions issued loans without a state guarantee, and in some cases loans were given directly to the LG enterprises without an LG guarantee. Since LGs lacked experience in commercial lending and many finance specialists lacked training in long-term budget planning, LGs were not always able to correctly assess their repayment capacity. Furthermore, foreign credit institutions offered loans with a grace period of two to three years, which (given the expectation of an economic growth) did not seem risky. Since the banking crisis of the mid-1990s (with the exception of the period of the Russian crisis), macroeconomic indicators have improved significantly which certainly, has an impact on LG borrowing. That was seen very clearly during the Russian crisis, when interest rates for loans doubled. Another important aspect that LGs often did not consider when planning larger investment projects was the decrease of utility service users after the breakdown of Soviet centralised communal services. This led to a drop in fee collection rates and, therefore, difficulties in repaying debts.

After Latvia overcame the banking crisis of 1995, the government decided to tighten fiscal and monetary policy. As local budgets are a part of the public budget, the CoM established the Council of Control and Supervision of Local Government Loans and Guarantees (hereinafter Council) in 1996. The Council's main tasks included supervision of local financial activities related to loans and guarantees, and planned loans and guarantees, and advising LGs on their financial operations. One of the purposes of establishing the Council was to create a unified recording system of LG liabilities in the country. Based on the Council's decision, the LGs are allowed to take short-term and long-term loans. Short-term loans may be used to cover a temporary deficit – these loans are made exclusively from the national budget and have to be repaid by the end of the financial year. Short-term loans are generally made to purchase fuel for district heating. Long-term loans are used for implementation of economic and social programmes requiring investments. Depending on the state and municipal priorities prevailing at the time, the purposes of the loans change from year to year.

Based on the Law on LG Budgets, LGs may take out loans in Latvia or abroad by issuing bonds or signing loan agreements. In 2002, however, amendments were passed by the Parliament to prohibit issuing LG bonds and stipulating that all planned leasing deals and long-term financial liabilities must be submitted for review by the Council. The Law was also amended with a clause requiring that 'local governments make loans by signing an agreement with the State Treasury'. The Minister of Finance, taking into account an LG's application for a specific project, may approve another lender, if its terms are more favourable than the ones for loans issued by the state budget. These latest amendments limit LGs' rights to free access to local and foreign capital markets, contradicting Paragraph 8 of Section 9 of the Charter. This paragraph is the only one not accepted by the Parliament.

Since the liabilities of LGs are included when calculating total national liabilities and the fiscal deficit, a maximum increase in LG loans and guarantees, including stabilisation loans, has been defined since 1997 by the annual state budget law (see Table 10.3). The total increase of LGs' loans and guarantees is fixed in the protocol of negotiations between the LALRG and the MoF. Notably, agreement on the limit has not been reached in any of the past years.

Table 10.3 Total permitted increase of LG loans and guarantees, 1997–2005 (in LVL million)

Year	Total	Loans (including internal)	Including stabilisation	Guarantees
1997	46.8	46.8	n.a.	n.a.
1998	38.0	20.0	8.0	n.a.
1999	10.6 +1.75	8.1	0.35	2.5
2000	18.5	11.5	0.5	7.0
2001	17.4	10.4	1.0	7.0
2002	25.5	16.5	1.0	9.0
2003	24.6	15.6	1.0	9.0
2004	29.3	20.3	1.0	9.0
2005	43.3	29.3	1.0	14.0

Source: State Treasury.

To ensure fulfilment of LGs' liabilities in the case of unforeseeable conditions, the law specifies that after receipt of the authorisation of the Minister of Finance, total loans may be increased by LVL 1.75 million (EUR 2.49 million). Latvian commercial banks have always tried to compete with the State

Treasury, but the proportion of commercial bank loans to LGs has remained insignificant (at 5 to 10 per cent) after 1997.

Currently, only the Law on Stabilisation stipulates that an LG's finances must be 'stabilised' if its debt obligations for the regular fiscal year and for the previous year exceed 20 per cent of the total LG budget for the regular fiscal year. In Latvia, loans represent the greatest share of debt liabilities, the majority of which are long-term loans. On average, short-term loans for budget management represent 3 to 5 per cent of budget expenditures. Another 10 per cent is loans for the purchase of heating fuel. As mentioned before, the practice of issuing bonds has not yet been developed.

Analysis shows that there is no direct link between debt liabilities and size or location of local government. As mentioned in the section on stabilisation, there are LGs with large debt liabilities in all regions. Debt liabilities are closely related to LGs' fiscal policies, management and even the thinking and accountability of the leaders. Along with those that successfully implement their fiscal policy, at least half of Latvian LGs have never taken loans. This fact may be explained by various factors, including the consequence of 'Soviet thinking', when it was assumed that borrowing is a bad thing.

CONCLUSION

It is difficult to assess the level of efficiency of the system of intergovernmental fiscal relations in Latvia, or even degree of local autonomy. First, the main source of LG revenue in Latvia, the PIT, is defined in different ways. OECD publications, which characterise Latvia as a centralised state, consider PIT a transfer payment or shared tax. On the contrary, official publications of the EC define PIT as 'own revenue' and rank Latvia among the highly decentralised countries. Latvian LG and finance specialists consider the PIT as local government own revenue.

There are clearly a number of positive aspects to the intergovernmental fiscal system in Latvia. Decentralisation of functions has been implemented and many critical functions are delegated to local governments. These functions cover most of the responsibilities that must be implemented by authorities in close proximity to the population. Also, Latvia has established one of the most effective central and local government negotiation systems in Europe, a fact proven by the budget adoption process. In the tax area, the PIT and real estate taxes represent a reasonable choice for the main sources of local government revenue. The equalisation system of local government finance is stable, and Latvia has established a strong, unified control system for local governments, institutions and entities. The State Audit ensures, for example, efficient control over local finances and the Council of Control and Supervision of LG Loans and Guarantees effectively supervises the limits of borrowing.

There still exist a number of negative aspects in the intergovernmental fiscal system that need to be addressed. Funding for assigned public service functions is insufficient. Local governments in Latvia perform almost all the same functions as the Northern European countries, but the Latvian local LGs' share in the GDP is only half of that of the Northern European countries. Therefore, when delegating new functions to local governments, Latvia's central government must ensure an adequate funding.

Tax policy affecting LGs needs to be improved, since local governments currently have limited rights to define tax rates and district governments have no tax income. First of all, local governments need to be involved in the administration of the PIT. Moreover, LGs must be allowed to determine real estate tax rates, and the corporate income tax needs to be defined as a tax of the regions or districts.

The fact that earmarked grants represent the largest share of total grants also is not favourable. In the field of equalisation grants, after the implementation of regional reform, a separate equalisation systems need to be introduced for the lowest level LGs and district governments.

Latvian LGs presently have limited rights in attracting credit resources. Section (8) of paragraph 9 of the Charter needs to be ratified by the Parliament, and local governments must be allowed to borrow freely in local capital markets.

NOTES

1. Adopted by the Parliament in 1994.
2. Law on the State Budget for 1993.
3. Law on State Budget for 1994.
4. Law on Real Estate Tax.
5. Law on PIT.
6. Law on Lottery and Gambling Duty and Tax.
7. Law on Natural Resources Tax.
8. Regulations of the CoM on Order in which PIT is transferred to the LG Budgets.
9. Art. 5 of Law on Real Estate Tax.
10. Law on Equalisation of LG Finances.
11. Based on the information prepared and submitted by the MoF to the Commission for the Stabilisation of LG Finances.

BIBLIOGRAPHY

Balcuns, A., M. Priede, M. Pukis and A. Strazda (2001), *The Country Report – Regulation, Competition and Contracting in the Local Government Utility and Communal Sector*, Budapest: Open Society Institute – Local Government and Public Service Reform Initiative.

Budget laws (1991–2001).

DEXIA (1997), *Local Finance in the Fifteen Countries of the European Union*, Brussels and Paris: DEXIA.

Phare, The National Association of Local Authorities in Denmark (1999), *Report on the Present System of Local Government Grants and Equalisation in Latvia and Future Possibilities for Changes*, Copenhagen: Phare.

The Urban Institute (2000a), *Analysis of the Legal Framework, Local Government Management and Finance Project*, Washington, DC: The Urban Institute.

The Urban Institute (2000b), *Manual of Municipal Finance Management and Accounting; Report on Municipal Management and Finance Project*, Washington, DC: Urban Institute.

Vanags, E. (1997), *Organisation and Economics of Local Governments*, Riga: The University of Latvia.

The World Bank (2000), *Latvia Strengthening Fiscal Decentralisation and Balanced Development: Current Situation and Policy Options for Reform*, Washington, DC: The World Bank.

11. Local government finance in Lithuania

Gerda Žigienė, Jadvyga Čiburienė and Mark W. Chandler

INTRODUCTION AND HISTORICAL OVERVIEW

The roots of self-government in Lithuania are centuries old. History shows that municipalities were formed in Lithuania during 1918–19. However, their roots go back to the 13th century, when self-governments formed rapidly, following the example of German towns, which were based on Magdeburg Rights or their modifications (Stačiokas, 1991a). The Law on Municipalities was in effect in Lithuania between the World Wars. These municipalities were eliminated after WWII when the USSR occupied Lithuania (1941–89). Control by the Communist Party enveloped all levels and areas of state administration, which meant that municipalities had no independence and decision-making powers (Baltušnikienė, 2004).

Once the independence of the country was re-established in 1990, the Supreme Council of Lithuania, elected by the free will of its citizens, formed conditions for creating a democratic state with a decentralised government. The transformation from a centralised party-controlled government was possible by virtue of the Provisional Basic Law of the Republic of Lithuania. Town and regional councils were elected at the end of March 1990 by virtue of the Law on the Fundamentals of Local Government. Executive boards of towns and regions were formed later.

Realistically, however, local governments still conveyed a weak presence. Municipal institutions continued being considered a composite part of the state government and a unit of its administrative bodies. Local governments owned no property or had independent budgets of their own; they were dependent on the Government. The passing of the Constitution of the Republic of Lithuania in 1992 provided an essential breakthrough in the system for local government. The Constitution contains six articles on local self-government. Norms for the

Constitution were composed reflecting the European Charter on Local Self-Government provisions and requirements. Passage of the Constitution provided the basis for an essential change in the legal system, regulating local government in Lithuania. New types of laws were drafted and passed with regard to the experience of Western democratic countries. These were: the Law on the Government Representative for regulating legal proceedings of local government institutions (in 1993); the Law on Local Self Government and the Law on Elections to Local Government Councils; and the Law on the Territorial Administrative Units of the Republic of Lithuania and their Boundaries (in 1994).

BASIC LEGAL FRAMEWORK AND LOCAL GOVERNMENT FINANCE REGULATIONS

The reform of the economic system took place in 1990 after the statehood of Lithuania was re-established and market relationships began forming. Earlier centralised procedures for taxation were quickly changed to new relations for taxing. The main features of the Law on the Fundamentals of Local Government involved the elimination of any sort of intent by state governing bodies to regulate the functioning of the local government system and its organisational and social relations by their normative acts or instructions (Stačiokas, 1991b). The Law on Budget Structure of the Republic of Lithuania, passed on 29 June 1990 (Law No. I-430), established the structure for the state budget, the taxes that comprise the budget, and procedures for its formation and use. The new financial system for the country was becoming institutionalised (the budget, its formation, taxes, banks, finances of economic entities); meanwhile, administrative subordination of economic entities to USSR governing structures were being eliminated. The changes in administrative territorial divisions and residential areas are shown in Table 11.1. Command economy administrative territorial units were changed from the beginning of 1990 and a two-level system with five types of administrative territorial units was created: towns, cities, townships, administrative regions and rural districts. This system was criticised from its introduction because it was based on the territorial division that existed during the Soviet period. Stasys Kropas, a local government expert, defined the deficiencies of this period as (1) the absence of a coherent system of regional and local government, (2) undefined functions of the central and local government, (3) the absence of a realistic economic-financial base for local governments, (4) an imperfect system of internal administration in local governments, (5) an insufficiently clear strategy of local government development and (6) undefined rights and duties of local government employees (see: Bekšta and Petkevičius, 2000).

The reform of administrative units of the territory of Lithuania has been divided into two stages. Under Stage 1, in 1995, ten new higher administrative units, that is regions, were formed; rural districts were abolished and local administration units (elderships) were created. The Law on the Territorial Administrative Units and their Boundaries was supplemented in 1999 and 60 municipalities were created. Under Stage 2, it is planned to increase the number of municipalities to 93.

Table 11.1 Administrative territorial divisions and settlements (as of 1 January 2007)

Administrative territorial units	1990–1993	1994–1995	1996	1997	1998	1999–2000	2000–2003	2004–2005
First level:								
1. Towns and / cities	92/11	92/11	92/11	92/11	108			
2. Townships	22	19						
3. Administrative regions	44	44						
Second level:								
4. Rural districts	426	427						
5. Regions/Counties			10	10	10	10	10	10
6. Districts			44	44	44	44		
7. Local administration units (elderships)			446	449	449			
8. Municipalities						56	60	60
9. Settlements: cities and towns						107	106	103

Source: Statistical Office, 1993–2006.

The average size of a municipality, excluding the capital, Vilnius, is approximately 60,000 inhabitants. This unusually high average population is due to the extensive area of each municipality; 80 per cent of the territories extend between 1,000 and 2,000 km^2. Almost two-thirds of municipalities have between 30,000 and 100,000 inhabitants.

The amendment to the Law on Local Self-government (2000) provided one of the key elements of reform: it distinguishes a functional division of self-government into autonomous, delegated (limited autonomous), state (transferred to self-government) and conventional (for the full list of the functions, see Table 11.2).

Table 11.2 Distribution of functions according to levels of government

Functions	Munici-palities	Regional/ District or Urban Governments	Central Government	Remarks
I. Education				
1. Preschool	X			Governmental institutions can establish educational institutions
2. Primary	X			
3. Secondary	X			
4.Technical	X	X	X	
II. Social Welfare				
1. Nurseries	X		X	
2. Kindergartens	X		X	
3. Welfare Homes	X	X		Can be private or affiliated with religious organisation
4. Personal Services for Elderly and Handicapped	X			
5. Social Services and Social Housing	X			
III. Health Services				
1. Primary Health Care	X			Can be private
2. Health Protection	X			
3. Hospitals	X	X	X	Can be private
4. Public Health			X	
IV. Culture, Leisure, Sports	X	X	X	
V. Public Utilities	X			Electricity and Central heating – decentralisation in process

Source: Bekšta and Petkevičius, 2000.

DEMOCRATIC LEGITIMACY AND FINANCIAL REPORTING

The main territorial administrative units are counties and municipalities. All municipalities of the country are at one level. The following institutions exist at city and county municipalities: the council is an institution of representation that resident voters elect; the mayor holds the executive power and the controller handles control. Council members of a municipality are elected for a three-year term of office (two years until 1997) by a secret ballot according to the proportional electoral system. The council elects a mayor from amongst its members; the mayor then heads the council. This means that the representative and executive powers of governing are not separated. Quite possibly, executive power is considered to be above the representative branch of governing. The mayor is even able to perform a triple role: executor of the executive branch, head of the council when a collegial executive institution is formed, and head of the council as the representative institution. The mayor is directly responsible and accountable to the council that elected him/her for the independent execution of their rights of authority.

Execution of certain functions of the central government is delegated to all municipalities. Municipalities hold an independent level of governing which means the following rights (Astrauskas, Bulovas and Svetikas, 1994): to pass independent decisions; the rights of ownership; independently plan a part of budget expenditures and establish revenues to cover such expenses. The agenda of Municipal Council meetings is announced on the information stand of the municipality and an Internet Web page. The minutes of Council meetings are posted on the municipality's Web page and are published in one of the daily newspapers no later than within five days. The mayor, municipal administration director and controller report to the Council for the past year no less frequently than once a year.

In order to assure the implementation of municipal principles and rights, the municipal council interacts with residents in the following ways: Agendas of Council, Committee and Commission meetings are announced on the Municipality's Internet Web page and one daily newspaper; the mayor reports to voters on the operations of the Municipality and Council no less frequently than once per year. These reports are posted on the Municipality's Internet Web page and published in one daily newspaper. The controller provides an analogical report. Residents are able to state their opinions in an advisory nature on a public issue regarding municipal matters through local resident surveys (announced via public informational media).

LOCAL GOVERNMENT REVENUE SOURCES

Tax Revenue

Until 1998, personal income tax and the profit tax of legal persons were common sources of revenue for both the State budget and local government budgets. The *Seimas* (Parliament) used to set the proportion of appropriations (in percentage terms) for the budgets of local governments. The proportions of personal income tax and the profits tax of legal persons used to be set separately by virtue of the Law on Confirmation of Financial Indicators of the State Budget and the Budgets of Local Governments for the year in question.

Personal income taxes were used largely for financing local authorities, although the national government controls this source. That dichotomy created problems for the efficient administration of the tax. It may be that part of the reason why revenues were so low from personal income tax is that the institution in control of collection, the national government, had a significantly weakened incentive to improve collection, since local authorities receive the vast majority of the revenues. Local governments could have become a strong interest group for an improvement in the efficiency of the administration of personal income tax. The local governments did not, however, take on this role, probably calculating that they would be unable to retain the benefits from such an improvement in collection (Chandler, 2002).

However, as of 2002, the proportion of personal income taxes in Lithuania allocated for local governments is again a share of general taxes after deducting payments to the Compulsory Health Insurance Fund and the state budget (see Table 11.3). The share of personal income taxes allocated to local government budgets has increased each year – 43.46 per cent in 2002; 45.78 per cent in 2003; 47.14 per cent in 2004 and 47.4 per cent in 2005 (Law on Confirmation of Financial Indicators of the State Budget and the Budgets of Local Governments, 2002, 2003, 2004, 2005). Nonetheless, the fact that the personal income tax, which had been within the limits of local government authority became part of common taxes, reflects increased centralisation. At the end of each year, the *Seimas* (Parliament) ratifies the Law on Confirmation of Financial Indicators of the State Budget and the Budgets of Local Governments, which specifies the share of personal income taxes that is to be allocated to all local government budgets in the following year.

Fiscal autonomy means the capacity of local governments to fix the bases and rates of taxation, as well as non-taxation revenues, independently. Local governments in Lithuania are not fully autonomous in the determination of the base and rates of tax revenues. The laws of Lithuania designate taxes and

Table 11.3 The composition of local government revenue

Local government revenue (in LTL thousands)

	1995	1996	1997	1998	1999	2000	2001	2002	2003	2004	2005
Tax revenue	1,765,464	1,998,864	1,968,072	2,739,550	2,904,116	2,829,828	2,803,502	1,393,486	1,417,592	1,502,663	2,001,500
Non-tax revenue	64,697	122,615	139,056	198,625	68,910	74,903	71,326	124,835	72,076	55,533	390,110
Grants	686,366	649,058	862,261	781,775	189,394	351,573	383,544	1,980,617	2,068,149	2,199,469	2,251,440
Total	2,516,527	2,770,537	2,969,389	3,719,950	3,162,420	3,256,304	3,258,372	3,498,938	3,557,817	3,757,665	4,643,050

Local government revenue (in USD thousands)

	1995	1996	1997	1998	1999	2000	2001	2002	2003	2004	2005
Tax revenue	441,366	499,716	492,018	684,888	726029	707,457	700,876	381,745	515,748	594,784	732,809
Non-tax revenue	16,174	30,654	34,764	49,656	17,228	18,726	17,832	34,199	26 ,223	21,981	142,831
Grants	17,592	162,265	215,565	195,444	47,349	87,893	95,886	542,590	752,434	870,594	824,320
Total	629,132	692,634	742,347	929,988	790,605	814,076	814,593	958,534	1,294,405	1,487,359	1,699,960

Composition of local government revenue (per cent)

	1995	1996	1997	1998	1999	2000	2001	2002	2003	2004	2005
Tax revenue	70	72	66	74	92	87	86	40	40	40	43
Non-tax revenue	3	4	5	5	2	2	2	4	2	1	8
Grants	27	23	29	21	6	11	12	57	58	59	49
Total	100	100	100	100	100	100	100	100	100	100	100

Note: *Forecast

Source: Ministry of Finance (1999, 2000, 2001, 2003, 2005a), Projects of Financial Indicators of the State Budget and the Budgets of Local Governments, Vilnius.

other payments to budgets. The State Tax Inspectorate administers all taxes except the value added tax and excise tax, which are administered by Customs, and the state natural resources tax, oil and gas resources tax and pollution tax, which are administered by the Ministry of the Environment.

The taxes and other payments to municipal budgets are only set by law on a multi-annual basis. The State Tax Inspectorate, which comprises the central tax administrator and territorial state tax inspectorates (local tax administrators), administers taxes, that is keeps records of taxpayers' and other payments to the state (municipal) budget, controls computation of payments into the state (municipal) budget, exacts interest for late payment and penalties that are imposed in accordance with tax laws, and also refunds surplus payments and wrongly exacted taxes, interest and penalties. It implements municipal decisions regarding the provision of tax relief, collections and deductions from the budget, apportions taxes and other payments into state and municipal budgets, and so on.

Non-tax Revenues

The municipal council in Lithuania has the right to impose a small part of its own revenues, which is assigned to non-tax revenues. Such revenues include municipal budgetary revenues that are obtained for services rendered and local levies, the base of which is set by the Law on Local Levies. According to this law, a local levy is an obligatory fee, set by a municipal council decision from fee payers, and is in force only in the municipal territory and paid to the municipal budget. By its own decision, the municipal council: (1) sets the rate of the local levy, (2) approves regulations for the local levies, and (3) defines privileges to the taxpayers. The base of these revenues is not wide due to general economic conditions. It is planned to extend the base in the future.

GRANT TRANSFERS

Grants to Lithuanian local governments are funds received only from the central state budget. Such grants are subsidies from the state budget (the amount is set according to the Law on the Methodology of Determination of Municipal Budgetary Revenues) and other funds from the state budget, as determined by the *Seimas* and the Government.

General Grants

There are two main purposes for general grants in Lithuania: levelling/equalisation of municipal personal income tax revenues and levelling of differences in the structure of municipality expenditures which are brought about by objective factors that do not depend on municipal activity. The changing of principles regarding the formation of grants during the transition period in Lithuania could be divided into three stages as follows: (1) until 1998, (2) 1998–2001–02 and (3) after 2001–02.

The principle for the formation of municipal budgets was quite simple until 1998. The process of preparing financial indicators of municipal budgets was based on the volume of expenditures at each municipality for which forecasted revenues were assigned (for certain territories of the municipality). If there were insufficient revenues, then the difference was covered by general grants from the state budget. When forecasted revenues exceeded the amount required to cover the volume of expenditures, the excess was assigned to the state budget. Accordingly, shares of personal income tax and legal income tax assigned to municipal budgets were approved each year.

Overall transfers in Lithuania prior to the 1997–98 equalisation reform increased the disparity in revenues across municipalities in contradiction of a major goal. From 1998, a significant step was made towards the development of a modern, reliable and sustainable system of municipal budget revenues. In 1998, revenues from income taxes of legal persons were allocated to the state budget, whereas personal income taxes became the primary source of revenues for local governments. The formula-based mechanism for levelling revenues, validated by law, became much more objective. A distribution of revenues between the two levels of governing was introduced with respect to World Bank recommendations (Ministry of Finance, Fiscal Policy Course on Internet). The system sets the overall volume of municipal expenditures, as well as the principles and procedure for the allocation, calculation and transfer of revenue sources that are assigned to this volume. The *Seimas* passed the Law on the Methodology of Determination of Municipal Budgetary Revenues based on budgetary co-operation. One of the principles of the law is that the main financial indicators should be established by negotiations between the central government (represented by the Ministry of Finance) and the municipalities (represented by the Municipal Association). The drawback of such a procedure is that the lower-level administrative levels are unclear about the expected amount of revenues. The local government becomes dependent on decisions by the central government on fiscal issues. Another important principle is that the assessment of a municipality's fiscal requirement is based on calculated expenditure requirements which are determined upon a three-year basis. The amount of general grants is determined according to the amount of expenditures expected for the planned years of all municipalities, minus the expected amount of tax and non-tax revenues of all municipalities and minus special grants planned to be assigned from the state budget.

The overriding theme is that a well-functioning intergovernmental fiscal system is key to most of the transition economies' major reform objectives (Bird, Ebel and Wallich, 1995). In 2001–02, the implementation of the state and local government budget reform began. In the 2002 national budget, general-purpose grants to municipalities are only used to compensate for changes to overall projected revenues between 2001 and 2002 and for partial compensation of the revenue shortfall from 1997 to 2000. This contrasts with the 2001 budget in which municipalities received general-purpose grants to compensate for the shortfall of tax revenues in the previous year and for functions newly delegated to them by the state government. This latter form of compensation is mandated by the Constitution. However, there is additionally a general grant from local governments back to the state budget from those municipalities whose projected revenues have risen by more than 7 per cent from the revenues projected for the last year. Revenue forecasts for the municipalities are thus significant determinants of the size of their general grant. An example of the sometimes rather ad hoc nature of the Lithuanian municipal grants system is provided by the phenomenon of interest free loans for which the Finance Ministry later does not require repayment. This happened in 2001, when interest free loans from the Finance Ministry were kept as grants by municipalities to cover revenue shortfalls from personal income taxes. This dispensation might be labelled grants for needy areas, those that received less than projected from the income tax, although they also form part of the equalisation system. The process then forms part of the story on the timing and mechanism of payment of revenue grants to local governments (Chandler, 2002).

Specific Grants and the Equalisation System

The number and types of specific grants have varied throughout the transition period in Lithuania. They are established not only in the budget law passed before the year begins, but also in amendments passed during the year itself. The only consistent grants have been for investment. In 2002, specific grants became much more important in the structure due to the radical reorganisation of local government financing. Functions that are classified as state functions, which are only delegated to local authorities for administration, are now funded by specific grants. Most notable is the shift of education funding into a specific grant called the pupil basket.

The equalisation system was reformed quite markedly in 2002. The previous system was based on a total equalisation state grant for local governments (the forecast level of expenditures for all municipalities, *minus* the forecast revenues from tax and non-tax sources, *minus* total specific grants). Hence, the forecast of revenues had a direct impact on the state allocation for equalisation. This total grant was then divided between three sub-funds. Revenue shortfall funds went to towns whose revenues were below the amount that had been forecast. Revenue equalisation funds were for those towns whose per capita revenue was below the average. Expenditure needs equalisation went to all towns whose indices of expenditure needs were above the lowest. Expenditure needs equalisation funds were supplemented by formula determined payments to the fund from local governments with above average tax revenue per capita. In all, 20 municipalities paid into this fund.

One of the main criticisms of the system of equalisation in 2001 was that it depended directly on revenue forecasts. Hence, the new system was based on actual receipts instead. Another change was the removal of the formula for distributing funds for revenue shortfalls. The new system contains only equalisation for towns with below-average revenues and equalisation of expenditure needs. The formula for payment into the expenditure needs equalisation fund was removed and replaced by a payment of a specified proportion of tax revenues by a specified group of eight municipalities. The portion of personal income taxes by per cent, forecast for allocation to the budgets of each respective municipality, has been calculated (see Table 11.4).

Table 11.4 Portion of personal income taxes allocated for municipality budgets

Municipality	Share of personal income tax (per cent)
Vilnius city (capital city)	40
Kaunas city	74
Klaipėda city	64
Palanga city	70
Panevėžys city	84
Šiauliai city	96
Ignalina district	78
Mažeikiai district	55
Remaining 52 municipalities	100

Source: Law on the Change of Law on Methodology of Determination of Municipal Budgetary Revenues, 2001.

The second element of the equalisation system is the calculation of revenue equalisation grants to municipalities. Local governments receive these payments each month that their personal income tax revenue per resident the previous month was less than the national average.

The portion of funds remaining in the state treasury account is distributed to level out those differences in the expenditure structures, caused by objective factors rather than municipal operations, of all municipalities. The Municipal Association submits to the Ministry of Finance groups of expenditures and demographic, social and other indicators and coefficients that are necessary for the distribution of funds to level the structure of municipal expenditures.

Table 11.5 Grant structure (in mill. USD)

	1995	1996	1997	1998	1999	2000	2001	2002	2003	2004	2005[a]
General grants	124.5	137.6	120.2	98.9	31.8	44.1	22.4	0	0	0	0
Specific grants	0	0	0	91.3	0	10.6	3.6	532.9	733.1	848.6	819.7
Funds from the state budget	44.7	23.9	92.9	5.2	6.9	4.1	13.1	0	0	0	0
Debt from the state budget	2.3	6.0	2.4	0	14.9	4.9	20.2	0	0	0	0
Compensation grants	0	0	0	0	0	24.2	36.8	9.7	19.3	21,9	16.6
Total:	171.5	162.2	215.6	195.4	47.3	87.9	95.9	542.6	752.4	870.6	836.2

Note: [a] Non-final data.

Source: Ministry of Finance, 1999, 2001, 2003, 2005b (Projects of Financial Indicators of the State Budget and the Budgets of Local Governments); calculations.

The changes in the funding of state functions for 2002 implied a large increase in the amount of funding from special purpose grants (see Table 11.5). To balance this, there was a large fall in funding from general revenues, particularly personal income taxes. Hence, the new revenue structure has grants providing the majority of funding, which personal income taxes did before (Chandler, 2002).

LOCAL GOVERNMENT EXPENDITURES

Over the past decade, the relative importance of the local government sector has declined somewhat (by roughly 7 per cent) in relation to the national budget. The decrease in the relative importance of municipal budgets was pronounced in 1997 and, to an even greater extent, in 2005.

Table 11.6 National and local budgets (in mill. USD)

	1994	1995	1996	1997	1998	1999	2000	2001	2002	2003	2004	2005▫
National budget	1,433	2,264	2,568	3,319	2,622	2,628	2,659	2,508	2,872	4,080	5,464	5,735
General government budget	960	1,544	1,831	2,559	1,752	1,793	1,822	1,717	1,966	3,502	4,668	5,074
Local budgets	473	720	737	760	870	835	837	791	906	1,331	1,666	1,496
GDP	4,227	6,489	8,185	9,999	10,748	10,664	11,462	12,141	14,231	20,655	24,715	25,661
LB as % of GDP	11.2	11.1	9.0	7.6	8.1	7.8	7.3	6.5	6.4	6.4	6.7	5.8
LB as % of NB	33.0	31.8	28.7	22.9	36.8	31.8	31.5	31.5	31.5	32.6	30.5	26.1

Source: Ministry of Finance, 1999, 2000, 2001, 2003, (Projects of Financial Indicators of the State Budget and the Budgets of Local Governments); Bekšta and Petkevičius, 2000 (1994–1997 data).

Table 11.7 Municipal expenditures by sector in Lithuania (per cent)

	1995	1996	1997	1998	1999	2000	2001	2002	2003
Education	36.5	39.6	48.5	55.3	52.9	53.1	58.0	56.8	56.8
Health care	23.2	22.8	5.3	0.6	0.5	0.4	0.4	0.4	0.6
Social care	9.0	9.7	11.0	12.0	12.3	12.3	14.5	14.2	14.2
Sports and culture	3.5	3.5	4.3	4.7	5.4	5.5	4.5	4.4	4.6
Administration	2.9	3.1	4.1	4.1	4.8	4.8	4.9	4.8	4.9
Public works	0.7	0.5	0.8	0.8	0.8	0.8	0.8	0.8	0.8
Defence	0.0	0.0	0.0	0.0	0.0	0.0	0.1	0.1	0.1
Housing and municipal economy	16.7	12.5	13.6	10.8	14.0	14.0	6.5	6.4	6.7
Energy supply	0.0	2.2	2.0	3.0	2.8	2.8	2.5	2.4	3.5
Other	7.5	6.1	10.4	8.7	6.5	6.3	7.9	9.8	7.9
Total	100.0	100.0	100.0	100.0	100.0	100.0	100.0	100.0	100.0

Source: Ministry of Finance 1999, 2000, 2001, 2003, (Projects of Financial Indicators of the State Budget and the Budgets of Local Governments); calculations.

Municipal governments now handle expenditures worth about 6 per cent of gross domestic product (GDP) – half the level of the first years of independence (see Table 11.6). Traditionally, the most important component of local expenditures has been the social sector, which includes education, culture and recreation, and health and social assistance (see Table 11.7). Municipal expenditures for social services constitute about three-quarters of total expenditures. Education absorbs the major part of the expenditures. Social security and welfare consumes about 0.6 per cent of total expenditures. The figures for 1997 reflect the shift of responsibilities for health services from local governments to the Compulsory Health Insurance Fund. The number of health care institutions funded from municipal budgets decreased and, as of 1 July 1997, was very small. From 1998, municipal budgets financed primary health care services only.

The relative importance of social service expenditures in local budgets has increased throughout the transition. This reflects a change in priorities, especially toward education and social care (see Table 11.8).

The changes in municipal budgetary expenditures over the past decade show that the budgetary resources allocated for social services remain stable and are even increasing, notwithstanding the changes in municipal revenue sources. The fact that municipalities are responsible for more functions than only in the sphere of social services (expenditures for defence from 2001) could explain this increase.

Much power in local government affairs is vested in the Lithuanian Ministry of Finance, due to its control of budgetary revenue allocations to local governments. Revenues are general, and taxes are not assigned to any particular spending category. This effectively removes one aspect of the budgetary process from local control. The more controversial question is how much control local governments have over their expenditure. The existence of expenditure norms, used by the Finance Ministry in calculating budget allocations, may have considerable influence on local governments. Local governments may be heavily constrained by these norms politically, since spending less than the norm could be used as strong political ammunition against the ruling party on the local council. If no area receives less than the norm, there is no flexibility to increase spending in any area. Also, however, spending less than the norm could be self-defeating for local governments if the Ministry of Finance reacted by reducing allocations for local governments in that area the following fiscal year. Within broad spending categories governed by norms, municipalities may have more flexibility. Even here, though, they are constrained by decisions at the national level, such as nationally determined teachers' wages (Chandler, 2002). However, since tax and non-tax revenues, which, by law,

Table 11.8 Fluctuation of municipal expenditures by sector in Lithuania (in USD thousands)

	1995	1996	1997	1998	1999	2000	2001	2002	2003
Education	223,991	279,277	351,226	479,528	432,242	442,355	481,144	544,809	734,355
Health care	142,563	161,253	38,637	5,237	4,480	3,317	3,202	3,625	7,120
Social care	55,275	68,631	79,362	103,888	100,160	102,493	120,189	136,092	184,188
Sports and culture	21,286	24,874	30,959	40,697	44,433	45,466	36,920	41,804	59,118
Administration	17,676	21,654	29,733	35,614	39,282	40,221	40,682	46,065	63,590
Public works	4,225	3,872	6,014	6,640	6,687	6,843	6,826	7,729	10,382
Defence	0	0	0	0	0	0	565	640	1,042
Housing and municipal economy	102,432	88,113	98,711	93,515	114,125	116,794	53,790	60,907	86,143
Energy supply	0	15,429	14,502	26,053	22,976	23,517	20,491	23,202	44,791
Other	46,164	42,886	75,085	75,715	53,116	52,351	65,144	94,000	102,024
Total	613,611	705,989	724,226	866,885	817,500	833,356	828,951	958,874	1,292,755

Source: Ministry of Finance 1999, 2000, 2001, 2003 (Projects of Financial Indicators of the State Budget and the Budgets of Local Governments); calculations.

are attributed to municipal budget revenue sources, are not tightly bound to specific municipal expenditures, they must be used, and, since there is no regulation about which particular tax revenues should be used to finance a certain sector, it is not possible to identify which municipal expenditures for a certain sector are financed with non-tax revenues (OECD, 2001).

ACCOUNTING RULES, REGULATIONS AND THE LOCAL GOVERNMENT BUDGETING PROCESS

Social, economic and other programmes and accounts of funds required to implement municipal functions, which the municipal council approves, comprise the basis for forming a municipal budget. Generally speaking, the normative arguments supporting a balanced budget rule imply that the overall budget, or account, of a government tier must be in equilibrium; that is, in each fiscal year current tax collection, user charges and received transfer payments have to balance with public spending for both consumption and investment purposes (Dafflon, 2002).

The Concept of Budget Structure, passed by the Government in the spring of 1998, stimulated budget reform. The next step was the new Law on Budget Structure passed in July 2000, which took into account all essential changes in state development strategy and budgeting and introduced three-year budget planning; programme-based budgeting principles; increased public awareness of the budget; basically reduced the non-budgetary management of state funds; set norms for the adoption of legislation affecting state income; revised the responsibility of state institutions in the budgeting process; and improved the expenditure control system and other budget management systems (OECD, 2001).

Appropriation managers prepare programmes and draft expenditure estimates on the basis of strategic goals (priorities) defined by the Government. The following three stages have been distinguished in the Government-formulated 'Procedures and execution of state and municipal budgets':

Stage 1: drafting projects for financial indicators of municipal budgets by the Ministry of Finance. The Government submits to the *Seimas* the state budget draft and financial indicators of the municipal budgets no later than 75 days before the end of the budget year. The draft of the Law on the Approval of the State Budget and Financial Indicators of Municipal Budgets shall specify the following: the total amount of revenues and its distribution according to the type of revenue; the allocation of payments into the state budget that will be used for the funding of special programmes by appropriation managers;

the total amount of appropriations and their distribution, per institution, for the implementation of programmes approved by the Government; the distribution of the total amount of state budget appropriations according to their functional classification; the resources for the formation (replenishment) of the state budget's working capital; the annual ceiling for public debt; the limit for requested government guarantees during the budget year; the limits for municipal borrowing; the amounts of general and targeted grants to municipal budgets and the compensation of the general grant; the amount of budget tax revenue for each municipality; the portion (by per cent) of personal income taxes distributed to municipal budgets.

Stage 2: execution of budgets and execution accountability that encompasses the following: designation for municipal budgets; revenues for municipal budgets; allocations of municipal budgets, and turnover funds.

Stage 3: schedule for drafting and confirming municipal budget projects. The projects are announced on the municipality's Internet Web page and one daily newspaper, as well as at the Finance and Public Relations Departments of municipality administration and the Reception of the municipality for public considerations by residents. City residents and legal persons submit comments and suggestions regarding the budget project within seven days. Committees are obligated to deliberate the project within the scope of their authority and submit their decisions to the Budget and Finance Committee no later than seven days from the receipt of the project. Council factions submit their opinion on the Project to the Budget and Finance Committee within seven days from the date of its receipt.

The Municipality administration summarises the replies received from residents and legal persons and submits such to the Budget and Finance Committee. The Budget and Finance Committee deliberates the project upon receipt of the conclusions from factions and committees regarding the replies from residents and legal persons and submits its conclusion, including indications of commentaries and major conclusions from Faction Committees, to the director of the municipality administration. The Budget and Finance Committee must indicate specific reasons in its conclusion in instances when it does not concur with recommended adjustments. Once all Committees have considered the project, and following a public discussion of the project, the director of the municipality administration submits the project to the Municipal Council. If the Council passes a decision to adjust the project, the deliberation is postponed no longer than 20 days, when Committees will again consider it. Once budgets are approved, the mayors of municipalities submit them to the Ministry of Finance. If any municipality fails to approve the budget within the allotted time, a 1/12 portion of the funds from the last fiscal year is transferred to the applicable municipality until budget approval has been completed.

SUPERVISION

Prior to 2004 there were two external control institutions subordinate to the *Seimas*: the ombudspersons and the state controller, whose activities were regulated by the Law on *Seimas* Ombudsmen (1994) and Law on State Control (1995). The ombudspersons investigated citizens' complains concerning abuses of power or prohibitively bureaucratic activities of the officials. The ombudspersons may request that local government institutions abrogate, suspend or amend decisions that conflict with laws and legal acts. They also may request the imposition of disciplinary penalties on local government officials or bring to court requests to abrogate a disputable decision.

The State Control Office supervised the legal and effective use of state property, the fulfilment of the budget and financial discipline of state institutions. While performing its functions concerning local self-governments, the State Control Office determined if local authorities are using state funds appropriately and efficiently and, if necessary, evaluated municipal budget performance and the economic and financial activities of municipal offices and enterprises.

Initially, supervision over the legality of local government activities was conferred on the government representative, in accordance with the Law on the Government Representative (1993). Later, however, this position was abolished. In accordance with the Law on Amendments and Supplements to the Law on Country Management and the Abrogation of the Law on Government Representative (1997), these functions were transferred to the office of county governor. However, the constitutional provision on representatives of the government was not repealed. As a result, in 1998 the Law on Administrative Supervision of Local Governments was adopted, which re-established the institution of government representatives (Bekšta and Petkevičius, 2000).

Implementation of the new audit concept occurred in 2004 after the amendments to the Law on Local Self Government of the Republic of Lithuania went into force. The controller's office became the institution for an external audit, supervising the use of budget funds, as well as the legal and effective management and use of municipal property. However, the functions of control remained with it. The qualitative turning point in the financial control system at municipalities occurred during the year 2004. The laws of the Republic of Lithuania demand that external audit and control operations can only be grounded on principles of legality, openness, neutrality and professionalism and state audit requirements. The task for an external financial audit was to disclose the actual situation, and assess and declare an opinion about whether financial reports contained true, correct and thorough information and whether they were made according to laws. Operating procedures for internal control – their sufficiency and effectiveness – of the subject under audit are accented while performing an external financial audit. Once audits are completed, the subjects of the audits are observed regarding correction of errors and implementation of recommendations. This auditing area is a new sphere of work for the Controller's Office (The report of Kaunas Municipality Controller's Office, 2005).

The Law on Internal Control and Internal Audit went into effect. The Internal Audit Department was established. As of 1 January 2004, the status of the Controller's Office changed – the role of inspector and punisher was rejected in exchange for that of an assessor and advisor. In addition to the external financial audit, the Controller's Office also performs an audit of operations. It assesses the public and internal administration of the subject undergoing the audit from the perspective of frugality, effectiveness and results-orientation. Priorities were distinguished each year for the operations of the Controller's Office in each municipality (used as the basis for forming action and work plans) (Kaunas Municipality Council Activity Rules, 2004; the report of Kaunas Municipality Controller's Office, 2005).

FURTHER DEVELOPMENTS: LOCAL GOVERNMENT AND FINANCIAL MARKETS

Lithuania has no municipal bond issuing experience. The main problems associated with municipal bond issuing are the inadequate legal basis and the absence of the models for municipal bond issuing. According to the present legal composition of municipal budgets and the regulation of the borrowing procedures, Lithuanian municipalities may not issue bonds. The prerequisite is a change in the legal situation, which should be implemented in three ways: changing the *determinate order of municipal borrowing* and setting the *order of municipal bond issuing and turnover* (in cases of local and international issuing), and the setting of the *responsibility of the central power* with respect to municipalities' debts (Žigienė, 2004).

Procedures for Borrowing

The Government of the Republic of Lithuania Resolution On Approval of the Procedures for Borrowing by Municipalities (2001) regulates borrowing by municipalities in Lithuania. This resolution specifies that a municipality may borrow by virtue of a decision by the municipal council only for the following purposes: (1) financing projects that are planned by the state investment programme; (2) financing municipal investment projects; (3) covering short-term revenue shortages when there are insufficient turnover funds for this purpose in a municipal budget.

The essential provisions of this resolution, which influence issuance of municipal bonds, are several. The first is that the *Seimas* establishes the limits on borrowing by local governments by passing the Law on Confirmation of Financial Indicators of the State Budget and the Budgets of Local Governments for the following year.

The limits on municipal debts in Lithuania (see Table 11.9) were changed during recent years. The overall debt of a municipality cannot exceed the approved budget revenues for the year (excluding grants for special objectives, allocated from the state budget of the Republic of Lithuania).

Table 11.9 Limits on municipal debts in Lithuania

Year	Annual borrowing limit* (per cent of realised revenue)	Additional limit
2000	20	30 per cent Vilnius municipality
2001	22	35 per cent Vilnius municipality
2002	35	50 per cent Vilnius municipality
2003	35	50 per cent Vilnius municipality
		40 per cent Kaunas municipality
2004		50 per cent Vilnius municipality**
2005	35	50 per cent Kaunas municipality**

Notes: *excluding grants for special objectives allocated from the state budget for the municipality and interest-free loans designated for covering temporary, short term shortages in budgetary funds.
**Additional 6 per cent for municipalities, implementing EU support programmes.

Source: Law on Confirmation of Financial Indicators of the State Budget and the Budgets of Local Governments, 1999, 2001, 2002, 2003, 2004.

Article 6 of the resolution under discussion specifies that 'by decision of its council, a municipality may borrow directly from creditors locally and from abroad'. This point does not foresee emissions of municipal bonds but it does not prohibit them either. It also permits loans with a state guarantee in accordance with legal acts, which regulate the procedures for internal and foreign loans, received with a state repayment guarantee. Such a provision, which is applicable to emissions of municipal bonds, can greatly strengthen the positions of local governments with respect to investors because rating agencies and investors assess state guaranteed municipal loans favourably.

According to Article 9 of Resolution 110, 'long term loans', which generally exist when issuing municipal bonds, are capital that 'a municipality may only acquire to finance investment projects', that is to finance projects planned in the state investments programme or municipal investment projects.

Meanwhile, Article 12 on borrowing procedures envisages that 'a municipality undertakes its own liabilities by assuring performance with its own budgetary funds'. This means that Lithuanian laws on local governments do not establish opportunities for issuing bonds by which the income realised from the project provides the guarantee. Here, a conflict arises between these two articles (9 and 12) of the resolution and opportunities for issuing bonds because commonly, it is specifically project revenue bonds that are emitted to finance investment projects. The revenues from the project being financed guarantee their buyouts. The resolution, meanwhile, only foresees the guarantee for bonds from municipal budgetary funds (Žigienė, 2004).

Procedures for Issuance and Circulation

The laws of the Republic of Lithuania define the procedures for the issuance and circulation of government securities for different emissions with nominal values in national and foreign currencies. The Resolution of the Government of the Republic of Lithuania on Procedures for the Issuance and Circulation of Securities (hereafter 'Procedures') (1997) describes the issuance and circulation of government securities in emissions with nominal values in LTL, which are issued to the Lithuanian securities market.

The main provisions of this resolution would also applicable to the issuance and circulation of municipal bonds with corrections and amendments to certain articles. The first would be to the name of the resolution and all articles which mention government securities. The concept of this object needs to be enlarged to include municipal bonds as well, not only government securities.

In 2001, the Government approved a resolution regarding procedures for the issuance of Government of the Republic of Lithuania securities in international financial markets, signatures of other liability debt documents and receipt of foreign loans (Procedures for the Issuance of Government of the Republic of Lithuania Securities in International Markets, Signatures of Other Liability Debt Documents and Receipt of Foreign Loans, 2001). This resolution could be applicable to municipalities for borrowing in international capital markets. It would not require any major corrections. Municipal bonds simply need to be added to the object of this resolution.

Laxity of management procedures related to issuing municipal bonds, an inadequate legal base, as well as a lack of knowledge on this tool and the possibilities of its usage in municipal administration prevent Lithuanian municipalities from buying credit finances by issuing municipal bonds. Raising external finances through issuing municipal bonds would increase municipalities' independence and the possibility for equal competition in European and world markets.

CONCLUSION

Lithuanian local government operates in a rapidly changing environment. The structure of Lithuanian local government finance is continually being revised as well. Throughout the 17 years of transition, changes have been made to the number of layers of local government, the number of municipalities, the taxes used to fund local government, and the types of grants paid by the state to municipalities (see Chandler, 2002). These changes continue up to the present day after a fairly radical reorganisation of municipal funding in 2002. Command economy administrative territorial units were changed from the beginning of 1990 and at present, the territory of Lithuania is divided into administrative units: counties and municipalities. Sixty municipalities have self-government rights. It is planned to increase the number of municipalities to 100. The essence of local self-government reforms in Lithuania is to bring the local government closer to residents and provide conditions for people to be publicly active. Administrative units are formed to resolve issues relevant to economic and social development of towns and other areas. The issue regarding a division of the limits of authority and functions between different levels of governing and administration has not been conclusively resolved in Lithuania to date. Since there is no clear definition of functions, problems arise regarding a duplication of functions.

Municipal budgets accumulate part of the national income allocated for education, culture, health care, social and welfare maintenance, development of the entire economy of the county and other functions. Social, economic and other programmes and accounts of funds required to implement municipal functions, which the municipal council approves, comprise the basis for forming a municipal budget. These provide the conditions for residents to consider the project on the budget by procedures that the regulation establishes. The main principles for municipal budget formation are constant execution of functions, thrift and frugality, the principle of realistic cash flow operations, budget adequacy, coverage of general expenditures, the principle of openness and the principle of a balanced budget. However, only one of the general regulatory principles relevant to procedures for forming the budget and executing accounting and control, as well as accountability, has been legally validated – the principle of a balanced budget – for use in Lithuania.

Almost all revenue sources for local governments are controlled by the state and this weakens local government. The power of municipalities to make policy decisions over expenditures has oscillated since 1990. Overall, there is a generally low opinion of local government in the general public according to regular opinion polls. Local government is often perceived to have a low capacity to fulfil its responsibilities and this induces resistance to expanding their responsibilities any further. The main body responsible for fiscal and other relations between the local and central government is the Association of Local Authorities in Lithuania. Until 1998, the personal tax income and the profits tax of legal persons was a common source of revenue for both the state budget and local government budgets. From 1998, personal income taxes became the basic revenue source for municipal budgets, and it was a positive tendency in forming a base for local government budgets. However, as of 2002, the proportion of personal income taxes in Lithuania, allocated for local governments, is again a share of general taxes and it reflects increased centralisation.

The principles for the formation of grants in Lithuania were changing during the transition period. In Lithuania, legislation grants are divided into compensation grants, specific grants and equalisation aid. Compensation grants are given to towns that received less income than was forecast for them. Grants became a much larger part of municipalities' incomes in 2002 as part of the reform of local government finance. According to the present legal composition of municipal budgets and the regulation of the borrowing procedures, Lithuania municipalities may not issue municipal bonds. Raising external finances through issuing municipal bonds would increase the municipalities' independence and the possibility for equal competition in European and world markets.

The main problem of Lithuanian local government has still not been solved. This is the issue of giving municipalities some control over their revenues. Lack of control over income inevitably leads to lack of independence in expenditure and administrative decisions. It also implies the absence of mechanisms to link decision-making on services to costs and benefits.

BIBLIOGRAPHY

Astrauskas, A. (1999), Savivaldybių biudžetų sudarymo principai ir metodai [The Principles of Municipalities Budgets Constructing], *Viešųjų institucijų valdymas*, [*The Management of Public Institutions*], Kaunas: Technology, 6–12.

Astrauskas, A., E. Bulovas and Ž. Svetikas (1994), Vietos savivaldos sistema, vykdant Lietuvoje administracinę-teritorinę reformą [The System of Self-government in Pursuance of Administration Territorial Reform], *Savivaldybė* [Municipality], 4, 26–30.

Baltušnikienė, J. (2004), Fiskalinės decentralizacijos teoriniai ir metodologiniai aspektai [Theoretical-methodological Aspects of Fiscal Decentralisation], *Pinigų studijos* [Money Studies], 1, 89–101.

Bekšta, A. and A. Petkevičius (2000), Local government in Lithuania, in T.M. Horvath (ed.), *Decentralisation: Experiments and Reforms*, Budapest: OSI/LGI, 165–216.

Bird, R.M., R.D. Ebel and C.I. Wallich (eds) (1995), *Decentralisation of the Socialist State*, Washington, DC: The World Bank.

Chandler, M. (2002), *Grant Transfers and Financial Supervision in Lithuania*, paper presented at the 10th NISPAcee Annual Conference: Delivering Public Services in CEE Countries, 25–27 April, Krakow, Poland.

Country studies. Lithuania http://www.country-studies.com/lithuania/

Dafflon, B. (2002), *Local Public Finance in Europe: Balancing the Budget and Controlling Debt*, Cheltenham, UK and Northampton, MA, USA: Edward Elgar.

Kaunas Municipality Controller's Office (2005), Kauno miesto savivaldybės kontrolieriaus tarybos 2004 metų veiklos ataskaita [The Report of Kaunas Municipality Controller's Office of 2004], Kaunas Municipality, http://www.kaunas.lt/savivalda _/ kontrolierius/2004_veiklos_ataskaita.doc.

Kauno miesto savivaldybės tarybos veiklos reglamentas (2004), [Kaunas Municipality Council Activity Rules], http://www.kaunas.lt/savivalda_/taryba/reglamentas.shtml.

Kornai, J. (1992), *The Socialist System: The Political Economy of Communism*, New York: Princeton University Press.

Lietuvos Respublikos biudžeto sandaros įstatymas (1990), [Law on Budget Structure of the Republic of Lithuania], I-430, http://www3.lrs.lt/cgi-bin/preps2?Condition1 =224660&Condition2=.

Lietuvos Respublikos vietos savivaldos įstatymas (2000), [Law on Local Self-government], VIII-2018, http://www.lsa.lt/teises/I-533.htm.

Lietuvos Respublikos teritorijos administracinių vienetų sistemos tobulinimo konsepcija (2003), [The Conception of Development on the System of the Territorial Administrative Units], News, No. 59-2679, Appendix 1.

Lietuvos Respublikos konstitucija (1992) [Lithuanian Constitution], Vilnius: Public News, Vol. 33, publication No. 1014.

Martinez, J. (1998), *Municipal Finance in Lithuania: An Opportunity for Economic Success* (Volume 2: Analytical Background), Washington, DC: The World Bank.

Ministry of Finance (1999, 2000, 2001, 2003, 2005a), *Project of Financial Indicators of the State Budget and the Budgets of Local Governments*, Vilnius: Ministry of Finance.

Ministry of Finance (2005b), Internetinis finansų ministerijos Fiskalinės politicos kursas [Ministry of Finance. Fiscal Policy Course on Internet], Interactive, http://www.fmmc.lt/lit/world/paskaita11-2.htm, accessed on 2005 08 29.

OECD (2001), *Fiscal Design across Levels of Government. Country Report: Lithuania.* Survey prepared by the Trading Centre at the Ministry of Finance of the Republic of Lithuania, May.

Savivaldybių biudžetų pajamų nustatymo metodikos įstatymo pakeitimo įstatymas (2001), [Law on the Change of Law on Methodology of Determination of Municipal Budgetary Revenues] IX-566, http://www3.lrs.lt/cgi-bin/preps2?Condition1=15343 4&Condition2=.

Savivaldybių biudžetų pajamų nustatymo metodikos įstatymas (1999), [Law on the Methodology of Determination of Municipal Budgetary Revenues, VIII-385]. http:// www3.lrs.lt/cgi-bin/preps2?Condition1=41848&Condition2=.

Stačiokas, R. (1991a), *Lietuvos savivaldybių raida* [The Development of Municipalities in Lithuania], Vilnius: Research and teaching centre of Vilnius University.

Stačiokas, R. (1991b), *Metmenys savivaldos pagrindų įstatymo komentaro*, [The Draft of Self-government Law Commentary], Vilnius: Research and teaching centre of Vilnius University.

Statistical Office (1993–2006), Lietuvos statistikos metraštis [*Statistical Yearbook of Lithuania*], Vilnius: Statistical Office.

Valstybės biudžeto ir savivaldybių biudžetų finansinių rodiklių patvirtinimo įstatymas, [Law on Confirmation of Financial Indicators of the State Budget and the Budgets of Local Governments], IX-2550. http://www3.lrs.lt/cgi-bin/preps2?Condition1=264962&Condition2=.

Žigienė, G. (2004), *Savivaldybių obligacijų išleidimo modeliavimas Lietuvos sąlygomis. Daktaro disertacija* [Modelling of Issuing Municipal Bonds in Lithuanian Conditions. PhD thesis], Kaunas: KTU.

12. Financing local self-government in the Republic of Macedonia

Borče Davitkovski and Ana Pavlovska-Daneva

INTRODUCTION

Regarding decentralisation in Macedonia it must be said that its finalisation did not happen because of the requirements of the local self-government units (even though the municipalities had constantly requested decentralisation after the adoption of the first Law on Local Self-Government 1995), but as a result of the armed civil unrest in Macedonia during 2001. The Ohrid Framework Agreement was signed after the conflict in August 2001, when one of the provisions for peace in the country between the Macedonian and Albanian ethnic community was carrying out territorial decentralisation. This provision was legally brought into operation in the Ohrid Framework Agreement with the adoption of the amendments in the Macedonian Constitution on 20 November 2001 with three of the 15 amendments (Amendment 5, Amendment 16 and Amendment 17) being related to the local self-government's status in the Republic of Macedonia.

Therefore, the citizens did not succeed in carrying out their constitutional rights on local self-government, but this came about because of a compromise at the time of the signing of the Ohrid Framework Agreement that was inflicted by weapons and verified by the international community. It appears that in Macedonia there is an enforced or 'gifted' decentralisation which is legally verified through the Constitutional amendments and relevant laws. While the technical and functional decentralisation process is carried out in Europe, in Macedonia, unfortunately, territorial decentralisation is carried out as a result of a peace agreement.

The Macedonian local administration's position regarding the central authorities varied, depending on the historical circumstances. During the period of the Yugoslavian Federation (1945–1991), we could cite three diametrically opposed positions.

The Constitution of the Federal Peoples Republic of Yugoslavia (1946) imposed a so-called Administrative Period. The whole administration at that time was centralised and focused on the central authorities (ministries), at the federal level and the republican level. By adoption of the Law on Municipality System Law (1955) the local self-government units obtained the profile of a political-territorial community with particular local, administrative and governmental jurisdictions, similar to other political-territorial communities (federation, republic, province, region and municipality);

The Constitutions of 1963 and 1974 introduced even more independent municipality status. During this period, the local units had the right to introduce certain local taxes without consulting the republic or federal authorities. The independence of the local administration regarding the central authorities was placed on a level of relations between two equal authorities and the predomination of the local over the central authorities was very often the case. During that time, large municipalities were created; the existence of the regions was halted and the local bodies' policy towards the central authorities was created depending upon the economic power/resources of a certain municipality.

Afterwards, by the Constitutional amendments (the federal as well as republic) during 1988–89, the municipality system was terminated; the municipalities' authority was transferred to the central bodies and a legal vacuum was created in the regulation, which lasted until the disintegration of the former Yugoslavia. Without an accurate legal framework, both the legality and legitimacy of the existing local authorities became questionable.

This chapter gives an insight into a very complicated process, which began recently in the Republic of Macedonia – the implementation of fiscal decentralisation together with a new territorial organisation. Considering that this is an ongoing process and not likely to be completed in the near future, it is currently concentrating on the legal framework, analyses of available data, which unfortunately is insufficient, and forecasts for the future development of local self-governments in the country.

BASIC LEGAL FRAMEWORK AND LOCAL GOVERNMENT FINANCE REGULATIONS

Contemporary local administration in Macedonia was introduced with the Constitution of the Republic of Macedonia in November 1991 and since then we can distinguish three sub-periods (Ministry of Local Self-government of the Republic of Macedonia, 2004a).

The first one began in 1991 and lasted until the adoption of the first Law on Local Self-Government in 1995. The Constitution of 1991 established a single level self-government organisation. Besides the municipalities as units of the local self-government, the Constitution defines the City of Skopje as a special local self-government unit that is organised in accordance with a special law. In the spirit of the European Convention on Local Self-government of 1985, the Constitution guarantees local self-government units with sources of income of their own, as well as additional funds from the state.

Local self-government's position in the Republic of Macedonia did not come into effect until 1996, when the Law on Local Self-government[1] and the Law on the City of Skopje[2] were adopted. Prior to this, the central authorities carried out a complete centralisation at local level and the local self-government authorities really had no significant rights with regard to the central bodies.

Therefore, at the beginning of 1992, by a Decision of the Government, the former administrative bodies were transformed into the ministries' local units and all functions and estates of the former local government bodies were transferred to the central authorities. The same transformation happened to the local units' facilities that were transferred from local to state property.

The second phase began with the Law on Local Self-government adoption in 1995 and the Law on the City of Skopje in 1996. Following this, the existing 34 municipalities on the territory of the Republic of Macedonia were divided into 123 new municipalities with the City of Skopje having the special status of a separate local self-government unit.

According to the Law in 1995, there were three types of local self-government bodies' competencies:

1. Concrete activities that the local self-government executes independently.
2. Activities that the local self-government executes in accordance with the responsible state authorities.
3. Conducting certain State bodies' activities that have been given to the local self-government units as their entrusted duties.

The third sub-phase of the development of local self-government began in 2001 with the Constitution's amendments,[3] which came into operation with the adoption of the new Law on Local Self-Government[4] of 29 January 2002. The entire Macedonian legal decentralisation arrangement process was completed by November 2004 with the adoption of the new Law on the Territorial Division of the Local Self-government Units and the Law on Financing of the Local Self-government Units. However, one has to know the number of the municipalities that will be established in order to be able to perform certain simulations and analyses of the financing. In the Macedonian case, the Law on Financing of the Local Self-government Units became Government procedure before the Law on Territorial Division. For this reason, the transfer of authority to the municipalities is gradual and in phases as demonstrated in Table 12.1 (Open Society Institute Macedonia, 2005).

Table 12.1 Review of transfer of authority in Macedonia

Phase	Start	Transfer of authorities	Conditionality
First	1 July 2005	1. Transfer of own tax incomes (sharing of personal income tax) of municipalities (Government) 2. Preparation of transfer methodology of capital and restricted assets (Government) 3. The local self-government will start implementing the plan of resolving remaining debts accumulated by 31 January, 2001 (SGU)	If 90% of all municipalities that consist of 90% of the total population provide: 1. At least two financial officers 2. At least three tax experts
Second	Conditional	Transfer of authorities (for a block of transfers): 1. Culture 2. Social and child protection (kindergartens and homes for elderly) 3. Education (primary and high schools) 4. Health (public health institutions and primary care)	1. Conditions of the first phase are met 2. Good financial results for a period of 24 months for timely and correct reporting confirmed by the Ministry of Finance 3. No remaining obligations towards creditors 4. Relevant Commission assessed that all conditions are met 5. Existing written request from the municipalities to the relevant ministry and the Ministry of Finance for the block of transfers

Source: OSI Macedonia, 2005.

DEMOCRATIC LEGITIMACY AND FINANCIAL REPORTING

The Law on Local Self-Government introduces mainly two types of competencies:

1. Independent competencies, and
2. Delegated competencies.

The first novelty is that the common competencies that were carried out in approval of the central bodies no longer exist. Then, in contrast to the former Law, the new Law gives a wide list of competencies and responsibilities (which looks more like a wish list than a list of real authority and duties), that the municipalities, according to their economic and human resources, have to accomplish. Still, it is not clear through what mechanisms and organs the municipality will be able to carry out professional and expert supervision of the new duties within its authority.

Regarding the delegated competencies, they are transferred only to the mayor as a local self-government units' official. The state authority which delegates its competences is still the subsidiary responsible for the realisation of the delegated duties. Whilst the municipalities are carrying out these duties, the Law allows them to create public services or to delegate the work to other subjects based on public contracts. In this case, the municipality has the subsidiary responsibility.

In the Republic of Macedonia, there are several types of state supervision over the local self-government administration:

1. Supervision of the municipalities' original competences
   (a) Control of the legality
   (b) Revision and control over the financial activities
2. Supervision of the delegated competences
   (a) Control of the legality and
   (b) Control of the efficiency
3. In cases determined by the Law, there is a prior supervision that covers prior state approval for some local regulations.

The Ministry of Local Self-Government carries out the supervision of the legality of the local regulations. The Ministry of Finance carries out the control of the material and financial work of the municipalities. The local material and financial work's revision is carried out by the State Revision (Audit) Bureau according to the Law on State Revision (Audit). Finally, supervision of the delegated competences is the responsibility of the state authority, whose duties are delegated to the municipality. The legislator attempted to put the municipality on an equal footing with the central government bodies and where there is no reaction from central government, the law prefers to use the regulations and activities of the municipality.

Regarding financial reporting practices, it is believed that there are three very important reasons that financial reports must be prepared (Ministry of Local Self-government of the Republic of Macedonia, 2004c):

1. Financial reports help fulfil the obligations of the local self-government units to be publicly evaluated and to provide information about whether the current revenues are enough for the payment of current expenses or not.
2. The financial reports should help users in the evaluation of the local self-government's operation results in any particular year. Financial reports should also give information about whether the financial position of the self-government units has improved, or worsened, as a result of their total activities over the year.
3. Financial reports should help to evaluate the level of services that can be provided by the local authority and also its capability to fulfil those obligations.

In accordance with the Macedonian Law on Accounting of Budgets and Budget Users, the local self-government units are required to prepare basic financial reports, including: balance sheet, balance of revenues and expenses, consolidated balance of capital property (index of capital property), liability balance and financial reports notes.

The basic financial reports, together with their explanations, make up the annual account of the units of local self-government. Even though the Law has precisely specified the reporting obligations for the local self-government units, the data can show whether or not they respected the instructions from the Ministry of Finance regarding that field of their work. The fact that there are no penalties for wrongly preparing financial reports hides the possibility of 'filtering information' in favour of those submitting the reports. Moreover, the financial reports, which are budget oriented, cannot be directly prepared from the municipality's accounting system, due to, among other reasons, diversity, inappropriate organisational arrangement and the low level of training for the personnel that arrange the appropriate reports.

In future, it will be necessary to pay special attention to the manner of organising and realising financial-reporting practices for the municipalities, with the goal of achieving their uniformity and uniform use.

INDEPENDENT LOCAL GOVERNMENT REVENUE SOURCES

The revenues of the local units are divided into original, non-tax, capital, transfers and donations. The revenue structure of the municipalities in Macedonia is shown in Table 12.2 (Ministry of Local Self-government of the Republic of Macedonia, 2004b).

Table 12.2 Revenues of local units in 2001

Revenues	In million denars	Per cent
1. Tax (Original) revenues	840.4	26.3
2. Non-tax revenues	1,158.0	36.2
3. Capital	8.4	0.3
4. Transfers	1,176.7	36.7
5. Donations from abroad	15.7	0.5
Total	3,199.2	100.0

Source: Ministry of Local Self-Government (2004b).

The municipalities generate 62.8 per cent of the total revenues from personal revenue sources (non-tax revenues, original and capital revenues) and 37.2 per cent are generated from outside sources. The original revenues of the local self-government budgets are divided into revenues from taxes and revenues from so-called specific taxes – communal taxes. The structure of the original revenues is presented in Table 12.3.

Table 12.3 Structure of tax (original) revenues

	1998	1999	2000	2001	2002
Taxes	72	84	85	87	85
Duties	28	16	15	13	15
Total	100	100	100	100	100

Source: Ministry of Finance.

The basic local taxes are: property tax, inheritance and gift tax and the sales tax on real estate and rights. The centralised manner for registering and paying taxes, as well as their administrative arrangements, are the basic reasons for the restricted fiscal power of the municipalities. The local administration has no insight into their tax bases. The central authority, making this concept the largest obstruction of successful financial management of the municipalities, defines the rate/amount beforehand. With regard to the above, there are a number of remarks that most municipalities have a low tax payment percentage, especially the property tax as a traditional local tax.

The basic problem is the administration of property tax. In accordance with the Property Tax Law[5] (which covers the sales tax on real estate and rights and inheritance and gift tax), this tax is determined according to data from the tax payer's report and other data that is available from the Public Revenue Board. The property tax is paid every three months.

But, in practice, these provisions are conducted with a number of shortages, and as a result of this practice, we have a low degree of property tax payment, which for the period from 1999 to 2005 was under 50 per cent:

- 58 per cent for 1999
- 59 per cent for 2000
- 52.6 per cent for 2001
- 57.7 per cent for 2005
- 55.4 per cent for 2006

The low degree of property tax payment is a result of:

- Insufficient commitment by the central government;
- Exclusion of municipalities in the administration of these taxes;
- Inefficient preparation and adoption of decisions from the Public Revenue Board;
- Incomplete and non-updated registration of the property by municipalities;
- Unreal tax restrictions;
- No application of legal punishment provisions;
- Insufficient transparency in this field.

Communal taxes, which, according to Macedonian classification, are called taxes for specific communal services are:

1. Communal tax for a temporary stay (which are in fact tourist charges),
2. Communal tax for exposing a firm on the buildings,
3. Communal tax for roads and registering vehicles, and
4. Communal tax for using public lighting and other communal taxes.

The communal taxes are paid according to the Law on Taxes for Temporary Stay[6] and the Law for Communal Taxes.[7] The revenues from the communal taxes are own resources revenues of the municipality where they were collected. The percentage of these revenues, according to the registration in the Treasury of the Ministry of Finance, in the total scope of revenues, amounts to 10.5 per cent. Its percentage is solid, but of course there are many unused reserves. According to the data, in the total scope of communal taxes, the largest revenue (more than half) is from the communal tax for public lighting, then for the communal tax for using streets and registering vehicles.

The non-tax revenues are:

1. Revenue from property;
2. Profits from public communal enterprises;
3. Other revenues from property and
4. Other administrative services

In the municipalities in Macedonia, there is weak property management, especially with real-estate, which results in very low revenue collected. The tax potential of this type of revenue is still an unknown quantity. This is the result of the fact that the municipalities do not own much real estate. They can earn this income by renting real estate, selling premises that are of no public interest, as well as by leasing property. The participation of revenues that the local units achieve from the property is still very low, even though there are municipalities with high value property. We may consider that this group also includes, as municipality revenues:

1. Compensation for arranging construction land, communes and
2. Compensation for arranging construction land, city rent.

The compensation for arranging construction land, in fact, is the largest individual local source of revenue. According to available data, it accounted for around 20 per cent in the structure of local revenues in 2001. The basic characteristic for this type of local revenue is the low degree of payment, which is around 60 per cent. Apart from other factors, the low scope of payment is also the result of the frequent release (full or partial) of payment duties for this type of compensation function, as well as medical, sport and other types of administrative facilities. We should be aware of the fact that sequences of payments are regulated by way of compensation between the municipality and the investors, which are not always transparent. The compensations are most often of an enforced form, as a result of several year obligations by the municipality for certain construction firms' projects. This is an indication that great opportunities exist for misuse and disallowed initiatives. An analysis must be performed on the manner of establishing strict regulations, including a stricter system of sanctions.

A second local source of revenue, with a share of over 10 per cent of the total revenue, is the compensation for the use of construction land and city rents.

Public utility companies in the Republic of Macedonia *de facto* do not make a profit. So far, none of these companies has ever demonstrated a profit but unfortunately they generate losses or, at best, they end the year with break-even results, that is with all costs covered and funds provided for future investments.

The capital revenues, in accordance with the classifications, encompass the revenues from the sale of capital resources – privatisation (facilities, furniture, equipment, land and non-material investment) and capital transfers from governmental and non-governmental sources (capital or grant). This type of revenue will be able to be achieved soon after the decentralisation process where there will be a transfer of facilities for education, social care, sport and culture to the municipalities.[8]

GRANT TRANSFERS

Transfers, according to their size and the reason for them, are the largest source of revenue in Macedonian municipalities. In the revenues for 2001, their participation was 36.7 per cent. All transfers in the Republic can be grouped into general and applicable. In the basic transfers, there are transfers for equalisation or so-called general fiscal aid. Only the local units that cannot really cover their budget expenditure from their own sources should utilise the right to these transfers. The fiscal requirements of the municipalities and the requirements for financial transfers in accordance with the well-known criteria for equalisation (estimated according to special formulas), based on transparency, stability, rightness and objectivity must be constantly evaluated. All other transfers are applicable. They are distributed as follows:

1. The State Budget. The largest source of transfers is the State Budget. There are five types of transfers (grants). The most important are so called Block-transfers, which will be transferred in the second phase of decentralisation (starting from September 2007), in 30 per cent of the municipalities (which passed the first phase according to the specific conditions).
   For the realisation of economic infrastructure projects, the Ministry of Finance approves transfers for non-returnable financing of construction, modernisation and reconstruction of local roads, construction and recon-

struction of local water plants, micro accumulations for investment in specific regions up to 80 per cent, and for investing in rural centres, 60 per cent. Before fiscal decentralisation (1999–2004), the transfer of those grants was mostly based on political criteria. It can be said that the approving resources criteria are of a general political nature. Otherwise, For example, over 500 million denars were transferred to the municipalities through this budget each year, or, in other words, their participation in the total transfers amounts to around 30 per cent. According to the new legislation (2004–07), there are new conditions attached to mathematical formula and objective criteria, that makes the transfer of grants more transparent and objective.

2. The fund for major and regional roads in accordance with the Law on Public Roads. This fund makes available the resources for the municipalities' local roads and streets, prescribed in Article 106 based on the annual programme for construction, reconstruction, maintenance and protection of local roads and streets. The annual scope of transferred resources to the municipalities, as well as their participation in total transfers, is identical to the first type of transfer. The same remarks are also relative to the manner of their distribution and registration.
3. The Water Supply Programme. By decision of the Government, the Ministry of Transport and Communications is authorised to transfer the budget resources to the local self-government units for water supply and other transfers for local governments' infrastructure requirements. For this purpose, each year, around 150 million denars are transferred to the municipalities and their participation in total transfers is 10 per cent.
4. The Urban Organisation Plan Programme. This is presented each year and includes the total amount and concrete purposes. The annual amounts for this programme vary from year to year (for 2001 it amounted to around 24 million denars, with participation in total transfers of around 1.6 per cent).
5. The Programmes for revitalisation of villages, together with the programme for electrification of villages, are small and minor according to their importance. Both add up in total transfers to 2 per cent.
6. The Local Media Programme. Ongoing transfers to public media at a local level are distributed by decision of the Government through the Information Agency into 12 equal portions during the year. The resources, in an annual amount of around 16 million denars, with no concrete explanation, are distributed to the local Radio Broadcasting Networks in percentiles/fixed amounts. Their participation in total transfers amounts to 1 per cent.
7. The last are the transfers for projects that are financed with resources from the sale of Telecom, proposed by the Budget of the Republic of Macedonia for 2001, 2002 and 2003.

With regard to total transfers, it is characteristic that during the evaluation of the data for their payments from the final account of the Budget of the Republic of Macedonia and those from the final accounts of the local self-government units for 2001, there is a difference of around 500 million denars. This difference is probably the result of the transfer payments not being recorded on a regular basis.

Foreign donations are important for investment for all municipalities in the Republic of Macedonia, especially capital donations. It should be mentioned that foreign donations are a result of individual efforts. Often, the mediators between the donators and the local authority are the non-governmental organisations. The donations are paid directly to the investor. The donators require transparency and a report of the donation given. On the other hand, as a result of these conditions, only a small part of them are registered and expressed in accounting reports in the local self-government units' budgets. In this way, for 2002, the total registered revenue, on this basis, amounted to around 13.5 million denars, or 0.4 per cent of the total local revenues.

The previous analysis leads us to conclude that the participation of tax revenues, as the most important personal finance source, is very low in relation to government transfers, which indicates the necessity for a certain degree of fiscal decentralisation.

LOCAL GOVERNMENT EXPENDITURES

The total amount of the local expenditures, according to data for 2001, is very low at 2.578 millions of denars. Their part of total expenses is approximately 3 per cent, in the central budget around 4 per cent and in GDP 1.1 per cent. According to this data, local expenses per capita are 1,327.40 denars or 22 euros.

The relevance of the accountancy base of information (as a unique source of information) should be looked at with some reserve due to the following:

1. The above-mentioned is not unified in all municipalities with regard to the main accounting principle (finance or accounting)
2. The inclusion of registration of expenses is not complete for two reasons:
   (a) not all municipal consumption units are included;
   (b) not all expenditures from different kinds of financing are being registered (the expenses based on donations, capital expenses and central transfers);
   (c) many transactions are not being registered.

The participation of local expenses in the total public expenses of the Republic of Macedonia can be above 8 per cent and 3–4 per cent from the expected GDP. Compared to the final account of the local self-government units for 2001 which was 2.578 millions denars, this amount is three times higher. However, we should bear in mind that this is not a total budget consolidation of the local self-government units and that after consolidation is finished, this percentage could possibly be higher. If this plan is to be realised, one can conclude that local incomes are contributing with more then 10 per cent of total public income of the Republic of Macedonia.

An analysis of all functional local expenses in the Republic of Macedonia for the past period is impossible to carry out because of the shortage of data. The only thing possible, regarding the existing facts, is a rough classification, shown in Table 12.4.

Table 12.4 Functional classification of the local public expenses for 2001

Expenses	Participation (%)
1. General public services	34.5
2. Communal services	65.5
Total	100

Source: Ministry of Finance.

Compared to the different transition countries, this structure is rather inviolate, although compared to the Macedonian municipalities they are conducting fewer functions. As a matter of fact, if in these countries the participation of the general public services is moving from minimum of 2.8 per cent in Belarus and 25.6 per cent in Russia, Macedonia with its 35.5 per cent is well above the maximum (see Dabla-Norris and Wade, 2002), as presented in Table 12.5.

Table 12.5 Structure of expenditures

Expenses	Participation (%)
Current expenditures	73
Capital expenditures	27
Total	100

Source: Ministry of Finance.

The situation is completely different as regards the categories in Table 12.6.The expenses for salaries, rents and supplements are 24 per cent of the total current expenses of the local units.

Table 12.6 Classification of expenditures

Category	Participation (%)
Current expenses	100
Salaries, rents, and supplements	24
Commodities and other services	64
Current transfers	12
Capital expenses	100
Buying of capital goods	82
Capital transfers	18

Source: Ministry of Finance and author's calculations.

The following conclusions can be made:

- The participation of the total local expenses in the total public expenses (above 10 per cent) is still low, and this fact points to a low level of fiscal decentralisation;
- Local expenses per capita also continue to be very low;
- The explanation for the changes which have occurred in the total amount by years, as well as the separate municipality expenses, cannot be given because of non-existent information over the past years, or because of their incomparability for other reasons;
- In the administrative budgets, the percentage of salaries and rents is very high, as well as the supplement for commodities and other services;
- The participation of the capital component is low;
- More control of the balance between the incomes and expenses is needed and equalisation transfers for budget deficits in less developed municipalities;
- Monitoring schemes need to be established to cover the financial situation;
- In the second phase of decentralisation, the municipalities are allowed to borrow on the capital market and to issue local bonds. Therefore there is need for an enforced State Audit.

ACCOUNTING RULES, REGULATIONS AND LOCAL GOVERNMENT BUDGETING PROCESS

Fiscal decentralisation is a process of transfer of authority and management responsibilities for the process of fiscal decision making to the lower levels of government in a devolved government system (Boex, 2001). The transfer is a process of shifting responsibilities for government duties and for the consumption from the central to the local government, where the local self-government is given the authority to make its own decisions.

The key issue in the implementation of the new municipalities' competencies is the development of result-oriented management as a type of administrative philosophy. This determination is a result of the efforts to introduce real decentralisation in the Republic of Macedonia by paying special attention to the achieved results. Instead of the traditional procedural approach, the new strategies of quality management are increasingly focused on the quality of the results and the consequences realised with public sector measures. The goal is to achieve a transition from the *ex ante* resource control operational model, with excessive regulations designed to prevent the abuses and *ex post* control, in order to provide for the respect of the legal provisions, towards a model that will secure continuous monitoring of the quality of the work and management and reporting of the results (efficiency, cost-efficiency, effectiveness, service quality, financial operations). Traditional values such as neutrality, integrity and equality have to be combined with the demands of present times, that is. value for money and service quality criteria.

The following requirements have to be taken into account when defining the role of each layer of government: (1) closeness of the services to the users; (2) ability of the government institutions to adapt to the needs and the circumstances (flexibility); (3) quality, efficiency, effectiveness and cost-efficiency of the services; and (4) compatibility of the work of the public administration (Ministry of Local Self-government of the Republic of Macedonia, 2001). The competencies have to be clearly distributed and the responsibilities of each echelon have to be properly defined, understood and accepted by all parties. The state has a primary responsibility to provide all citizens with access to quality services and they have to have some competence in the fields of general planning, coordination and supervision. The local authorities, whenever it is applicable and consistent with national policies, should play an important role – direct or in partnership with other agencies – in the provision of appropriate services. Within the scope of their responsibilities, local authorities should have a greater level of discretion in the provision of their services. When competencies are transferred to local authorities, it is important to provide them with financial or other resources necessary for the completion of delegated tasks.

Measuring the performance on offering public services on the part of authorised bodies appears as a type of management tool, with the help of which the movement towards achieving the ultimate goal – greater efficiency – is made visible. The creation of appropriate indicators for measuring the performance of public bodies is based on two principles: first, the concentration of programme outcomes, that is existing results, rather than the quantity of services offered by the organisation; and second, upon defining the anticipated result, the performance measurement is focused on the citizens/consumers (see Mark and Nayyar-Stone, 2002).

Speaking about the current Macedonia, little attention is given to the need for improving the public services offered by the public sector and also to the possibilities offered in this regard by the creation of indicators for measuring performance. None of the measures taken by the public subjects can be said to be service-oriented and even the proposed reforms that are partially implemented seem to represent a marketing ploy in light of the coming elections. The main preoccupation of the direct participants in providing services (public servants) is holding on to their jobs (or positions), wherein they admit that, despite the possible willingness to introduce the use of indicators for measuring the results of their work, they are faced with the problem of a funds shortage. Inexperience, and a lack of experts to aid their training, present an additional problem. The influence of politics (unfortunately, even petty politics) plays a major role in taking the steps that lead to an improvement in services.

SUPERVISION AND CONTROL: THE STATE AUDIT

The financial control system of the municipality should include three levels: internal control, internal audit and external audit. The financial control and audit are mainly composed of an inspection of the accounts of the liquid and other assets of the municipality, as well as its liability.

There is a difference between the financial control and audit, depending on who is responsible for conducting those activities and what the scope of the appropriate competences is. Internal personnel of the local self-government units usually carry out the internal control. The internal audit can be conducted by internally authorised inspectors such as individuals or by an authorised inspection body of the local self-government units. The internal inspection can sometimes be confined to an independent expert authorised by the local authorities to conduct systematic inspections of the municipalities' financial conditions and to advise them about future financial decisions. In the end, authorised revision institutions can conduct the external audit. It can also be conducted by professional accounting firms, such as Pricewaterhouse Coopers, KPMG, Ernest & Young and others, or by financial institutions which are often under state control such as the State Bureau for Revision (Audit), which is active in the Republic of Macedonia.

The system of internal control over the local units of self-government by regional units of the Ministry of Finance has little or no possibility of real control over the assets collection in the municipality. It makes the system extremely sensitive. In fact, in most cases, the system is useless. However, the experience of the internal control system in other countries shows that, under correct internal control, mistakes in the financial transactions of the local self-government units appear very rarely; they are easy to detect and correct. An accurate internal control can help prevent attempts at bribery and corruption, even though in practice it is difficult to detect. Accordingly, the internal control system is an extremely important component of the supervisory system of the municipality, and it should not be underestimated or disregarded.

The Mayor of the municipality orders the internal revision, after prior approval from the Government of the Republic of Macedonia. If the Mayor does not establish an internal audit, then the Ministry of Finance's inspectors carry out this activity (but then it is not an internal audit). Even if there was an established internal audit, this would be a control body without well-trained personnel for the execution of such tasks.

The Ministry of Finance, through the central audit, should carry out an audit of the financial reports (and the budgets) of the units of local self-government. However, they are faced with various financial problems. It is partially a result of the current system of local financing, partially a result of bad financial management. At the same time, the Ministry has insufficient or no information at all on this issue, and does not provide any assistance for dealing with the problems. This imposes the need for total reconsideration of the supervision process and establishing its modern forms such as the supervision of local activities carried out. This includes supervising the local economic performances. The Macedonian local financial systems nominally have a limited number of relatively small independent income sources. However, in practice, the central authorities determine the level of these. It is commonly accepted in other European countries that the central grants are an important element of local finances, such as in the Republic of Macedonia. If the local financial problems are not appropriately solved at a local level, they should be under the jurisdiction of the central authorities. Theory suggests not to intervene, but to prevent the creation of deficits with a large number of rules and control. However, assistance from the central authorities is necessary, at least in the near future, in order to solve two problems:

1. The financial information system must be created in such a way that will clearly discover how to recognise the real need for assistance.

2. Building a credible, objective and effective assistance policy that will reduce the discretion for assistance, due to political reasons.

The Ministry of Finance may follow the financial position of the local units through monthly reports and financial accounts that are requested from them. Besides this, at a Ministry's disposal, there is other independent information from its own control procedures, as well as from the reports of State inspectors. Data received from financial accounts are not sufficient because their credibility and eligibility are not confirmed by a revisers' report or by any independent external expertise.

Internal audit is not established in the local units, even if it is an obligation of the Budget Law of 2001. The State Audit Office continuously conducts audits during the year, but carries out an obligatory audit only once a year for the utilisation and spending of budget incomes. However, the findings of the State controllers are often left without any implications, either because they are not being examined at all, or because no measures are taken regarding them.

FURTHER DEVELOPMENT: LOCAL GOVERNMENT AND FINANCIAL MARKETS

The very fact that the municipalities and the city of Skopje as local self-government units have the status of legal entities enables them to appear on the capital market as independent entities. So far, this has not been allowed because the Law on Budgets, which is passed every year, stipulates a provision (which from 2006 does not exist) with which the self-government units are strictly prohibited from entering into debt with financial institutions in the country or abroad, except with the State Budget.

According to the new legal framework, besides their own incomes and incomes from donations, the municipalities can provide additional funding by borrowing in the country or abroad, either short or long term. However, there are several limits. The loans can have only fixed interest rates and for foreign loans prior consent is required from the Government of the Republic of Macedonia. The Law on Financing of the Local Self-government Units stipulates that the Government cannot guarantee or take over liabilities derived from debts of a municipality, including municipal public services, except in cases where a certain responsibility was taken over as a legal obligation.

In cases of short-term loans, the municipality can borrow in the country by paying the loan by the end of the current fiscal year. These loans can be used for covering an interim lack of cash, but cannot be used for payment of penalties and penalty interests. The total amount of the short-term debt during the year cannot exceed 20 per cent of the realised total revenues of the operational budget of the municipality in the previous fiscal year.

The municipality can have long-term debts for financing capital investments only if the payment of the debt is realised in equal or decreasing annuities. The decision for the long-term debts is made by the Municipality's Council and is valid only for the fiscal year in which it has occurred. The total amount of the annual instalment cannot exceed 15 per cent of the realised total revenues of the operational budget of the municipality in the previous fiscal year.

In the end it is important to point out that the possibility for the municipalities to borrow has delayed implementation, because in the transitional provisions of the Law on Financing of the Local Self-government Units it is stipulated that long-term loans in the country are possible, only after the Ministry of Finance determines that a certain municipality in a period of at least 24 months has regularly submitted positive financial reports and that in the last two years has no remaining liabilities towards creditors. This is a correct and logical solution because it will stimulate municipalities to use their funds prudently, and this will also contribute to strengthening the obligation for submitting correct and precise financial reports. In the context of the delayed implementation of the provisions for free access to the capital market by the municipalities, we can mention that at this moment in time, the total amount of debts of the municipalities is 1.6 billion denars of which 1 billion is for construction works and 50 per cent is for delayed payment interest rates.[9] This means that the municipalities need two years to cover old debts before they can start with new borrowing.

CONCLUSION

The Republic of Macedonia is undergoing an extensive endeavour – decentralisation and transfer of significant fiscal responsibilities to the municipal level. The Law on the Territorial Organisation of the Local Self-government Units in the Republic of Macedonia sets the number of municipalities in the territory of the country and defines the populated areas that form the municipalities. The Law on Financing of the Local Self-government Units defines the sources and the manner of their financing, that is, it defines the conditions that have to be in place in order to provide quality execution of each of the municipalities' responsibilities determined by the Law on Local Self-government. The Law on Property Taxes, as well as the Law on Utilities taxes, stipulates the manners of acquiring these revenues.

The fiscal capacity of the local self-government, defined as own income, should provide for the execution of responsibilities supported by own sources of revenues of each municipality (property taxes, utilities taxes, personal income tax). At the moment, the fiscal capacity of the municipalities in the Republic of Macedonia can be determined only by using parameters that are available and that according to their sources can be considered as reliable.

The decentralisation process in Macedonia began by transferring revenues to the local self-government and by distributing the consumption, which has not been adequately estimated. However, no efficiency analyses have been made for the newly-adopted limits because this process is under strong political influence.

To overcome this condition, first there should be official data on municipal GNP. Afterwards, the municipalities with under-average fiscal capacity should be stimulated to increase their fiscal efforts by:

- Increasing the scope of taxpayers, that is, expanding the tax base;
- Improving the administration and collection of taxes;
- Choosing adequate tax rates, according to the economic stature of the population.

NOTES

1. Official Gazette of the Republic of Macedonia No. 52/1995.
2. Official Gazette of the Republic of Macedonia No. 52/1996.
3. Official gazette No. 91/2001.
4. Official gazette No. 5/2002.
5. Official Gazette of the Republic of Macedonia No. 80/93, 3/94, 71/96, 54/2000, 61/2004.
6. Official Gazette of the Republic of Macedonia No. 19/96 and 26/02.
7. Refined text in the Official Gazette of the Republic of Macedonia No. 17/97.
8. Government of the Republic of Macedonia, Plan adopted at the meeting held in July 2005.
9. Government of the Republic of Macedonia, Information adopted at the meeting held in February 2005.

BIBLIOGRAPHY

Boex J. (2001), *An Introduction Overview of Intergovernmental Fiscal Relations*, Fiscal Policy Simmer Training Courses at GSU, Atlanta: Georgia State University.

Dabla-Norris, E. and P. Wade (2002), *The Challenge of Fiscal Decentralization in Transition Countries*, IMF WP/02/103, Washington, DC.: World Bank.

Government of the Republic of Macedonia (1999a), *Strategija za reforma na državnata uprava vo RM* [The State Administration Reform Strategy], Skopje: Government of the Republic of Macedonia.

Government of the Republic of Macedonia (1999b), *Strategija za reforma na lokalnata samouprava vo Republika Makedonija* [The Local Self-government Administration Reform Strategy], Skopje: Government of Macedonia.

Mark, C. and R. Nayyar-Stone (2002), *Assessing the Benefits of Performance Management in Eastern Europe: Experience in Hungary, Albania and Georgia*, Paper presented at the NISPAcee Annual Conference, Krakow.

Ministry of Local Self-Government of the Republic of Macedonia (2001), Action Plan for the Local Self-government Reform Implementation (2002–2004), Skopje: Ministry of Local Self-government.

Ministry of Local Self-Government of the Republic of Macedonia (2004a), *Study on the Administrative Communication between the Central and the Local Government*, Skopje: Ministry of Local Self-government.

Ministry of Local Self-Government of the Republic of Macedonia (2004b), *Assessment of the Controlling Mechanisms and Supervision of the Operations of the Municipalities*, Skopje: Ministry of Local Self-government.

Ministry of Local Self-Government of the Republic of Macedonia (2004c), *Study on the Financial Management in the Local Self-government Units in the Republic of Macedonia*, Skopje, Ministry of Local Self-government.

OECD (1999), *The Government Performance Project*, PUMA(99)2, Paris: OECD.

Open Society Institute (OSI) Macedonia (2005), Measuring the Fiscal Capacity of the Local Self-government units in the Republic of Macedonia, Skopje: Open Society Institute Foundation – Macedonia and Centre for Economic Analyses.

Pavlovska-Daneva, A. (2001), The Concept of Local Administration in the Republic of Macedonia, *Ius Forum*, **2**(10-12).

Siljanovska-Davkova, G. (1999), Za (ne)usoglasenosta na makedonskata lokalna samouprava so Evropskata povelba za lokalna samouprava [On the discrepancy between the Macedonian local self-government with the European Convention of the Local Self-government], in *Zbornik vo čest na Evgeni Dimitrov*, Skopje: Faculty of Law, 461–77.

13. Local government finance in Moldova

Clare T. Romanik, Eugeniu Hristev and Maria Salabuga*

INTRODUCTION

In contrast to many other countries across the region, the numerous attempts of reforming public administration system in Moldova during the 1990s can be viewed as a 'parade of lost opportunities'. Central authorities were reluctant to undertake thorough administrative reforms and few local governments were ready to make use of those aspects of decentralisation that would bring more resources and opportunities. Moreover, emerging political parties regarded local government reform only in the context of political gain, to criticise the opposing party for its approach. Public administration reform incurred frequent changes, producing four distinct generations of reforms, all affecting local governance finance.

BASIC LEGAL FRAMEWORK AND LOCAL GOVERNMENT FINANCE REGULATIONS

The First Generation of Reform (1991–1994)

The first generation of local government reforms began with euphoria, but proceeded in a very difficult macroeconomic environment. A steep drop in GDP (in 1994 the country's GDP was only 40 per cent of the 1990 level), a massive stoppage of enterprises, depreciation of bank deposits, and hyperinflation which exceeded 1,000 per cent in 1992 are just some of the bitter

* The authors would like to thank Andrei Cantemir for providing expert feedback on policies and legislation affecting local finance.

characteristics of that period. Furthermore, the military conflict in Transnistria and political strain in the South (Gagauzia) fuelled the vulnerability of administrative changes.[1]

On 10 July 1991 Parliament passed the Law on the Basis of Local Self Governance. The law framed the design of local autonomy and outlined bold ideas concerning democratic values in the practice of local administration. Principles of accountability, broad community participation, citizen consultation, transparency and information are highlighted as the foundations for a democratic self-governance. The goal of the law was to relinquish the legacy inherited from the soviet political-administrative system. Part of the transformation was to consolidate administrative territorial units (ATUs), eliminating the district (*rayon* – a Russian word) as the 2nd tier of sub-national government and introducing the county (*judet* – a Romanian word). But because the law was too ambitious, it was never put into force.

In its place, the GoM (on 23 July 1991) enacted another normative act, the 'Temporary Regulations on Functioning of Local Governments', which was in effect until December 1994. The spirit and content of the Temporary Regulations differ dramatically from the Law on the Basis of Local Self Governance. The Law promotes radical changes while the Temporary Regulations makes cosmetic modifications, not addressing the core administrative functions and responsibilities. The Temporary Regulations preserved the soviet district (*rayon*) system. Old soviet logos and stamps were still valid and largely used by the local governments.

The Second Generation of Reform (1994–1997)

Conventionally, the second stage of administrative reform began with the adoption of the new Constitution on 29 July 1994. The new Constitution embodied many fundamental norms and procedures in line with international principles of local governance. Of specific importance are the provisions stipulated in Article 109 that legitimise the pillars of a genuine local administration: (i) local autonomy, (ii) decentralisation of municipal services, (iii) elections of public officials and (iv) citizen consultation on issues of major interest for the community.

On 7 December 1994, Parliament adopted three laws at once, the Law on Territorial-Administrative Structure, the Law on Local Public Administration and the Law on Local Elections. Under the Law on Territorial-Administrative Structure the territorial division consisted of two administrative tiers: (i) villages (communes) and towns and (ii) districts (*rayons*) and cities with the status of municipality. Thirty-eight districts and 859 1st level local governments were formed. The four largest cities were granted the status of municipality. Also, the law specifies that Gagauz-Yery has a special autonomous status, to be regulated by a special organic law. The Law on Local Public Administration reiterates the principles of self-governance, that is local autonomy, decentralisation of municipal services, election of public officials and citizen consultation. The initial legislation package was amended 14 times, aiming to strengthen the influence of the central government over local affairs.

The Third Generation of Reform (1998-2002)

As the centre-right coalition gained control of Parliament in March 1998, a new stage of reform emerged, with the aim of establishing a system of local public administration in compliance with the European Charter of Self Governance, which Moldova ratified in October 1997. A broad legislative framework was created, consisting of laws to regulate the main aspects of local public administration: finance, property, local taxes/fees and provision of public services. *Judets*, first conceptualised in 1991, were now to become a reality. As larger administrative units, *judets* were to create economies of scale, with sufficient economic and fiscal power to deliver a diverse range of public services.

The *judet* system introduced an elected system of government at the county level (that is, the *judet* council) and, in parallel, central government representation at the county level (that is, through the prefect). The prefect had the authority to assure the legitimacy of local decisions and to promote national interests within the *judets*. The prefect also manages de-concentrated services, that is public services of central ministries and departments deployed in the respective *judets*. The relations between elected public authorities and the prefect were intended to be collaborative and consultative, not subordinate.

The 1998 reform produced both positive and negative results. Among the strong points are legitimacy of democratic principles, separation of power, community participation, identification of municipal property, community oriented service provision and others. The procedure for the election and recall of mayors was in full compliance with democratic principles – via universal, direct and secret suffrage – which had a positive impact on transparency and accountability. However, the high degree of independence of the mayor's office led, in many cases, to controversies between mayors and local councils.

The Fourth Generation of Reform (2002–2005)

The Communist Party won an overwhelming majority in the February 2001 parliamentary elections, allowing them to implement significant changes to the local government system. On 27–28 December 2001 the Moldovan Parliament passed legislation that fuelled controversial debates in and outside the country. These were a new Law on Administrative-Territorial Organisation that reintroduced the district (*rayon*) system, and several amendments to the 1998 Law on Local Public Administration that introduced a new procedure for electing local public officials. The international community and, in particular, the Council of Europe saw this as undermining local autonomy and reversing decentralisation reform. Several municipal associations and the parliamentary opposition factions expressed similar criticisms of the intention to reshuffle the county government system.

According to the LLPA, 1st tier ATUs have both a legislative and executive branch (compared to monolithic government at the 2nd tier), with each branch independent of the other and from higher-order authorities and accountable only to the citizens. In practice, however, the real distribution of powers between tiers of government or between executives and legislatures varies greatly, depending on party affiliation, their relationship with the district chair, and the personality of the mayors and district executives. As discussed below, the finance departments of the 2nd tier ATUs hold great financial power over the 1st tier ATUs.

DEMOCRATIC LEGITIMACY AND FINANCIAL REPORTING

During the first generation of reform (1991–1994), the old soviet approach of drafting local budgets and shaping the financial basis of constituencies was still in force. There was a strict subordination to central government as mayors of cities and the heads of district (*rayon*) executive committees were appointed and dismissed by the President of Moldova.

Despite the passage of the Law on Local Taxes and Fees during the second generation of the reform (1994–1997), local governments still had insignificant financial autonomy. Little discretion was given to local governments in terms of budgeting. The Ministry of Finance (MoF) continued to be the key player in the local budget cycle, with the exclusive authority to guide the development of, oversee and check local budget drafts. At any time, the MoF could interfere in the budget process or make amendments affecting local budgets. Local budgets were very dependent on state budget transfers, which made them sensitive to macroeconomic indices and vulnerable to nepotism and favouritism. As a consequence, the efficiency and effectiveness of public funds was quite low and the enthusiasm and entrepreneurship of local governments were undermined.

The third generation of the reform (1998–2001) that introduced the *judet* system did not represent much of an advance with regard to the local budget process. A positive element was the balanced budget requirement. Otherwise, the same traditional approach of direct guidance from the MoF, pre-budgeted commitments, and heavy transfers from the state budget was in place. Prepared budgets of the 1st level ATUs were presented to the *judet* financial departments for review and revision, while *judet* budgets were submitted to the MoF for preliminary consultation. Local governments had little financial autonomy as more than half of their planned budget expenditures were committed upon normative directions issued by the Ministry of Finance.

Amendments initiated in 2001 gave the prefect (the representative of the central government) more discretion to intervene directly in local governments' financial affairs. The General Finance Division, together with other functional departments, was reassigned from the *judet* council to the prefecture. The prefect was invested with the power to prepare the draft *judet* budget and to present it to the *judet* council for approval, in effect, becoming the chief executive of *judet* finances.

According to the 2003 Local Public Finance Law, special purpose transfers from the 2nd tier ATUs cover the labour expenses related to educational and cultural facilities. This continues the trend of most planned expenditures of 1st tier ATUs being committed *a priori*. In addition to these competencies, 1st tier ATUs have entrusted duties for social protection, including for the unemployed, public health, use and protection of natural resources, nature reserves, public order and civil protection. Despite language espousing local financial autonomy, the law does not imply substantial changes to the financial authority of local governments. Local councils and mayors are granted the same power and responsibility as stipulated in previous legislation concerning the procedure of drafting, approving and executing local budgets.

INDEPENDENT LOCAL GOVERNMENT REVENUE SOURCES

Own Revenues

First tier ATUs have insignificant own revenue sources, amounting to only 12–13 per cent of their budget in recent years. Although own revenues reached 20 per cent of the local government budgets in 1999, this was more a result of the severe reduction of state budget revenues in that year, than of growth in own revenues. The own revenues of 1st tier ATUs include proceeds from sale of land, houses, apartments, lease of land, local taxes and fees, fees for services provided by the local government or local public institutions, and 'profit' from enterprises partially or wholly owned by the local government. The fees for services provided by the local government or local public institutions are about 3 per cent of total revenues, as is the 'profit' from enterprises partially or wholly owned by the local government. Annual sales of land and property amount to less than 3 per cent of total revenues. Fees for natural resources use and the leasing of state real estate generate much less revenue and make up less than 1 per cent of total revenues.

Table 13.1 Own revenue sources as per cent of total revenues (2004)

Revenue Source	% of Total Revenues
Local taxes and fees (established by Title VII of Fiscal Code)	3
Fees for services provided by local government or local public institutions	3
Fees for natural resource use, state property and land	<1
'Profit' from shares in local enterprises	3
Sale of land and property (capital revenues)	3
Total: Own Revenues	13

Source: Ministry of Finance.

Revenues from local taxes and fees[2] amount to less than 3 per cent of total revenues. Over the period 1996–2004, they ranged from a low of 2 per cent of total revenues in 1996 to a high of 5 per cent in 1998. For the last three years, they have held steady at about 3 per cent. Of these local taxes and fees, the most important are the tax for territory maintenance, market fees, and licence fees for establishing commercial trade.

Shared Revenues

There are two types of shared revenues received by the 1st tier ATUs: regional revenues (from the land and real estate taxes) and general government revenues (from the corporate income tax (CIT), personal income tax (PIT), and previously the VAT). The land and real estate taxes are approximately 11 per cent of total local budget revenues (Table 13.2). The 2nd tier ATU determines how revenue from the land and real estate taxes will be shared between the 1st and 2nd tier ATUs. From 1996 to 1998, the 1st tier ATUs received a greater share of the regional revenues; in 2000 and 2001, the split was roughly even.

Since 2002, the 2nd tier ATUs have retained a greater share of these revenues for their budgets. In 2003 and 2004, the 2nd tier ATUs retained three times as much revenue as they distributed among the 1st tier ATUs.

Table 13.2 Shared revenue sources as per cent of total revenues (2004)

Revenue Source	% of Total Revenues
Land and real estate taxes	11
Personal and corporate income taxes	13
Total: Shared Revenues*	25

*Note:** Parts do not sum to 25% because of rounding.

Sources: Ministry of Finance.

When Title VI of the Fiscal Code (2004) is finally fully implemented, the country will have an *ad valorem* real estate tax. So far, the government has developed a methodology for estimating the value of urban residential units and has carried out one pilot appraisal project. Implementation of the *ad valorem* tax in rural areas will be delayed for some time. Title VI does not change the authority of 2nd tier ATUs to determine the 1st tier ATUs' share of the real estate tax, so this limits the ability of the real estate tax to become a source of self-governance and financial autonomy for Moldova local self-governments.

The annual budget law determines how general government tax revenues (PIT and CIT) will be shared with the central government and the 2nd tier ATUs. The 2nd tier ATUs, in turn, determine how much of the general government tax revenues (PIT and CIT) will be received by the 1st tier ATUs. In recent years, the share of regional and general government revenues received by 1st tier ATUs amounts to about one-quarter of their total budget. From 1997 to 2001, these revenues were approximately half of their total budget. Earlier, when the 1st tier ATUs received a share of the turnover tax (then VAT), the shared tax revenues were even more significant in their budget, almost 80 per cent of their total budget in 1996.

Evolution of Local Government Revenue Generating Capacity

During the first generation of local reform (1991–1994), the taxable resources of local government were scrawny. In July 1994, Parliament enacted the Law on Local Taxes and Fees, which introduced new taxes, although their contribution was insignificant at the beginning. Local authorities had the right to select from a list of 14 local taxes/fees established by Parliament, as well as establish the approach of tax levy and tax exemptions. But the maximum threshold of the tax/fee rates was the prerogative of Parliament. In practice, only half a dozen local taxes were used. The most frequently used were: tax for territory maintenance[3] (used by four out of five jurisdictions), licence for establishing commercial trade (used by seven out of ten jurisdictions), market fees (used by one out of two jurisdictions) and licence to render public transport (used by one out of seven jurisdictions).

Figure 13.1 Average own revenues (per capita) in cities and villages

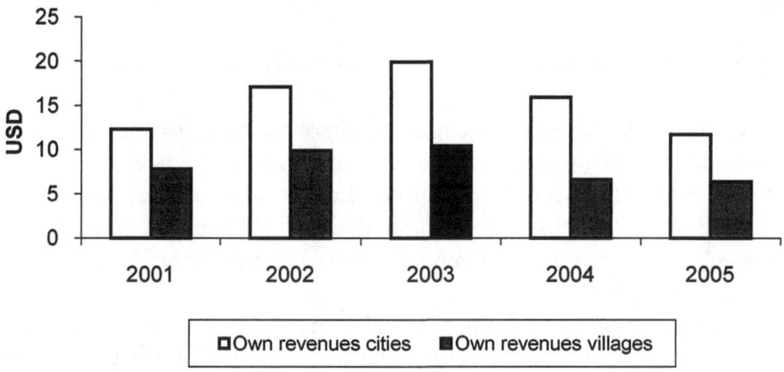

Source: Ministry of Finance.

As one might expect, the fiscal capacity of 1st tier ATUs varies by size. Over the past five years, per capita own revenues of villages have ranged from 42 per cent (in 2003) to 63 per cent (in 2000) of the per capita own revenues of towns and cities (see Figure 13.1). More than half of the total revenues generated by local taxes and fees are collected in Chisinau. In the most extreme case of the licence to render public transport, Chisinau generates 95 per cent of the revenue generated by this tax.

During the third generation of the reform (1998–2001), a very serious problem was the non-transparent manner in which the main sources of shared revenues were distributed between the 1st and the 2nd tiers of government units at the discretion of the *judet* authorities. First level government units were forced to continuously negotiate to gain access to resources collected in their territories. This practice was codified in the 2003 Law on Local Public Administration, which grants the 2nd tier governments the authority to determine how regional and general government revenues are shared between the two tiers of local government.

The most recent and significant legislation governing local taxes is Title VII of the Fiscal Code enacted through Law 93-XV of 1 April 2004 which entered into force on 1 January 2005. Title VII supersedes the Law on Local Taxes and

Fees (1994) and eliminates three of the local fees, namely, a border-crossing fee, a fee for the right to sell in customs zones, and a fee for the right to make movies and TV programmes. Of these, only the border-crossing fee had been a significant revenue source for local governments. According to the new Fiscal Code, the local taxes in Moldova include the tax for territory maintenance, lottery tax, tax on advertisements, tax on the use of local official symbols of the jurisdiction, licence for establishing commercial trade, market tax, hotel tax, resort tax, licence to render public transport, car parking fees, tax on dog owners.

Current Challenges in Local Government Revenue Collection

Title VII of the Fiscal Code attempts to empower local governments to take more responsibility in administering their own revenues and establishing the tax rate. For example, according to the new Law, local authorities should collect local taxes from companies based within their jurisdiction on a quarterly basis. Previously, local governments generally relied on the State Tax Inspectorate for tax collection.

Even before passage of the new Fiscal Code, many local governments had attempted to improve their tax administration and collection capacity, but they encountered several difficulties. They lack automated systems and databases of the local taxpayers, which considerably slows down the process of tax collection and monitoring. They also lack legal expertise, which means that sometimes taxes are adopted by local councils that are not expressly provided for in the law, are outside of their competencies or are contradictory to existing laws.

GRANT TRANSFERS

The 2003 Law on Local Public Finance identifies both general transfers for operating revenues and two types of special purpose transfers. Together, these amount to more than 60 per cent of the local government budgets. The LLPF does not define transfers intended to cover capital investment costs; these are funded through a Social Investment Fund that has very limited resources.

General Transfers from Financial Support Fund

Article 10 of the LLPF specifies that transfers from the Financial Support Fund for Administrative Territorial Units should cover the gap between projected revenues and necessary operating expenditures, in order to balance the budget of local governments. Each year, the Ministry of Finance defines expenditures norms for all types of local government expenditures, which local governments should use to plan their budget. These transfers, calculated based on the Ministry of Finance's established norms and expected revenues, attempt to compensate for the different fiscal capacities of individual local governments. In other countries these might be called equalisation grants.

The formula provided in the LLPF for per capita transfers is: $t = cf - v$, where c is per capita expenditure norm, f is the adjustment factor to the per capita expenditure norm, and v is the projected per capita revenues. The adjustment factor is intended to allow the Ministry of Finance to make an adjustment in the case where ATUs need to incur specific additional expenditures imposed by the law. In practice, the adjustment factor tends to favour the larger cities, justified by the fact that they have to provide more services (for example, sewerage, heat) than rural jurisdictions.

Transfers are allocated from the central budget from the special Financial Support Fund for Administrative Territorial Units. The Fund is supplemented both from the central budget and from the surplus of the revenues of local administration whose per capita revenues exceed the average per capita expenditures of the ATUs from the same district (*rayon*) by more than 20 per cent (that is, where $v > 1.2 * cf$).

Special Purpose Transfers

Article 11 of the 2003 Law on Local Public Finance defines special purpose transfers intended for when the central government delegates additional functions to the local government, or if it passes laws or regulations which either take away revenue or change the administrative territorial structures (such as when *judets* were replaced by *rayons*). These special purpose transfers are to be decided by the annual budget law. There is no formula for special purpose transfers as these are intended to be irregular in nature.

Article 8 (3) of the 2003 Law on Local Public Finance defines another type of special purpose transfer for the salaries and social fund payments for employees of educational and cultural facilities, except for museums. These special purpose transfers are made to 1st tier local governments from the budgets of 2nd tier local governments.

Evolution of Grant Transfers

Transfer levels have varied widely, as a result of frequent changes in the regulations governing transfers and shared revenues. As the amount of shared revenues received by 1st tier ATUs has diminished, the amount of transfers has increased to compensate. In the late 1990s, shared revenues were half of the 1st tier ATU budgets and transfers were less than one-third. In the past few years, the shared revenues were reduced to one-quarter of the 1st tier ATU budgets and transfers increased to more than 60 per cent. (The main reason for the decrease in shared revenues and increase in transfers in recent years is that the VAT ceased to be a shared revenue.) In other countries this would be seen as an undesirable development, as shared revenues are generally more predictable than revenues. However, shared revenues are extremely unpredictable in Moldova as the annual budget law determines the shares of general government revenues to be distributed among 2nd tier local governments and these, in turn, determine how the general government and regional revenues will be distributed among the 1st tier local governments (or retained by the 2nd tier local government).

Figure 13.2 Transfers and shared tax revenues received by 1st tier local governments

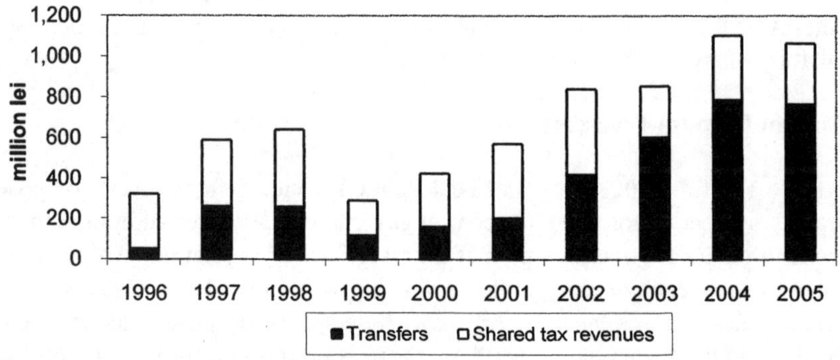

Figure 13.2 illustrates the increase of both transfers and shared tax revenues received by 1st tier local governments since 1999. While shared tax revenues increased and then decreased somewhat during this period, transfers steadily rose. One would expect with the increase in transfers (both absolutely and as a share of local government budgets) calculated with a formula based on projected revenues, local governments would have a greater incentive to underestimate own revenues and perhaps, even less incentive to collect own revenues.

LOCAL GOVERNMENT EXPENDITURES

As described in the section above on transfers, expenditure norms defined by the Ministry of Finance are fixed according to the number of population living in a particular town or village, or the number of particular beneficiaries such as pupils. Despite the fact that the transfer is intended to compensate for differences in fiscal capacity, generally, the more money a community can earn the more it can spend. According to the Law on Local Public Finances, no community can spend more than its annual estimated or generated amount of revenues.

Expenditures by Function

The Moldovan local government budget categories according to function are:

- Administration,
- Education,
- Culture, arts, sports, youth activities,
- Health protection,
- Social assistance, and
- Public housing, utilities, roads and public transit.

Table 13.3 Distribution of expenditures by function (in per cent for the 1st tier local government)

	1998	1999	2000	2001	2002	2003	2004
Local administration	6	11	14	15	14	13	11
Education	51	71	71	67	67	68	69
Culture/sport	3	3	3	4	4	4	4
Health	12	3	1	1	1	1	0
Social protection	5	4	1	1	1	1	1
Housing, utilities, roads, public transit	12	5	6	7	7	5	5
Other expenditures	12	4	4	4	6	7	10
Total expenditures	100	100	100	100	100	100	100

Source: Ministry of Finance.

As shown in Table 13.3, listing expenditures by function for local governments, education is by far the largest expense, each year amounting to more than half of the total budget. In 2004, education expenses were ten times greater than the next highest category of expenditures, which was administration of the local government. In previous years, other expenditure categories of importance were public services such as roads, streetlights and park maintenance.

Expenditures by Economic Structure

The Moldovan local government budget categories according to economic structure are:

- Salaries,
- Social fund payments,
- Goods and services,
- Other operating expenditures, and
- Capital expenditures.

Table 13.4 Distribution of expenditures by economic structure (1st tier local government)

	2000	2001	2002	2003	2004
Salaries/wages	40	35	32	36	48
Social Fund payment	11	12	9	10	13
Goods and services	29	29	25	27	29
Other operating expenditures	10	10	9	10	6
Capital expenditures	10	17	27	16	4
Totals	100	100	100	100	100

Source: Ministry of Finance.

Table 13.4 shows, with data from 42 1st tier local governments, the marked increase and then decline in capital expenditures of 1st tier local governments. What is also clear is the dominance of salaries and social fund payments, which are mostly not discretionary expenditures as the number of employees and salaries for schools and other local government functions are established centrally. As noted above, the salaries and social fund payments of employees of educational and cultural facilities are paid through a special purpose transfer from the 2nd tier ATU.

One sees a very different picture in terms of the capacity to fund capital expenditures, with the combined expenditures of 1st and 2nd tier local governments (see Table 13.5). Clearly, this means that 2nd tier local governments are making most of the capital investments at the local level.

Table 13.5 Distribution of expenditures by economic structure, in per cent for the 1st and 2nd tier local government)

	1998	1999	2000	2001	2002	2003	2004
Operating expenditures	87	87	83	84	83	86	77
of which:							
Salaries	31	40	37	33	34	37	30
Social fund	6	5	9	9	10	10	8
Goods and services	30	28	25	29	26	24	18
Interest rates payment	7	3	1	1	0	0	0
Current transfers	10	8	8	9	8	11	17
Other current expenditures	3	4	4	3	4	4	4
Capital expenditures	13	13	17	16	17	14	23
of which:							
Capital investments	8	7	10	9	9	7	15
Capital refurbishments	2	3	3	3	5	3	4
Other capital expenditures	3	2	4	4	4	3	4
Total	100	100	100	100	100	100	100

Source: Ministry of Finance.

Evolution of Local Government Expenditures

Local government expenditures relative to GDP have varied from very low, roughly 2 per cent during the first generation of reform, to quite high, up to 18 per cent in the second generation of reform, back to a moderate level from 8 to 10.9 per cent in the third and fourth generations of reform.[4] After the high level of local government expenditures during the second generation of the reform, they dropped precipitously in 1998 and 1999 when VAT ceased to be a shared tax revenue. In both 1998 and 1999, 1st tier local government expenditures on education were reduced by 30 per cent compared to the previous year.

The low level of local government expenditures during the first generation of reform is explained by the fact that the central government was still directly financing most of the local community expenditures from the state budget. For instance, road repairs (including those within villages), water and sewerage were financed by the central government. Local governance dealt mainly with socio-cultural institutions.

Beginning with the second generation of reform, the most important local expenditures became schools, hospitals, libraries, and cultural community centres. As mentioned above, most of the related expenditures were pre-budgeted commitments, established in accordance with the Ministry of Finance norms.

Local government expenditures jumped sharply from 1999 to 2000, at the time that shared revenues increased. However, when the VAT ceased to be a shared revenue, local governments had to respond to diminishing revenues by looking for ways to reduce their expenditures and financial obligations. One way to do this is to reduce educational expenditures, as it is not clear how these should be shared between local and central authorities. These are, in effect, unfunded mandates, where the responsibilities and authorities given to the local governments are not covered by the revenue sources.

ACCOUNTING RULES, REGULATIONS AND LOCAL GOVERNMENT BUDGETING PROCESS

Moldova has a unitary budget. Article 19 of the LLPF (2003) establishes the budget process. This begins with the MoF sending methodological guidelines to the 2nd tier ATUs, along with macroeconomic projections, information on relevant government policy, and projected rates of contribution from general government revenue. The Finance Departments of the 2nd tier ATUs share this information with their respective 1st tier ATUs who then make revenue projections based on this information. The budgets prepared by 1st tier ATUs are reviewed by the Finance Departments of the 2nd tier ATUs who submit the collective budgets to the MoF for review. The 1st tier ATU then submits the local budget for review and approval by the local council. Until the local council approves the budget that has been approved by the higher authorities, the ATU will not receive transfers or shared revenues.

While this process appears rational, the timing is problematic, as local governments do not have sufficient information to estimate budgets until the last minute. Although the shared tax revenues are fairly predictable from the central government to the 2nd tier ATU, the amount transferred to each 1st tier ATU is less predictable. Decisions regarding transfers lack any predictability. This decision comes very late in the year, making budget planning a near impossible task. It is not uncommon for a town to find out on 1 December the exact amount of transfers, when 15 December is the deadline for submitting the final budget to the Ministry of Finance, before which time it should be approved by the local council. This allows very little time for the local council to review the budget, as specified in Article 20 of LLPF, in two readings, with at least five-day intervals between the readings. The effective timetable means little possibility of real dialogue on the budget, unless the council has been involved in the preparation process.

It became usual practice during the 1990s to minimise initial budget estimations and readjust them during the budget year to reflect reality. Unrealistic estimations and overloaded commitments led to significant discrepancies between the revenue and the spending sides of the budget. Ultimately, this deficit was covered by the state budget through direct transfers or bank loans. Because local budgets had a shaky and unstable source of own revenues, paying off these debts became a thorny issue in the intergovernmental relations. A more frequent solution at that time was mutual debt write-off. This approach was especially popular in netting out energy debts, unpaid bills for communal services, debts to the Social Insurance Fund and salary arrears.

Article 12 of the LLPF (2003) attempted to address this by requiring a budgetary balance. Annual budgets may not be approved or executed with a fiscal deficit. However, another provision of the same law discourages accurate revenue projections. Article 3 states that all surplus revenues collected beyond the project revenues shall remain with that local government's budget. Naturally, this reinforces the practice of under-projecting revenue collection. In 2003, the so-called 'surplus' accounted for about 600 million lei, or 60 per cent of local governments' total final budget. However, only one-third of that amount actually remained with the local governments and the remainder was diverted to central government expenditures.

Mayors are considered the main executor of the 1st tier local budget, responsible for drawing up the budget proposal, generating revenue, managing property/assets, and ensuring good accounting practices, such as regular preparation of budget execution reports and maintaining the balance sheet. During the year, local government budgets are usually modified on a quarterly basis by the decision of the local council.

Cash execution of the budgets is carried out through the treasury system, through revenue and expenditure accounts. The territorial treasuries allocate transfers from the respective budgets to local ones, as well as contributions to those budgets from the general government revenue and real estate tax. Given the dependency of local governments on these transfers and shared revenues, a perennial complaint of local government officials is the delay by the territorial treasury in providing the necessary cash.

SUPERVISION AND CONTROL: THE STATE AUDIT

The Ministry of Finance has very strong financial controls over the preparation and execution of local government budgets. Article 36 of the Law on Local Government Finance (2003) identifies the Ministry of Finance and the Finance

Departments of the 2nd tier local governments as the auditors of budget preparation and execution of 1st tier local governments.

A governmental decision of 1 November 2005 establishes that the Ministry of Finance, through the State Treasury, the Department of Financial Control and Audit, and its ten local branches, shall exercise the following functions related to the supervision and control of the local budgets and financial operations: approve standard reporting forms for the local government accounting and budgeting divisions; review local budget preparation and execution for accuracy; actually execute local budgets through local treasuries; monitor bank accounts, if any (this would only be in the rare case of a local government having a loan); and prepare operating reports for central and local authorities on cash operations within the execution of the local budgets.

The State Treasury of the Ministry of Finance both executes and regulates all financial transactions of local government. The local branch of the Department of Financial Control and Audit carries out audits of ATU budget execution on a bi-annual basis. The results of the audits are reviewed by the respective local public officials and then published. The other institution responsible for auditing is the Chamber of Control and Audit of the Court of Accounts. The Chamber performs random audits or if there is a problem.

Articles 16 and 19 of the Law on Local Government Finance (2003) provide the general responsibilities of local government for record keeping and supervision over budget execution. Finance departments or finance units of each ATU should prepare quarterly and annual budget execution reports. They should also maintain a loan registry to account for all loans on an annual basis. The local councils have a budgetary committee that meets on a quarterly basis, during which the executive branch presents the budget report. In addition, any council member may solicit budget information at any time.

FURTHER DEVELOPMENTS: LOCAL GOVERNMENT AND FINANCIAL MARKETS

The 2003 Law on Local Public Finance allows ATUs to take long-term loans or float bonds, only for capital expenditures. This applies to loans from domestic or foreign financial institutions. The law specifies that within the loan agreement, revenues to repay the interest and principal must be identified from the jurisdiction's own fiscal revenues. The law is also clear that the central government may not act as a guarantor of loan repayment. Article 14 specifies that the loan may not exceed 20 per cent of the total annual own revenues.

To date, several towns have obtained loans, mostly on a concessionary basis through the Ministry of Finance from the World Bank loans or other donor organisations. No bonds have been floated and there are no local government staff experienced in such issues. Even administration and maintenance of accounting records of the current loans is a rather unusual experience for the average local government accountant.

Several towns have received World Bank loans to rebuild their water supply system and other infrastructure, without real projections of their ability to pay back these loans. There is a critical need to develop basic legislation for municipal financial markets and to develop sufficient, stable revenue sources that the towns can count on in projecting revenues to pay back infrastructure loans.

CONCLUSIONS AND RECOMMENDATIONS

Moldova meets some of the democratic prerequisites for local government finance. The local councils and the mayor are democratically elected through universal, direct and secret vote. However, local governments cannot determine their own internal administrative structures in order to adapt them to local needs, including determining the staffing structure and salaries of local government employees. An annex to the local government budget includes the staff limits for public institutions funded from the budget.

On the expenditure side, local government functions are generally assigned according to the principle of subsidiarity. That is, responsibility for performing a function is assigned to the lowest tier of local government capable of performing that function effectively. In general, the 2003 Law on Local Public Finance makes clear distinctions in the assignment of functional responsibilities between the two tiers of local government. There is some overlapping of functions between the two tiers of local government in the field of social assistance.

On the revenue side, the Moldovan local government finance system is further from fiscal decentralisation. As demonstrated by the low level of own revenues, local governments do not have sufficient own resources that they can freely use. Much of their budget is made up of special purpose transfers for salaries and social fund payments for employees of educational and cultural facilities. The amount of funds received by 1st tier local governments from intergovernmental transfers and shared revenues is solely determined by 2nd tier local governments and this decision-making process can be accurately described as an inscrutable black box.

The first recommendation is to reduce the arbitrary power of the 2nd tier local governments over the finances of the 1st tier local governments. Most importantly, this means the 2nd tier local governments should follow a clear formula for distributing shared revenues and transfers, including how much they retain themselves.

A second recommendation is to make the new *ad valorem* real estate tax a tax of the 1st tier local government tax, instead of a shared tax. This is general practice in most countries. Preferably, the 1st tier local governments would also have the authority to set the real estate tax rate, perhaps within a range, and the tax base.

A third recommendation is to remove disincentives to raise own revenues and project them accurately. The system rewards underestimating revenues, by allowing (in law, if not always in practice) the local government to retain all revenues generated above the projected amount. This creates a strong incentive for downward bias in budget revenue projections. Final budgets may show little resemblance to original budgets as 'found surplus revenues' are added, as well as additional expenditures.

The method by which the general transfers are calculated also creates disincentives for local governments to project revenues accurately, and possibly may affect their collection efforts. The formula should not consider projected revenues, but fiscal capacity. A proxy for fiscal capacity can be revenue from taxes for which the local government does not have collection responsibility. The transfer formula should not punish local governments for greater fiscal efforts.

In general, local governments should be granted greater financial autonomy by allowing them to set the rates of their own taxes. However, if these disincentives persist, local governments are unlikely to utilise financial autonomy and increase their taxing efforts.

A fourth recommendation is to develop legislation to support a municipal capital market. Given the different fiscal capacity of Moldovan towns and cities, the authority to obtain loans or float bonds may be differentiated by the size and type of local government.

A fifth recommendation is to introduce multi-year strategic planning for capital investment. A small share of local governments in Moldova have gone through a comprehensive community-based strategic planning process with a public hearing on the strategic plan before it is approved by the local council. In these cases, the local governments are incorporating the priorities established in the strategic plan in their annual budgets. This is the closest to multi-year capital investment planning in Moldova. As these local governments gain experience in doing this, they should begin to make sectoral and programme allocations in their budget, based on a multi-year plan. Then, on an annual basis, the capital portion of the local budget can be reviewed and approved in concert with approval of a revised and extended strategic plan or capital investment plan.

A final recommendation is to allow local governments greater authority in establishing administrative staffing plans. Instead of following norms laid out by the central government, local governments should be able to decide which positions are needed and how many staff to hire.

NOTES

1. Transdniestria is a breakaway region in the eastern region of Moldova that won quasi-independence after a brief war in 1992 and has survived ever since on Russian military support, money and cheap gas, plus a thriving arms business and other smuggling activities. Gagauz-Yery, in the south of Moldova was granted a wide range of administrative and political autonomy.
2. Determined by the 1994 Local Taxes and Fees, until 2004 with the passage of Title VII of the Tax Code.
3. The tax for territory maintenance is similar to a Business Improvement District 'BID' in that it taxes commercial entities or individuals engaged in entrepreneurial activities to cover the costs of street sweeping, park maintenance, and so on
4. These are all local government expenditures. Expenditures for 1st tier local governments have been equal to 3 to 4 per cent of GDP for the past six years.

BIBLIOGRAPHY

Anderson, J. (2000), *Moldova Local Government Finance Laws: Review and Recommendations*, Washington, DC: Urban Institute Project 06901-007.

CASE-Moldova (2005). *Financing Local Governments in Moldova – Summary of Current Situation*, Chisinau: Moldova.

Institute for Development and Social Initiatives (IDIS) and 'Viitorul' (2003), *Legal and Practical Developments in the Sphere of Local and Regional Democracy in Moldova*, Chisinau, IDIS.

Ionita, V. (2004), *Fiscal Decentralization in SEE countries: Case of Moldova*, Presented at the Stability Pact Conference.

Law on Local Public Administration (2003).

Law on Local Public Finance (2003).

Title VII of the Tax Code (2004).

APPENDIX
LEGISLATION OF THE FOUR GENERATIONS OF LOCAL GOVERNMENT REFORM SINCE 1991

The First Generation of the Reform (1991–1994)

- *Law on the Basis of Local Self-Governance (1991).* Outlines the framework of local governance in compliance with basic principles of democracy, citizen participation, decentralisation and the like. Introduces notions of prefect, mayor and *judet* (county). Too ambitious, not put into force.
- *Temporary Regulations on Functioning of Local Governments (1991).* Preserved the old district system and enacted cosmetic reshufflings in terminology, that is replaced chief of executive committee, with mayor and executive committee, with local council. In effect, replaced the Law on the Basis of Local Self-Governance. Retained the soviet system for the 2nd level of sub-national government.

The Second Generation of the Reform (1994–1997)

- *Constitution (1994).* Article 109 of the Constitution calls for local autonomy, decentralisation of municipal services, election of public officials, and citizen consultation on issues of major interest to the community. Retained the soviet system of 2nd level sub-national government.
- *Law on Territorial-Administrative Structure (1994).*
- *Law on Local Public Administration (1994).*
- *Law on Local Elections (1994).*
- *Law on Special Juridical Status of Gagauz Yery (1994).*
- *Law on Local Taxes (1994).*
- *Law on Public Service (1995).*

The Third Generation of the Reform (1998–2002)

- *European Charter on Local Self-Governance. (Ratified by Moldovan Parliament 1997).*
- *Law on Administrative and Territorial Organization (1998).* Replaces *rayons* with counties (*judets*) and consolidates the smallest villages into communes.
- *Law on Local Public Administration (1998).* Establishes that cities and communes are not subordinated to the regions and have the right to finan-

cial autonomy. Identifies and expands local government competencies to achieve decentralisation of social public services.

- *Law on Local Public Finance (1999).* Identifies revenue sources and expenditure assignments. States the principles and mechanism of the (equalisation) transfer system
- *Law on Public Patrimony (1999).* Delimits state and local public property by type and guarantees local governments the right to public patrimony.
- *Law on Tax on Immovable Property (1999).* Introduces *ad valorem* property tax with provisions for re-evaluating and indexing property values. Local councils (for cities and communes) are given the authority for setting the tax rate between 1–2 per cent of market value.
- *Law on Local Elected Officials (1999).*

The Fourth Generation of the Reform (2002-2005)

- *Law on Administrative and Territorial Organization (December 2001).* Returns to the *rayon* system of 2nd tier local government, replacing the *judet.*
- *Amendments to 1998 Law on Local Public Administration (December 2001).* Abolished prefectures and replaced them with district (*rayon*) executive committees. Mayor to be elected by local councillors and also to serve as chair of local council.
- *Law on Local Public Administration (2003).* Identifies competencies of local governments (including asset management), but does not eliminate overlapping competencies of 1st and 2nd tier ATUs. States that local governments should receive additional resources for entrusted duties and the financially weaker government should benefit from financial re-distribution.
- *Law on Local Public Finance (2003).* Reinforces the role of the 2nd tier level governments in guiding the budget development for and determining revenue share and transfers received by 1st tier local governments.
- *Title VII of the Tax Code (2004).* Supersedes Law on Local Taxes and Fees of 1994. Empowers local governments with some additional tax administration and collection authorities.

14. Local government finance in Montenegro

Djordjije Blažić

INTRODUCTION

The goal of this project is to present research on local self-government financing in Montenegro during the transition period. Our main intention is to describe the local self-government financing system, focusing mainly on various resources of local revenues and their classification, mostly by analysing the legislative and institutional framework of local self-government in Montenegro, which was first established by the Constitution of RCG in 1992 and the Law on Local Government in 1991. We will also share our observations of the political economy, budgeting process and principles of confidentiality and social responsibility. At the end of this project we will deal with issues of revision, that is control of local self-government performance. The purpose of this is to provide an authoritative overview of local self-government financing in Montenegro, highlighting the newly reformed financing system of municipalities adopted in July 2003 and which came into effect on January 2004.

Montenegro, as with Croatia, Bosnia and Herzegovina, FRY Macedonia prior to their independence, was a constituent republic of the Socialist Federative Republic of Yugoslavia. After a one-party system, dating from after WWII, the first plural election in Montenegro took place in 1990. The breaking up of the SFRJ resulted in the creation of the Federal Republic of Yugoslavia. The new country shared the same destiny as its predecessor after the Montenegro conflict with Milošević's regime and its later fall on 5 October 2001. The clash continued with the following Serbian political establishment over the call for a referendum on the autonomy of Montenegro. Misunderstandings existed amongst the leaders of Serbia and Montenegro over this issue, with the contribution of international political factors and their influence in the situation, resulting in the passing of the Constitutional Charter of Union of States of Serbia and Montenegro as the legal act of the highest importance.[1]

Local self-government in the Republic of Montenegro was created at the beginning of the 1990s. Its first legislative shape began with the Constitutional amendments 106–108 from 1991 (Constitution of SR Montenegro from 1974) and in the first Law on Local Government from 1991 (Blečić, 2000). Development of local self-government continued through the adoption of the new Constitution of the Republic of Montenegro in 1992, the Law on Transfer of Government Affairs on Local Self-Government Bodies[2], the Decree of the Government of Montenegro on entrusting governmental affairs to local self-government[3], the Law on the Capital City in 1993[4], and especially the amendments to the Law on Local Government in 1995.[5] Serious processes of decentralisation and empowerment of municipalities began in 1988 and are still ongoing (Government of Montenegro, 1998; 2001).

MAIN LEGAL FRAMEWORK AND REGULATIONS OF LOCAL SELF-GOVERNMENT FINANCING

There are several laws and other regulations regarding local self-government in Montenegro: the new Law on Local Government[6], the Law on Financing of Local Government[7], the Law on Mayor's Election[8], the Law on Territorial Division of SR Montenegro into Municipalities[9], the Law on Historical Capital[10] and the Law on Election of Councillors and Deputies.[11] The Law on Capital City and the new Law on Historical Capital are under preparation. An important framework for financing local self-government is set out by the Law on Budget and the Law on Debt Issuance, as well as a number of other various material laws.

The new system of local self-government has some major characteristics:

- System of division of power (managerial type);
- Omnibus system of responsibilities of local units;
- One level local self-government, and
- Monotype concept of organisation of municipalities.

The only municipality that differs from this model is the historical capital city, which has some particular responsibilities, different from the other municipalities.

With the new concept of the law on local self-government (see Blažić, 2004), the combined model of establishing local self-governmental affairs was accepted (system of enumeration and general clause) along with setting down the presumption (of responsibility) of local self-government for affairs which are not prescribed as being governmental bodies' responsibility or other bodies and organisations that act as a public authority. The law creates a space for local units to conduct affairs of interest to the local population, which are not prescribed as a responsibility of governmental bodies. The new system of local self-government retains three groups of local affairs. The first group is the so-called own affairs of local self-government, which local self-government independently arranges, conducts and finances from own funds. The second group is the so-called delegated (transferred and devolved) affairs, that is affairs which, by their legislative nature, belong to the State and are financed from the State budget, but which are delegated by the State to local self-government to be carried out. Municipalities are and can only be founded by the law. Currently, there are 21 municipalities in Montenegro. More precisely there are 19 'classical' municipalities and one Historical Capital (Cetinje) with another having the status of Capital City (Podgorica).

Financing of the municipalities and relations between municipalities and central government in this area are regulated by the Law on Financing of Local Government. Major functions of local self-government are the autonomy in making ordinances and the control, collection and disposal of collected revenues. The new Law on Local Government prescribes only the principles of financing, while the Law on Financing of Local Government and certain tax laws closely regulate it.

The structure of local self-government bodies is defined by the Law on Local Government and municipal ordinances. Namely, the law prescribes the founding of local bodies for the conduct of municipal affairs, municipal assembly as a citizen representative body and the mayor (president of a municipality) as an executive body. Local bodies with the responsibility for conducting municipal affairs can be: secretariats, directories, offices, bureaux, and so on. For the operation of specific affairs, the following local bodies can be set up: community police, service for protection and information centre. For the conduct of affairs that demand expert knowledge and autonomy, agencies can be founded.

The new concept of local self-government is particularly focused on relationships between local self-government and Government bodies, based on the principles of co-operation but also limited control of the central over local bodies. Local self-government in this new concept is defined as a right and the possibility for citizens and local bodies to, within the limits set by the law, arrange and manage certain public affairs under their own responsibility and in the interest of the local population, exercised by the principles of democracy, decentralisation, autonomy of local self-government, mutual cooperation between the State and the municipalities and the legality and professionalism of local bodies' performance.

DEMOCRATIC LEGITIMACY AND FINANCIAL REPORTING

The new law promotes municipal influence on government bodies' decisions, especially regarding the lawmaking processes, related rights and responsibility of the municipalities, as well as processes out of their jurisdiction but of interest to the local unit. In that light, the right of local self-government to participate in creating laws on the position, rights and responsibilities of local self-government and other legal acts of that nature, to participate in drafting of laws and regulations and to pass judgment on proposed drafts, are prescribed by the law. However, in practice, the obligations of government bodies towards the local bodies are often not followed through. A typical situation of not following the law's procedure of municipal involvement in passing the regulations of interest of local self-government is reflected in the adoption of the Law on the Budget of the Republic of Montenegro for 2004, where budget grants to Cetinje, as a historical capital, and other municipalities are set out. Through the above law and in accordance with the Law on Financing Local Government, the so-called 'conditional grants' are set for financing capital investments in municipalities. The budget for 2004 allocated conditional grants for municipalities in the amount of 785,005.41 Euros and for financing Cetinje, 305,000.00 Euros. The total amount of government grants for the municipalities is forecast to be 1,090,005.41 Euros.

The Law on Local Government and the Law on Financing of Local Government distribute the competences between the municipal parliament and the mayor regarding the budgeting. The mayor, as an executive body, proposes the Budget and is responsible for the budget discharge, while parliament decides on its adoption and adoption of the annual budget report. The new Law on Local Government clearly prescribes the public and transparent procedure of budget adoption with an active involvement of citizens of municipalities and all interested parties. The mandatory nature of public and transparent adoption of the budget allows active influence on its forming and distribution of funds. The eventual adoption of the budget outside the prescribed procedure of publicity and transparency has, as a legal consequence, the declaring of the budget as illegal by the Constitutional Court and repeating the adoption process in accordance with the law. However, even with the prescribed procedure of budget adoption, its transparent and public (with citizen participation) features are not yet fully in practice, although a small number of municipalities (Pljevlja, Kotor, Tivat, and so on) are already using it.

Municipal budgets, after public discussion, are adopted by the municipal parliament. The mayor sets out the Budget Proposal and submits it to the municipal parliament by the end of November of the preceding year for adoption. Any local self-government for which conditional grants are being provided from the State budget has to keep those funds independently and to use them only for the purposes they were assigned to. In practice, municipalities apply legal regulations, but the Republic often does not act in accordance with this, as is evident in the example of Cetinje where the State did not fulfil its legal obligations towards the historical capital in the amount of 305,000 Euros.

INDEPENDENT REVENUE SOURCES OF LOCAL GOVERNMENT

The Law on Local Government prescribes that local self-government must have its property and revenues at full disposal, in accordance with the law. Also, the law states that local self-government autonomously determines the controls and collects the local revenues. Thus, local public revenues change owners, from the State to the municipalities. However, due to this shift of responsibilities, new problems occurred in municipal bodies relating to the collection of revenues, considering that they are not yet adequately organised and there are no qualified staff or technical equipment (computers and software) for this kind of work in assessing, as well as in the collection and control of, the revenues. This indicates the necessity for urgent organisation of special local bodies in charge of public revenues, purchase of technical equipment and training the employees who would deal with local revenues management at the local level

Together with the right on municipal property, another fundamental right is the autonomy to determine, control, collect and dispose of own revenues. The Law on Local self-government arranges the principles of financing which are reflected in the following municipal rights:

- The municipality has the right to conduct its own affairs, with public revenues.
- Local self-government, for its own affairs, can set taxes and fee standards, in accordance with the law.
- Revenues and expenditures are to be presented in the form of a municipal budget.

- The financial means necessary for operating local bodies are provided from the municipal budget.
- Local self-government disposes of its revenues independently.
- The financial means necessary for conducting transferred and devolved affairs are provided from the State Budget.

From the global aspect, local self-government has four revenue sources: (1) own revenue; (2) joint revenues (state taxes and concessions), (3) State Treasury and (4) Equalisation Fund. Own revenues are presented in Table 14.1.

Table 14.1 Own revenues of local self-government

Taxes	Surtax on personal income tax Real estate tax Tax on consumption Tax on vacant construction plots Tax on company or title
Fees	Use of construction land Arrangement of construction land Protection of the environment
Other taxes and fees	Administrative Tourist Communal
Concessions	For conducting communal activities For conducting concession affairs called for by the municipality Part (30%) of concession fees collected by the state
Property	Revenues from the sale or lease of property Revenues from property rights Revenues from shares held or stocks in public enterprises and institutions founded by the municipality
Self-contributions	
Donations and subventions	Revenues collected from international organisation
Other revenues	Fines gathered from petty offence proceedings, as well as property confiscated in those proceedings Revenues from local body activities Revenues from interests on deposed funds

Source: Law on Local Self-government.

Joint revenues of local self-government are those revenues introduced by the State but which are shared percentage-wise between local self-government and the State. An overview of joint revenues is presented in Table 14.2.

Table 14.2 Central–local government joint revenues (in per cent)

Type of revenue	State Treasury	Municipal Budget
Tax on personal income	90	10
Tax on real estate trade	50	50
State concession fees	70	30

Source: Law on Local Self-government.

GRANT TRANSFERS

Introduction

Unlike equalisation and incensing grants, conditional grants are grants given by the State from the State Treasury to municipalities to finance investment projects of special interest for a municipality or municipalities. The right to conditional grants from the State Treasury is only for those local self-governments that have adopted a multi-year investment plan. The multi-year investment plan determines: capital demands (list of needs necessary for achieving the optimal level of public services), capital provisions (means and equipment), environmental impact and impact on the budget, financial resources and justification for each project in the plan. The multi-year investment plan is for a period of five years. They can approve a maximum of 50 per cent of foreseen costs of an investment project realisation for a municipality.

The amount of conditional grants is determined in accordance with the level of own municipal revenues collected per capita, compared to average revenue per capita of all municipalities for the year previous to that of the investment project realisation. The government decides on the allocation of conditional grants on the proposal of the Minister of Finance.

The Law on the Budget of the Republic of Montenegro for the year 2004[12] and in accordance with the new Law on Financing of Local Government prescribes that so-called 'conditional grants' for capital investments in municipalities are determined by the State Treasury. The budget for the year 2004 forecasts conditional grants for municipalities in the amount of 785,005.41 euros and for financing historical capital of 305,000 euros. The total amount of grants from the State Treasury to municipalities is planned to be 1,090,005.41

euros. In 2005 year the aggregate sum of conditional grants has amounted to euros 455,139.70 for 21 municipalities.

Equalisation Fund Revenues

Differences in demography, geography, the economic and particularly fiscal capacity of municipalities demanded an instrument of fiscal equalisation for those underdeveloped municipalities with the others and stimulation of municipal revenue collection to be integrated into a system of municipal finances. Fiscal equalisation and stimulation of municipalities are exercised through an Equalisation Fund, that is through equalisation and incensing grants. A Commission for Financing of Local Self-Government consisting of seven members (five of whom are appointed by the Association of Municipalities and one per Ministry of Finance and Ministry of Justice) manage the Equalisation Fund.

Funds from the Equalisation Fund are provided from the tax on personal income in the amount of 10 per cent of income, and are deposited on a special Equalisation Fund account by an authorised carrier. These funds are used for equalisation grants – 90 per cent of total funds, and incensing grants – 10 per cent of funds. Municipalities with revenue from tax on personal income, value added tax and tax on profit per capita lower than average revenue from the same sources at the state level have a right to the Equalisation Fund.

Unlike equalisation grants with the purpose of helping municipalities which, due to low fiscal capacities, cannot regularly self-finance their functioning, incensing grants have the role of stimulating municipalities to increase their revenues. For that reason, the right to incensing grants is only given to those municipalities that have increased their own revenues in the current year compared to the previous one. The amount of incensing grants per municipality is established, based on the nominal increase of own revenues of the municipality compared to others. In 2004 all 21 municipalities earned the right to incensing grants.

COSTS OF LOCAL ADMINISTRATION

Municipal Participation in Total Public Expenditures

One of the most important issues in overseeing the fiscal position of municipalities is their participation in public expenditures, as well as participation in the Gross National Product. Regarding public expenditures, the biggest share is taken by the national budget, Retirement and Disability Fund, Health Fund, job centres and municipalities. Details are contained in Table 14.3.

Table 14.3 Estimate of total public expenditure (in million euros)

	2004	2005	2006
Budget of RCG	379.60	390.05	404.06
Retirement and Disability Insurance Fund	147.80	158.32	167.94
Healthcare Fund	104.00	108.16	111.39
Job Centre	13.37	14.32	15.19
Municipal	63.00	67.48	71.59
Total	707.77	738.33	770.17

Source: Ministry of Finance.

Analysis of Total Public Revenues of Municipal Budgets for the period January–June, 2004

Considering that the new system of finances came into effect on 1 January 2004 and that at the time of writing this document we have official data for the first six months, we will present the realised revenues for the period 2004. Table 14.4 shows the local public revenues classified by type and amount that were collected in 2004.

Table 14.4 Own local revenues in municipal budgets

Type of revenue	Amount in euros	Participation (in %)
Municipality of taxes	20,467,647.09	25
Local administrative taxes	1,171,054.85	1
Local communal taxes	4,150,628.29	5
Fee for use of communal resources of common interest	19,071,128.30	24
Construction land fee	4,316,821.33	5
Fee for construction land maintenance	12,258,971.55	15
Local roads fee	1,561,093.00	2
Other fees	934,397.99	1
Other revenues	17,371,711.00	22
Total	77.568,453.26	100

Source: Central Bank of Montenegro.

Analysis of own local revenues shows a variety and large nominal variation in the percentage of the share of some local revenues in the municipal budgets.

Regarding devolved revenues allocated to municipalities, we have the situation shown in Table 14.5.

Table 14.5 Collected devolved revenues from municipal budgets

Type of revenues	Amount in euros	Share in %
Tax on personal income	9,026,776.25	42.8
Tax on real estate traffic	1,849,747.70	8
Tax on inheritance and gift	8,357.96	0.2
Concession fee	396,414.57	1
Tourist fee	708,375.45	3
Grants of state	9,433,301.62	45
Total	21,422,955.55	100

Source: Central Bank of Montenegro.

At the other end of the spectrum are: tax on personal income, grants from the State Budget and tax on real estate traffic. With regard to revenues distributed to municipalities from the Equalisation Fund we have the situation shown in Table 14.6.

Table 14.6 Financing means distributed from equalisation funds to municipalities in Montenegro

Year	Type of revenue	Amount in euros	Total
2005	Equalisation grants	8,010,000	8,900,000
	Incensing grants	890,000	
2006	Equalisation grants	8,640,000	9,600,000
	Incensing grants	960,000	
2007	Equalisation grants	8,550,000	9,500,000
	Incensing grants	950.000	

Source: Central Bank of Montenegro.

Regarding the total revenues in municipal budgets and their percentage for the period observed the situation is as shown in Table 14.7.

Analysis of municipal revenues collected, after the introduction of the new system of financing, shows a high degree of autonomy of municipalities in establishing and collecting public revenues. Analyses of municipal revenues collected in the old system of financing for the period 2000–2003 show that the structure and share of local revenues in municipal budgets were different. The dominant share of devolved revenues and grants from the State Treasury characterised this period, together with a smaller participation of own revenues. This indicates that in the period mentioned, municipal budgets depended mostly on State revenues and municipalities had a smaller degree of fiscal autonomy. In practice, budget grants were often distributed, based on political will or the orientation of the local self-government, choosing municipalities where the political ruling party at the national level had power, meaning that a political 'selection' of municipalities which were helped by the State was present. Table 14.8 shows the overview of particular revenues in municipal budgets for the period 2000–2005.

Table 14.7 Overview of revenues in municipal budgets, 2005

Source of revenue	Collected municipal revenues	Share (in %)
Local (own) revenues	63,703,002.19	73
Devolved revenues	14,360,498.24	16
Equalization fund grants	8,048,818.00	9
Conditional grants	455,139.78	2
Total	8,667,458.21	100

Source: Ministry of Finance of the Republic of Montenegro.

Table 14.8 Municipal budgets revenue structure

Year	Share of local revenues (%)	Share of devolved revenues (%)	State Treasury grants (%)
2000	46.71	49.66	3.63
2001	46.10	51.04	2.86
2002	48.89	49.12	1.99
2003	57.14	40.91	1.94
2004	71.14	16.53	0.21
2005	72.65	17.18	0.54

Source: Ministry of Finance.

MUNICIPAL BUDGET COSTS

Prior to the 2003 reform and the Law on Local Self-government of 2003, local government bodies did have very little jurisdiction, as all – education, healthcare, social and childcare, public works and so on – were almost exclusively in the hands of the central government. With the difficult economic situation in Montenegro it can be said that insufficient municipal budget funds were distributed exclusively for meeting the citizens' needs in the utility area, urban planning, construction land planning, constructions, local roads and local traffic and in sport and culture, that is financing public enterprises and institutes of this nature and an oversized administration. This left not too much leeway for investment in infrastructure. In summary, it can be said that limited municipal funds were distributed primarily to cover the operating costs and basic needs of municipalities.

FINANCIAL RULES, REGULATIONS AND BUDGETING OF LOCAL SELF-GOVERNMENT

Local Self-government Budget

Local self-government has its own budget. In the municipal budget all municipal revenues and expenditures that fall under municipal responsibility are shown. The budget is adopted for a period of one fiscal year, which corresponds with the calendar year. The municipal budget is composed of revenues, budgetary expenditures, financial sources and uses. Budgetary expenditures are composed of unpaid commitments plus expenditures for which a cash outlay has been made. The budget shows revenues by source and expenditures by units, functions and their economic purpose. Revenues, budget expenditures, sources and uses must be balanced. Operating expenditures and uses can be financed only from revenues and budget reserves, including short-term loans for anticipated revenues in case they are used to maintain liquidity in the short term.

Budget Execution

Upon the budget enactment, the competent local government authority for finance informs the spending units about appropriated funds. Budget funds are used for the purposes determined by special laws and regulations of municipalities. During the year, budget funds will be, as a rule, put at the disposal of all bearers and users of those funds within the realised revenues and depending on liabilities due, if a law or an enactment of a municipality or a contract with a bearer or user of budget funds does not regulate otherwise.

The spending unit shall use the appropriated funds in compliance with the proposals approved by the Mayor. If, due to an uneven inflow of budget revenues, the discharge of planned expenditures cannot be carried out, the following may be used to cover those expenditures: reserve funds and short-term loans within the limits provided for in this law. The Mayor is accountable for the budget discharge and the budget implementer is responsible for the proper utilisation of budget funds.

Budget Reserves

Within the budget, part of planned revenues will not be allocated in advance, but kept for the current budget reserve. These funds are used for unforeseen or insufficiently foreseen activities which are financed from the budget. Funds from the current budget reserve are put at the disposal of the Mayor in compliance with the Municipal Assembly decision. The Mayor may authorise a budget implementer to manage the funds of the current budget reserve (up to a certain amount).

The budget provides funds for a permanent budget reserve, which is presented as a separate item in the expenditures. The permanent budget reserve is used for financing expenditures made for the participation of municipalities in eliminating the consequences of unexpected circumstances (droughts, fires, floods, environmental and other natural disasters) and other extraordinary events that can jeopardise the lives and health of inhabitants and cause large-scale damage. The permanent budget reserve may be used for the temporary execution of budget liabilities created due to lower revenues. The Municipal Assembly body in charge of the budget makes a decision on the utilisation of the funds from the permanent budget reserves in individual cases, up to the amount of 10 per cent of the permanent budget reserve. The Municipal Assembly makes decisions on the utilisation of the funds from the permanent budget reserve which is higher than 10 per cent of the permanent budgetary reserves.

At the end of the budget year, the Assembly of a municipality adopts the annual budget report. The format of the local budget is strictly defined by law. The proposal of the annual budget report is determined by the Mayor, who submits it to the Assembly by the end of May of the current year. The proposal of the annual budget report is then presented for information to the Ministry of Finance within 30 days from the day of enactment. As well as the annual budget report, the Municipal Assembly is presented with the bills of profits and losses of public institutions and companies, the permanent reserves and the balance of property dated 31 December of the year the budget refers to. Public companies and institutions established by the municipality must submit their annual financial reports to the municipal body in charge of finances for inspection within 30 days after adopting their annual financial report.

Investment Policy of Local Self-government

Municipalities implement their investment policy in compliance with good financial management practices. The decision of a Municipality Assembly on investment policy is based on the availability of unused funds, types of securities where unused funds may be invested, investment diversification policy, the quality of instruments the money is to be invested in, and other issues significant for investment policy. The Mayor makes the decision on investments, in compliance with the established investment policy and at the proposal of the body in charge.

Local Government Treasury

An important innovation in the finance system of local self-government is the introduction of a treasury system for operating the disposal of municipal budget funds. The local government body in charge of financial activities opens a consolidated treasury account and the money is deposited in that account. No payment shall be made from the consolidated treasury account without justification in the budget. The local government body in charge of financial activities is authorised to approve the opening of sub-accounts, that is, of other accounts as an integral part of the consolidated treasury account. The local government body in charge of financial activities keeps the treasury ledger book. Separate records are kept in the treasury ledger book for every user of the budget. Transactions and events recorded in the ledger book must at all times be in compliance with the transactions in the treasury ledger book and reconciled to the local consolidated bank account.

The local government body in charge of finance activities performs treasury duties by executing the following functions: (1) financial planning, (2) cash management, (3) expenditure control, (4) debt management, (5) budget accountancy and reporting, and (6) managing financial information systems.

MONITORING: STATE AUDIT

Regarding the control over the implementation of the Law on Local Government Finance, this law envisaged several forms of monitoring: an external form of control by the Ministry of Finance and by a competent auditing body. Internal monitoring is conducted as follows: policy control (purpose monitoring) is performed by the Municipal Assembly and the mayor; the administrative body and finally the judicial (court) control is performed by the Constitutional Court and the administrative Court.

Internal Control

A Municipal Assembly shall monitor the budget execution and proper utilisation of the funds that are in the budget, appropriated for certain purposes in compliance with the Statute. The Municipal Assembly debates the financial report and decides on the annual budget report. Monitoring can also be performed alternatively as regulated in the Statute. A Mayor shall present the report on financial control to the Municipal Assembly within 30 days and shall inform the Ministry of Finance about the measures taken. A Mayor shall perform the monitoring of financial, material and accountancy operations of spending units as regards their purpose, volume and utilisation of the funds in compliance with the Statute. The competent local government body, together with the Chief Administrator, performs the administrative monitoring of the implementation of the law. The Chief Administrator performs high-instance (second level) monitoring, ruling on complaints against first level administrative acts, which determine the tax liabilities of citizens and other legal and physical entities.

External Control

The Ministry of Finance shall monitor the legality of the work of local government bodies in the implementation of the Law on Local Government Finance. The Ministry of Finance may require the government body in charge of auditing to review the financial operations of a municipality regarding: security, reliability, cost-efficiency, effectiveness and purposefulness of using local government budget funds related to the tasks devolved or delegated to a municipality. Municipalities are obliged to present to the Ministry of Finance the data on revenues and expenditures, as well as on budget borrowing, quarterly, 30 days prior to the end of the quarter. Constitutional and legal controls of municipal regulations by which municipal budget and tax and other liabilities of citizens are set, are performed by the Constitutional Court of Montenegro. In that process, the court may decide on the legal status of municipal regulations, which cease to be valid with the enactment of a court decision.

The Law on the State Audit Institution[13] which was recently adopted launched the State Audit Institution and set out its rights, responsibilities and methodology. The subjects of audits are bodies and organisations in charge of budgets and state property, municipalities, funds, the Central Bank of Montenegro and other legal entities where the state has a share. This Institution monitors the regularity, effectiveness and efficiency of the business of the subject. Monitoring of regularity is the control of business conduct regarding regulations, general standards of revenue collection, expenditure finance, disposal and management of property, fulfilling commitments, keeping records of revenues and expenditures, and property and management of affairs. Investigating effectiveness is an examination of the level of achievement of the planned goals. Efficiency reviewing is a control of goal achievement with minimal investment. An audit is performed for the purpose of providing relevant information on the management of the budget, property and economy, regularity of the business conduct of the subject, improving his business capacity and prevention against misconduct.

The Institution independently decides on audit subjects, the amount and type of audit, and the timeframe and methodology. The Institution must perform once a year, an audit of the annual budget report of the Republic of Montenegro. It then informs the subject on completion of the audit and presents its findings of the audit in a report. This report on revision consists of conclusions and suggestions for the correction of any irregularities. The institution is obliged to provide public access to the annual report.

FURTHER DEVELOPMENT: LOCAL GOVERNMENT AND FINANCIAL MARKET

Raising capital on the financial market by a municipality is regulated by the Law on Local Government Finance, Law on Debts Issuance and Law on State Treasury. The Law on Debts Issuance[14] prescribes that the emitter of debts issuance can be a municipality. A municipality may borrow by debts issuance or by taking loans. A municipality may perform debt issuance in compliance with the law. Municipalities cannot borrow abroad, except according to the law. Municipalities may take short-term loans intended for satisfying short-term needs for liquidity. A short-term loan is any credit in which the principal repayment schedule does not extend beyond 12 months. The decision on taking out a loan shall be published in the Official Gazette of the Republic of Montenegro.

A municipality may raise long-term loans and give guarantees. A long-term loan is any commercial credit in which the principal repayment schedule extends beyond 12 months. A municipality may take long-term loans only for the purpose of financing capital investments or for the purchase of major capital assets, in compliance with the approved Capital Investment Plan. Long-term loans may not be used to finance current expenditures. Contracts for taking out loans, on the basis of the Assembly's decision, are concluded by the Mayor. A municipal body in charge of finance keeps records of the existing debt of a municipality, short-term and long-term loans taken, and guarantees given. Municipalities may contract debt so that the total repayment of the principal and interests, in a specific year, does not exceed 10 per cent of realised revenues in the year preceding the year of borrowing. Public companies, institutions and other legal entities founded by a municipality can contract debts only with the approval of the founder. The Municipal Assembly gives approval for contracts on taking out loans. In practice, municipalities have not taken a role in the financial market.

CONCLUSION

Local government finance, after 1990, that is after constituting the Federal Republic of Yugoslavia (FRY), created from the former member republics of the Socialist Federal Republic of Yugoslavia (SFRY), suffered changes and adjustments several times, mostly due to the needs of the state authorities. Only after the adoption of the Law on Local Government in 2003, and a set of new tax laws, was a new system of municipal finances established. It was characterised by a high degree of autonomy in prescribing, regulating, collecting, controlling and disposing of municipal financial means. However, the principle of autonomy – fiscal sovereignty of municipalities – strengthens the responsibility of local self-governments and the local population to fulfil and finance local needs. The principle of democracy, that is the possibility of a citizen to actively participate in the decision-making process on public expenditures at the local level was promoted. Public control of municipal budgetary funds' management, together with the strengthening of both external (administrative) and internal forms of control, have bound municipal bodies to a rational and economic use of funds. An important element of internal controls of public expenditures is the new municipal treasury system.

The wide range of responsibilities in the determination of, collection of and control of municipal revenues brought to municipalities a number of staff and technical problems. The lack of staff specialised in tax and tax collection, inspection control of public revenue collection and adequate technical equipment has had a large impact on a still inefficient and insufficient public revenue collection. Municipalities mostly rely on revenues coming to municipal budgets by default, with no active participation by the municipal bodies, such as devolved revenues and equalisation grants, much less their revenue collection.

The differentiation of revenues and responsibilities of central and local authorities in this area has importantly improved the local self-government system, but still leaves a problematic amount of division of public revenues between the state and municipalities. Glancing through municipal revenues (own, devolved, equalisation grants) it can be seen which municipalities dispose of a wide range of resources. However, the particularities of different municipalities, of which more than half are under-developed, implies that realisation of their fiscal capacity is of minor importance and cannot influence to any real extent a stable provision of municipal services. Bringing in the Equalisation Fund with its equalising and incensing grants provided significant security and stability for municipal budgets, where, considering the level of underdevelopment, full collection of all municipal revenues could not fulfil the minimum municipal needs.

The abandonment of centralistic management, development of local self-government and increase in municipal responsibilities, with the introduction of a market economy, coupled with the bad political and economic situation in Montenegro and the region and the bad shape of the infrastructure, and so on results in frequent conflicts between the state and the municipal authorities regarding public revenue distribution. Public revenues allocated to the municipal sector often cannot sufficiently cover the basic functions of local government, or provide capital investments. Another common problem between State and municipal (often opposition) authorities is failing to follow through the State's financial obligations to municipalities. In addition, the unsolved issue of differentiation between state property and municipal property (a very important item in revenue collection for them) creates problems in municipal finances.

Bearing in mind the above, we can conclude that the new system of local self-government and finance has made important progress in strengthening the fiscal autonomy of municipalities, but the process must be ongoing, upgrading and profiling the particularities of the development of the economy in under-developed municipalities, broadening revenue sources – especially possible lucrative ones – clearly defining property resources at municipal disposal, changing the attitude towards the financial market and taking an active role in it, and so on. The latter is extremely important due to fact that municipalities' real estate provides a guarantee for attracting capital and possible investments in the municipalities.

NOTES

1. Official Gazette of the State Union of Serbia and Montenegro, No. 1/03.
2. Official Gazette of the Republic of Montenegro, No. 30/92.
3. Official Gazette of the Republic of Montenegro, No. 28/92.
4. Official Gazette of the Republic of Montenegro, No. 56/93; Blažić (1994).
5. Official Gazette of the Republic of Montenegro, No. 16/95.
6. Official Gazette of the Republic of Montenegro, No. 35/2003.
7. Official Gazette of the Republic of Montenegro, No. 42/03.
8. Official Gazette of the Republic of Montenegro, No. 42/03.
9. Official Gazette of the Republic of Montenegro, No. 56/9.i.
10. Official Gazette of the Republic of Montenegro, No. 16/00.
11. Law on the Budget of the Republic of Montenegro for the year 2004 (Official Gazette of the Republic of Montenegro, No 25/05).
12. Official Gazette of the Republic of Montenegro, No 28/04.
13. Official Gazette of the Republic of Montenegro, Nos. 59/00 and 10/01.
14. Official Gazette of the Republic of Montenegro, Nos. 11/04 and 13/04.

BIBLIOGRAPHY

Begović, B. (2000), Economic Aspects of the Management of a Municipality towards an Increase in Economic Efficiency, in Begović, B., Z. Vacić, B. Mijatović and A. Simić, *Upravljanje lokalnom zajednicom, putevi ka modernoj lokalnoj samoupravi* [Managing a Local Community. Ways towards Modern Local Self-government], Belgrade: Centre for Liberal-Democratic Studies, 64-77.

Begović, B., Z. Vacić, B. Mijatović and A. Simić (2000), *Upravljanje lokalnom zajednicom, putevi ka modernoj lokalnoj samoupravi* [Managing a Local Community. Ways towards Modern Local Self-government], Belgrade: Centre for Liberal–Democratic Studies.

Blažić, Dj. (1994), *Istorijska prestonica i sistem lokalne samouprave u Crnoj Gori – Komentar Zakona o istorijskoj prestonici* [The Historic Capital and the System of Local Self-Government in Montenegro – Comments on the Law on Historic Capital], Podgorica: Udruženje pravnika Crne Gore.

Blažić, Dj. (2004), *Lokalna samouprava* [Local Self-Government], Podgorica: Centre for Tolerance and Dialogue.

Blažić, Dj, and S. Dujić (2004), *Foundations of Public Administration in Montenegro*, Podgorica: PaRIM Project of European Union – European Agency for Reconstruction.

Blečić, M. (2000), *Finansiranje lokalne samouprave u Crnoj Gori* [Local Self-Government Financing in Montenegro], Cetinje: Obod.

Damjanović, M. (2001), Realiteti lokalne demokratije [Realties of Local Democracy], in M. Damjanović (ed.), *Lokalna demokratija, stanje i prespektive* [Local Democracy, Situation and Perspective], Belgrade: Magna Agenda.

Djordjević, S. (2001), Modernizacija lokalne samouprave i vlasti [Modernization of Local Self-Government and Authorities], in M. Damjanović (ed.), Lokalna demokratija, stanje i prespektive [Local Democracy, Situation and Perspective], Belgrade: Magna Agenda.

Fira, A. (1995a), Lokalna samouprava I [Local Self-Government I], Belgrade: Political Economy.

Fira, A. (1995b), Lokalna samouprava I [Self-Government II], Belgrade: Political Economy.

Government of Montenegro (1998), *Documents of Local Self-government Reform in Montenegro*, Podgorica: Ministry of Justice- Expert team.

Government of Montenegro (2001), *Local Self-Government Finance System*, Podgorica: Ministry of Justice –Team of Experts.

Horvath, T. (ed.) (2000), *Decentralization – Experiments and Reforms*, Budapest: Open Society Institute, Local Government and Public Service Reform Initiative.

Ilić, M. (1996), *Lokalna samouprava u Jugoslaviji* [Local Self-Government in Yugoslavia], Niš: Gradina.

Ilić, M. (2001), *Grad u lokalnoj samoupravi* [City in Local Self-Government], Niš: Balkan Centre for Research on Local Self Government.

Kandeva, E. (2001), Introduction to Comparative Local Government in Central and Eastern Europe: A Balkan Perspective, in E. Kandeva (ed.), *Stabilization of Local Government*, Budapest: Local Government and Public Service Reform Initiative, 19-39.

Lilić, S. (2001), Pravna država, javne sluzbe i lokalna samouprava [State of Law, Public Services and Local Self-Government], in M. Damjanović, (ed.), *Lokalna demokratija, stanje i perspektive* [Local Democracy, Situation and Perspective], Belgrade: Magna Agenda.

Marinković, R. (2000), *Lokalna samouprava, stara i nova pitanja* [Local Self-Government – Old and New Questions], Belgrade: Institute for Political Sciences.

Milovanović, D. (1994), *Pravno ustrojstvo lokalne samouprave* [Legal System of Local Self-Government], Belgrade: University of Belgrade – Faculty of Law.

Pusić, E. (1963), *Lokalna zajednica – Prilog proučavanju odnosa lokalnih samoupravnih zajednica i društvenih grupa* [Local Community – Contribution to the Study of the Relationship between the Local Communities and Social Groups], Zagreb: Narodne novine.

Pusić, E. (1981), *Komuna i općina* [Commune and Municipality], Zagreb: Informator.

Special Administrative Region of Hong Kong (2000), *Efficiency Unit of the Government of the Hong Kong SAR, Best Practice Guide on Performance Measurement in Government*, Hong Kong: Government of Hong Kong.

Šević, Ž. (2001), Local Government in Yugoslavia, in E. Kandeva (ed.), *Stabilization of Local Government*, Budapest: Local Government and Public Service Reform Initiative, 417–469.

Simić, A. (2000), Pravni aspekti upravljanja lokalnom zajednicom [Legal Aspects of Governing a Local Community], in Begović et al., *Upravljanje lokalnom zajednicom, putevi ka modernoj lokalnoj samoupravi* [Managing a Local Community, Ways towards Modern Local Self-government], Belgrade: Centre for Liberal-Democratic Studies, 28–63.

Skenderović Ćuk, N. (2001), Regionalizacija i njen uticaj na status lokalne samouprave – komparavini prikaz evropskih koncepcija [Regionalisation and its Impact on the Status of Local Self-Government – A Comparative Overview of the European Concepts], in M. Damjanović (ed.), *Lokalna demokratija, stanje i perspektive* [Local Democracy, Situation and Perspective], Belgrade: Magna Agenda.

UNDP (2000), *The Challenges of Social Cohesion, Vulnerability Trends and Perceptions*, Report No.2 (Serbia) of the Early Warning Systems for FRY, Belgrade: UNDP.

Vacić, Z. (2000), Politički aspekti upravljanja lokalnom zajednicom {Political Aspects of Governing a Local Community], in Begović et al., *Upravljanje lokalnom zajedni-*

com, putevi ka modernoj lokalnoj samoupravi [Managing a Local Community. Ways towards Modern Local Self-government], Belgrade: Centre for Liberal-Democratic Studies, 11–27.

Vlatković, M. (1994), *Lokalna samouprava u Srbiji: prilog kritici uredjivanja i ostvarivanja* [Local Self-Government in Serbia: Contribution to the Critics of Organisation and Realisation], Belgrade: Zajednica opština i gradova Jugoslavije.

World Bank (2000), *The Road to Stability and Prosperity in South Eastern Europe: A Regional Strategy Paper*, Washington, DC: The World Bank

15. Local government finance in Poland

Piotr Bury and Paweł Swianiewicz

15.1 INTRODUCTION

Local government was re-introduced in Poland in May 1990, first at the basic, municipal (*gmina*) level. From the very beginning it was charged with a set of tasks, important for local societies and equipped with separated sources of revenue.

Until 1999, municipalities were the only tier of local government. In 1999, two 'upper' government tiers were introduced: the county (*powiat*) and regional (*województwo*) levels. With these measures, the intended reform of public administration was more or less complete.

Issues discussed in the following sections include the local government reform and the related reform of local government finance (Section 15.2), the structure and tasks of local government (Section 15.3), the municipality's independent sources of revenue: local taxes and shares in central taxes, fees, user charges and income from communal property (Section 15.4), central government grants (Section 15.5), borrowing (Section 15.6), expenditures (Section 15.7) and financial supervision (Section 15.8).

15.2 LOCAL GOVERNMENT REFORM

Prior to 1990, the highly centralist doctrine of real-socialism left no space for local self-governance. Local administration was hierarchically dependent on the upper tiers and the branch ministries of central government; local discretion with regard to financial issues or forms of service delivery was almost non-existent. The constitutionally dominant position of the communist party limited any reforms aimed at real democratisation of local life. The turning point was the roundtable negotiation (between the 'Solidarity' opposition and the ruling communist party) in 1989. The local government reform was the only topic in which final agreement was not reached and a 'statement of disagreement' was signed. Nevertheless, the main directions of the future reform had already been delineated.

The present structure of local government in Poland is a result of two waves of decentralisation. The first wave took place in 1990, when the system of local government was introduced at the municipal level. Quick, but intensive, preparations paved the way for the enactment of the new Local Government Act in March 1990, which was followed by local elections in May 1990 and a radical decentralisation of financial regulations in January 1991. The 1990 reform introduced elected local government at the municipal level only, whilst the upper, regional tier of territorial division remained under state administration. This solution was treated as provisional. It was argued that those 49 small regions introduced by the communist administration in the mid-seventies were dysfunctional and required modification. It was assumed that a new, elected regional government should be introduced, together with a reform of the territorial division. The second stage of the reform took place in 1999 and resulted in two new tiers of elected sub-national governments: the counties and regions.

Local government finance is regulated by legal acts of four categories. The first is the Constitution which states some general rules, similar to those specified in the European Charter of Local Government adopted by the Council of Europe. The next category is the Act on Public Finance which regulates all public finance within the country. The third act refers to local government revenues, while the fourth consists of many legal acts which regulate particular taxes, fees, methods of distribution of general grants, rules of financing budgetary entities, and so on.

In 1990, new local governments had to operate within the confines of the old financial system, changed in 1991 by a new Act on Local Government Income and General Grants. The 1998 reform was also prepared very quickly. The specific directions of the government proposal were formulated at the beginning of 1998, the election to county and regional councils were held in October and new tiers of government began operating in 1999. Again, as in 1990, many important legal regulations were approved at the last minute (or even later). The vote on the Act on Local Government Income followed the October 1998 elections. Moreover, the Act was only temporary: its validity for 1999 and 2000 was specified in its title. The government and parliament agreed that substantial revisions would be necessary after a year or two of the new system's operation. Also, precise regulations on the division of competencies between tiers of government and between local government and state administration were discussed by the Parliament even after the 1998 county and regional elections. In both the municipal and the regional reforms the temporary financial regulations continued in effect beyond the intended period; first, the 1991 Act for two years, until a more stable Act on Financing Local Governments was passed at the end of 1993, then in the second wave of reform, the provisional and unsatisfactory Act on Local Government Revenues was extended for the 2001–2003 period. Since 2004, local finance has been regulated by the new Act on Local Government Revenues.

15.3 STRUCTURE AND TASKS OF LOCAL GOVERNMENTS

As a result of the decentralisation process, there are currently three tiers of territorial governments: almost 2,500 municipalities, 315 counties (plus 65 large cities with county status) and 16 regions which replaced 49 smaller units. Both at the municipal and county levels, local government is the only form of public administration. At the regional level there is a dual structure: elected local government on the one hand and a governor nominated by the Prime Minister with his/her own administrative apparatus on the other. Functions of the regional, state and local government administrations are (at least in theory) clearly separated and there is no hierarchical subordination between them; the same holds for the tiers of local government.

In every case, a local council is elected proportionally to the number of inhabitants. At the municipal level it varies from 15 to 45 councillors, for the county from 15 to 39, and for the region 30 plus 3 for every 500,000 inhabitants above 2 million. The executive power at the municipal level is held by the Mayor directly elected by all citizens (since 2002, before the municipal executive was collective and appointed by the council), and at the county and regional levels by the collective Executive Board appointed by the council. Apart from these regular forms of representative democracy, local communities can take important decisions directly through referenda.

The goal of local government reform was to separate functions distinctly as well as the policy areas between the tiers of government and to eliminate the vertical dependency of the lower tier upon the higher. The three levels of subnational government have been established. Obviously municipal, county and regional levels co-operate, for example, in economic development policies, but in terms of specific service delivery, the separation is close to perfect. The situation is much more complicated regarding the relationship between the central and local government levels. In some cases (such as for education or for some social welfare benefits) nationwide regulations are so strict that the local government's role is, to a huge extent, reduced to the role of central government's agent in the implementation of central policies.

Fortunately, Poland avoided the radical territorial fragmentation experienced by several countries in the region.[1] The average size of Polish municipalities is around 16,000 inhabitants (for rural ones, over 7,000) and 125 square kilometres. Only a few of the Polish municipalities are smaller than 2,000 and none of them have fewer than 1,000 inhabitants. Thus, the Polish municipality is quite large from the European comparative perspective.[2]

The reforms have granted a wide range of functions to the municipal governments while the list of the functions of the counties and regions is much shorter. Polish municipal governments are responsible for the provision of a wide range of essential municipal services.

Some of these functions include:

- spatial order, physical planning;
- local roads, and local public transport;
- street cleaning, refuse collection, waste disposal and sewage treatment;
- market places, green areas and cemeteries;
- provision of gas, water and central heating;
- municipal housing;
- education (pre-school and school for children up to 15 years old);
- culture and leisure centres;
- several functions related to social care;
- local promotion and co-operation with other local governments and organisations.

During the 1990s, there were two significant changes in the scope of functions provided by municipal governments. The first was in 1994 when extended functions were granted to select large cities (mostly those exceeding 100,000 in population size). This action, called the Pilot Programme, offered an opportunity to take over some of the tasks of state administration. Since both joining the Programme and the scope of the tasks transferred were voluntary, financial support was given in the form of specific grants. Transferred tasks became obligatory in 1996 under the Act on Large Cities. The point of these two actions was to see if the future county level governments could function effectively.

The second change concerned the responsibility for primary schools. In 1990, several factors (including fear of teachers' trade unions) caused a delay in transferring schools to the local governments. It was decided that the transfer would be delayed until 1994 and that before that date the schools would be managed locally, only by those localities which made a formal application to do so. Later, the deadline for the transfer of the schools was postponed to 1996, when primary education (including financing teachers' salaries) was actually transferred to the municipal governments. This shift made education the most important task of the local governments at the municipal and county levels (see below). The method of funding education is described in Section 15.5.

County government responsibilities include:

- secondary education;
- health care (investments and management; current medical operations are mostly financed by separate health insurance system);
- roads of county importance;
- labour offices (coping with unemployment problem);
- natural disasters protection;
- land surveying and building administration;
- public order and security.

In case of regions direct delivery of services is very limited, seldom going beyond higher education or regional roads. They are mostly focused on strategic planning and regional development programmes. They play very important role in implementing EU regional policies, managing over 30 per cent of structural funds available for Poland.

All local government tasks consist of three groups. The functions enumerated above as 'own tasks' are of the first type. Second, local administration also performs functions delegated by the state – these are generally administrative tasks, for example registering births and deaths, issuing drivers' licences and registering automobiles, and organising national elections and referenda. Delegated tasks are financed through separate specific grants, which are supposed to be sufficient to perform these tasks. In practice, local governments often complain they must cover at least part of the costs from their own revenue sources. The third group consists of tasks performed by local administration on the basis of agreements with the governor or with other local governments.

15.4 INDEPENDENT LOCAL GOVERNMENT REVENUE SOURCES

According to the Constitution, local governments in Poland are financed through a mixture of (1) revenues from own sources, (2) general purpose grants and (3) specific grants.

The first group is the largest and most complex, consisting of different kinds of revenue sources including local tax revenues, shares in central taxes, fees, user charges and revenues from communal property. Shares in central taxes have long been treated as a separate group of revenue source. Since 1998, however, due to the new Constitution, they have been classified as one of the own revenue sources. Since local governments have no direct possibility to influence these revenues, however, such a classification is considered improper.[3] Therefore, in the general structure of revenue sources, in 2001, tax shares are shown as a separate category (see Table 15.1).

Table 15.1 Revenues of local governments in Poland in 2006

	Munici-palities	Cities of county status	Counties	Regions
Total (in '000 Polish zloty, 1 euro = 3.8 PLN)	51,724,275	40,985,861	14,649,539	9,485,847
Structure of revenues (%)				
Revenues from own sources	32.2	38.9	15.9	14.5
of which property tax	14.0	11.9	0	0
Shares in revenues from central government taxes (PIT and CIT)	15.2	28.8	14.2	49.3
General (unconditional) grants	32.6	21.3	46.6	21.9
Conditional grants for current expenditures	19.3	9.8	21.0	6.7
Conditional investment grants	0.7	1.2	2.3	7.6

Notes:
1. Municipal and county local governments do not include large cities with county status.
2. Local government revenues do not include: (a) most fees and charges for local services collected by budgetary enterprises or other service delivery units, (b) local borrowing and privatisation of municipal assets, which are counted as 'sources to cover budget deficits defined as the result of total expenditures – total revenues'.

Source: Authors' own calculations based on reports from local budgets' execution.

Local Taxes

The municipal government is the only tier of local government with limited powers of taxation. Both county and regional governments are financed almost exclusively by central, general and specific grants, shares of central taxes and a few very minor revenue sources of their own (Bury, 2003).

There are eight taxes for which the full revenues accrue to the municipal governments; the most significant are the property tax, the tax on agriculture, the tax on vehicles and the tax on civil law activities. Three of the former are administered and collected by municipal administration, the remainder by the national tax offices. Maximum rates for the three taxes (for property, for vehicles and for dog licences) are set by central legislation; local governments may select their own rates, but they must not exceed the 'ceiling level'. Local governments can also use other instruments of their own tax policies.

Property tax

This is by far the most important source of local own revenues. In 2006 it delivered as much as close to 14 per cent of the municipal total income (see Table 15.1). The property tax is paid both by physical persons and by legal entities. The tax includes buildings, other constructions and plots of land which are not subject to agriculture or forest taxes.

Buildings and land are taxed 'per square metre' and tax rates are annually adjusted for inflation. The rate depends on type of property, and in general it is several times higher for commercial than for housing properties. The maximum rate per square metre of housing flat is close to 0.15 euros, while for commercial buildings it exceeds 4.5 euros. For 'other constructions' the tax depends on the value used for the depreciation of the taxed objects or at the maximum rate of 2 per cent of their market value. The latter category of property provides an insignificant portion of the revenues from the property tax. The Act on Local Taxes and Fees specifies several tax exemptions, including public roads, properties used by local administration and those used by foreign embassies and the local council may add its own exemptions.

The tax on agriculture

This tax delivered just 1.5 per cent of the total municipal revenues in 2006, but it happens to be important source for small, rural local governments. In general, this is the only tax levied on farmers. The tax is paid per hectare, but the land area is weighted by factors showing the quality of soil and the economic and climatic environment for farming activity. The maximum rate for one (weighted) hectare equals the average market price of 250 kilograms of rye over the first three quarters of the previous year. There are several tax exemptions declared in the Act on the Tax on Agriculture, the most significant of which is for soils of the lowest quality, which means that more than one third of all agricultural lands cannot be taxed (see Bury, 2002).

Other local taxes (tax on civil law activities, on vehicles, on forests, on dogs, on legacies and donations, flat rate income tax for small businesses) have a minor importance for local budgets and are not going to be discussed in detail in this chapter.

Fees and User Charges

All user fees in Poland may be divided into two groups: hidden taxes and real fees paid in receipt of a public service. Of the many fees collected by local governments, mostly at the municipal level, we select for discussion only one example – the market fee.[4]

The market fee

The market fee is paid to a municipality by all persons selling goods at open places, covered markets and halls designed for fairs, and exhibitions. The market fee appears to be a tax levied on commercial activity. The total revenues from this fee provide just 0.2 per cent of municipal revenues, but there are single cases of local governments for which it is a major source of revenues.

User charges

Charges such as for kindergartens, water provision, waste water, solid waste collection and public transportation and so on are usually collected by the servicing unit. These revenues frequently do not appear in the municipal budget, as the money is kept by the delivery unit (for example, budgetary establishment or a municipal company) and is used to cover the costs of service provision. In some cases, local government may subsidise these services or the local budget may receive the surplus, so what does appear in the budget is just a balance of charges collected and the amount spent on the actual delivery of the service.

Over the last decade, local governments and delivery organisations have gradually been gaining larger and larger discretion over fees and charges for services. Consider the current situation for the most important services:

- city transport – the local council decides on the price of tickets; private competitors (if they exist) are free to determine their own rates;
- waste collection and disposal – tariffs are negotiated between the provider and the client; the local council may (although it has done so rarely) set the maximum price per unit;
- water and sewage – the municipal entity (in most cases a company) proposes the tariff, which needs to be approved by the local council;
- central heating – the price is set by an entity delivering the service on the basis of national general rules; prices are controlled by the Office for Energy Regulation;
- communal housing – the local council sets the rent on the basis of general rules established in law; in practice, for political reasons, the council often sets rents below the real cost.

Revenues from Communal Property

There is an information problem in identifying revenues from communal properties because the income from privatisation is not treated as normal revenue. But available data suggests that in the entire country this has never been a source of significant revenue for local governments. In 2001 income from privatisation represented about 1.5 per cent of local income and rentals another 1.5 per cent. In some local governments these rates were, of course, much higher. It should be noted, however, that revenues from renting space for shops and offices in communal buildings are usually revenues of off-budget units dealing with municipal housing, and are not shown in local government budgets. From other data, we know that revenues from rentals of shop and office space covered between 12 per cent (in the period 1999–2001) and 25 per cent (in 1994) of the costs of maintenance for communal houses.

There is a growing criticism that this category of revenues is not clearly separated from operating revenues. Such a separation would allow for a distinction between operating and capital budgets and enable better monitoring of financial situation as well as control of the purpose of borrowing (see also Section 15.6 of this chapter).

Shares in Central Taxes

Each local government receives a share of two main income taxes: Personal Income Tax and Corporate Income Tax (PIT and CIT). Since 2004 these shares have been transferred to the relevant local budgets at the following rates:

- to municipalities: PIT: 36.2 per cent; CIT: 6.71 per cent;
- to counties: PIT: 10.25 per cent; CIT: 1.4 per cent;
- to regions: PIT: 1.6 per cent; CIT: 15.9 per cent.

There are a few features of the Polish tax-sharing system which make it different from that existing in many other countries of Eastern Europe:

1. The shares are based on amounts based by tax-payers living (located) in each local government unit. In case of PIT share goes to local government according to place of residence, not place of work of the tax payer.
2. There is no territorial redistribution mechanism, that is, each share goes to the local government of the territory where the tax was collected (for the PIT) or 'worked out' (for the CIT); this redistribution was in place until 2000 for the municipal PIT shares.

3. Percentage shares for each tier of local government are established in the Act on Local Governments Income and remain stable for long periods.

As shown in Table 15.1, shares provide significant proportion of sub-national revenues – between 14 per cent in counties and over 40 per cent in the case of regions.

Local Taxes in Poland – An Evaluation

Of all the local taxes, it is the property tax which remains the subject of a long and ceaseless debate. There are two general lines of criticism of this tax. The first is that it still does not raise sufficient revenues, especially in big cities. The second is that the property tax is unfair, since it depends on the type and the area of the property rather than its value. Currently, the owner of a poor, village house located in the countryside far from any urban centre has to pay the same tax as the owner of a home of similar size but of many times greater value in the centre of Warsaw.

The result is a call for a reform leading to an *ad valorem* tax. This has also been typical advice from the USAID or from World Bank advisors over the last decade. The draft of new regulations for a value-based property tax was prepared by the Ministry of Finance and approved by the Government in 1995. In a survey by the Centre for Public Opinion Research (CBOS) in 2000, 31 per cent of the respondents were of the opinion that the new tax would be less fair than the present one, while only 27 per cent expressed a positive opinion on its fairness. Twenty-nine per cent of the respondents expected to be negatively affected by the reform, while only 4 per cent expected a positive change. In any case, the value-based property tax remains an official long-term goal of the Polish government, but its introduction in the near future is unlikely both due to political and technical reasons. The whole system of local taxes in Poland may be assessed in terms of theoretical 'fiscal federalism' criteria as follows (see Swianiewicz, 2003):

1. The allocation of tax yields is not proportional to the allocation of functions. This applies primarily to the situation of the county and regional governments which do not have own tax revenues. The allocation is much better at the municipal level. The ratio of revenues from own sources to total budget revenues is somewhat lower than in some West European countries (for example, Denmark or Sweden), but similar or even higher than in most of the others (for example, the United Kingdom, The Netherlands or Spain). The negative thing, however, is the gradually diminishing role of

revenues from own sources in municipal budgets: it was around 47 per cent of total budget revenues in 1992, 40 per cent in 1995 and only 33 per cent in 2001. As a result a strong vertical equalisation mechanism.

2. Uneven geographical distribution of the tax base. In 2001, own revenues represented well over 40 per cent of budgets in the cities, but just over 20 per cent in the rural areas. Inequalities among the regions are even larger.
3. The system of local taxes is fragmented and complicated. There are many local fees and taxes (such as the tax on dogs) which do not raise significant revenues but are costly to collect and unnecessary complicate the system.
4. Tax is well defined in geographical space. Polish local taxes do not produce major problems in this respect. Taking tax sharing into account, there are problems with defining the local share in the CIT from companies which are registered in one municipality but operate branches in various locations. Allocation to municipalities proportional to the number of employees working in each of the local branches seems to be far from perfect.
5. Visibility of the tax. Most Polish local taxes are visible.
6. The low elasticity of tax yields with respect to inflation. Because the property tax, the tax on vehicles and small local fees and taxes are not elastic with respect to inflation, their rates are adjusted annually. Exceptions are the tax on agriculture and the tax on forestry; these are related to the market price of crops and wood respectively.
7. The tax base is relatively immobile. The property tax, which provides by far the most important local own revenue, conforms completely to this principle.

15.5 GRANT TRANSFERS

Role and Purpose of Grants

There are several theoretical arguments for state grants to sub-national governments (Bramley, 1990, Swianiewicz, 2003). It is very difficult to say which of these arguments has been most important for the development of the current Polish grant system, since they have never been clearly spelled out. We can only guess from the general tone of the discussions occurring during the different stages of the decentralisation reform.

Probably the most important purpose of grants has been to secure minimal standards for important services. This argument is sometimes closely connected with the horizontal equity argument. In the Polish grants system, these arguments are definitely at the heart of the educational grants as well as the former highway and equalisation grants. The current system of general grants also fits this idea (see below).

Certainly the argument for the stimulation of spending on preferred merit goods is very popular in the sector ministries of the central government and it has been behind the rapid development of the specific purpose grants (it was especially successful in 1998 when the system of financing county and regional governments was formed). But such a goal has never been explicitly formulated by any governments; rather, it has been a side-effect of the strength of the central bureaucracy. Other arguments (such as the reduction of spill-over effects and the enhancement of location efficiency) were hardly a part of the public discussions and cannot be considered significant for the Polish system.

There is still another argument which is missing among the theoretical features of the 'ideal local financial system', but which was very important in Polish conditions. The revenue power of local governments is not sufficient to cover the costs of mandated service provision. This is true, not only for certain geographical areas (since the tax base is inevitably allocated unevenly across the country, regardless of which revenues are defined as local taxes), but also generally. The so-called 'own' revenues are not sufficient to cover minimal needs related to functions performed, even in relatively affluent local governments. There are only a very few exceptions to this rule. In such circumstances the role of grants is simply to support local budgets.

This function of the grant system has become increasingly visible over the past decade. At the beginning of the 1990s there was a reasonable balance between the revenue power and the scope of functions of municipal governments. But since that time, several new functions have been transferred to local governments with no parallel increase in the scope of local own revenues. Instead, new functions were financed through the grants system. The most powerful example of this phenomenon is the transfer of responsibility for primary schools (a process which ended in 1996). It is intended that this function, which in some local governments consumes more than half of the total budget, be financed first and foremost by the general purpose grant. Thus, when the schools were transferred to the municipal level, the amount of the grant increased significantly and the share of own revenues in the total municipal budget decreased significantly.

As can be seen from the discussion above, the emerging grant system is a result both of consciously formulated purposes and spontaneous development influenced by various actors with their specific interests. Local governments in Poland receive two types of grants from the state budget: general and specific.

General Grant

The current system of general grants has been in operation since 2004. The grant consists of three parts: educational, equalising and balancing (in the case of municipalities and counties) or regional (in the case of regions).

The educational part is the largest one, constituting over 75 per cent of the total general grant. It is calculated according to the formula prepared by the Minister of Education, which is based mostly on the weighted number of pupils and number of teachers. The most important weights include location of schools – due to higher unit costs rural schools receive a higher per pupil grant. This regulation is not questioned; however it is disputable that the weight is identical for every rural community, regardless of its population density or specific location (for example as a rich suburb of a large city). Other weights take into consideration type of school (higher weights for some vocational schools), number of handicapped pupils, national minorities, and so on. Another disputable element is a weight referring to number and salaries of teachers. This factor does not represent needs (demand for the service) so theoretically it should be excluded from the formula, but local government associations rightly argue that local authorities have no control over the number and salaries of teachers so the full cost of this spending item should be compensated.[5]

The equalising part consists of two funds: basic and supplementary. Lower than average (in case of municipalities below 92 per cent of national average) per capita own and shared revenues are required for intervention. The potential (applying maximum available rates and no local tax exemptions) rather than actual tax revenues are taken into account in the calculation, so the grant is neutral from the point of view of local tax policy. The rule is that they receive significant, but not full compensation of the difference to the average level, so the grant should not provide a disincentive for the efficient tax collection. The supplementary fund is much smaller (not more than 5 per cent of the total general grant) and is granted to local governments of the municipal and county tier whose indicated parameters differ from the average for the whole country: it consists of the population density and the unemployment rate. For the regions, the relevant parameter is their population; the grant is assured only when there are 3 million or fewer inhabitants.

The balancing and regional parts represent the horizontal equalisation mechanism (the so-called 'Robin Hood tax'). The funds come from revenues of the richest local governments, which have to pay percentage of their revenues (up to 30 per cent in the case of municipalities and up to 98 per cent in the case of counties) above a certain threshold level of per capita revenues. Distribution of the equalising parts depends on the decision of the Minister of Finance, with very general guidance from the Act on Local Government Revenues.

Specific Grants

There are three types of specific grants. One is for current spending on tasks delegated to local governments (see Section 7); the second is related to current expenditures on the local governments' own functions and the third is for local government investments.

Grants for delegated tasks

The only relevant regulation in the Act on Local Governments' Revenues is that the amount of these grants should ensure the execution of the relevant tasks. Such regulation, being far from precise, was a reason for bargaining and quarrelling between central and local governments. The local governments have frequently complained that many functions delegated to them are under-funded and that grants received are hardly enough to cover the salary costs of required personnel. Therefore, the delegation of new functions has sometimes been seen as a method to decentralise budget problems. Central government usually argued that similar amounts were sufficient for the provision of services before passing them to local governments and that decentralisation should lead to some efficiency gains and related saving in necessary spending. They failed to note that the sums involved would be insufficient to avoid arrears in payments. Moreover, for most of the last decade the inflation rate was underestimated in official predictions, which also provided an occasion to 'save' something on grants for delegated tasks. As a consequence, local governments commonly 'subsidise' delegated functions from their own revenues or from general purpose grants which are supposed to support provision of other municipal functions.

Grants for local governments' own current tasks

This category is the most difficult to describe, since regulations are extremely fragmented and unclear. Grants related to various functions are regulated by legislation pertaining to diverse sectors (such as acts related to education, social care, housing, and so on). Only in a few cases is it clearly defined what the amount of the grants should be and how they should be allocated among individual local governments. A good example of this is the grant to support housing benefits for poor tenants, although even in that case, bargaining discussions over methodology and questioning the accuracy of government calculations have not been avoided. In most other cases central bureaucracy has the broad discretion to make decisions, so the final allocation is the result of bargaining processes between the central and local governments.

At the beginning of the decentralisation reform, there was an assumption that specific grants for own functions should be the exception rather than the rule, and that local governments should be financed mostly by their own revenues and general subsidies based on clear, transparent criteria. In the second half of the last decade, however, the system of financing has gradually been rendered ineffective. That change was not due to any change in official policy, but was rather the result of incremental changes – a series of small victories by the central sector bureaucracy which aspires to more strict control over the structure of local government spending. Compared to the initial assumptions of the authors of the Polish decentralisation reforms, the share of this category of revenues in county and regional budgets is disastrous (well over 10 per cent).

Grants for local governments' investments

This category of grants is regulated in the most detailed way, although its allocation criteria are still far from transparent. Starting in 2001, investment grants can be allocated only for investments specified in the regional development strategy and related to goals formulated in the regional contract (signed between local and central government leaders of the region). Investment grants cannot exceed 50 per cent of total investment costs. Investment grants from the central budget are not the only form of state support for local government investments. Another is through funds used to promote national purposes. The most significant among such funds are the National and Regional Funds for Environment Protection and Water Management, which offer both grants and cheap loans for investments such as sewage treatment or waste disposal plant.

During the last few years EU structural funds have became the most important category of investments grants. In 2006 almost 30 per cent of local government investments were financed or co-financed by EU funds. It is regional government that is the most powerful authority in decision making on allocation of EU funds to individual local projects.

Grants Mechanism Reassessed

The main features of the current system may be summarised in the following points:

1. The allocation of most general purpose grants is based on formulas which depend on objective and easily measurable criteria. The system is influenced by neither the subjective decisions of bureaucrats nor political

clientelism and it helps to build genuine, not merely declarative, autonomy for local policies.

2. The total amounts of the components of the general grants are fixed annually in the Budgetary Act. This solution seems to be less satisfactory than the old (1990s) one in which the funds were defined as percentages of central budget revenues. On the other hand, in most cases, the adopted criteria do not allow manipulation of the amounts of the grants. That still may happen, however, with the most significant education grants.
3. The rules for grants distribution are relatively stable which ensures stability for local finance and allow for long-term financial forecasts by local governments.
4. The allocation formulas for equalising and balancing parts poorly reflect variation in spending needs. They mainly refer to per capita own revenues, disregarding – for example – specific spending needs of big cities (which serve many 'free-ride' consumers from other municipalities and which have specific spending needs due to congestion and social problems).
5. General grants are based more on objective criteria than special purpose transfers. Their overall amount is not defined by law, which makes them vulnerable to the process of annual state budget bargaining.
6. The criteria for special grants allocation are also much less clear (with some exceptions, such as the case of support for housing allowances). That leads to subjective decisions and may smack of political clientelism. There is no doubt that adopting clear and sharp criteria in the case of specific grants (especially those related to capital investments) is much more difficult than for general grants. But there is still much to be done in moving toward greater transparency and fairness in the system.
7. From a political point of view, greater dependence on central transfers may be even more convenient for local politicians. It allows avoiding unpopular decisions (for example increasing local taxes) and permits the blame for possible reductions in local services to fall on the central government.

In general, the strengths of the grant system seem more significant than its weaknesses, even if the list of the latter is longer. The current grants system is quite well structured and includes several elements which are worthy of retention.

15.6 LOCAL GOVERNMENT BORROWING

Legal regulations do not specify the purpose for borrowing, so local governments can borrow both for capital and for current expenses. Potential specification of legal purposes for borrowing would be very difficult in any case, since there are no separable operating and capital budgets in Poland. Nevertheless, in practice, local governments take credits or issue bonds primarily for capital investments. Borrowing to cover current expenses is relatively rare and happened on a massive scale only once when several local governments faced severe problems with financing a compulsory teachers' salaries increase in 2000.

The size of local government debt (other than short-term debt which must be repaid within the same budget year) is limited in several ways:

- the Polish Constitution states that overall, public debt cannot be higher than 60 per cent of GDP; if the debt is larger than 50 per cent (which happened in 2003) special limitations apply, provided by the Act on Public Finance, which make new borrowing more difficult;
- the standard overall limit of local government debt cannot be higher than 60 per cent of annual revenues;
- the standard debt service in a given year cannot exceed 15 per cent of local government budget revenues.

In the first half of the 1990s, local governments were very reluctant to borrow money, but later on many municipalities became active on the capital market. Until recently, the dominant share of local government loans was in the form of preferential loans (with the interest rate lower than for commercial loans) offered by state funds, especially by the National and Regional Funds for Environmental Protection and Water Management. The procedures they used played a significant educational role, preparing local governments to operate in the commercial market as well. Since 2001, the debt holdings of private banks are larger than loans offered on preferential conditions; bonds take third position. Most local governments are still very prudent and the level of local debt is usually far from the legal limit.[6]

A potentially weak point of the borrowing rules is lack of regulations for local government bankruptcy. Moreover, the Act on Public Finance provide special grants for local governments having difficulty with debt repayment. In spite of limitations imposed on these grants, such a regulation may provide a moral hazard encouraging irresponsible behaviour of both banks and local governments.

At the moment, one of the most important barriers for local borrowing is the level of public debt. Although local government debt is very low in macroeconomic terms (below 2 per cent of GDP), the overall debt of the public sector exceeded 50 per cent of GDP in 2003. This structure of public debt belies the fact that local governments finance well over half of total public investments (see Table 15.2). Local governments borrow to finance investments while the central government issues bonds or takes credits to finance social spending. It may happen that the ability of local governments to use credit instruments will be limited, in spite of their generally prudent policies, simply because central government policies exhaust the dominant share of the public debt limit. This possibility may be a particular danger in the next few years, just at a time when local governments may dramatically need borrowed resources in order to utilise European Union regional structural funds.

Table 15.2 Expenditures of the central and local governments in Poland, 1991–2001 (in millions of zlotys and in per cent)

	1991	1994	1997	2000	2003	2006
Local government spending as % of total budget expenditures	16.3	18.9	25.3	39.8	35.8	40.7
Local government spending as % of GDP	5.5	7.1	8.6	11.0	10.0	n.a.
Local government investments as % of total public investments	42.6	52.0	55.5	64.0	59.3	72.0

Source: based on Statistical Yearbooks of the Republic of Poland.

15.7 LOCAL GOVERNMENT EXPENDITURES

General information about local government expenditures in both current and real prices, as well as their relation to central government spending since 1991 is shown in Table 15.2. The ratio of local government expenditures to total budget spending grew consistently throughout most of the period analysed. This ratio was lower for all tiers of local government in Poland in 1995 than for Denmark (53 per cent) and other Nordic countries (32–36 per cent), and most other countries of Northern Europe. On the other hand, it was much higher than in most South European countries such as Portugal (10 per cent) or Greece (11 per cent) (Bury, 2002). In Poland the ratio has reached as much as 39–41 per cent since 1999. This recent 'jump' was the result of two newly established tiers of local government, the county and regional levels. It means that currently, two out of every five zlotys are eventually spent from public budgets by the local governments.

The importance of the tasks fulfilled by each tier of the local government in terms of budget expenditures is shown in Table 15.3. In municipalities, large cities (that is towns of county status) and counties, education is a dominant item of current expenditures. In the regions, transport takes first place.

Table 15.3 Expenditures of local governments in Poland by tiers and sectors in 2006 (in per cent)

A. Municipalities

	Current expenditures			Capital expenditures		
	Cities of county status	Urban munici-palities	Rural munici-palities	Cities of county status	Urban munici-palities	Rural munici-palities
Education	39.2	44.8	50.1	7.8	13.8	19.6
Social care	16	22.1	19	1.5	0.8	0.5
Culture	3.2	3.5	2.6	3.1	2.5	1.2
Physical culture	1.2	1.8	0.7	6.1	6	2.3
Health care	1.3	1	0.8	4.1	1	1
Communal services	3.3	5.1	4.7	16.9	38	41.9
Housing	5.7	2.8	1.1	10.7	8.7	2.7
Transport	14.4	3.4	3.3	41.9	23.1	26.2
Administration	7.9	11.8	14.2	3.6	2.5	2.2
Other	7.8	3.7	3.5	4.3	3.6	2.4

B. Counties and regions

	Counties		Regions	
	Current expenditures	capital expenditures	current expenditures	capital expenditures
Education	46.7	17.4	16.5	1.9
Social care	20.6	7.2	5.3	0.6
Culture	0.5	0.1	13.8	6.3
Physical culture	0.1	0.4	1	1.7
Health care	3.2	15.2	7.3	19.3
Public safety	5.8	5.8	0	0.3
Transport	6.7	47	33.1	48.6
Administration	12.7	4.9	8	4.9
Other	3.7	2	15	16.4

Notes:
Data on local government spending do not include the full amounts spent on many services such as water provision, central heating, public transportation and municipal housing. Resources collected from service users in the form of fees and charges are not included, but data in the table include only local budget subsidies to that service provision.
Communal services – water and sewage in urban areas, streets, street lighting, public transportation, solid waste disposal, street cleaning, central heating, and so on

Source: Authors' own calculations based on reports from local budgets execution.

As mentioned in Section 15.2, Poland avoided the radical territorial fragmentation experienced by several countries in the region. That does not mean that in territorial organisations or in the allocation of functions, no mistakes were made. Solid waste management, for example, is the responsibility of the municipal tier, although available analyses suggest that economies of scale may be achieved for a market of 70,000–100,000 citizens. Thus, waste management is a natural candidate to be a county function. But instead, central government made their municipal allocations with the suggestion to organise in single-purpose associations. Another example is related to excessively small counties, especially those surrounding big cities, with poor infrastructure in education, health care and other crucial services. In secondary education this leads to considerable spill-over problems (see Swianiewicz, 2002).

15.8 FINANCIAL SUPERVISION

According to the Constitution, the supervision of local government activities is limited to checking its conformity with the law. It is the Prime Minister and regional governors who are responsible for the general supervision, but there are also 16 Regional Accounting Offices (RIO), which were created in 1993 and which are responsible for the supervision and control of local government finance.

In practice, each resolution of the local council which is related to financial office is sent to RIO, who checks its legality. If it is found to be illegal, the governor has the right to invalidate the resolution. If the local government disagrees with the governor's opinion, it may take the issue to court for a final decision. In addition to the supervision of financial resolutions, RIO exerts also external control (at least once every four years) checking books of local governments.

The local council usually controls financial activity through its Committee of Finance and, in special cases, through the Scrutiny Committee. In an increasing number of local governments, there is also a separate unit (within the structure of the local administration) responsible for internal control. Twice a year, the local council is obliged to analyse and accept (or reject) information about the execution of the budget. It is obligatory for the Scrutiny Committee to prepare and present to the council its opinion, before voting.

It has already been mentioned that the RIOs are institutions which were created especially to deal with the control and supervision of local government finance. RIO Presidents are nominated by the Prime Minister and their position is surprisingly stable and not dependent on any political changes in the

Parliament or central government (more than half of RIO presidents have held their position since 1993, in spite of several central government changes).

Aside from checking the legality of each local resolution related to finance, the RIOs have several other duties. They collect reports from budget execution and provide training for local government officers. In the case local council is unable to approve the budget until 31 March, the RIO may impose its own budget. The RIO's opinion on creditworthiness is also required when a local government wants to take bank credit or issue bonds, but this is usually limited to check if the legal limits of the debt are observed.

The system described above works relatively smoothly, although it is not problem-free. One of the most frequently raised problems is a variation in interpretations of legal regulations by individual RIOs. It happens that what is allowed according to one RIO, is forbidden by another in a different region of Poland. Also, standards and procedures of control vary considerably across the country. In 1997 the National Council of RIOs was created in an attempt to address the problem of standardisation. But the National Council can only suggest or propose solutions; it does not impose them. Another attempt at increasing the quality of RIO inspectors and standardising of their work methodology was the edition of the relevant manual (British Know-How Fund, 1999). In spite of the evident progress due to these efforts, there is still much to be done in the standardisation of RIO procedures and their interpretations of the law.

15.9 CONCLUSIONS

Many conclusions were drawn in the discussion of particular topics. Some of the more general ones are reviewed below:

1. The system of municipal revenues has generally been the same since its inception, that is since 1991. The structure of local government revenues in general and the structure of grants in particular have been gradually worsening. First, the proportion of own revenue in total budgets of municipal governments has been decreasing. But still, the proportion of municipal revenues coming from own taxes (with some amount of local discretion in tax policy) is higher than in most of the other countries of the region. Second, specific grants are losing their function of supporting investments and becoming an element of finance for current tasks of the local governments.
2. Own sources of revenue are especially unimportant in the county and regional units of local government. These two tiers of sub-national govern-

ment have no own tax revenues, a fact which does not comply with the Constitution, which states that 'local government units have a right to set rates of local fees and taxes'.

3. The grant system in spite of specific criticism in section 5, seems to provide a stable and source of financing local government spending, based on objective formulas.
5. The overall legal framework allowed a relatively (compared to other countries of the region) developed market of local borrowing, allowing the financing of a considerable proportion of investment spending through bank credits and municipal bonds.

NOTES

1. For territorial fragmentation in CEE countries and its consequences for service delivery – see Swianiewicz (2002).
2. See, for example, Council of Europe (1995).
3. For an extensive discussion of the definition of local own revenues see Swianiewicz (2003).
4. For a full description of municipal fees see Bury (2002).
5. For more complete discussion of educational grants and of financing education by local governments, see Levitas and Herczyński (2002).
6. For more details see Kopańska and Levitas (2003).

BIBLIOGRAPHY

Bramley, G. (1990), *Equalisation Grants and Local Expenditure Needs*, Aldershot: Avebury.

British Know-How Fund (1999), *Kontrola finansów komunalnych* [Control of Communal Finance], Warszawa: British Know-How Fund, Local Government Assistance Programme.

Bury, P. (2002), *Finanse lokalne z elementami finansów państwa*, Kielce: WSU.

Bury, P. (2003), Zasadność istnienia samorządowych powiatów i województw w aspekcie finansowym, in *Finansowe aspekty rozwoju lokalnego i regionalnego u progu XXI wieku. Doświadczenia i perspektywy*, Wrocław: WSZiF, Zeszyty Naukowe, No.15.

Council of Europe (1995), *The Size of Municipalities, Efficiency and Citizen Participation*, Local and Regional Authorities in Europe, No. 56, Strasbourg: Council of Europe.

Dexia (2002), *Local Finance in the Fifteen Countries of the European Union*, Paris: Dexia.

Kopańska, A. and T. Levitas (2004), The Regulation and Development of the Subsovereign Debt Market in Poland: 1993–2002, in P. Swianiewicz (ed.), *Local Government Borrowing: Regulations and Practice in Central and Eastern Europe*, Budapest: OSI-Local Government and Public Services Initiative, 25–78.

Levitas, T. and J. Herczyński (2002), Decentralisation, Local Governments and Education Reform in Post-Communist Poland, in K. Davey (ed.), *Balancing*

National and Local Responsibilities, Budapest: OSI-Local Government and Public Services Initiative, 113–90.

Swianiewicz, P. (ed.) (2002), *Consolidation or Fragmentation? The Size of Local Government in Central and Eastern Europe*, Budapest: O OSI-Local Government and Public Services Initiative.

Swianiewicz, P. (2003), *Foundations of Fiscal Decentralisation. Benchmarking Guide for Countries in Transition*, LGI Discussion Papers, No. 26, Budapest: OSI-Local Government and Public Services Initiative.

16. Local government finance in Romania

Claudiu Doltu

INTRODUCTION

The first bodies of local governance in the modern history of Romania were created in 1864. After the First World War, in 1925, new laws on public administration were passed. Between 1947 and 1989, local governance was completely subordinated to the Communist Party and its role consisted exclusively in implementing Government decisions. Elections for mayors and local councils were just a formality and the population was totally deprived of the possibility of selecting its representatives and leaders. Although the ideas of decentralisation and local governance followed the modern and contemporary history of Romania, society in general did not seem to understand or appreciate the practical importance of these concepts. It can be said, with few exceptions, that a dependent spirit in local governance is deeply rooted in the country. Among civil servants, at the central government level, local autonomy was hardly accepted in 90 years. Decentralisation started to accelerate after 2003 and had been consolidated from a financial perspective in 2005–06.

The European approach of regional development has penetrated slowly into Romanian society (Regional Policy Unit, 2002). The EU accession was a strong incentive for Romania to adapt its approach of local governance and decentralisation to the European spirit of these concepts (Funk and Pizzati, 2003). The conclusions of this study address mainly the financial independence of local authorities, that is, the conditionality for the local governance capacity to design and implement policies aimed at promoting communities' interests.[1]

BASIC LEGAL FRAMEWORK AND LOCAL GOVERNMENT FINANCE REGULATIONS

The administrative structure of Romania includes municipalities, towns and communes, which may include one or more villages. These local entities are distributed over 41 counties plus Bucharest. Bucharest municipality has special status, functioning both as a municipality and a county. Local entities range in size from 2 million in Bucharest to an average of just under 4,000 in the communes. The remainder of the population is distributed as follows: 36 per cent in the municipalities, 10 per cent in the towns and 45 per cent in the communes.

Table 16.1 Structure and population of local governments

	Number	Share of Total (%)	Population	Share of Total (%)	Average Population
County Councils	41		22,533,156		549,589
All local councils	2,951	100	22,533,156	100	7,636
Bucharest	1		2,027,512	9	2,027,512
Municipalities	83	3	8,032,804	36	96,781
Towns	179	6	2,320,375	10	12,963
Communes	2,688	91	10,152,465	45	3,777

Source: Ministry of Public Administration.

There are two tiers of local government in this administrative structure: local councils and county councils. Between these two tiers there is no hierarchical relationship. The local councils and the mayors are the authorities of the public local administration. They operate as autonomous administrative authorities. Each county has also a Prefect appointed by the Government as its local representative. Between the Prefects on one side and the mayors and local and county councils on the other side, there are no hierarchical relations.

The Mayor is elected by public scrutiny with a mandate of four years in each commune and town. Councillors, with a four years' mandate and also elected by public scrutiny, make up the local councils. Each county has a Prefect, appointed by the Government. The Prefect looks over the legality of the activities performed by the mayors and local and county councils and supervises the decentralised activity of the Ministries and of the other central bodies within the territory. The Mayor is the head of the local public administration and is responsible to the local council for the operation of all public local services. The local council, based on the Mayor's submission, approves the organisational chart, the number of personnel and the rules for governing the public services, the designation and the dismissal of the head of these services.

At the Government level there is the Ministry of Public Administration and the Interior. This Ministry is in charge of fulfilling the Government's attribution regarding the local public administration, and to oversee the Mayors' performances in realising the delegated attributions. Division of power between the local government and the central government is inspired by the dual system. There is a clear line between the powers of the two representation bodies. Some Ministries have their own representation bodies at the local level and perform their specific activities, other than the tasks of the local authorities; for instance, the Ministry of Public Administration and Interior (responsible for public order), the Ministry of Economy and Finance (responsible for tax collection, financial controls and customs), the Ministry of Labour and Family and the Ministry of Education and the Ministry of Agriculture.

The European approach to Regional Development has been relatively recently introduced in the general priorities of the government. Based on this regional development approach, the 41 counties and municipalities of Bucharest have been separated into eight regions and each should be administered by a Governor appointed by the Government.

The financial responsibilities in the administration of the local public finance fall under the Mayor's and the County Council President's responsibilities. Based on the Mayor's project, local and county councils prepare the budgets for their communities. The county council distributes the transfers from the state budget to the local municipal councils, city and village councils and to its own budget.

DEMOCRATIC LEGITIMACY AND FINANCIAL REPORTING

Local governments' responsibilities are related to public administration, pre-university education and culture, social assistance, transport and communication, and public works and housing. These responsibilities are divided between basic level local governments (municipalities, towns and communes) and the counties. The counties are responsible for child protection and care of disabled children, county public services and county roads, as well as county cultural institutions (museums, libraries, and so on). Municipalities, towns and communes carry out more direct service provision: urban transport, sanitation and public utilities and maintain roads, sidewalks, parks and green areas. They are also responsible for pre-university education and other social assistance (such as the minimum income guarantee programme), local culture and sports services, local economic development and markets.

In 90 years, the local governments were strongly financially dependent on the central government, despite the large area of administrative competence, and they had an administrative role rather than a significant position in policy formulation. After the year 2000, the local governments' financial independence from the central government increased slowly, but continuously. The degree of independence is revealed by the amount of the local budgets' participation in total public spending (10.8 per cent on average for 1990–99 and 17.7 per cent in average for 2000–06), and by the significant changes in structure of expenditures (see Table 16.2).

Table 16.2 GDP total government expenditures and local government expenditures

	GDP annual change (%)	Total government expenditures (% of GDP)	Local government expenditures (% of GDP)	Local government expenditures relative to total government expenditures (%)
1995	7.1	34.7	4.5	12.9
1996	3.9	33.8	4.5	13.4
1997	-6.1	33.6	4.1	12.0
1998	-4.8	34.5	3.6	10.1
1999	-1.2	34.7	3.8	10.5
2000	1.6	35.3	4.1	11.1
2001	5.3	33.4	6.0	17.3
2002	4.5	32.1	6.1	17.9
2003	5.2	32.1	6.7	18.9
2004	8.4	31.4	6.6	19.0
2005	6.5	32.0	6.5	18.6
2006	8.2	33.5	7.6	21.0

Note: Total public expenditures represent all expenditures included in the state consolidated budget: state budget, social insurance budget, special funds and local budgets.

Source: Author's own calculations; based on Romanian Ministry of Economy and Finance data.

In the first years of transition (1990–99) the local budgets' participation in the total budget spending increased very slowly and was correlated with the general evolution of the economy (Table 16.3). This correlation reflects an attempt by the central government to centralise the resource allocations during periods of financial stress in the economy. For example, during the recession years (1997–99), local budgets' participation in the total budget spending decreased from 12 per cent to 10.5 per cent and general government expenditures increased from 33.6 per cent of GDP to 34.7 per cent of GDP.

Table 16.3 Local government expenditures in total government expenditures (%)

	Public administration	Education	Health	Social assistance	Public works and housing	Transport
1995	26.4	13.7	19.4	2.9	87.0	38.0
1996	27.9	15.2	20.2	3.2	89.6	39.7
1997	30.7	12.6	20.1	2.0	91.0	33.8
1998	35.5	9.9	0.6	3.2	89.3	29.4
1999	41.4	11.6	0.5	2.9	86.4	21.6
2000	37.9	10.3	0.3	4.9	80.1	22.4
2001	38.1	69.4	0.6	5.6	81.6	21.9
2002	38.1	69.9	0.7	8.1	72.5	20.3
2003	37.3	72.1	1.1	10.6	74.0	12.3
2004	37.6	72.3	1.5	9.5	67.1	20.9
2005	38.5	64.9	1.3	9.2	60.0	22.4

Source: Author's own calculations; based on Romanian Ministry of Economy and Finance data.

The local governments could hardly develop their own policies in the main fields of interest for their citizens. Sometimes responsibilities and financial resources are given to the local authorities by the central government, but they cannot decide the policy in the respective fields. For instance, hospitals and pre-university school buildings have been transferred to the local authorities' patrimony, but they are not in a position to change the function of these buildings. The local authorities have to cover all the maintenance costs for these buildings, but only the Ministry of Health and the Ministry of Education can decide to close down the respective activities or to change the function of the buildings.

Despite the fact that the local authorities are directly elected by local citizens, there is no established culture of citizens' participation in local government. The financial reporting plays only a formal role in the relationship between local bodies and citizens. The county councils and local councils are not at all involved in any real co-operation or even permanent dialogue with the local citizens. The Mayors and the Presidents of the county councils are accountable only to the Audit Court.

INDEPENDENT LOCAL GOVERNMENT REVENUES SOURCES

The evolution of the local government's revenues reveals a slight increase in the degree of financial decentralisation of public finances. It also shows a modest capacity of local government to design policies around the political interests of the central government. Local authorities have a limited capacity to introduce local taxes and to establish a tax base. Local councils, county councils and the General Council of Bucharest municipality establish local taxes, respecting the legal limits imposed by the central government.[2] The list of local taxes and the upper and bottom limits for the tax base are established by the central government through laws. The Directorate of Local Public Finance – a separate central government body – is responsible for local tax collection and reports to the Ministry of Economy and Finance.

There are six local government revenues sources. In order of importance these are: amounts received from the state budget, own revenues, subsidies, loans, receipts from credit granted, contributions and sponsorships (Tables 16.4 and 16.5).

Table 16.4 The structure of local government revenue sources (%)

	1995	1996	1997	1998	1999	2000	2001	2002	2003	2004	2005
Own revenues	27.7	22.6	19.0	24.7	44.6	36.3	22.1	22.0	46.0	46.5	44.6
Amounts received from the state budget	36.1	39.5	44.4	37.1	46.7	55.1	71.5	76.1	46.6	47.4	48.9
Subsidies	36.0	37.0	36.2	37.6	7.0	8.5	6.4	1.3	5.6	5.8	5.3
Receipts from credit granted	0.0	0.0	0.0	0.0	0.0	0.0	0.0	0.0	0.0	0.0	0.0
Contribution and sponsorship	0.0	0.0	0.0	0.0	0.0	0.0	0.0	0.0	0.0	0.1	0.1
Loans	0.3	0.9	0.5	0.5	1.6	0.1	0.3	0.6	1.8	0.2	0.1
Total	100	100	100	100	100	100	100	100	100	100	100

Source: Author's own calculations; based on Romanian Ministry of Economy and Finance data.

Own revenues consist of current revenues (fiscal and non-fiscal revenues), capital revenues and revenues with a special destination. Capital revenues proceed from capitalisation of goods belonging to public institutions and from selling houses built with state funds and revenues with a special destination, account for the remaining 15 per cent of own revenues. Fiscal revenues represent, on

Table 16.5 Local government revenue sources (USD million)

	1995	1996	1997	1998	1999	2000	2001	2002	2003	2004	2005
Own revenues	454.2	366.7	276.8	375.0	646.8	559.4	540.9	621.2	1,810.44	2,272.24	2,984.10
Amounts received from the state budget	591.7	639.9	648.0	563.1	678.2	849.6	1,752.3	2,146.7	1,835.17	2319.48	3,267.17
Subsidies	590.1	599.7	528.8	569.5	102.0	131.5	156.0	35.5	221.35	281.95	418.08
Receipts from credit granted	0.0	0.0	0.0	0.0	0.0	0.0	0.1	0.3	0.15	0.34	0.68
Contribution and sponsorship	0.0	0.0	0.0	0.1	0.0	0.0	0.0	0.0	0.00	5.92	8.06
Loans	5.0	15.2	6.9	8.2	23.7	1.3	7.5	16.7	72.06	9.02	7.97
Total revenues	1,640.9	1,621.5	1,460.5	1,515.9	1,450.6	1,541.8	2,449.9	2,820.3	3,939.17	4,888.95	6,686.06

Source: Author's own calculations; based on Romanian Ministry of Economy and Finance data.

average, about 56 per cent of own revenues and about 16.5 per cent of total revenues. They consist of direct tax, which represents, on average, about 90 per cent of fiscal revenues, and indirect tax. Direct tax comprises tax on profits, taxes on the population, tax on using state-owned lands, tax on buildings and lands owned by legal persons and other direct tax – car tax on legal persons, tax on agriculture land and other direct tax.

Taxes on population (income tax on self-employment, tax from civil persons' buildings, and land and car tax, income tax from rent, stamp duties and other taxes) are among the largest fiscal revenues. Tax from legal persons on buildings and land, tax on using state-owned lands and tax on profits are also important revenue sources. The indirect tax is much less important, as fiscal revenues accounted on average, for 1995–2005, for only 10 per cent of fiscal revenues. The indirect tax consists of: tax on shows, stamp duties from legal entities, penalties on delayed payments and other indirect taxes.

Non-fiscal revenues represent, on average, about 15 per cent of own revenues. They consist of quotas from net profit of Regies Autonomes (RA) locally subordinated, quotas from public institutions (tax on driving licence exams, driving licence issuance and other car and road taxes) and sundry revenues such as: revenues from recovering lawsuit expenditures, revenues from fines and penalties, restitution from budget financing from previous years, royalties and other revenues.

Transfers from the central budget are the most important finance source for the local government. Annually, transfers from the central budget (state budget, social insurance budget and special funds) represent, on average, almost 50 per cent of the total local government revenues. Amounts received from the state budget decreased from 84.1 per cent of the total local government revenues in 1992 to less than 50 per cent between 1993 and 1999, and increased again above 50 per cent (on average) between 2001 and 2005. County councils can use 50 per cent of the amounts transferred from income tax to balance the local budgets. Twenty-five per cent of these funds are kept in the county council's budget and the remaining 75 per cent is used as follows: 50 per cent is divided among local budgets (municipalities, towns and communes) using an equalisation formula and 50 per cent is distributed at the local level, based on certain criteria defined each year by the local councils. These criteria normally should reflect local needs, priorities and interests. Supplementary, local budgets can use an additional 50 per cent from the 17 per cent of quotas from income tax, in order to balance the local budget, using the same methodology.

On this basis, in 2003, local government (for the entire country) had the discretion to allocate ROL 3,914 billion (about USD 58.9 million or EUR 52.2 million). At the county level, significant differences (between counties) exist, as a result of using the equalisation formula for transferring from the state budget funds of income tax. Poor counties benefit more from the methodology used in the Romanian public finance system than better-off counties. At first sight, these amounts seem to be insignificant on a county level, bearing in mind that Romania has 41 counties (plus Bucharest as a distinct administrative-territorial entity) and each county has a multitude of needs.

However, the amounts could not be ignored – in fact each county has the discretion to allocate, on average, more than USD 1 million/year. Also, there are counties, especially poor counties, which have the discretion to allocate more than USD 2.4 million/year (DFID, 2003). For instance, in 2003, Vaslui (a poor county) had discretion to allocate ROL 86 billion (about USD 2.6 million or EUR 2.3 million) based on seven criteria defined by the county council. Sibiu (a rich county) shows that in 2003, local authorities have the discretion to allocate only ROL 29 billion (about USD 870,000 or EUR 770,000).

Subsidies also come from the central budget and have various allocations: from heating and urban transport, to child protection, disabled persons and to investments partially funded through external loans. The amount of subsidies in the total local government revenues decreased from 46.1 per cent in 1993 to 1.3 per cent in 2002, and remained above 5 per cent for 2002–2005. This decrease has been accompanied by an increase in own revenues.

Own revenues' share in total revenue increased mainly starting with 2003. If for 1991–2002 they represented on average just 25 per cent of total revenues, for 1991–2005 this average increased up to 29.4 per cent. This increase is due to the change of the legislation on local public finance (introduced in 2003) that allowed own revenues to increase as a share in total revenues on 46 per cent in 2003 (up from 22 in 2002) to 46.5 per cent in 2004 and 44.6 per cent in 2005. These evolutions are a clear sign of local governments' increased financial independence in recent years.

The other legal financing sources of local government – credits, contributions and sponsorships and loans – were almost never used between 1991 and 2002. Loans have been rarely used, representing 1.6 per cent of the total revenues in 1996 and 1.8 per cent in 2003. Local authorities started to consider more loans as a financial source only after 2005, when they made a strong political lobby for amending the legislation to allow them to raise more money borrowing from the financial markets.

The structure of the local government revenue sources reveals that the decentralisation in Romania's public finance increased very slowly in the first years of transition and accelerated when the macroeconomic stability was confirmed and the EU accession was almost achieved. During the 1990s, there were no significant changes. The strong financial dependence on the Government has

Table 16.6 The structure of revenues from taxes, 1991–2002 (USD million)

	1995	1996	1997	1998	1999	2000	2001	2002	2003	2004	2005
Fiscal revenues	361.2	283.2	212.5	279.0	381.3	283.2	288.9	358.2	550.0	667.1	828.7
Direct tax	338.7	268.1	197.6	272.0	374.1	273.2	276.4	339.7	415.7	488.0	633.8
Tax on profit	9.8	9.9	2.0	25.0	25.5	18.8	7.4	6.4	14.6	13.0	13.3
Taxes on population	108.0	92.0	68.2	146.1	246.9	140.5	103.9	157.8	179.2	208.1	263.1
Tax on using state owned lands	18.4	11.0	7.2	8.2	5.3	5.2	5.9	5.0	8.4	5.0	4.4
Tax on buildings and lands from legal persons	130.8	87.6	49.7	58.8	67.0	77.7	92.6	132.1	176.1	219.3	299.4
Other direct tax	71.6	67.5	52.8	34.0	29.3	31.0	35.6	38.4	37.4	42.5	53.6
Car tax from legal persons	21.8	15.8	8.2	10.9	11.1	12.2	14.0	16.9	18.7	22.6	27.3
Tax on income from agriculture	29.0	180.3	2.9	0.0	0.1	0.1	0.0	0.1	1.3	1.5	2.9
Other direct tax	20.8	33.6	41.8	23.1	18.1	18.7	21.5	21.4	17.4	18.4	23.4
Indirect tax	22.5	15.1	14.9	7.0	7.2	10.0	12.5	18.6	134.3	179.1	194.9
Tax on shows	1.1	1.0	0.9	1.1	0.5	0.4	0.5	0.5	0.7	1.0	1.0
Other indirect tax	21.4	14.1	14.0	5.9	6.7	9.6	12.0	18.1	133.6	178.1	193.9

Note: Values are converted in USD using the annual average exchange.
Source: Author's own calculations; based on Romanian Ministry of Economy and Finance data.

Table 16.7 Non-tax revenues of local government, 1991–2002 (USD million)

	1995	1996	1997	1998	1999	2000	2001	2002	2003	2004	2005
Non-tax revenues	68.7	67.69	54.7	82.7	89.7	86.4	95.1	114.2	138.6	174.7	252.3
Quotas from net profit of RA locally subordinated	2.4	5.06	4.1	8.5	8.6	11.2	10.3	6.6	9.3	9.3	11.0
Quotas from public institutions	27.2	30.93	26.8	35.5	36.6	16.6	22.2	30.4	38.5	45.4	62.8
Other revenues*	39.2	31.70	23.8	38.7	44.5	58.6	62.6	77.2	90.8	120.0	178.4

Note: * Includes: revenues from recovering lawsuit expenditures, revenues from fines and penalties, restitutions from budget financing from previous years, royalties and other revenues. Values are converted in USD using the annual average exchange
Source: Author's own calculations; based on Romanian Ministry of Economy and Finance data.

led to abnormalities in local authorities' political structure. Over the years, many Mayors have abandoned their political parties or their political independence and entered the ruling party, which is a way of attracting more funds from the Government.[3] Starting from 2003, the financial independence of the local authorities has increased significantly (see Tablc 16.6 and 16.7).

GRANT TRANSFERS

The process of the allocation of the equalisation grants begins with the State budget. This consists of three parts. First, each county receives a sum from the central budget. The county council then shares this sum between its own budget and the balance for allocation to each local council in the respective county. Second, from the central budget, each county receives a specific sum as part of the heating subsidy. Third, the Budget Law mandates the county councils to use a specific formula to allocate equalisation grants to the local councils. This formula is included as an Annex to the State Budget Law and is aimed at measuring the relative financial capacity of county and local councils. Since 2003, the fiscal capacity is calculated as follows:

$$QSe = \frac{\dfrac{(ORc + ITc) : Pc}{(ORe + ITe) : Pe} \; x \; \dfrac{Pe}{Pc}}{\sum_{e=1}^{n} \left[\dfrac{(ORc + ITc) : Pc}{ORe + ITe) : Pe} \; x \; \dfrac{Pe}{Pc} \right]} \; x \; QSc$$

where:
QS(e) = Divided amount from income tax on administrative-territorial entity
OR(c) = County's own revenues
IT(c) = Income tax on county level
P(c) = County's population
OR(e) = Administrative-territorial entity's own revenues
IT(e) = Income tax due to administrative-territorial entity
P(e) = Administrative-territorial entity's population
QS(c) = Divided amount from income tax on whole county

Two lessons result from analysing this equalisation formula: (1) data shows that poor counties benefit more than the rich from this equalisation formula and (2) the county councils are not adhering to the legal requirement on using a formula-based approach to allocate the distribution grants. Instead, they are using an ad-hoc allocation.[4] There are several factors that make the ad-hoc allocation more doable for the local authorities. These factors are related both to the revenues and to the expenditures of local councils (World Bank, 2002).

Two factors related to revenues constrain the use of a formula-based approach. First, the county councils suspect that the local councils are not doing enough to raise revenues through their own taxes and fees, thus increasing their reliance on equalisation grants. Second, the county councils are also concerned that some local councils have lost revenues due to objective factors.

Three factors are related to expenditures. First, the investment expenditures are not linear – they may inflate during certain years while a large project is under construction then decrease as the project is completed. Second, some expenditure needs are not shared by all local councils (hospitals or institutions that care for institutionalised children do not operate in all local councils). Third, county councils are also responsible for helping local councils that have financial problems. For example, some local councils accumulate debts for public utilities or fail to maintain schools in good shape so that the county councils must transfer to them additional funds.

There have been some interesting developments in subsidies for investments partially financed by external loans. These transfers were not particularly important for their financial volume – they represent only a small fraction of the total local government revenues. They are interesting, especially for different interest groups linked by the local investment projects. Bucharest – the capital of Romania – is a special case. Investment projects financed by external loans also involve domestic co-financing. The municipality of Bucharest – represented by the Mayor – obtained important financial credits from the European Investment Bank and from the European Bank for Reconstruction and Development in 2000. The projects' implementation was delayed several times because of conflicts between the Mayor, politically supported by one party, and the local council, dominated by another party. After the general elections at the end of 2000, the Mayor's party lost power and the political colour of the government changed. Afterwards, the local council – supported by the Prefect and encouraged by the Government – rejected the investments' documentation. They could do this because they approve the investment projects and also, funds for co-financing investment projects financed by external loans come from the Government. For almost three years, all the Mayor's major investment projects were blocked. Finally, the conflict was resolved after a political negotiation, mediated by the President of Romania himself!

Table 16.8 Subsidies for investments partially financed by external loans

	1998	1999	2000	2001	2002	2003	2004	2005
ROL million	255,003.4	632,746.7	811,618.8	945,044.3	736,659.6	950,003.0	602,506.0	236,276.0
USD million	28.73	41.26	37.41	32.52	22.29	28.6	18.5	8.1
% of total revenues	1.9	2.8	2.4	1.3	0.8	0.7	0.4	0.1

Source: Author's own calculations; based Romanian Ministry of Economy and Finance data.

LOCAL GOVERNMENT EXPENDITURES

Local government expenditures include two major classes – by object and by function. The sum of expenditures by object is always equal to the sum of expenditures by function. The expenditures classification by object consists of: current expenditures, capital expenditures and financial operation (Table 16.9).

Table 16.9 Local government expenditures by object (%)

	1995	1996	1997	1998	1999	2000	2001	2002	2003	2004	2005
Current	69.8	72.2	74.3	74.1	77.4	78.9	86.5	87.0	85.9	88.7	88.7
Capital	30.2	27.6	25.3	25.7	22.1	20.1	13.3	12.6	13.5	10.5	10.3
Fin. Ops.	0.1	0.2	0.4	0.2	0.5	1.0	0.2	0.4	0.6	0.8	0.9
Total	100	100	100	100	100	100	100	100	100	100	100

Source: Author's own calculations; based on Romanian Ministry of Economy and Finance data.

The classification by function includes: general public services, socio-cultural expenditures, public works services, community development and environment, economic activities and other expenditures (Table 16.10).

The current expenditures mobilise most of the local government's spending – a minimum 69.8 per cent in 1995 and maximum 87.7 per cent of total expenditures in 2004 and 2005. For 1995–2005, they accounted, on average, for about 80 per cent of total expenditures. Current expenditures consist of: personnel, materials and services and transfer and subsidies. Personnel expenditures include all direct and indirect personnel expenses (salaries, benefits, staff travel and training). Materials and services expenditures consist of the purchase of expendable supplies, equipment and contracts with third parties for certain activities (for example, street cleaning) and payment for public utilities. Transfers and subsidies consist of all funds provided to others – from income support payment as a transfer to payments to other public institutions, which are classified as subsidies.

Table 16.10 The structure of local government expenditures by function (%)

	1995	1996	1997	1998	1999	2000	2001	2002	2003	2004	2005
Public authorities	7.3	6.9	7.9	13.4	14.0	14.4	9.7	9.6	9.4	9.6	10.2
Education	10.4	11.9	10.0	9.0	8.9	7.8	36.5	36.3	32.7	33.4	34.1
Health	12.5	12.4	12.8	0.5	0.4	0.3	0.4	0.5	0.6	0.8	0.9
Culture, religion, sport and youth	4.3	3.2	4.7	4.9	4.3	4.6	3.4	4.0	4.2	4.3	4.2
Social assistance	6.0	6.3	4.6	9.3	8.0	11.5	9.3	13.2	15.2	14.6	14.1
Public development, housing, environment	38.9	37.6	39.0	41.3	40.4	36.0	25.4	22.4	25.9	20.3	19.6
Transport and communication	19.9	19.9	19.6	20.3	12.3	11.7	8.1	7.2	7.5	13.5	14.0
Other	0.8	1.8	1.3	1.2	2.3	3.3	1.6	2.3	0.7	1.1	0.7
Special earmarked expenditures	0.0	0.0	0.0	0.0	9.5	10.3	5.7	4.5	0.0	n.a.	n.a.

Source: Author's own calculations; based on Romanian Ministry of Economy and Finance data.

Capital expenditures represented on average only 19.2 per cent of total spending for 1995–2005. They decreased from a maximum of 30.2 per cent in 1995 to 10.3 per cent in 2005. Between 1999 and 2003, almost 25 per cent of local government investments were established by the central government, through earmarked expenditures. Almost 60 per cent of these were oriented towards the public works and transport. Financial operations include loans, temporary loans for establishing public institutions and public services by local interest, principal, interest and charge payments for credits, and so on. This expenditure category is insignificant and has never exceeded 1 per cent of total expenditures.

Expenditures on general public services represent local administration expenditures, which include the operating costs of the local government. They do not include the operating costs of other public institutions subordinated to the local government. Local administration expenditures account for about 10 per cent of the total expenditures. They mobilised a minimum of USD million 110.5 in 1992 and a maximum of USD million 655.1 in 2005. Socio-cultural expenditures include expenditures on education, culture, sports and religion and social-assistance. The local government's responsibility regarding education is only to ensure the operation and maintenance of the local schools. Accordingly, the education expenditures are strictly related to these administrative activities as well as to repairs and capital expenditures. Expenditures on education accounted on average for 21 per cent of total expenditures for the period 1995–2005. They increased significantly in 2001 to 36.5 per cent of total expenditures (from 7.8 per cent in the previous year), and stayed above 30 per cent until 2005. Since 1995, when local government was charged with responsibilities regarding education, these expenditures represented a minimum of USD 119.2 million in 2000 and a maximum of USD 2,197 million in 2005 (Table 16.11).

Expenditures on health accounted, on average, for 3.8 per cent of total expenditures. Their share in total expenditures significantly changed over the years, from zero per cent at the beginning of the 1990s to 15 per cent in 1994, staying above 12 per cent between 1995 and 1997 and then decreased to less than 1 per cent between 1998 and 2005. Culture, sports, religion and youth expenditures include local budget support for cultural and sports organisations – museums, libraries, operas and houses of culture. They account on average for only 4.2 per cent of total expenditures, and over the years they have preserved their share in total expenditures relative constantly. Social assistance weight in total expenditures increased from 1 per cent (USD 7.4 million) in 1991 to 13.2 per cent (USD 370 million) in 2002. At the county level, these expenditures include child protection services and at local council level, they include both payments of social benefits and support for social institutions.

Public development, housing and environment have the biggest share in the total local government expenditures – on average 31.5 per cent between 1995 and 2005. This expenditure category is the most important among other expenditures and includes funds for water and heating companies, operations on public markets, street cleaning and repair, and housing and waste disposal. Transport and communication expenditures include funds provided to local public transport and to regional airports. This is the second most important expenditures category for local government and accounts, on average, for 14 per cent of total local government expenditures between 1995 and 2005. In monetary terms, this expenditure category slowly decreased from USD 319.6 million in 1996 to USD 292.1 million in 2003 and then increased to USD 664 million and USD 900 million in 2004 and 2005.

Earmarked expenditures were a functional category introduced in 1999.[5] It accounted for 9.5 per cent (USD 134.1 million) in 1999 and 4.5 per cent (USD 125.8 million) in 2002. These are expenditures financed by targeted funds, for example, the public roads fund, housing fund, and so on, and are annually established by the central government through an Annex to the Public Budget Law. Since 2003, these earmarked expenditures are no longer used in the local budgets.

On one hand, the expenditures structure and evolution could be interpreted as revealing unstable functional responsibilities of the local government

Table 16.11 Local government expenditures by function (USD million)

	1995	1996	1997	1998	1999	2000	2001	2002	2003	2004	2005
Total	1,605.9	1,607.5	1,446.8	1,507.7	1,408.6	1,535.7	2,432.0	2,804.0	3,871.2	4,761.8	6,607.2
General public services	116.5	110.5	114.7	202.4	196.8	221.1	236.2	270.4	362.4	456.2	655.1
Socio-cultural expenditures	532.6	544.1	464.9	357.8	305.1	371.0	1,205.7	1,513.2	2,040.7	2,530.0	3,422.4
Education	166.3	191.5	145.2	136.2	125.3	119.2	886.7	1,018.1	1,265.8	1,591.7	2,197.0
Health	200.8	199.7	184.8	7.7	6.2	4.9	10.2	12.8	24.6	38.2	47.5
Culture, religion, sport and youth	69.1	50.8	67.9	73.7	60.8	69.9	81.5	111.5	163.5	205.6	268.2
Social assistance	96.4	102.1	66.9	140.1	112.7	177.0	227.2	370.8	586.8	694.6	909.7
Public development, housing, environment	624.8	604.9	564.0	623.3	568.7	553.1	618.7	629.0	1004.2	967.3	1,260.7
Economic activities	319.1	320.1	284.7	306.3	185.6	184.4	206.8	215.1	314.8	675.2	949.4
Agriculture	0.0	0.0	0.0	0.0	11.0	4.7	8.7	10.2	13.8	16.5	14.1
Transport and communication	319.1	319.6	283.8	305.5	173.6	179.1	196.7	202.9	292.1	644.0	900.8
Other	0.0	0.5	0.9	0.7	1.0	0.5	1.4	2.1	9.0	14.8	34.5
Other activities	11.8	24.4	12.6	14.8	11.4	27.6	16.6	31.9	25.6	52.9	47.1
Guarantee and redistribution	0.0	0.0	0.2	0.6	0.7	1.6	1.8	2.4	4.5	5.4	8.0
Transfers	0.0	0.0	0.0	0.0	0.0	4.0	5.2	5.1	7.0	8.2	8.0
Credits granted	0.0	0.0	0.0	0.0	0.0	0.2	0.2	3.7	0.4	0.3	0.2
Interest repayment and other expenditures	0.0	0.1	0.4	0.2	0.6	0.7	0.9	2.7	7.0	33.4	27.5
Repayment loans	1.0	3.3	5.2	2.3	5.6	13.1	2.3	8.0	16.9	32.8	50.2
Special earmarked expenditures	0.0	0.0	0.0	0.0	134.1	158.9	137.6	125.8	87.7	0.0	0.0

Source: Author's own calculations; based on Romanian Ministry of Economy and Finance data.

Table 16.12 Local government overall balance

	1995	1996	1997	1998	1999	2000	2001	2002	2003	2004	2005
Surplus (+)/deficit (-) ROL	71,166.7	43,323.5	98,015.5	72,718.6	644,391.9	228,353.0	520,318.5	539,335.5	225,410.7	415,101.4	703,904.5
Surplus (+)/deficit (-) USD (mil.)	35.0	14.1	13.7	8.2	42.0	6.1	17.9	16.3	67.9	127.2	241.6

Source: Author's own calculations; based on Romanian Ministry of Economy and Finance data.

(World Bank, 2002). On the other hand, this could be interpreted as a normal development in a transition period which is more or less a learning-by-doing process. As services provided by the local governments are determined each year through an Annex to the State Budget Law, the role of local government is defined to a great extent by the central government and the local authorities cannot significantly influence how their positions and responsibilities are changing. Also, when financial management is subject to permanent uncertainty, the implementation of local policies and development plans is difficult because the local authorities do not know what expenditure assignments for the next year will be. As a result, local governments have weak incentives to develop financial management policies.

Local governments are responsible for all investments in public works (water, heating and public housing) and public roads (county and local roads, streets, bridges). Investments may be carried out by both the local government, or a public institution subordinated to it, and by local public companies owned by the local government. Local and county councils approve investments totally financed from the local government's own sources, if they do not exceed ROL 80 billion (almost USD 2.3 million). The Government must approve investments above this limit. The local governments' financial sources for investments consist of net operating savings, transfers from the Government and debt and borrowing issues. Since 1999, the net savings rate increased above 10 per cent and financed almost 60 per cent of investment expenditures in 1999 and about 50 per cent in 2000 (Urban Institute, 2001).

Local governments' overall balance shows a permanent surplus (see Table 16.12). The annual surplus remaining after regulation with the state budget is used to repay the possible residual debts and to constitute a floating fund. The floating fund is held in a distinct account, opened to each administrative-territorial unit, at the state treasury. It can be used in the current year to cover some temporary discrepancies between revenues and expenditures and to cover a possible deficit at the end of the tax year. The floating fund can also be used to finance some investments aimed at developing local public services for the community.

LOCAL BUDGETING PROCESS

The local government budget process begins in May or June of the previous year. The budget projects are designed based on local public administration own budget projects and based on projects drafted by the institutions and locally subordinated public services. The main credit coordinators of local budgets implement budget financing through programmes elaborated by the institutions and public services of local interest.[6] The main credit coordinators submit the local budget project to the Directorate-General of Public Finance and Financial State Control up until 15 May, and they submit to the Ministry of Economy and Finance the local budgets at county level by 1 June. By 1 July the Ministry of Economy and Finance (MEF) transmits to the Directorate-General of Public Finance and Financial State Control the limits for funds divided from certain state budget revenues and for the earmarked transfers and also the distribution criteria on administrative-territorial entities. By 20 July, within these limits, the main credit coordinators elaborate the new proposals for the budget project and submit it to the Directorate-General of Public Finance and Financial State Control, which prepares the budget project and forwards it to the MEF by 1 August. Further, the MEF elaborates the project for the Budget Law and submits it to the Government by September. The Government prepares the Budget Law and submits it to Parliament by October. Parliament must then approve the Budget Law for the next year. If, at the beginning of the fiscal year, the Budget Law still has not been approved, the local governments receive authorisation from the Ministry of Public Finance to spend, each month, one-twelfth of their total actual expenditures from the prior year.[7]

Thirty days after the Budget Law is issued by Parliament, the Mayor lays down the project for the local budget and submits it for approval to the council. The budget project must be published in the local press and is accompanied by the Mayor's report and by the county council's report. According to the law, citizens can submit litigations against the local budget project. The county council then solves these litigations, and finally adopts the local budget project.[8]

The credit coordinators are responsible for framing their own budget, for following up the revenues collection and for organising and keeping up to date the accounting system (to submit the balance sheet and the budget execution account). Expenditures from budget credits approved in the budget can be made only with the approval of the credit coordinator and must be previously endorsed by the internal financial preventive control, which testifies the legality of the expenditures, that is the limits and the destination of the budget credits. The financing of expenditures from local budgets is made through credits opened by the credit coordinators within the limits of the budget credits approved by the local budget. Quarterly accounts are produced by the main credit coordinators that are sent to the MEF. This provides detailed information on expenditures incurred. It also contains some data on commitments and expenditures.

SUPERVISION AND CONTROL: THE STATE AUDIT

Two other systems of ex-post control of local government operations exist: internal audit carried out by every spending agency and co-ordinated by the Ministry of Economy and Finance, and external audit performed by the Court of Audit. Internal audit is not only concerned with financial control of budget execution and detection of fraud and misuse of funds, but also involves an assessment of the effectiveness and efficiency of a unit's operations. Internal auditors are considered 'consultants' to management. The Court of Audit is responsible for auditing on a broad basis, including the effectiveness and efficiency of the provision of public services.

Infringements of the law and punishment are mentioned in the Law on Local Public Finance. Infringements carry a prison sentence of from one to three months or a penalty of from RON 5,000 to RON 10,000 (about USD 2,000 and USD 4,000, respectively) for the following: (a) exceeding the maximum limits for the sums approved, in the expenditures part, by the budgets foreseen in the framework of which payments are engaged, authorised for release and effected; (b) exceeding the approved budgetary credits for the engagement of expenses; (c) using the funds coming from contracting local public debt for purposes other than those they were approved for, and (d) delivery of wrong data for substantiating the documentation presented in order to obtain the authorisation for contracting/guaranteeing external loans.

The list of contraventions and sanctions is much broader and refers to actions which do not comply with the provision of certain specific articles of the Law. Contraventions are sanctioned with penalties. The finding of contraventions and the application of penalties are carried out by the Court of Accounts, the Ministry of Economy and Finance and by other persons empowered in this sense, according to the law.

FURTHER DEVELOPMENTS: LOCAL GOVERNMENT AND FINANCIAL MARKETS

Local councils can contract domestic or external loans, either medium or long term, for public investments and for refinancing the local public debt. The local public debt resulting from borrowing must be reimbursed from the local financial resources, with the exception of earmarked transfers from the state budget. Local governments can use, as debt instruments, bonds and credits from commercial banks and other credit institutions. The local governments can issue bonds both directly and through specialised agencies or other institutions. External loans can be contracted only with the approval of a special commission composed of the representatives of the local public administration and Government.

The local public debt is not considered to be a Government liability and must be totally reimbursed from revenues used as collateral for the respective loans. Local authorities are not allowed legally to exceed the limit of 30 per cent of the total current revenues of the local budget when considering public debt. Before 2005, local authorities seemed to be reluctant to use financial markets, not only because of their lack of experience in this field or because they had limited assets that could be used as collateral, but mainly because of the general conditions on the financial markets. After 2005, once the liquidity of the financial markets increased, local authorities were more interested in accessing them. The financial market liquidity and increased competition have moved the supply of finance closer to the local authorities. The local authorities' development needs and their appetite for accessing financial markets explained the strong lobby made during 2005 to increase the ceiling for borrowings from 20 per cent to 30 per cent of their total current revenues. Most probably, in the coming years, the local government borrowings from the financial market will increase rapidly.

CONCLUSIONS

The decentralisation of the local government public finance followed the same pattern as the general process of reform adopted in Romania (stop-and-go). The local governments' financial independence from the central government increased slowly, but continuously. Although during the 1990s the local governments were strongly financially dependent on the central government, after 2003, but mainly starting from 2005, the local governments' financial independence became relevant. The structure of local government revenue sources reveals that the decentralisation in Romania's public finances increased very slowly in the first years of transition and accelerated when the macroeconomic stability was confirmed and the EU accession was almost achieved. On the one hand, the expenditure structure and evolution could be interpreted as revealing unstable functional responsibilities by the local government; on the other, this could be interpreted as a normal development in a transition period which is more or less a learning-by-doing process.

NOTES

1. Although the analyses cover the period 1990–2006 not all the data are presented in the tables which contain only data for 1995–2005. Because the Romanian authorities recently changed the budgetary classification, data for year 2006 are not yet available to be included in this study.
2. The Law No. 189/1998 establishes the basic legal frame for public local finances. This law has been amended several times by Government ordinances.
3. Media and reports drafted by civic and political organisations consider this kind of change as political blackmail.
4. A study realised by the Urban Institute (2001), points out that Government's attempt to impose a single formula for allocating the equalisation grants in 2000 did not work in the case of the four relevant counties included in that analysis. The World Bank (2002) also remarked that anecdotal evidence suggests that other county councils failed to follow the formula.
5. This expenditure category is often criticised by the local authorities, which affirm that certain Ministries want to recapture control over local spending decision. On the other hand, the Government considers that through these special earmarked expenditures they can be sure that funds are used for the purposes for which they are allocated.
6. The Presidents of county councils and the Mayors are the main credit coordinators. The heads of institutions or public services – legal persons – subordinated to local councils are secondary credit coordinators or tertiary credit coordinators.
7. In Romania the fiscal year starts on 1 January and ends on 31 December.
8. Although the citizens have access to the local budget project and can submit litigations, they don't use this right. In general, citizens have a passive role *vis-à-vis* the community problems and seem not to be aware of their potentially active role.

BIBLIOGRAPHY

Agentiile de Dezvoltare Economica a Judetelor, Arad, Caras-Severin, Hunedoara si Timis (1998), *Concept de Dezvoltare Regională* [The Concept of Regional Development], Timsoara: Editura Orizonturi Universitare.

Consiliul Judetean Timis (2000a), *Ghidul Consilierului Local* [Handbook for Local Counselor], Timisoara, Timisoara: Consiliul Judetean Timis.

Consiliul Judetean Timis (2000b), *Ghidul Primarului* [Handbook for Mayor], Timisoara: Consiliul Judetean Timis.

Department for International Development (DFID) (2003), *Support for the Commission for Poverty and Social Inclusion*, October, London: DFID.

Funk, B. and L. Pizzati (eds) (2003), *European Integration, Regional Policy, and Growth*, Washington, DC: The World Bank.

Law No. 189/1998 on Local Government Public Finance.

Law No. 215/2001 on Local Public Administration.

Law No. 69/1991 on Local Public Administration.

OUG [Government Emergency Ordinance] No. 219/24.11.2000 on Local Government Public Finance.

OUG [Government Emergency Ordinance] No. 45/5.07.2003 on Local Government Public Finance.

OUG [Government Emergency Ordinance] No. 61/28.12.1998 on Local Government Public Finance.

Regional Policy Unit (White Paper) (2002), *Office of the Deputy Prime Minister: Your Region, Your Choice: Revitalising the English Region*, May, London: Regional Policy Unit.

Urban Institute (2001), *Romania Local Public Expenditures Report*, July, Washington, DC: The Urban Institute.

World Bank (2002), *Romania Public Expenditures Review*, Washington, DC: The World Bank.

World Bank (2003), *Romania Poverty Assessment*, Washington, DC: The World Bank.

17. Local government finance in Serbia

Thomas Meekel

INTRODUCTION

Despite the Serbian long tradition of local self-government (*lokalne samouprava*) dating back to the time of the Ottoman Empire and the significant role played by local authorities and their leaders in the national liberation throughout the first half of the 19th century, the nascent Serbian central state continuously attempted to reduce this local political power. The willingness to build a modern central state, modelled by the elite after a strongly centralised state, combined with the autocratic or oligarchic rule of the Serbian princes and dynastic opponents (Obrenović and Karadjordjević) justified constant legal changes, aimed at limiting local self-government. 'In the struggle between local leaders (*knezovi*) and local military commanders on one hand, and central government and educated people (often living in the Diaspora), on the other, the local forces were defeated. New institutions, often copied from foreign models, were strictly centralised and served as the main source of power and livelihood for the elite' (Solić, 2002). The central State tended to reduce the number of elected tiers of local administration by transforming them into administrative districts; also by nominating the village leaders and by closely supervising their work and by controlling local decisions before their implementation, in other words to set up tutelage over local communities. Obviously, local authorities offered continuous resistance to these centralisation and modernisation trends. Given the development of a nationalist context, where three expansionist wars broke out (in 1885 against the Bulgarians, in the First Balkan War against Turkey in 1912, in the Second Balkan War against Bulgaria in 1913), the decentralisation of power to any other entity other than the central State could simply not be accepted and carried out, which does not mean that in practice municipalities could not experience, to a certain extent, freedom of self-government.

By the end of the First World War, in which Serbia lost more than 25 per cent of its male population, the newly created state, Kingdom of Serbs, Croats and

Slovenes, faced a serious challenge. The former Serbian state bureaucracy was overwhelmed by a population that had more than doubled and by a territory three times the size of Serbia. Thus, despite the 1921 Constitution, which centralised political authority and strengthened the power of the royal government in Belgrade, the six regions (*Oblast*) of this unitary country were considered as local self-governments and enjoyed as such a certain freedom, even though controlled by the *Okrugi* (state regional districts). For instance, they were granted the right to choose which law would regulate the local authorities located in their territory (municipalities – *Opštine* and cantons – *Srezovi*). However, this autonomy of local self-government was drastically limited as King Aleksandar I suspended the constitution, dissolved the *Skupština*, proclaimed a royal dictatorship and renamed his country the Kingdom of Yugoslavia in the year 1929. It was then reorganised in 1931 into regional divisions (*Banovinas*), which, as State local bodies, exerted a strict control over all local authorities. The head of the Ban appointed one-third of the municipal assembly members and could dismiss the mayor or any councillors of a municipality under his authority. Municipal finance was also under State control.

This lack of autonomy persisted until the 1950s, when the government of the newly established Federal People's Republic of Yugoslavia (FPRY) decided to eradicate the specific bureaucratic management linked to the immediate post-war reconstruction period and to decentralise powers to the local level. The municipalities regained their self-government functions, powers and authorities. Introduced in 1953, the concept of self-management was further developed in the 1963 and 1974 Constitution. This latter empowered the member republics with further capacities but, at the same time, protected municipalities from any republic or provincial move towards centralisation (Art. 248 of the 1974 Constitution[1]). Until the end of the Socialist Federal Republic of Yugoslavia in 1992, the municipality became the basic state organ and political unit of the country (not to mention a small State in itself, because it did play a legislative, executive and judicial role), obtained further financial autonomy and independence, and often controlled, via the public firms, the local economic activity. A complex election system of delegates to the Municipal Assembly was put in place and direct democracy tools were promoted (referendum) even at the community level (*mesne zajednice*). Nevertheless, this local self-government system was fairly constrained 'by the political supremacy of the Union of Communists, the only political party allowed, which was fully centralised up to the republican/provincial level' (Šević, 2001). The party selected any incumbent to an elected position beforehand; it also, in practice, controlled the main decisions taken by the municipality which in return encouraged a lack of local initiative.

During the 1990s and the secession of the constituent republics, all former Yugoslav local authorities experienced a high centralisation trend. In Serbia, following the 1990 Constitution, the central government has constantly limited the autonomy of self-local government through various restrictive laws that remain today globally unchanged. The central State closely managed municipal resources, nationalised all municipal properties in 1995 and reintroduced in 1992 the districts (*Okruzi*) as a State administrative body in order to control the municipalities politically. In the main municipalities, which were won by the political opposition in the 1997 local elections, continuous demonstrations were held against the Milošević regime. Grateful for their support, the first democratic government (2001–2004) engaged a decentralisation process[2] even though no global strategy was developed. One of the major achievements of this period is by far the Law on Local Self-Government (2002) which granted municipalities significant additional financial means.

Despite long-lasting difficulties in forming a stable government at the central level, this trend towards an improved fiscal decentralisation framework has been strengthened in the recent period (2005–2007) with the enactment of the Law on Financing Local Self-Government (July 2006) and culminated with the recent ratification of the European Charter on Local Self-Government in July 2007. Pursuing the reform of the municipal finance system, profoundly disturbed by the introduction of VAT in 2005, the Law on Financing Local Self-Government considerably improves the fiscal equalisation system by enhancing its predictability, transparency and equitability. The new Constitution of the Republic of Serbia (November 2006), by restating that there were only two Autonomous Provinces in Serbia (Kosovo and Vojvodina), did not resolve the politically sensitive question of the fate of the Autonomous Province of Kosovo, which is, since June 1999, managed by the United Nations Mission in Kosovo (UNMIK), but also confirmed the prevalence of the municipalities in the Serbian local government system in denying the generalisation of a regional or provincial level as was expected.

This very positive change must not hide from view that some key issues have not yet been tackled. Besides the lack of local government capacities, often linked to poor human resources management within Serbian local governments and the lasting political instability of many Municipal councils, the current lack of a structured territorial development policy remains problematic. Because Serbia is unlikely to be able to sustain an unbalanced regional development in the long term without internal clashes, namely between a thriving North, Vojvodina, and a sinking South Serbia, a global development plan could be developed and implemented for the country (Meekel, 2004).

BASIC LEGAL FRAMEWORK AND LOCAL GOVERNMENT FINANCE REGULATIONS

With the full independence of the Republic of Montenegro (June 2006) ended the State Union of Serbia and Montenegro (SCG), proclaimed in 2003 in replacement of the Federal Republic of Yugoslavia. Thus, the new Constitution of the Republic of Serbia (October 2006), the first since the break up of Yugoslavia, does not refer any more to the federal level. In 2005, Serbia without Kosovo accounted for a bit less than 7.5 million inhabitants (Kosovo is estimated around 2.5 million inhabitants) and 88,361 square kilometres.

The Republic of Serbia appears as a classical 'Napoleonic-style' unitary state, over-strengthened by a decade of high centralisation. Legislative authority is no longer shared with the provincial level as it was previously, under the 1974 Constitution; it remains exclusively the responsibility of the *Narodna skupština*, the national assembly. Sub-national governments do not exercise general regulatory power. The 1990 as well as 2006 Constitutions strictly list their competences and avoid any general competence or presumption of competence in favour of municipalities (see Milkov, 2000, for the 1990 Constitution). Serbian local governments cannot alone determine their fields of action. As a consequence, it is easier to contest the powers and responsibilities of the local authorities through a single law, which has been a common practice in Serbia during the 1990s. For instance, since the nationalisation of all municipal properties through the Law on Assets Owned by the Republic of Serbia (1995), local authorities do not have any property right which impedes their economic development and allows control from the central government. Moreover, the Central State allowed itself to dismiss a municipal assembly for dubious reasons (not to mention political reasons) without any judicial control (Art. 45 of the 1991 Law on Local Self-Government, Art. 213 of the 1999 Law on Local Self-Government).

Under the Milošević rule, more than 19 municipalities were concerned by this direct threat to local self-government. However, the new Law on Local Self-Government (2002) did not remove the ability of central government to dismiss a municipal assembly: during the 2001–03 period, the new government discharged 30 local authorities (mainly located in Southern Serbia considered as a fortress of the Milošević, Socialist Party). Furthermore, the 2006 Constitution in Article 192 confirms this right of dismissal. Legal protection of the sub-national government has been in practice but also weakened by the general inefficiency of the judiciary and review mechanisms. It remains extremely difficult for a municipality to appeal about a central governmental decision. Administrative departments in district courts (first instance level) and administrative departments of the Constitutional Court (second instance court) are entitled to these requests. The establishment of an Administrative Court, postponed since 2001 and expected by the end of 2008 or 2009, should limit the overload of the Supreme Court.

The Republic of Serbia is divided into 29 administrative circumscriptions (25 without Kosovo) called districts (*Okrugi*). These Districts were established by a Governmental decision in 1992 as local state bodies and not elected local authorities. Nevertheless, this should not be considered as a deconcentration[3] process since there was no real transfer of responsibility from central ministries to the districts. A district is a territorial unit where departmental bodies of certain ministries and agencies of the republic are brought together in a single administrative centre for that particular area. The district head has no hierarchical power over the local bodies of the central ministries he coordinates. Districts are mainly responsible for administrative control and some inspection duties, as delegated by a ministry on an ad hoc basis. Therefore, districts do not have similar duties and tasks and should not be considered as a prefect system. The City of Belgrade also has the functions of a district.

If we skip the Autonomous Province of Kosovo and Metojiha, under an international administration in accordance with United Nations Security Council resolution 1244, the Republic of Serbia has the following local authorities: the Autonomous Province of Vojvodina, 160 municipalities, three cities (Novi Sad – 250,000 inhabitants; Niš – 200,000, Kragujevac – 140,000), and the City of Belgrade (1.5 million inhabitants), which consist of 17 municipalities.

The Serbian local government system relies on a single tier of administration – the municipality. A municipality has, on average, approximately 35,000 inhabitants, which is one of the highest rates in Europe. In order to provide better information to citizens and allow them to discuss specific issues, a municipality may establish and organise communities (*mesne zajednice*) within its territory. The three cities have globally the same functions as the municipalities. Financing is the only difference between municipalities and cities, which are entitled, together with the City of Belgrade, to an additional percentage of the taxes shared by the Republic. According to the Constitution of the Republic of Serbia of 2006 and the Law on Local Self-Government of 2002, the main municipal functions are urban and town planning, housing, communal services such as water supply, sewage systems, refuse collection, local transport and roads, heating, kindergartens and preschools, local economic development as well as sport and cultural facilities. It must be stressed that these competences have remained stable as they are similar to the ones listed in the 1990 Constitution. Sub-national governments may also be entitled by law or regulation to perform a central government function as entrusted duties, such as maintaining civil records. In practice, the scope of duties delegated by the Republic is extremely narrow. Some duties are shared with the Republic. In primary and secondary schools teachers' wages are paid by the Republic, while school facilities' operating and investment costs are financed by the municipality. With regard to social care, social welfare centres are paid by municipalities, while staff and benefits are financed by the Republic.

The unique supra municipal local authority is the Autonomous Province of Vojvodina, which has no hierarchical power over the municipalities located in its territory. The Province is responsible for regulating various matters of provincial interests (such as 'agriculture, water economy, forestry, hunting, tourism, vaterins, spas...' according to the Art. 183 of the 2006 Constitution) but the majority of these fields see the Republic and municipalities directly involved (urban planning and development, education, social care, health, and so on). Within the context of high centralisation in Serbia, and despite its recognition in the Serbian Constitution, the real role of the Province has been strictly limited. The 2006 Constitution refused to generalise or to create a new regional sub-national government, disregarding the experience of other transition countries such as Poland, where such a regional level was created with the express aim of gathering and attracting European structural funds. However, with a view to avoid unfunded mandates, the new Constitution provides an innovative measure in Article 184 as it sets for the first time a fixed percentage (7 per cent) of the Republic budget to be channelled towards the Autonomous province of Vojvodina's budget.

DEMOCRATIC LEGITIMACY AND FINANCIAL REPORTING

Since the 2001 change of government, Serbian local Government has benefited from a significant rise in their revenues (from 4.3 per cent of the GDP in 2001 to 6.9 per cent in 2006) without an increase in their service responsibilities. However, the total share of public revenue (excluding public enterprises) dedicated to municipalities, has remained globally stable at about 14 per cent since 2002 (see Table 17.1). Furthermore, local revenues amount to at least 22 per cent of the republic budget revenues over the period.

These stable percentages show that there might have been a policy of the Republic government aimed at providing local authorities with a constant flow of revenues. Some authors raise strong doubt about such a policy: 'The most important decision – decision on the total amount of resources to be distributed to municipalities and towns – is not reached on the basis of objective criteria

Table 17.1 Local government revenues as a share of GDP and budget revenues and budget expenditures in current prices (million CSD)

	2001	2002	2003	2004	2005	2006	2007*
GDP	708,400	919,200	1,091,724	1,311,283	1,600,664	1,928,894	2,221,896
General Government Revenues	275,675	407,181	474,900	592,700	723,500	854,500	984,300
Republic Budget Expenditures	132,339	216,076	314,417	363,225	430,579	480,295	537,699
Republic Budget Revenues	121,703	177,326	271,046	350,113	443,384	522,730	602,134
Local Government Revenues	30,434	55,319	68,195	81,420	99,391	132,516	
General Gov Revenues as % of GDP	38.9	44.3	43.5	45.2	45.2	44.3	44.3
Republic Budget Expenditures as % of GDP	18.7	23.5	28.8	27.7	26.9	24.9	24.2
Republic Budget Revenues as % of GDP	17.2	19.3	26.3	26.7	27.7	27.1	27.1
Local Government Revenues as% of GDP	4.3	6.0	6.2	6.2	6.2	6.9	
Local Gov Rev as % of Gen Gov Rev	11.0	13.6	14.4	13.7	13.7	15.5	
Local Gov. Rev. as% of Budget Expenditures	23.0	25.6	21.7	22.4	23.1	27.6	
Local Gov. Rev. as% of Budget Revenues	25.0	31.2	25.2	23.3	22.4	25.4	

*Note:** 2007 is planned and not actual revenues.

Sources: IMF Country Report n°06/384, October 2006; Serbian MoF. Local Government Finance System and Fiscal Equalization in the Republic of Serbia.

of needs for financing of local communities, but is arbitrarily reached, during formulation of the General balance of public revenues and expenditures, and mostly based on transfer level of previous years and results of political negotiations' (Begović et al., 2003). Such a bargain has been occurring annually between the Ministry of Finance and the biggest municipalities, which are able to relay their specific requests and demands to the central government via the Standing Conference of Towns and Municipalities, a national association grouping all Serbian local authorities. Nonetheless, following the local finance reform initiated in 2001–02 and pursued in 2004, this last habit is especially targeted by the recent Law on Financing Local Self-Government (2006) which aims at a predictable, transparent and equitable fiscal decentralisation system in Serbia. Within this context, it is noticeable that the new Law enhances local government democratic legitimacy by prohibiting the practice of unfunded mandates in Article 3.

Enacted in April 2002, the Budget System Law (BSL) paved the way for greater accountability of local government to their citizens as it reinstates the budget as a fundamental process. The Law initiated clear procedures for budget preparation (especially by listing the key information to be presented in the budget and through a legal calendar stating deadlines by which the budget has to be presented to the municipal assembly) and budget execution for every public entity. Due to the lack of information and capacities, the Law has been implemented with difficulties, especially in smaller municipalities. Instead of the central government, some development agencies have provided financial management training to about half the Serbian local authorities and have engaged them in developing public access sessions on the municipal budget, even though the only publicity that requires the Law is the official publication of the budget in the Official Gazette of the Republic of Serbia. Results are mitigated with the more developed and politically stable municipalities being those able to build on the training received. However, it seems that informing citizens about the municipal budget is a growing concern for Serbian local authorities.

The Ministry of Finance did not seize the opportunity of the Law to issue a decree or sub-legal act proposing a unique budget model and/or a similar final statement for Serbian municipalities. As a matter of fact, this lack of a common budgetary framework limits comparative analysis and impedes the development of reliable basic information and data transfer to its citizens. There is also a lack of consolidated data, including all financial information about the City Hall and its public utility companies, as the law does not request any consolidation of the local budgets.

Moreover, financial reporting on local infrastructure investment projects is generally deficient or non-existent. Consequently, it is almost impossible for a citizen to learn about the final cost of a facility through the financial documents provided by the City. The main reason for this stems from the lack of a sound reporting mechanism between the municipality and its public utility companies (PUC), which usually implement such infrastructure. Despite the 2002 Chart of Accounts and the MoF 2004 recommendation that a delineation between operating or capital expenses should be made, the municipal assembly grants large subsidies to local public utility companies without detailed explanations as to their purpose (either to cover recurring expenses linked to the daily operations of the utility, to develop new investments, to finance maintenance of the utility infrastructure or for any other purpose). Once the subsidy has been delivered, it seems extremely difficult for the municipal assembly to track and therefore to control its use, even if there was any willingness to do so. Fierce negotiation between local parties occurred at every mandate to capture the presidency of the wealthiest utilities, the most resourceful usually being the city construction land utility (providing the rent of green and brown fields to firms). For significant investment projects partially financed by an international funding source (a development bank and/or donor) and implemented by local public utilities, accountability towards the lender is to some extent ensured, namely through the establishment of specific project implementation units positioned within the PUC.

INDEPENDENT LOCAL GOVERNMENT REVENUE SOURCES

Since the reforms in 1994, local government revenues in Serbia are structured in three basic groups:

1. ‘Original Revenues’ (*izvorni prihodi*) consists of a group of local fees, charges and taxes, which can be considered as own revenues of the municipality for the following reason. Local authorities have some say as to the rates of each of these revenues, except for the local administrative fees (which account for less than 1 per cent of total local government revenues during the period), which are set by the Republic. Because the most productive taxes go to the Republic, the own revenues of local government are insufficient to finance necessary expenses.
2. ‘Unlimited’ Shared Revenues (*ustupljeni prihodi van ogranicena*) consist of a variety of shared taxes (shared wage taxes which have replaced the shared sales taxes and shared property taxes) between the Republic and the local level. The Republic government in principle fully controls the rates

and basis of these shared taxes and collects them. Through these shared revenues, the Republic provides a sort of vertical balancing, enabling all municipalities to meet their basic needs. They are termed unlimited because only a percentage of the yield of these taxes given to local governments is fixed, as opposed to limited shared revenues, where the rates change annually and the global amount of shared revenues given is fixed and limited.

3. Transfers and grants from the State – formerly termed 'Limited' Shared Revenues (*ogranicena ustupljeni prihodi*), have been considerably reformed in 2004 and especially in 2006; with the new Law on Financing Local Self-Government designing an improved horizontal balancing mechanism, allowing less-developed municipalities with low fiscal capacities to achieve a minimum standard in public service.

The 2001 and 2002 intergovernmental finance reforms maintained this structure whilst significantly improving local government revenues, increasing them from 42 billion dinars in 2001 to 132 billion dinars in 2006 (an increase of 209 per cent – see Table 17.2). In addition to the clarification of the duties of municipalities, the main aim of the Law on Local Self-Government enacted in 2001 and 2002 was indeed to offer sufficient autonomy to local governments through adequate, ensured and permanent financial resources (Raičević and Stojanović, 2002): one-third of the 154 Articles of the 2002 Law regulate financial issues. Following the suppression of the payroll tax in 2004, and with the introduction of Value Added Tax (VAT) on 1 January 2005, the Serbian intergovernmental system needed a radical transformation, realised by the 2006 Law, effective in 2007. The Law increases the discretion of local governments towards their own revenues and sets a coherent grant transfers framework. Recent changes to each of the three local revenue groups (detailed in Appendix 17.1A: Local Governments Revenues 2000–06 in stable CSD) will be explained forthwith.

Defined in Article 6 of the Law on Financing Local Self-Government, own revenues accounted for more than 40 per cent of total local government revenues in the 2001–2003 period. This rather high percentage, when compared to regional standards, decreased in 2005 and 2006 to about 30 per cent due to the suppression of its major tax revenue, the payroll tax (effective on 1 July 2004) and its replacement by a financial transfer from the Republic government. However, from 2007 onwards, own revenues will drastically increase as the 2006 Law transferred the property tax to local governments that will be free to fix the rate (which represented 5 per cent of local government revenues in 2006). Moreover, the Law makes local governments responsible for the collection of all own revenues as of 1 January 2007 (Article 60) and therefore plans for State Tax Administration employees to be transferred to the respective local governments (Article 61). Even if such a move might have been motivated on the Republic side by the Tax Administration's willingness not to be further burdened by a time-consuming and inefficient task (given the cost of collection and the yield of revenues provided to the Republic), this situation opens stimulating developments for Serbian local governments over the medium term.

Table 17.2 Growth of local government revenues in stable 2006 CSD

	2001	2002	2003	2004	2005	2006
Local Gov. Rev.						
(Million CSD)	42,822	91,616	98,380	116,119	116,983	132,516
in USD (Million)	633	1,553	1,801	2,004	1,620	2,209
Average per Capita*	5,711	12,219	13,121	15,487	15,602	17,674
in USD	84	207	240	267	216	295
Growth over previous year	n/a	113.9%	7.4%	18.0%	0.7%	13.3%
Growth over 2001	n/a	113.9%	129.7%	171.2%	173.2%	209.5%

Note: * Population of Serbia without Kosovo (census 2002): 7,498,001.

Source: Serbian MoF (Local Government Revenues), National Bank of Serbia (Inflation and Exchange Rate).

Regulated by the Law on planning and construction (Art. 73–77), enacted in 2003, the two most significant own revenues are the fees for the development of construction land (11 per cent of total local revenue in 2006 – line 7) and for the use of construction land (5 per cent in 2006 – line 8). Prior to 2003, these fees were not considered public revenues and were not recorded as budget revenues of the municipality but as resources of the local public utility company dealing with this matter, the Directorate for the city construction land. This explains why the fee for the development of construction land, related to the provision and maintenance of public utilities for urban properties, almost tripled in 2003 but only in appearance: it was, for the first time, allocated to the municipal budget of thriving local authorities such as Belgrade. Once the rate is established by the municipal assembly, the fees are collected by the Directorate for the city construction land or a dedicated PUC in charge of billing and collection, such as Infostan in Belgrade.[4]

Besides these fees, only the income from the lease of property in the disposition of municipal governments[5] (line 10) and local communal fees (line 3 – it regroups 16 local communal fees as defined in Art. 83 of the Law on Financing Local Self-Government) provide important resources (respectively 5 per cent and 2 per cent of total local government revenues in 2006). Following the

2001–2003 reform, local governments have been given the right to specify these fees and set their rates. The municipal assembly defines the procedures for administering and collecting these fees, carried out in practice by the local public utility companies.

For information, the payroll tax (line 1 of Appendix 17.1A) was introduced in 2001 as a replacement to a variety of charges on businesses for their use of public space, roads and utilities. All local governments soon imposed the payrolls of companies operating within their jurisdictions at the maximum rate, 3.5 per cent. As a consequence, the payroll tax became a key resource of local government representing one-fifth of their total revenue in 2003. However, mainly because this tax burden put 'a further strain on wages and salaries, which increases the price of labour and encourages its transferral to the grey economy' (Begović et al., 2003, p. 32), the new government established in March 2004 swiftly subsumed it into an additional percentage of the wage tax[6] (Law on Repeal of the Law on the Payroll Tax). The willingness to show progress in the global reform of the Serbian fiscal system, and especially the aim of reducing taxes imposed on businesses, was preferred at that time to the stabilisation of local government own revenues.

Even though it is of small financial significance, voluntary contributions (line 11) or '*Samodoprinos*', that are redefined in Art. 20–31 of the Law on Financing Local Self-Government and which are a legacy from the former Yugoslavia, are notable for being widely used and, for some local authorities, crucial. Citizens agree collectively through referendum to create additional revenue for specific investments (for instance, electrification of the village, and so on). The revenue basis (which can be one of the existing tax bases or a contribution of any kind) and rates are defined by the municipal assembly. The Republic Tax Administration previously in charge of collection (Begović et al., 2003, p. 23) will hand it over to the local government.

Unlimited shared revenues have accounted for about 40 per cent of total local government revenues since 2002 and steadily increased since 2004 to amount to more than 50 per cent of local government revenues in 2005 and 2006, and will decrease due to the transfer of the property tax in 2007. The rates and bases of these shared taxes are controlled and collected by the Republic government. These revenues were divided into three groups: shared sales tax, shared property taxes and shared income taxes.

Until 2005, local authorities were granted a share of the sales tax levelled in their jurisdictions (line 24): 8 per cent for all municipalities, 10 per cent for the cities (Niš, Novi Sad and Kragujevac) and 15 per cent for Belgrade (as stated in former Art. 98, Law on Local Self-Government). If we take into consideration the additional percentage which local governments received as part of Serbia's equalisation system (lines 30 and 31), about 27 per cent of local governments revenues effectively stemmed from the sales tax. 'Shared sales taxes are extremely popular with local governments because not only their yields tend to increase automatically with economic growth, but unlike own revenues, local governments bear no political responsibility for determining their rates with their electorates. [As it is self-assessed by the tax payer], they are technically simple to administer' (Levitas, 2003, p. 23). However, sales tax has been replaced in January 2005 by VAT, which cannot be divested on a territorial basis. With a view to compensating local governments, the share of wage tax dedicated to the municipalities has increased from 25 per cent to 40 per cent in 2005 (line 25) and 50 per cent for cities. It must be stressed that since July 2004, in order to balance the end of payroll tax (line 1), 25 per cent of the wage tax had been dedicated to local government (line 29).

Regarding the shared property taxes (lines 15–18) only property transfer tax and property tax are significant (respectively 9 per cent and 5 per cent of total revenues in 2006). Administered and collected by the tax administration until 2007 and regulated by the Property Tax Law, both taxes rely on self-assessment. Thanks to the 2001–2002 reform, their yield has been fully transferred to local government. The fact that property transfer tax (levied at a rate of 5 per cent of the transaction price on the sale of real estate) constantly exceeds property tax (which is levied on a progressive tax rate – starting at 0.4 per cent of the market value of all properties up to 6 million dinars) is an anomaly. This can be explained by the relatively low rate of property tax in contrast to the excessive real estate sales tax rate, 'a low property tax base, estimated far below the market value, and relatively widespread evasion of the property tax'. (Begović et al., 2003, pp. 119–121) in comparison with a high level of tax collection for the property transfer tax (due to the fact that it must be paid to gain title of ownership). For both taxes, taxpayers see the benefit of understating the market values, as there is little systematic checking in the tax branch offices. The yield of these taxes might be improved with the collection being transferred to local governments.

Since 2002, local governments have also been entitled to the whole share of a number of income taxes (lines 19–22), whose returns are low and collection costs high (not to mention the horizontal inequity of such taxes). Given the end of the sales tax and the need to replace the significant role played by the shared sales tax in local government revenues (27 per cent of the total in 2004), the decision was taken to vest 40 per cent of the revenues generated from the wage tax to local governments in 2005. With 29 per cent of all local government revenues in 2006 (see line 26), shared wage tax is the main local government revenue.

Previously defined in Article 99 of the Law on Local Self-Government, limited shared revenues were considered as additional financial transfers from the State supposedly meant for the poorest local governments (a kind of horizontal balance mechanism). They have provided between 12 and 20 per cent of total local government revenues in the 2001–04 period and consisted of two main revenues: 5 per cent tax on wages for all local governments and on an additional percentage of sales tax, which has been replaced in 2005 by an additional tax on wages. This additional participation in sales tax was set down in an annual law, which also prescribed those revenues stemming from wage tax. The limited shared revenues were for its main part allocated according to a list of criteria (territory size, number of citizens, number of classes, number of elementary and secondary schools, number of children covered by child welfare and number of child welfare facilities, expenditure level in culture, and so on) but these were weighted differently by the MoF without any clear justification and transparent process.

However, a major shortcoming concerning limited shared revenues had been spotted by authors: they did not equalise wealth between municipalities. Conversely, the poorest local authorities gained, on average, 1,000 dinars per capita whilst the richer cities obtained twice as much per capita, because of their political capacity to bargain with the Ministry of Finance. As a result, the inequality in wealth between local authorities, that is to say, the horizontal imbalance of the intergovernmental financial system, remained startling. This irrelevant system was reformed in 2006 and a coherent equalisation system is being put in place, leading to a phased reduction of this vertical imbalance.

GRANT TRANSFERS

The new Law on Financing Local Self-Governments enacted in 2006 introduces two types of grant transfers, unconditional (such as a general revenue grant and equalisation grants – which are freely disposable) and conditional (municipalities can use it only for a specific purpose – a specific investment or a function to be implemented by the local authority) and indexes the total volume of unconditional grant at 1.7 per cent of the Gross Domestic Product (Article 37).

Four transfers are designed by the Law. (1) A general transfer aiming at providing local governments with both general revenue support is granted to all local governments on the basis of a clear and set formula in Article 42. Population and territory size account for 84 per cent of the weighting within the formula. (2) An equalisation transfer is planned for local governments whose average per capita shared taxes revenues are below 90 per cent of the municipal average (Article 38). Therefore, local governments with lower fiscal capacity will be proportionally compensated. It must be stressed that this mechanism safeguards any increase made in own revenues collection: the amount of equalisation transfer is not linked to the level of own revenues but to the effective yield of shared taxes. (3) A so-called compensation transfer is provided for local governments in order to compensate any losses due to changes in tax legislation (Article 39). Finally, (4) a transitional transfer (Article 40) is planned to smoothen the implementation of the equalization system until 2010. In practice, this transitional transfer will decrease the hardship of the reform on the cities and lengthen the transition period over three years.

In addition to 1.7 per cent of the GDP dedicated to these four unconditional grants, the Law offers the possibility to the Government to establish earmarked transfers. These transfers are determined by line ministries which submit their proposals to the Ministry of Finance. A Commission for intergovernmental finance, composed equally of members of the national association of local governments (Standing Conference of Towns and Municipalities) and Ministry of Finance representatives, will overview the new mechanism and ensure its 'fairness, efficiency and transparency' (Article 50) as well as predictability (Article 47).

This new grant transfer system is expected to improve the vertical imbalance among Serbian local governments. Simulations show that transfers to municipalities should globally increase by 27 per cent, while at the same time, cities will see their transfers reduced from 28.6 per cent (Stipanović, 2006).

LOCAL GOVERNMENT EXPENDITURES

No reliable data is available on local government expenditure since there is neither a systematic collection of budget and final statement documents (even though this is compulsory according to the Law – Art. 14 and Art. 63 of the Budget System Law – BSL) nor coherence control at a central level. Even though a new chart of accounts, to which all budgeting units must adhere, has recently been passed in 2002, there have been too few guidelines and training given to municipalities in order to ensure a similar practice of registering their expenditures. Enforcement also remains extremely weak with no methodical check of the budget documents that the Ministry of Finance may receive.[7] With regard to final statements, some municipalities send their formal documents to the State Treasury (which took over the former Public Payment Agency – PPA – *Uprava za javna plaćanja – UJP*), which focuses, for statistical purposes, on municipal assets (stock) and not on the results of the budget execution (flows). As a matter of fact and despite regular requests issued by the IMF, the Ministry of Finance is roughly assessing the volume of local government expenditures from the level of revenues given to the local authorities, assuming that the latter cannot incur arrears indefinitely (local authorities cannot spend in the long term more than they receive). Such a philosophy shows a lack of interest towards the nature of expenditure incurred and in a global sense for internal budget reporting and budget control over local authorities.

This specific attitude may be explained by assessing the role of the PPA with regard to budget execution and especially reporting to the MoF and local government executive. Attached to the Ministry of Finance, the PPA is an institution that was performing the same functions as the former *Zavod za obračun i plaćanja* (ZOP) (clearing house, tax collection and statistical data) but now only for the public sector. Because each public payment has to be processed through the PPA (local budget is executed through the PPA), the PPA may indeed track all expenditure realised by a municipality, together with the beneficiaries of the payment orders.[8] This creates the misleading impression that municipal budget execution is somehow under control and thereby setting up a proper treasury system. Maintaining a Treasury General Ledger within the organisation, as imposed by the BSL, is an additional and useless burden (not to mention that the introduction of such a system in each local government, as imposed by the BSL, when not misunderstood, encountered an insurmountable lack of capacities in smaller municipalities).

However, even though an exhaustive analysis on local governments' expenditures could not be conducted over the period, some observations can be made from the study of several local government budgets, especially on the importance of the off-budget funds and the capital investments planned in a Serbian municipality. It must be emphasised first that Serbian local authorities have a fair amount of autonomy in deciding, within the set budgetary limitations, on the priorities regarding the realisation of public expenditures. Local governments regained this expenditure authority with the 2001–2002 municipal finance reform laws. For instance, even for salary levels, local authorities can manage to pay their staff up to 20 per cent more than national standards' requirements.

The subsidies allowed to local public companies, seen in many of the local government budgets, are often considerable. For example in Novi Sad, the wealthiest city of Serbia in relative terms, two-thirds of the 2003 budget consists of subsidies to local PUCs, which have their own budgets. There is no consolidation of these off-budget entities, whose functions are primarily to implement all necessary investments and operate the utilities for the municipality. With a view to implementing the new Chart of Accounts, rather than developing a separation of capital and operating budgets, the MoF recently requested municipalities to divide their subsidies into current and capital sections. Reports show that a significant part of the subsidy is dedicated to capital investments. Nevertheless, the lack of clear delineation between capital and current expenditures does not allow for any further analysis. As a working example, many local water PUCs do not include maintenance costs in their current expenditure – they consider them to be a specific investment to be financed through municipal subsidies. As a matter of fact, it does not seem that any of these municipal subsidies are repaid or returned, whether there is a temporary interruption of the works or a surplus at the end of the venture, or due to the operating revenues generated by the new investment.

Established capital budgeting techniques are widely unused even though progress is noticeable in the cities and municipalities that obtained an international loan. Once an investment has been decided by a municipality (needless to say this is often done without any financial planning[9]), the PUC in charge simply requests annual municipal subsidies to cover the cost. If their financial requirements cannot be met, the local authority tends to lobby the central government for additional funding or occasionally for a sovereign guarantee. For this reason, in 2003, the MoF justified the inequality of the equalisation system (and the allocation of the limited shared revenues) by pointing out that Belgrade and the three cities required additional financial transfers in order to finance some capital investments. However, arbitrary decisions and non-transparent negotiations might be limited thanks to the 2006 Law.

Regarding surpluses and deficits in local budgets, the Budget System Law is rather imprecise. While proclaiming the balance principle for both Republic and local government budgets (Art. 5), the Law also allows both entities to 'determine the use of the budget surplus or [to arrange] for financing the deficit' (Art. 13a). However, contrary to the Republic, local governments cannot take out loans for financing a budget deficit (Art. 35, Public Debt Law) but may as the Republic temporarily suspend implementation of the budget (Art. 42). Even though a deficit occurs at the end of the year, which is more likely to happen given the insecure realisation of local government revenues (collected on a monthly basis, their planned amount may not be realised by the end of the year), the current legal framework does not explain how a local government can resolve its deficit or transfer it to the next year. The accumulation of arrears seems to be the only practical solution in place to avoid deficit. Given the cash basis of accounting, the volume of a potential recorded deficit might be limited. Expenses are indeed paid only when enough cash is available – and suppliers often demand to be paid before servicing the local authority. It must also be stressed that the Law does not differentiate the operating and capital part of local government budgets and therefore is not establishing any kind of 'golden rule' which would forbid a deficit in the current budget.

According to analysis by an international financial institution, conducted on Serbian local government cash deposits, based on data collected by the PPA, certain Serbian local governments are said to have massive surpluses of up to 20 per cent of their budget. Obviously, this might concern only the wealthiest cities (especially Belgrade and Novi Sad). However, these statements, based on the observation of repeated liquidity surpluses, should be viewed with extreme care, as a daily treasury position cannot in itself provide anything on the effectiveness of the budget situation. It should be pointed out that despite an attempt from the national Treasury to gain control over local cash deposits, local authorities maintained their capacity of placing their available deposits in commercial banks. Therefore, albeit the PPA processes transactions, cash management practices pertaining to Serbian local authorities should be considered as highly decentralised.

ACCOUNTING RULES, REGULATIONS AND LOCAL GOVERNMENT BUDGETING PROCESS

After setting up the budget classification system (Art. 11), the BSL in Article 61 proclaims the authority of the Ministry of Finance to establish budgetary accounting regulations pertaining to local governments. A Chart of Accounts following the Government Finance Statistics Manual has been issued in 2002 for all public entities. However, given the lack of information and training delivered, it is likely that implementation at the local government level is unsatisfactory. As for the establishment of treasuries, fixed by the BSL at the local level by end 2004, smaller municipalities have been hindered by their lack of capacity and expertise to implement such reforms.

The traditional line-item budgeting techniques are used quite exclusively in Serbia. The BSL requests a set of documents to be presented and adopted during the budget process (Art. 15) but none is related to any performance analysis of programmes and services. The budget focuses on the input size of the services and not on the outputs. Performance budgeting is still exceptional and too often used only because a donor-funded project requires it. For instance, German technical assistance in selected local water companies placed the emphasis on performance indicators such as supply and consumption of cubic metres of water for analysing the PUC budgets and municipal subsidies.

The accounting system is cash-based in Serbia, which means that transactions and other events are recognised only when cash is received or paid.

In addition to the mandatory cash-based accounting, accrual accounting has only partially been introduced in the BSL, mainly through commitment management (Art. 36). In practice, only certain direct budget beneficiaries at the central level (especially selected ministries) have begun entering into commitments for processing expenditures – in these cases, expenditures are recorded when a liability is incurred.

The BSL sets up a detailed timetable for the local budgeting period (Art. 14, Item 2). According to the law, the preparation process begins formally on 15 June, when the local finance directorate issues instructions for preparing the proposed budgets. The major shortcoming was that the local authority often did not know at this time the level of state financial transfers it could rely on. The local authority had to begin internal budget discussions on the expenditure side without a clear view of the revenue side. This situation favoured a budget preparation based on the previous year's expenditure level. It also explains the wide use of amendments modifying the budget during its execution. With the improved predictability of grant transfers due to the 2006 Law on Financing Local Self-Government, such a situation might over time become less common. The Law specifies deadlines for formal submission of the draft budget between the main stakeholders of the budget-making: financial department, budget beneficiaries, the executive local government body and the municipal assembly. On 20 December, the budget should be approved by the municipal assembly. Nonetheless, if the local government failed to enact the budget before the commencement of the fiscal year, the law allows for a three months' funding (Art. 28). This possibility has been largely used in 2004.The final statement has to be approved by the municipal assembly on 1 June and passed on to the Treasury on 15 June (Art. 64).

SUPERVISION AND CONTROL: THE STATE AUDIT

The BSL in Article 66a defines responsibilities for internal control and the scope of work for internal controllers. Local authorities are to form internal control for those transactions relating to budgetary receipts and outgoings, assets management and debt management of local governments and, if prescribed by the Ministry of Finance, to organise a separate service of internal controllers. Besides internal control systems, the Law compels municipalities to establish Local Inspection and Audit Services (Art. 68), which shall carry out various audit functions (compliance audit, assessment of internal control systems, control of compliance with law, performance audit, advice and support). Developing such internal audit functions at the local level is new, since partial internal audits were previously conducted at the central level by the ZOP. Given the scarce skilled human resources, it is questionable whether local governments, except the largest, can comply, even in the medium term, with these requirements.

In addition to this local internal auditor, responsibility for the audit function of municipalities can be found with the Ministry of Finance and to a lesser extent with external private companies. The Budgetary Inspection and Audit Department of the Ministry of Finance may carry out inspections and audits over local authorities and their public utility companies if 'the public funds comprise more than 50 per cent of their revenues' (Art. 67). It also has 'a quality assurance role over the work of the Local Inspection and Audit Services… to ensure that inspection and audit approaches are applied consistently on the territory of the Republic' (Art. 69). In the field, because of the understaffing of the Budgetary Inspection and Audit Department and its broad mandate, local governments and dependent PUCs do not face regular controls. Audits in Serbia are exclusively ex-post and seem to have been focused on compliance audits.

Despite the 2006 Constitution (Art. 96) commanding its establishment and the Law on the State Audit Institution adopted on 14 November 2005, which specifies that this institution is to be set up within six months of the publication of the Law, it must be stressed that there is not yet any specific State Audit Institution (SAI) in Serbia. Additionally and coherently, the BSL refers also implicitly to it in Art. 68 in requesting the internal audit service of the MoF to liaise with the 'External Audit Institution'. However, intensive discussions are ongoing to appoint the five members of the SAI and it is expected in the coming months. It is noticeable that given the lack of SAI, the Serbian Parliament selected in 2004 qualified auditors for conducting external audits of the annual final accounts of the Republic budget, which was effectively done through tender.

FURTHER DEVELOPMENTS: LOCAL GOVERNMENT AND FINANCIAL MARKETS

The current legal framework for local public borrowing regulated by Articles 33–38 of the Public Debt Law enables local authorities to borrow in domestic and foreign currency, provided that the annual amount of debt service (capital repayment and interests) does not exceed 15 per cent of the previous year's recurring revenue and that the outstanding debt does not exceed 50 per cent of the previous year's recurring revenue (Art. 36). The Minister of Finance has a veto on any new debt contracted but only if exercised within 15 days.

Municipalities are not allowed to issue guarantees, which is quite irrelevant given the fact that local authorities heavily subsidise their local public utility companies, a move considered as a kind of implicit guarantee. Management boards of local public utilities may take the decision to borrow without any municipal guarantee.

Under the present financing system, a few municipalities with stronger economic bases constitute the foundations of an initially small municipal credit market. The borrowing capacity of the vast majority of Serbian local governments is, however, increasing slightly. According to the recently established Municipal Infrastructure Agency (MIA), a Serbian state agency currently ranking the creditworthiness of Serbian municipalities, a mere dozen municipalities out of the total 180 are able to borrow.

In recent years, five local authorities (Belgrade, Niš, Novi Sad, Kragujevac, Subotica) have signed foreign currency loans for a global amount of 227 million €. At this point in time, the two main lenders are the European Bank for Reconstruction and Development (EBRD) and the European Investment Bank (EIB). Belgrade City Hall has signed two loan agreements with the EBRD for a total of 110 million € without any sovereign guarantee and also a 90 million € loan with the EIB (with a sovereign guarantee) in order to repair and develop its infrastructure. Focusing on renovating their water systems, the Cities of Niš (6 million €), Novi Sad (5 million €), and Kragujevac (5 million €) asked for and obtained a guarantee from the State (Official Gazette of the Republic of Serbia), a rather long process where the Republican Parliament has to approve the loan. Subotica obtained 9 million € from the EBRD without any sovereign guarantee.

Concerning bank loans in domestic currency, a steady increase is reported even though the contracts are not systematically recorded at the central level. These domestic loans are frequently limited with a very short maturity. It seems that these loans are often short-term facilities offered repeatedly to cities by the banks that hold their deposits. Foreign private banks that settled in Serbia are now prospecting the market of local public borrowing. Recent changes in Serbian local finance that contributed to the rise of local government revenues should have a positive impact on the development of local public borrowing.

Further reform is also required regarding the insufficient forms of debt security provided to any lender. This is the reason why foreign development banks usually demand a sovereign guarantee. Pledging of physical assets is prohibited by the Law on Assets of 1995, which nationalised municipal property. However, even if such collateral were available, it is not certain whether this would be the most effective solution. Experience in many countries suggests that in practice, it is difficult for private creditors to foreclose on pledges of sub-national government real or immovable property in the event of defaults. Most developing and transition countries tend to rely heavily on general obligation financing – that is, debt secured by a pledge of local governments' budget resources. In order to promote such collateral within the Serbian legal framework, further steps will be required. Amongst these, designing the municipal budget model with a clear delineation between the current and the capital budget is of key importance. It would then enable easier assessment of the capacity for a Serbian municipality to generate a net operating surplus[10] and therefore be able to take and repay a loan.

CONCLUSION

Following the 2001 and 2002, 2004 and 2006 reforms, the Serbian local governments saw their revenues more than tripling in real terms while their assignment of public service responsibilities remained globally limited to traditional 'communal services' and some items of personal social services. Over this period, the financial autonomy or degree of discretion conferred on Serbian local governments has been significantly improved. Regarding expenditures, there are few restrictions on current spending (as well as a lack of transparency regarding capital expenditure, due to the insufficiently reported financial relationship between municipalities and local public utilities). On the revenue side, the recent 2006 Law on Financing Local Self-Government can be considered as decisive, even though its first results will be evaluated only in the coming years. Showing a clear commitment to stop past practices and methods, the new legal framework attempts to tackle for the first time the structural horizontal unbalance between the few wealthy cities and the majority of municipalities, through the establishment of a fair, predictable and transparent transfer system. Moreover, in giving them full responsibility over the property tax and collection duties for all own source revenues, local governments will increase the already considerable ratio of own revenues over total revenues (accounting for about one third). The Law opens new opportunities for local governments. In order to optimise their own source revenues and financing capacities, Serbian local governments now face the challenge to build and implement fiscal policies while integrating in the same time a significant number of former tax administration employees.

Given this legal breakthrough in the Serbian fiscal decentralisation framework, local governments might look at enhancing coordination and the cooperation mechanism to share amongst them good practices and lessons learnt. The fact that the Serbian national local government association, the Standing Conference of Towns and Municipalities, is expressly positioned as a natural counterpart of the Ministry of Finance regarding all matters pertaining to local finance, is instructive about the progress achieved and the dialogue that seems to have been established and developed between local governments and the Republic level, at least in the field of local finance.

Surely, many important issues remain pending, such as the municipal ownership of local assets or the lack of clarity between local governments and local public utilities, which strongly impedes local public infrastructure financing. However, it must be stressed that the financial situation and perspectives for Serbian local governments have never looked so positive in a long time.

NOTES

1. Within the Third part of the 1974 Constitution, which deals with the 'relations in the Federation and the Rights and Duties of the Federation', article 248 states: 'In addition to the constitutional rights which they enjoy in other social-political communities, the nationalities shall also realize their sovereign rights in the Communes as the basic self-managing and socio-political communities'.
2. Decentralisation: the transfer of responsibility to democratically independent lower levels of government, thereby giving them more managerial discretion, but not necessarily more financial independence.
3. Deconcentration means the transfer of responsibility from central ministries to field offices or more autonomous agencies, thereby becoming closer to citizens while remaining part of central government.
4. When such a PUC exists. In small municipalities, the Department in charge of urbanism of the municipal administration deals directly with it.
5. Regulated in the Law on Planning and Construction
6. The wage tax is payable by individuals on income earned from wages and salaries generated throughout the calendar year. The applicable rate is 14 per cent for salaries.
7. With reference to this anecdote, there is only one civil servant dedicated to municipal finance in the MoF, dealing mainly with financial transfers to municipalities.
8. Before processing the payment order, the system checks for sufficiency of funds in the originator's account. After the close of the business day, the PPA sums the total values of the payment orders received in each account.
9. For instance, in 11 municipalities within South Serbia, municipal investments plans should be considered as a 'wish list' and not an effective plan forecasting budget resources for its implementation.
10. Defined as current revenues minus operating expenditures minus debt repayments.

BIBLIOGRAPHY

Begović, B., G. Ilić-Popov, B Mijatović and D Popović (2003), *Reform of Taxation System*, Belgrade: Center for Liberal-Democratic Studies.

Budget System Law, Official Gazette of the Republic of Serbia, Nos 9/2002 and 87/2002.

Chart of the Accounts, Official Gazette of the Republic of Serbia, Nos 92/02, 64/03, 125/03, 58/04, 63/04, 85/04 and 99/04.

Constitution of the Republic of Serbia, Official Gazette of the Republic of Serbia, No. 1/90.

Čubrilović, V. and V. Ćorović (1938), *Srbija od 1858 do 1903* [Serbia from 1858 to 1903], Belgrade: Geca Kon.

Čubrilović, V. (1982 [1958]), *Istorija političke misli u Srbiji 19 veka* [19th Century History of Political Thought in Serbia], reprint Belgrade: Narodna knjiga.

Dexia (2002), *Local Finance in the fifteen countries of the European Union*, Second Edition, Paris: Dexia Editions.

Đorđević, S. (2002), Sistem lokalne samouprave u Srbiji i Jugoslaviji, 1804-2000 [System of Local Self-Government in Serbia and Yugoslavia (1804–2000)], in: M. Damjanović (ed.), *Uporedna iskusta lokalnih samouprava* [Comparative Experiences of Local Self-governments], Belgrade: Magna agenda, 241–78.

Hőgye, M. and C. McFerren, (2002), Local Government Budgeting: The CEE Experience, in M. Hőgye (ed.), *Local Government Budgeting*, Budapest: Open Society Institute – Local Government and Public Service Reform Initiative, 43-74.

IMF (2006), IMF Country Report no. 06/384, Washington, D.C.: International Monetary Fund.

Law on the Amount of Resources and Share of Municipalities and Cities in the Wage Tax and Sales Tax, Official Gazette of the Republic of Serbia, Nos. 15/02 and 87/02.

Law on Financing Local Self-Government, Official Gazette of the Republic of Serbia, Nos 62/06.

Law on Guarantee Fund, Official Gazette of the Republic of Serbia, Nos 65/05.

Law on Local Self-Government, Official Gazette of the Republic of Serbia, Nos 47/91, 49/99, 27/01 and 9/02.

Law on Planning and Construction, Official Gazette of the Republic of Serbia, Nos 47/03.

Law on Public Debt, Official Gazette of the Republic of Serbia, No. 65/05.

Law on the State Audit Institution, Official Gazette of the Republic of Serbia, No. 101/05.

Law on Ratification of the European Charter on Local Self-Government, Official Gazette of the Republic of Serbia, No. 70/07.

Law on Providing Contra-guarantees of the Republic of Serbia and Montenegro as a Guarantee for EBRD upon the Loan for City of Kragujevac, City of Niš, and City of Novi Sad, Official Gazette of the Republic of Serbia, No. 18/03.

Law on Repeal of the Law on the Payroll Tax, Official Gazette of the Republic of Serbia, No. 33/04.

Levitas, T. (2003), *Reforming Serbia's Local Government Finance System*, Paper presented to the Conference on Reforming Local Government Finance System, Belgrade, June 2003

Meekel, T. (2004), Serbie: Comment rebâtir la relation entre l'État et les collectivités locales? [Serbia: How to rebuild relations between the central state and local authorities?], Paris, *Revue d'Etudes Comparatives Est-Ouest*, **35**(1–2), 297–329.

Milkov, D. (2000), *The Structure of Public Administration in Yugoslavia*, Paper presented in the United Nations Public Administration Network, website: http://www.unpan.org/.

OECD (1997), *Managing across Levels of Government*, Paper presented to the Public Management Committee, Paris: OECD.

Petersen, J. and J. Crihfield (1998), *Linkages between Local Governments and Financial Markets: A Toolkit to Developing Sub-sovereign Credit Markets in*

Emerging Economies. Prepared for The World Bank by Government Finance Group, Arlington, Virginia: mimeo.

Property Tax Law, Official Gazette of the Republic of Serbia, No. 26/00.

Raičević, B. and S. Stojanović (2002), Lokalne finansije – iskustva i mogućnosti Srbije [Local Finance – Experience and Opportunities of Serbia], *Ekonomika preduzeća*, **50**(1–2), 55–63.

Šević, Ž. (2001), Local Government in Yugoslavia, in E. Kandeva (ed.), *Stabilization of Local Governments*, Budapest: Open Society Institute Local Government and Public Service Reform Initiative, 421-69.

Solić, A. (2002), *Elites and the Court in Belgrade in the 19th Century*, Bonn: Michael-Zikic-Stiftung.

Sowards, S. (1997), The Serbian Revolution and the Serbian State, Lecture number 5, *Twenty-Five Lectures on Modern Balkan History*, East Lansing, MI: Michigan State University Libraries [http://www.lib.msu.edu/sowards/balkan/].

Stipanović, B. (2006), *Local Government Finance System and Fiscal Equalization in the Republic of Serbia*, Belgrade: The Fiscal Decentralization Initiative for Central and Eastern Europe.

APPENDIX

Table 17.1A Local Governments revenues 2000–06 (in 2006 CSD/1000 and USD/1000)

		2000		2001		2002		2003		2004		2005		2006	
		actual	USD	actual	USD	actual	USD	actual	USD	actual	USD	actual	USD	actual	USD
	ORIGINAL REVENUES														
1	Tax on Salary Fund (3.5%)			7,205,490	107,797	13,936,957	217,116	14,604,193	254,259	10,112,555	174,549	535,381	7,413	325,909	5,434
2	Local Administrative Fees	46,659	2,740	138,935	2,079	299,350	4,663	478,140	8,324	568,047	9,805	563,987	7,809	377,713	6,298
3	Local Communal Fees	1,164,422	68,391	1,169,629	17,498	1,661,399	25,882	1,562,084	27,196	2,375,690	41,006	2,548,579	35,290	2,635,931	43,950
4	Tourist Fee	88,148	5,177	97,965	1,466	155,080	2,416	168,092	2,926	215,815	3,725	240,563	3,331	278,524	4,644
5	Company Tax	1,183,125	69,489	1,293,833	19,356	1,647,800	25,670	1,336,401	23,267	2,061,131	35,576	2,100,693	29,088	2,359,975	39,349
6	Belgrade Tax	6,116,656	359,254												
7	Communal Charges	7,821,078	459,361	3,547,022	53,065	129,237	2,013								
8	Ecological Charges	52,354	3,075	246,219	3,684	380,039	5,920	429,850	7,484	719,497	12,419	841,226	11,648	931,275	15,528
9	Construction Land	541,376	31,797	1,382,587	20,684	2,313,937	36,047	7,930,814	138,075	13,105,389	226,207	12,359,994	171,146	14,437,504	240,723
10	Construction Land Use	2,994,240	175,863	3,515,346	52,591	4,572,612	71,234	4,247,367	73,947	6,051,274	104,448	6,519,523	90,274	7,087,866	118,179
11	Other Charges	763	45	90,026	1,347	137,314	2,139	277,614	4,833	582,329	10,051	861,590	11,930	671,012	11,188
12	Lease	488,180	28,673	1,221,292	18,271	1,818,010	28,322	2,341,329	40,763	3,740,818	64,569	4,864,554	67,358	6,676,067	111,313
13	Self Contribution Fee	769,063	45,170	649,964	9,724	714,443	11,130	724,451	12,613	892,224	15,400	703,506	9,741	509,799	8,500
14	Other Fees	3,506,416	205,945	1,714,911	25,656	785,293	12,234	1,070,203	18,632	1,900,882	32,810	2,623,589	36,328	3,279,134	54,674
	Sub total	**24,772,479**	**1,454,979**	**22,273,218**	**333,217**	**28,551,470**	**444,787**	**35,170,540**	**612,319**	**42,325,651**	**730,565**	34,763,185	481,359	39,570,710	659,779
	Unlimited Shared Taxes														
15	Agricultural Land Tax	64,388	3,782	74,378	1,113	89,455	1,394	77,789	1,354	206,504	3,564	86,206	1,194	32,472	541
16	Property Tax	828,111	48,638	3,935,739	58,880	4,626,587	72,075	4,230,580	73,654	6,532,644	112,757	6,368,211	88,179	6,302,808	105,089
17	Inheritance and Gift Tax	191,767	11,263	235,550	3,524	270,163	4,209	217,581	3,788	357,044	6,163	500,448	6,930	538,983	8,987
18	Transfer Tax on Property	3,006,954	176,610	5,082,444	76,036	6,141,839	95,680	5,692,324	99,103	9,493,773	163,868	10,532,462	145,841	11,749,323	195,901
19	Private Business Tax					2,377,200	37,033	1,971,854	34,330	2,408,237	41,568	2,670,736	36,981	3,238,212	53,992
20	Revene from Immovables					276,910	4,314	463,112	8,063	994,864	17,172	1,539,966	21,324	1,916,952	31,962

Table 17.1A (continued)

	2000		2001		2002		2003		2004		2005		2006	
	actual	USD	actual	USD	actual	USD	actual	USD	actual	USD	actual	USD	actual	USD
21 Leasing on Property Tax					23,567	367	24,779	431	32,526	561	82,016	1,136	115,472	1,925
22 Tax on Gaming Income					37,150	579	44,749	779	54,784	946	0	0	126	2
Revenue from insurance persons									1,206	21	-175	-2	10	0
23 Other Taxes					2,993,202	46,629	3,253,400	56,642	4,866,605	84,000	4,655,476	64,463	5,759,183	96,025
24 Sales Tax	3,076,865	180,716	6,102,524	91,296	10,360,881	161,406	12,268,754	213,599	23,038,132	397,651	0	0	0	0
40% Share of Wage Tax											36,734,420	508,654	38,261,186	637,945
25 Local Road Tax	987,000	57,970	539,131	8,066	1,009,208	15,722	939,365	16,354	1,320,617	22,795	1,194,042	16,534	1,069,837	17,838
Other charges									0	0	385	5	1,279,668	21,336
SubTotal	**8,155,086**	**478,978**	**15,969,768**	**238,915**	**28,206,162**	**439,407**	**29,184,288**	**508,098**	**49,306,937**	**851,066**	**64,364,193**	**891,238**	**70,264,232**	**1,171,545**
Limited Shared Taxes														
26 5% Share of Wage Tax	1,663,345	97,694	2,193,479	32,815	2,828,872	44,069	2,954,002	51,429	4,286,022	73,979				
27 25% Share of Wage Tax									11,691,556	201,803				
28 Individualized Shared Sales Tax	2,770,440	162,718	5,170,994	77,360	7,431,083	115,764	7,468,045	130,019	6,861,293	118,430				
29 Shared Surplus-Sales Tax (50%)					1,782,440	27,768	41,665	725	870,669	15,028				
Annually fixed by Law											16,242,660	224,909	15,400,000	256,771
Other transfers											1,471,121	20,370	7,028,860	117,195
Sub-total	**4,433,785**	**260,413**	**7,364,473**	**110,176**	**12,042,394**	**187,601**	**10,463,712**	**182,173**	**23,709,539**	**409,240**	**17,713,780**	**245,279**	**22,428,860**	**373,966**
Donations									776,534		143,100	1,981	252,356	4,208
TOTAL	**37,361,350**	**2,194,370**	**45,607,458**	**682,307**	**68,800,026**	**1,071,795**	**74,818,540**	**1,302,590**	**116,118,661**	**2,004,275**	**116,984,258**	**1,619,857**	**132,516,158**	**2,209,497**

Sources: Serbian Ministry of Finance; Exchange rate and inflation information: National Bank of Serbia.

18. Local government finance in Slovakia

Juraj Nemec

INTRODUCTION

The history of Slovakia, as an independent country and of its public administration, is relatively short. The Slovak Republic was established only on 1 January 1993, as the result of the friendly breaking up of the former Czechoslovakia, following major changes after the 'Velvet Revolution' in 1989. The first important steps of public administration reform, to replace the old 'socialist' system, were undertaken in the early stage of the transition period in the common state.

The first democratic elections were held in June 1990 and became the basis for most of the changes in the public administration system in Czechoslovakia. By virtue of the National Council Act 369/1990, the system of local administration authorities was replaced by a system of local state administration (38 district local general state administration offices and 121 sub-district local general state administration offices) and local authorities. Local self-government was created by this act, with the main characteristics being similar to these in developed countries. From 1996 onwards, Slovakia implemented a second wave of public administration reform, characterised by the parallel themes of a radical change of the territorial and administrative structure of the state, and the establishment of a uniform two-tier system of offices of general state administration, with a broad range of tasks and responsibilities.

These important changes were reflected in two important laws, Law No. 221/1996 on the territorial and administrative sub-division of the Slovak Republic and Law No. 222/1996 on the organisation of the local state administration. The first of these had two parts. First, it addressed the issue of territorial sub-division, creating the legal framework for the establishment for the spatial execution of self-government functions. Municipalities were defined as the highest level in the hierarchy of territorial units, logically linked to their administration on self-government principles.

Second, it defined the administrative sub-division of Slovakia into 8 regions and 79 districts, at the same time limiting the authority of state bodies in local areas, unless these were given special powers by other laws. Regional and district offices of state administration were given a broad range of tasks in this structure. Other administration units included municipalities (and military counties, if they perform state administration responsibilities under special laws).

This '1996 reform' in Slovakia was aimed at increasing the effectiveness and quality of public administration and creating a customer-friendly and responsive system serving its citizens. The costs of reform were much higher than planned, but its results were very limited (Audit ustrednej statnej spravy, 2000).

After the general elections in 1998, the new Slovak government came back to the issue of public administration reform as a key goal. Because of the requirements of the EU accession processes, the main starting reform goals were the creation and operationalisation of regional self-government authorities. The later phases of this reform wave (after 2002 elections) focused on a massive transfer of competencies from the state to local and regional self-government and a radical change of the local state administration system (back to the specialised system and abolishing the district offices of general state administration). The realisation of the 2000–2004 reform measures created the current public administration system in Slovakia, where local and regional self-government deliver most of the public services, and a new system of fiscal decentralisation, in force from 2005, has significantly increased their own incomes.

BASIC LEGAL FRAMEWORK AND LOCAL GOVERNMENT FINANCE REGULATIONS

In this section we focus on the public administration structure and organisation in Slovakia, as the framework for local public finance. Because of massive changes resulting from the 2000–2004 reform waves, we need to distinguish the situation before 2002 and after.

Public Administration System in Slovakia 1990–2002

As already indicated, the basic public administration structures in Slovakia were created soon after 1989, and their main characteristics were similar till the end of the 20th century. This period is characterised by two, to some extent contradictory, features:

(a) a very high level of independence of local (municipal) self-government as the only self-government level in the country,
(b) a massive 'state' responsible for many public services that are normally delivered by self-government (such as primary and secondary education, local health care, and so on).

'The state'

All arrangements after 1989 followed the three-tier hierarchical structure of state administration. The first level was the national government as a supreme body of the executive power in the state. The lower levels were the district and sub-district levels (until 1996) and regional and district levels (after) of state administration controlled from the central level, and responsible for a large scale of state responsibilities. The scope of authorities of regional and district offices was really large. At the end of 1998 they carried out state administration in 32 sections of activities.

The system of relationships between central and local state administrations in Slovakia represented a very specific solution, and was based on the principle of sectored responsibility for the performance of state administration. In spite of the fact that regional and district offices were expected to be, in principle, responsible for territorial development within their jurisdiction, they represented more a complex of individual branch divisions of state administration 'under one roof', than a homogeneous organ of general state administration of the territory.

Local self-government in Slovakia

As indicated, by virtue of the National Council Act 369/1990, the system of local government is constituted in municipalities which are territorial and legal entities. Within limits set by the law, local governments have their own budgets and assets. Local governments may issue ordinances which are binding on all individual or corporate bodies within their jurisdiction. These ordinances may be superseded or invalidated only by parliamentary acts. In some cases, local governments may be delegated additional powers at discretion of the State, that is the central government, and have their execution financed by state funds. Interfering with the powers of local authorities is possible only by legislation passed by Parliament. With some statutory exceptions, local authorities are independent of state supervision. All valid decisions of municipalities and state authorities are reviewable by the Court on the basis of applying the 'cassation' principle, if the two instances of the decision-making process took part. A person who did not ask for a solution in the appeals procedure, does not have the right to sue.

Local government authorities are elected directly by the local population. Elected mayors head municipal offices. As the highest executive officer, the mayor summons and conducts the sessions of local representative bodies, represents the office and the municipality and decides in all matters of local administration, except those which, according to the law, are decided by the municipal assembly. Municipal offices consist of local administrative officials responsible for administrative and organisational matters in the work of the mayor and other activities of municipal bodies. In larger municipalities, the municipal office may be run by a principal appointed by the municipal assembly on the advice of the mayor. He is responsible to the mayor.

Each municipality has a chief auditor who is responsible to the municipal assembly and is elected by the municipal assembly on the recommendation of the mayor. He inspects local finances, accounts, management of local property and assets, and reports on the budget and final accounts. Local self-government authorities may freely associate with other local self-government authorities and thus may form regional or other interest organisations. Such associations, however, may decide and organise only those matters specifically referred to them by the local self-government.

The powers of municipalities exercising their self-government functions included, prior to the 2000 decentralisation, the following main responsibilities: management of movable property and realty; administration of local taxes and fees; guidance of economic activities in the municipality; creating and protecting healthy conditions and a healthy way of life and work for the municipality's population; protecting the environment; territorial planning; management of own budgetary organisations and subsidies; providing for public order in the municipality; local public transport in big cities; construction, maintenance and management of local roads and parking places; public space; public greens, public lights, market places, cemeteries; local water resources and wells, water supply networks, sewerage and water cleaning establishments in small municipalities; construction, maintenance and management of local cultural establishments, part of the sport, leisure and tourist establishments; infant homes, part of the ambulatory health services establishments, establishments of the basic social services (daily care); support of following activities – education, nature and heritage protection, culture and artistic hobbies, physical culture and sport, humanitarian activities; and the administration of the municipality including municipal police forces and the fire service.

Cities are municipalities that are declared as cities by the National Council of the Slovak Republic. At present, there are 138 cities in Slovakia. The legal status of the city of Kosice and of the capital, Bratislava, is regulated by special laws. The city parts of these cities have their self-government bodies and manage their own budgets.

Current Situation (2006)

The 'post 2000' reform changed the structure of the public administration system in Slovakia on a massive scale. In its first phase in a very (too) short time, all the necessary basic legislation was approved by Parliament (such as the Civil Service Code, the Public Service Code, the law to create territorial authorities, the law on elections to territorial authorities, the law on the transfer of competencies of the state to the regional and local self-administration, amendment of the law on municipalities, amendment of the law on municipal property, the law on the property of territorial authorities, amendment of the law on budgetary rules, and the law on financial controls and audit).

According to this legislation a large number of competencies were transferred in 2001–02. Municipalities received new responsibilities in the areas of road, communications, water management, social care, environmental protection, education (elementary schools and similar establishments), physical culture, theatres, health care (primary and specialised ambulatory care), regional development and tourism. Regional self-government became responsible for competencies in the areas of road, communications, railways, road transportation, civil protection, social care, territorial planning, education (secondary education), physical culture, theatres, museums, galleries, local culture, libraries, health care (polyclinics and local and regional hospitals), pharmacies, regional development, and tourism. A large portion of these competencies was re-allocated from direct ministerial responsibility (hospitals, education, and so on). The reform continued after the success of the Dzurinda coalition in the 2002 elections with its second phase in 2003 and 2004. The transfer of responsibilities was completed during this period, but real fiscal decentralisation began to function only in 2005, when the new system of financial allocations for municipalities and self-governing regions was adopted.

Problems pertaining

Reforms significantly increased the rights and responsibilities of self-governments; however certain aspects still need to be 'worked out'. We mention some of these in this chapter.

The new territorial regional structure of Slovakia does not fully reflect 'European requirements'. The newly established regions are too small to be accepted as NUTSII level regions and fragmentation is a problem at the local level. The number of municipalities is extremely high – 2,883 (and continuously increasing since 1989), and municipalities are too small – 68 per cent of municipalities in Slovakia are below 1,000 inhabitants.

Decentralisation and the principle of *subsidiarity* are very much based on the assumption that they will further revive local democracy and stimulate higher levels of citizen participation in local issues. According to many data, this assumption is not only unfulfilled in the conditions of Slovakia, but also in other CEE countries. Participation is limited in relation to the central level (Slovakia reached a record low level of participation in the 2004 EU Parliament elections – only 17 per cent), nor is it much better at the local level. It is obvious that citizens in transition countries are still not well prepared to exercise effective control over politicians and bureaucrats (Nemec et al., 2004). Swianiewicz et al. (2001) provide many interesting data concerning local democracy and participation by citizens at the local level in selected accession countries, including Slovakia. For example the most important issue for mayors from Slovakia was 'to make independent decisions'. The trust of citizens in local governments is still limited, but much higher that in national structures.

Local authorities still, in many cases, try to protect themselves from most forms of accountability. In Slovakia, own local and regional self-government finance was not subject to any external control before 2006. While central government has attempted step by step improvement of its reporting to citizens, many local authorities still do not feel the need to be accountable to local citizens, and some existing initiatives are more or less formal. The main problem is really non-transparent allocation of resources at the self-government level. Programme budgeting at the local level is expected to begin only from 2008. Clear evidence about non-transparent decision-making is provided through public procurement processes. For example, most decisions on suppliers of local public services are not competition-based.

INDEPENDENT LOCAL GOVERNMENT REVENUE SOURCES

This part includes three main topics. The first focuses on the situation prior to 2002, the second on recent changes, and the last one highlights the issue of intergovernmental transfers. The main general data to understand all local finance development trends are provided in Table 18.1.

Table 18.1 Slovakia – basic figures

	1993	1994	1995	1996	1997	1998	1999	2000	2001	2002	2003	2004	2005	2006
Number of inhabitants (mil)	5.32	5.34	5.36	5.37	5.38	5.39	5.39	5.40	5.38	5.38	5.37	5.37	5.37	5.37
GDP current prices (bil. Sk)	411	496	577	638	713	781	844	934	1.010	1.096	1.196	1.326	1.437	1.574
Unemployment rate (%)	12.2	13.7	13.1	11.3	11.8	12.5	16.2	18.6	19.2	18.5	17.0	14.3	11.6	10.9
Average monthly nominal income	5.379	6.294	7.195	8.154	9.226	10.003	10.728	11.430	12.365	13.511	14.000	15.630	17.290	18535
Consumer prices index	23.2	13.4	9.9	5.8	6.1	6.7	10.6	12.0	7.1	3.3	8.0	7.5	2.7	3.5
Foreign trade balance (bil. Sk)	-26.9	2.6	-5.7	-70.3	70.0	-82.9	-45.2	-41.7	-103	-96.6	-25.0	-47.0	-76.0	-91.6

Source: Statistical yearbook Slovakia, 2006, www.nbs.sk.

Municipal Revenue Sources, 1993–2001

The last valid system of municipal revenues was defined by the Law on the State Budget 2001 (472/2000 Z. z.). This law defined the structure of municipal incomes as follows: shared taxes (personal income tax, corporation income tax and road tax), property tax (own tax), local fees/taxes, non-tax incomes, credits and grants and transfers (see Table 18.2). Municipal revenues did not follow inflation trends for most years (Figure 18.1), and the level of fiscal decentralisation during the period 1991–2001 was very limited.

Table 18.2 Main municipal revenues 1991– 2001 (mil. Sk current prices)

	Shared and own taxes	Non-tax incomes	Credits	Grants and transfers	Total
1991	3,565	4,245	404	7,961	16,175
1992	7,542	6,451	n.a.	6,634	20,627
1993	10,945	5,999	1,004	3,018	20,966
1994	9,576	7,774	886	1,795	20,073
1995	8,545	8,966	1,173	1,495	22,236
1996	10,163	8,993	2,566	3,609	25,424
1997	10,569	10,295	2,733	5,026	28,786
1998	11,402	10,647	2,943	3,785	28,873
1999	11,609	9,117	3,163	3,362	27,344
2000	12,799	10,692	6,303	3,739	33,657
2001	13,992	10,925	2,731	4,773	32,718

Source: Ministry of Finance Slovakia.

Figure 18.1 Municipal revenues and inflation, 1996–2001

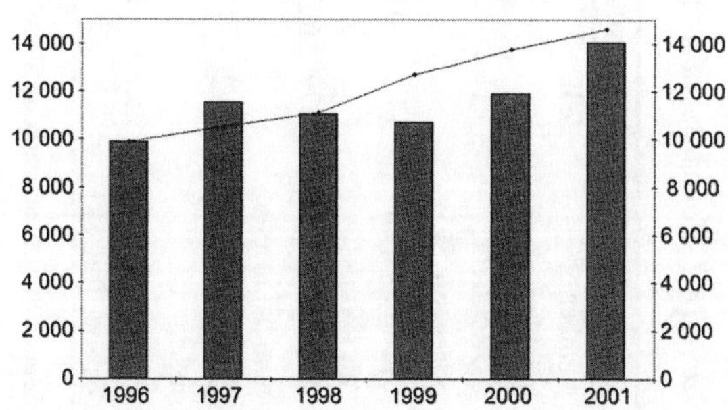

Source: Ministry of Finance Slovakia.

Shared taxes

Shared taxes represented the main income source for municipalities. Three types of central (centrally collected and centrally redistributed) taxes were used to finance local needs – personal income tax, corporation income tax and road tax. Concerning personal income tax, prior to 2000, the share was decided on a yearly basis by Parliament, as the percentage of total tax revenue for the respective tax. Revenues from shared income taxes were not distributed to municipalities on an even base, but the income per capita depended on the size of the municipality. The road tax was expected to support maintenance of local roads and its share is allocated to municipalities according to the number of inhabitants (surprisingly not according to the road structure). Table 18.3 highlights the development trends of revenues from shared taxes for the period 1993–2001.

Table 18.3 Revenues from shared taxes 1993–2001 (mil. Sk current prices)

	1993	1994	1995	1996	1997	1998	1999	2000	2001
Corporate income tax	-	1,637	1,564	1,200	782	1,357	980	1,227	1,515
Personal income tax	5,647	3,946	3,525	4,656	5,286	5,457	5,875	6,440	6,889
Road tax	-	389	412	458	461	451	515	629	959

Source: Ministry of Finance Slovakia.

Property tax

The property tax was the only real own tax of the municipalities. Its main sources were land tax, building tax and flat tax. In 2001, the size of land subject to taxation was 33,283 km^2, the number of buildings 1,696,986 and the number of flats 548,933. Municipalities had the right to set the tax rate within the interval provided by the law. The development trend of this tax is presented in Table 18.4.

Table 18.4 Property tax 1995–2001, mil. Sk current prices

	1995	1996	1997	1998	1999	2000	2001
Land tax	712	702	760	693	755	855	968
Building tax	1,007	1,440	1,852	1,667	1,926	2,065	2,134
Flat tax	-	-	-	27	41	55	66
Total	1,719	2,142	2,612	2,397	2,772	2,975	3,168

Source: Ministry of Finance Slovakia.

Local fees/taxes

This group of local revenues represents a specific issue. They were not real taxes, but also not typical fees/user charges recovering part of the costs of local public services. Table 18.5 provides data on revenues from this source for selected years.

Table 18.5 Local fees/taxes (mil. Sk current prices)

	1994	1997	2000	2001
Fee for dog	29.9	46.8	55.7	58.8
Fee for sale of alcohol and tobacco	314.0	418.4	372.7	375.3
Fee for playing machines	183.8	92.8	76.6	77.7
Fees for selling machines	2.1	1.0	0.5	1.0
Fees for the right to drive cars into historical centres	2.1	1.5	1.7	2.0
Fee for accommodation capacity	23.4	22.3	21.8	20.3
Fee for advertisement	13.8	32.1	39.7	50.2
Fee from incomes from entry fees to cultural and other activities	13.0	22.4	23.8	22.7
Recreation/spa fee	29.9	33.9	33.2	36.5
Fee for use of flat no other purpose	5.5	5.2	4.4	3.8
Fee for use of public space	105.2	168.9	239.0	274.7
Localisation fee	87.5	-	-	-
Fee for pollution of air	-	8.0	8.3	8.9
Fee for waste disposal	-	4.1	-	-
Other fees	6.1	9.3	7.8	7.5
Total	816.2	866.8	885.1	939.4

Source: Ministry of Finance Slovakia.

The total amount of revenues from local fees was increasing slightly, but below the inflation and total revenue rate. The administration and enforcement of fees was complicated, and tax evasion frequent.

Non-tax revenues

This group of revenues represented a large proportion of total municipal income. Its structure is highlighted in Table 18.6. This group includes public services fees/user charges, collected from inhabitants to recover costs of respective services.

Table 18.6 Non-tax revenues of municipalities 1996–2001, mil. Sk current prices

	1996	1997	1998	1999	2000	2001
Revenues from business and ownerships	634	600	578	519	704	449
Administrative and services fees	1,370	1,190	1,157	1,186	1,266	1,449
Capital revenues	2,266	2,971	2,759	2,123	2,536	2,525
Revenues from interests	331	420	444	337	247	192
Other non tax incomes	4,391	2,461	2,179	2,115	3,359	3,856
Transfers from municipal funds	-	2,650	3,529	2,836	2,579	2,453

Source: Ministry of Finance Slovakia

More main items are included in this group of incomes. The issues of frequent discussion are capital revenues, mainly obtained via the sale of municipal ownerships. Transfers from municipal funds represent more or less pure accounting income, as municipalities have to transfer the yearly budgetary surplus to municipal funds (mainly to the reserve fund) and re-transfer it back to current expenditure structure when needed.

Grants and transfers

Monetary transfers from the state to municipalities did not represent a major part of municipal incomes before 2002 (Table 18.1), but became temporarily important in 2003 and 2004 (see later text). According to valid legislation, municipalities were provided with general and specific grant schemes; current and capital grants separated. The main general grant was the equalisation grant for small municipalities, provided to municipalities below 3,000 inhabitants according to the scheme approved by the law on the state budget specifically for each year. The main source of specific grants was state funds, especially from the State Environmental Fund, State Water Fund, Fund Proslovakia (culture) and the State Housing Fund.

The total amount of resources provided by grants and transfers did not represent a stable income basis for municipalities for the period 1991–2001. For example this amount was 7,961 mil. Sk in 1991, but only 1,495 mil. Sk in 1995 and again 4,773 mil. Sk in 2001. The structure of main grants and transfers in 2001 was as follows:

A. Current expenditure transfers and grants – 2,134 mil. Sk, in it (main items):
   a. Equalisation grant – 585.2 mil. Sk

   b. Local public transport – 995.4 mil. Sk
   c. Regional development – 135.4 mil. Sk
   d. Individual needs grants – 113.0 mil. Sk

B. Capital expenditure transfers and grants – 2.639 mil. Sk. in it (main items):
   a. Environmental grants – 881.3 mil. Sk
   b. Local public transport – 428.3 mil. Sk
   c. Building of housing – 452.7 mil. Sk
   d. Building of schools – 155.0 mil. Sk

Outside of main structure of the state budget are grants provided to municipalities from revenues from lotteries – 137.5 mil. Sk in 2001.

Recent Changes

The 2003–2004 reform measures changed the municipal revenue system in a significant way. The processes of fiscal decentralisation defined the new system of own financial incomes of municipalities and self-government regions, providing much more resources to self-government. The legal base for fiscal decentralisation was voted by the national Parliament only in the autumn of 2004. For this reason, up until the end of 2004 the necessary amount of extra resources to finance new responsibilities at the municipal and regional levels was provided by 'decentralisation transfers'. From 2005 the fiscal decentralisation started to be functional and the remaining central grants covered most of the running costs of education facilities and costs of delegated responsibilities. The reflection of this situation on the municipal income level is shown in Table 18.7 (capital budgeting was introduced).

Self-government regions did not have their own substantial financial incomes, and all their needs to finance allocated responsibilities were covered via state grants. Only with the new fiscal decentralisation system did the revenue structure change (similarly to municipalities, central grants mainly cover running costs of education facilities). The situation is shown in Table 18.8.

Table 18.7 Main municipal revenues, 2002–2006 (mil. Sk current prices)

	Shared and own taxes	Non-tax incomes	Credits	Grants and transfers	Total all revenues
2002	16,891.0	5,837.2	1,553.1	13,789.2	57,489.6
2003	17,798.4	9,676.7	5,254.2	34,045.4	66,774.7
2004	19,737.0	7,638.7	8,343.8	28,302.6	64,022.1
2005	36,453.2	8,224.2	4,544.0	19,056.2	68,277.6
2006	40,793.8	8,628.6	5,208.3	20,372.3	75,003.0

Municipal revenues capital budget 2002–2006 (mil. Sk current prices)

	Own capital incomes	Capital transfers	Revenues from financial operations	Total
2002	3,516.4	9,139.8	369.3*	13,025.5
2003	3,181.8	7,016.6	121.9*	10,320.3
2004	3,316.8	5,547.2	3,199.6	12,063.6
2005	4,072.5	8,131.5	4,683.3	16,883.7
2006	5,680.0	7,449.8	11,085.7	24,215.5

Note: *different methodology.

Source: Ministry of Finance Slovakia.

Table 18.8 Regional self-government revenues 2002– 2006 (current prices mil. Sk/USD)

Year	Revenues total	Revenues current budget	Revenues capital budget	Revenues covered by grants	In it: Own taxes	In it: Shared taxes
2002	9,153.5	8,300.6	852.8	7,918.5	-	-
2003	18,425.9	16,579.9	1,692.5	17,304.2	-	-
2004	22,027.2	20,251.7	1,775.5	20,725.5	-	-
2005	23,689.3	22,630.0	1,059.3	10,069.2	2,799.5	8,896.4
2006	25,838.9	25,299.4	539.5	11,064.8	3,091.7	10,087.1

Source: Ministry of Finance Slovakia.

LOCAL GOVERNMENT EXPENDITURES

At the beginning of this section we must stress that the possibility of providing data describing expenditure patterns in local finance is limited by two large legislative changes – the switch to ISIC branch classification from 1 January 1996 and the introduction of a functional budgetary classification from 1 January 2002. For this reason, more detailed data can be provided only for the period 1996–2001. At the end we provide some figures for the recent period, presenting impacts from massive decentralisation after 2001.

Municipalities, from their establishment, were fully free to decide on expenditure patterns prior to 2002 (see later). The main expenditure items according to valid budgetary rules are:

1. Expenditures for realising self-governmental functions of the municipality.
2. Expenditures to finance budgetary and semi-budgetary organisations of the municipality.
3. Capital expenditures.
4. Repayment of credits and interest rate.
5. Expenditures to provide resources to citizens in an urgent need situation.
6. Transfers to municipal and other funds.
7. Expenditures on capital markets.
8. Other expenditures according to the respective legislation (for example grants and transfers to local business, supporting collective activities, and so on).

The municipality shall prepare a budget for every (calendar) year, in accordance with the budgetary classification set by the Ministry of Finance. The budget shall be made public a minimum of 15 days before its approval and citizens have the right to comment on it. The same applies to the final yearly account of the municipality and in case of borrowing decisions. The municipalities are not obliged to submit the budget proposal to any supervisory body.

Municipalities (as already indicated) shall establish municipal funds. The main resources of municipal funds are the remaining fund resources from previous years and transfers of budgetary surplus. Resources allocated to municipal funds are kept by the municipality and the municipal assembly decides on their future use. The main funds are the reserve fund and road maintenance fund. The reserve fund is the main source of solvency management of the municipality.

The final municipal account shall include all results from the financial operations of the municipality. It shall be approved by an independent auditor (probity audit). The principle of settlement of the financial year is a priority for covering all financial obligations to the state and state funds. There are no rules for liquidity management; municipalities are not protected from bankruptcy by external legal means. There are also no external measures, supervision or limits for capital expenditures.

The basic structure of municipal expenditures for selected years and according to availability (see above) is provided in Tables 18.9 and 18.10.

Table 18.9 Accounting structure of municipal expenditures 1996–2001 (mil. Sk current prices)

Indicator		1996	1997	1998	1999	2000	2001
610+620	Personnel costs	3,717	4,105	4,372	4,377	5,289	5,889
630	Goods and services	6,012	6,756	6,964	7,525	8,525	8,843
640	Transfers	3,095	3,665	3,736	3,844	3,927	4,114
650	Repayment of credits	577	673	889	1,030	1,107	1,027
700	Capital expenditures	8,387	10,017	9,735	7,020	7,366	8,754
800	Providing of credits	1,366	1,409	1,784	2,287	5,496	1,958

Source: Bercik (2003).

Table 18.10 Municipal expenditures 1993–2001, ISIC classification (mil. Sk, current prices)

Item	1993	1994	1995	1996	1997	1998	1999	2000	2001
Administration, safety	4,033	4,335	4,916	5,503	6,206	6,725	7,278	7,320	11,009
Services to inhabitants	10,211	9,885	9,046	11,146	12,642	12,528	10,395	12,383	14,060
Local economy	3,580	3,253	3,110	3,548	4,456	4,354	3,844	4,174	4,513
Financial and technical services	1,474	1,625	1,781	2,957	3,321	3,829	4,568	7,732	1,003
Total	19,298	19,098	18,853	23,154	26,625	27,436	26,085	31,609	30,585

Source: Bercik (2003).

The data after 2002 finally show the local self-government expenditures in more transparent way (see Tables 18.11 and 18.12).

Municipalities, as a whole group, do not have major problems with financial discipline. Only the two larger cities (Kosice and Banska Bystrica) were close to a cross-default situation, but have already started to recover from their financial problems. Expenditures are adapted to the revenue level, and all last year's fiscal surplus was produced at the municipal level.

Table 18.11 Municipal self-government expenditure, 2002–2006, functional classification (mil. Sk, current prices)

	2002	2003	2004	2005	2006
01 General public services	13,028	19,467	17,900.0	20,707.2	24,838.9
02 Military	7	7	7.4	9.2	24.0
03 Public safety	947	847	929.4	1,035.1	1,192.1
04 Economic area	7,948	6,479	7,693.3	9,390.1	12,295.6
05 Environment	5,362	5,416	5,276.7	6,475.1	7,080.9
06 Housing	9,929	7,608	6,956.6	9,170.1	11,610.9
07 Health care	134	189	189	173.5	187.2
08 Recreation, culture, religion	3,317	3,161	3,678.5	4,260.9	5,550.1
09 Education	11,554	23,736	23,816.5	25,241.2	27,324.4
10 Social care	852	1,995	2,509.6	2,753.0	3,211.3
Total*	53,462	68,905	68,957.0	79,215.4	93,315.4

Note: Fiscal operations and some specific items not included.

Source: Ministry of Finance Slovakia.

Table 18.12 Regional self-government expenditure, 2002–2006, functional classification (mil. Sk, current prices)

	2002	2003	2004	2005	2006
01 General public services	304.6	778.7	860.5	1,631.5	1,995.1
04 Economic area	835.1	1,189.8	3,890.1	4,129.2	5,366.2
05 Environment	0	0	0	0	36.6
06 Housing	0	3.9	7.2	2.2	0
07 Health care	0	527.9	430.6	401.2	239.1
08 Recreation, culture, religion	759.5	959.9	1,108.2	1,277.0	1,387.5
09 Education	5,432.8	11,443.3	11,094.2	11,827.7	12,357.4
10 Social care	1,443.9	3,372.6	4,602.4	4,722.3	4,895.3
Total*	8,775.9	18,276.0	21,993.2	23,991.1	26,277.2

Note: Fiscal operations and some specific items not included.

Source: Ministry of Finance Slovakia.

ties represented in the municipal and regional parliaments proposing a person for election may prefer loyalty to professional merit.

All decisions by the municipality and self-government region are subject to judicial control of administration. The mayor (lord-mayor, president of the region) shall report to the prosecutor any decision of the municipal/regional parliament if that decision is not in compliance with valid legislation (such cases are relatively frequent). Any citizen and legal body has the right to challenge the acts and activities of local government bodies before the court, even before the Constitutional Court. According to the civil law code they may claim any damage/loss incurred as the outcome of a malfunctioning of self-government. Such cases are also not too rare, but usually take a very long time to obtain a final decision (2–3 years). There are no specialised administrative courts in Slovakia.

As there is a legal requirement (see above) to have a yearly accounting audit, local governments usually hire professional private auditing firms to assess their standing and operations. However, compared, for example, to the Czech Republic, this audit is a formal financial audit, performance elements not included.

FURTHER DEVELOPMENTS

As indicated, the decentralisation reforms of 2000–2004 changed many aspects of self-governmental finances. From the point of view of municipal and regional revenues it created a new basis for local and regional finance revenues. From 2005, main revenue sources are own taxes (self-governments are free to set rates of local taxes from 2005), shared taxes (income tax was shared in 2005 as follows – 70 per cent municipalities, 22 per cent regions and 8 per cent the state), and own incomes. Grants and transfers are limited (the equalisation system was not yet comprehensively defined).

Except for this, the other main changes are the commercialisation of accounting rules, the introduction of a medium-term programme and performance budgeting, and setting of certain important financial rules for self-governments, namely:

1. The requirement to split the budget into current and capital budget.
2. The requirement to provide a balanced or surplus planned current budget.
3. The requirement to cover the deficit of the capital budget from reserves from previous years or by external revenues (temporary financial sources) from financial markets.

4. The definition of available temporary financial sources – credits or other borrowing, obligations, returnable financial supports/grants.
5. The requirement to obtain approval from the Ministry of Finance for credits over 75 mil. Sk (2.4 mil. USD in 2004).
6. Defining a maximum scale of credits and of credit recovery financial services.
7. The requirement to check the fulfilment of all the above-mentioned obligations in yearly external financial audits of the municipality or the region.
8. The right of the Ministry of Finance to introduce a 'forced financial management regime' status against municipalities not able to recover their financial obligations in time and to the necessary scale.

From 2005, municipal and regional budgets are prepared on an annual and medium-term cash basis, differentiating between capital and current expenditures. From 2008, resources will be allocated to programmes to limit the negative impacts of subjective allocation, clearly connected with the big opportunity for corruption. New programme-based performance budgeting is the tool to combat the negative impacts of subjective approaches to allocation of budgetary resources that brought the public administration system in Slovakia (including self-government level) to a critical point:

- resources were not allocated effectively, to activities where they were most needed (optimal allocation), and,
- resources were not used in an economic and efficient way (wasting of public money).

With all these changes, self-government finance will change from a quantitative (increase in revenues and expenditures) and a qualitative way (value for money/best value dimension of use of public resources). As of today, it is very difficult to predict how fast and how real qualitative changes would be. New rules try to respect some aspects of modern public financial management, but still some barriers persist – such as the non-existence of a real system of horizontal and vertical equalisation and of the effective audit of use of public resources.

Another problem (becoming more and more apparent) is achieving a real balance between extended responsibilities and available resources of self-governments. Because real financial needs to cover new duties were not calculated on the basis of long-run full costs data (Nemec et al., 2002), the existing system of fiscal decentralisation is just an estimate and compromise. Municipalities and regions have already started to claim insufficient resources and the Ministry of Finance is not willing to provide more (one argument is the necessity to be able to manage the process to enter the Euro zone – compliance with the Maastricht criteria).

CONCLUSIONS

Local government finance in Slovakia is characterised by a relatively high level of effective freedom of self-government structures concerning the financial management of their own affairs. This represents dominantly a positive situation, but invokes the need to continue with the creation of a real local democracy (mainly via education and information), and calls for the existence of certain mechanisms to combat potential corruption.

As a reaction to the dominant position of the state in local finance in the past, the volume of financial resources managed by local self-government has increased significantly recently as the outcome of massive decentralisation linked to the transfer of responsibilities from the state to the self-government.

Important changes to increase the effectiveness and efficiency of self-government resources were introduced by recent decentralisation and fiscal decentralisation reforms, but the necessity for further modernisation of public management and public financial management approaches still remains.

European governance values – openness, participation, accountability, effectiveness and coherence – shall be enforced in the daily practice of local self-government not only by proclamations, but also by effective legislation, regulation, and inevitably also by real daily practice. To manage local public finance better, the emphasis should be on accountability and effectiveness, where certain gaps still exist.

Mechanisms such as programme budgeting, formula and competition-based allocation of resources, equality of all ownership forms competing for the right to deliver local public services by fair and transparent rules, cost-centre accounting in larger cities, performance evaluation, careful performance management, performance-based audit and control, independence and professionalism of audit and control, and many others, must be addressed in the future.

NOTES

1. The problem of corruption represents a significant issue in Slovakia, as indicated also by the results of several researchers. Transparency International corruption perception indexes for Slovakia in 2001–2003 were almost similar (3.7), showing a slight improvement later, putting Slovakia into the group of countries with a high risk of corruption.

BIBLIOGRAPHY

Adamaschek, B. (ed.) (2000), *Efektivita vo verejnej sprave* [Effectiveness of Public Administration], Bratislava: Vydavatelstvo Bertelsmannovej nadacie.

Bercik, P. (1999), *Financovanie miestnych samospráv v Slovenskej republike* [Local Government Finance in Slovakia], Banska Bystrica: Ekonomicka fakulta UMB.

Bercik, P. (2003), *Ekonomický system miestnej samosprávy*, Banska Bystrica: Ekonomicka fakulta UMB.

European Commission (2001), *European Governance: A White Paper*, Brussels: European Commission.

Nemec, J., P. Bercik, and P. Kuklis (2000), Local governments in Slovakia, in: T.M. Horvath (ed.), *Decentralization: Experiments and Reforms*, Budapest: Open Society Institute Local Government and Public Service Reform Initiative, 297–342.

Nemec, J., P. Bercik, J. Liska, V. Sagat and M. Sumpiková (2002), *The Experiment on Assessments of Quality and Effectiveness of Performance of Local State Administration in the Slovak Republic*, IASIA conference, New Delhi.

Nemec, J., B. Meričková and L. Vitek (2004), *Contracting-out on local government level in transitional economies: Theory and selected evidence from the Czech and Slovak Republics*, IRSPM conference, Budapest.

Swianiewics, P. (ed.) (2001), *Public Perception of Local Governments*, Budapest: Open Society Institute Local Government and Public Service Reform Initiative.

Urad vlady SR (2000), *Audit ustrednej statnej spravy* [Audit of Central State Administration], Bratislava: Urad vlady SR.

Wright, G. and J. Nemec (eds) (2002), *Public Management in the Central and Eastern European Transition: Concepts and Cases*, Bratislava: NISPAcee.

Legislation

Ustava Slovenskej republiky [Constitution of the Slovak Republic]

Zakon SNR c. 369/1990 Zb. o obecnom zriadeni [Law on municipalities]

Zakon SNR c. 138/1991 Zb. o majetku obci [Law on municipal property]

Zakon NR SR c 39/1993 Z. z. o Najvyssom kontrolnom urade [Law on National Audit Office]

Zakon NR SR c. 221/1996 Z. z. o uzemnom a spravnom usporiadani Slovenskej republiky [Law on Territorial and Administrative Structure of Slovakia]

Zakon NR SR c. 222/1996 Z. z. o organizacii miestnej statnej spravy [Law on Organisation of Local State Administration]

Zakon NR SR c. 303/1995 Z. z. o rozpoctovych pravidlach (Law on Budgetary Rules]

Zakon NR SR c. 302/2001 Z.z. o samosprave vyssich uzemnych celkov [Law on Regional Self-Government]

Zakon NR SR c. 501/2001 Z.z. o financnej kontrole a vnutornom audite [Law on Financial Control and Internal Audit]

Statistical Sources

Internal materials of the Ministry of Finance SR

Statistical yearbooks Slovakia, 1995–2002

APPENDIX
EXCHANGE RATE SKK/USD

SKK/USD	Average/year	
	bid	ask
1993*	29	29
1994*	29	29
1995	29.52124	29.54354
1996	30.65699	30.67322
1997	33.60461	33.64582
1998	35.22319	35.30827
1999	41.34280	41.44739
2000	46.28456	46.37598
2001	48.30095	48.37049
2002	45.27484	45.35822
2003	36.72654	36.80684
2004	32.25307	32.33254
2005	31.04699	31.12553
2006	29.66829	29.74658

Note: * 1993, 1994 – author's data.

Source: www.oanda.com

19. Financing local communities in Slovenia

Davor Savin

INTRODUCTION

Slovenia is a country with a relatively low level of decentralisation. Its local administrative entities have only a single level: municipalities as a fundamental self-governing community. The Law on Local Self-Government (LLG, Official Gazette of the RS, 72/1993; 57/1999) allows for the organisation of other self-governing units, such as regions; however, so far these have not been established. The reason lies in the fact that, according to current legislation, regions can be established only on the municipalities' decision about their integrating into broader (local) communities. The municipalities, however, have in this regard different and frequently conflicting interests, which represent the primary obstacle to building an additional rank of decision making at the local level.

In 2006, approximately 11.9 per cent of total public finance (or 5.4 per cent of GDP) was made up of local finance. This represents about half the average figure in the 15 'old' EU member states. An additional indicator of decentralisation is the revenue from municipalities' own autonomous sources. The larger their share, the wider autonomy municipalities could acquire in implementing their current and development plans. Only around 34 per cent of all revenues of municipalities come from their own sources.

As a small country with 2 million people, Slovenia cannot allow any regions/areas to develop far below the country average for a long period of time. It is of key importance for the vitality of a small and (well)-developed economy – as proven by both the theory of regional economics and empirical data – that all regions progress as evenly as possible. If the conditions for balanced development of all geographic/economic areas in Slovenia are not established, the growth of GDP could be seriously slowed down. The traditional mechanisms of regional development are based on the assumption of spatial mobility of labour, capital and technology. However, some key factors that have a strong impact on regional development in a small economy are immobile. In particular, local capital facilities, transport, and institutional and social infrastructure belong to the category of immobile production factors. A new approach to regional development, on the other hand, emphasises the strengthening of internal resources within individual regions through associations with other entities so as to assure that economic growth in all areas of the country is as balanced as could be possible in a concrete situation. It is frequently emphasised that the formation of regions as an intermediary organisation between the state and municipalities would block both the tendency for all of the decision making at the state level to be centralised and the tendency of municipalities towards exaggerated decentralisation.

The Constitution of the Republic of Slovenia states: 'the territory of a municipality comprises a settlement or several settlements bound together by the common needs and interests of the residents' (Article 139). This definition is further developed in the Law on Local Self-Government, which states: 'a municipality shall, in accordance with the Constitution and law, independently regulate and perform the matters, duties and functions vested in it by law' (Article 2). This means that the municipality is an autonomous community, independently deciding about its own affairs, and that the central authority may not interfere in the forms and ways of life in local communities. The constitution stipulates that the state authority and local self-government act in the same way according to democratic, legal and social principles. Independence of municipalities can also be seen from the fact that the central authority cedes part of its own functions and duties under its jurisdiction to local communities, but only if they consent to it and if the state provides appropriate financial resources for them.[1]

According to the Law on Local Self-Government (Article 13), a territory can be organised as a municipality if it meets the following conditions: it must assure provision of (1) essential goods, (2) municipal services/utilities (drinking water, removal and purification of waste water, electricity), (3) eight years of education, that is, complete elementary schooling, (4) primary citizens' health care (health centre), (5) protection of citizens, (6) a postal service, (7) financial services of a savings bank or commercial bank, and (8) premises for local community administration. For establishing urban municipalities, the following additional conditions have to be met: to organise university and specialised libraries/information documentation centres; a hospital; telecommunication centre; a network of public services; local radio and television stations and press; vocational schools, colleges, and university departments and faculties;

sports and recreational areas and facilities; and scientific and research activities (LLG, Article 16a).

The development of a technological base in the manufacturing and service sectors showed that municipalities are becoming too small to perform all the necessary functions. This is especially noticeable in smaller municipalities that lack sufficient financial or human resources to promote and stimulate their development and, at the same time, fulfil their other obligations required by law.

There are currently 210 municipalities in Slovenia, among which 11 are registered as urban. The LLG requires that a municipality, as the fundamental self-government community, has a population of at least 5,000 unless there are geographic, historical or economic reasons that prevent it from meeting this condition. This legal criterion is currently not fulfilled by 110 municipalities. Next to that, nine municipalities have a population of less than 1,000 people while two urban municipalities, on the other hand, have more than 100,000 people (these are the capital, Ljubljana, with about 275,000 and Maribor, with 116,000 people). The predominant number of municipalities (about 46 per cent) have populations between 1,000 and 5,000 (See Table 19.1). Such a range is also found in municipalities for most large EU countries: around 95 per cent of all municipalities in France have populations up to 5,000; in Italy the share is 73 per cent and in Spain 86 per cent (OECD, 2002).

Table 19.1 Municipalities in Slovenia according to the number of residents in 2006

	Less than 1,000	Up to 5,000	Up to 10,000	Up to 50,000	Up to 100,000	More than 100,000
Percent of municipalities	4.3	52.4	22.4	23.8	0.5	1.0
Number of municipalities	9	110	47	50	1	2

Source: Government Office for Local-Self Government and Regional Policy.

The main goals that are to be achieved by the establishment of regions are the development of decentralisation, the assertion of the subsidiarity principle and balanced polycentric development of individual broader geographic/economic areas. By establishing regions, Slovenia would be comparable to the 15 'old' members of the European Union, which all have (with the exception of Luxembourg) two levels of local self-government. Among the countries that joined the EU in 2004, the Czech Republic, Slovakia, Hungary, Lithuania and Estonia have a single level of local self-government. To promote co-operation with neighbouring countries that have administrative regions, the formation of regions is particularly significant for Slovenia. Frequently, neighbouring regions cannot find an appropriate partner for their common projects in municipalities since most projects are carried out at a regional level. These kinds of projects, however, cannot be accepted at the level of small Slovenian local communities.

STATISTICAL REGIONS

Here we have to mention *statistical regions*. They are not organisations of local self-government, so their name could be misleading. Statistical regions of Slovenia represent a framework for data collection that is used for analytical and operative needs of the central government and agencies of the European Union. However, they do not represent an actual, institutionally existent level of local self-government. Statistical regional data is used for expert planning, assessing regional policy and comparing the latter with the policies of the European Union.

The category 'statistical region' was introduced in Slovenia in 1995, when previously larger local communities were reformed and split into smaller municipalities called *self-governing local communities*. Along with this reformation of local communities, the need arose for data aggregated at the level of several municipalities to be used for analytical and research purposes. Thus, 12 functional areas or inter-municipal cooperation areas were established. This regional structuring was dubbed 'statistical regions of Slovenia.' Territorial division was based on the Decree of the Government of Slovenia on Standard Classification of Territorial Units (SCTU), published in the Official Gazette of the Republic of Slovenia (no. 28/2000). The decree introduces a compulsory national standard for keeping records and collecting, analysing and presenting data on the territorial division of the country. According to the SCTU, the territory of the entire country is divided into 12 areas/regions.

Slovenian classification of statistical regions follows the Nomenclature of Statistical Territorial Units (NUTS), which passed in the European Parliament in 2003 (Regulation No. 1059/2003) and is thus integrated into the legal system of the European Union. In 2004, the nomenclature become legally binding for Slovenia.

The division into statistical regions in each of the ten new EU members became, as a result of bilateral negotiations in the accession process, an integral part of the NUTS classification of the European Union. Changing the size and the number of statistical regions is possible every three years, following the criteria of the required population for the entire country and each individual regional unit.

Table 19.2 Statistical regions – GDP per capita 2004

	Slovenia = 100	EU 15 = 100 Current prices
Central Slovenia	142.9	73
Coast and Karst region	103.2	53
Gorenjska region	86.1	44
Goriška region	95.8	49
Savinjska region	89.2	46
Southeastern Slovenia	90.9	46
Pomurska region	69.0	35
Notranjsko-Kraška region	77.0	39
Podravska region	84.5	43
Koroška region	77.5	40
Spodnjeposavska region	79.6	41
Zasavska region	71.8	37

Source: Statistical office of the RS, 2007; Eurostat Databases.

Data on statistical regions show that Slovenia exhibits quite unbalanced development in individual regions and the disparity between them has grown even larger over the last few years. The ratio of the most to the least successful (statistical) region, based on the gross domestic product per capita, rose from 1.8:1 in 1995 to 2.1:1 in 2004. Especially noticeable is an unbalanced distribution of labour-intensive sectors. For example, the share of textile, clothing, and leather sectors in total employment was 29 per cent[2] in the Prekmurje region, and only 10 per cent in the Gorenjska region (in 2004). These shares are much lower in other regions.

About 46 per cent of all companies have their seat in the most developed region (Central Slovenia, which includes the capital). About one-third of all employees in the country work in this region and they create about 43 per cent of the Slovenian gross domestic product. Central Slovenia reached 98 per cent of the EU15 average gross domestic product per capita (and even 107 per cent of GDP of the enlarged EU). In contrast, the Pomurska region, which has the lowest GDP per capita, reached only 48 per cent of the average of the EU15. Reducing the disparities in the development of individual regions is becoming an ever more important condition that has to be met to achieve the concept of polycentric and sustainable development in Slovenia in the future.

FINANCING OF MUNICIPALITIES

In accordance with the Law on Local Self-Government, all the local matters of public interest are independently decided upon and managed by the municipality. They include construction of housing, providing municipal utilities, day-care facilities and schools, issues regarding protection of the environment, maintenance of local roads and infrastructure, and so on. Financing of these functions is planned within the budget that the municipalities, in accordance with the Financing of Municipalities Act (FMA), prepare for a one-year period (Official Gazette of the RS, 80/94; 56/98; 89/99). The state may transfer by law the implementation of individual functions and tasks to a municipality subject to its prior consent, and if the necessary financial resources for these functions are provided. The state may co-finance individual public projects when it has an explicit interest in this. The state keeps control over the performance of these functions and tasks and over the management of the budget money intended for financing individual projects in municipalities. Thus, there is a formal distinction between the original functions and duties of municipalities that are carried out based on the Law on Local Self-Government (Articles 21 and 22) and the transferred functions and duties that were ceded or assigned to municipalities by the state (Article 24).

The Financing of Municipalities Act, passed in 1994 and subsequently amended several times, regulates the financing of local communities. It states that municipalities finance their functions and tasks from tax revenues, non-tax revenues, revenues from municipal property/assets, and transfers from the state budget (Articles 21, 22, 23). Recent analyses (Brezovnik and Oplotnik, 2003) of municipal financing confirmed the disparity between revenues collected in individual municipalities. Using an auxiliary analytical category of an 'average municipality' as a criterion, we can conclude that revenues from all sources in the budget of such an average municipality amount to € 712 per capita. Of this amount, around 60 per cent belongs to tax revenue, compared to less than 25 per cent in the smallest municipality. The expenditures are on average € 689 per capita. The share of current expenditures is 61.8 per cent, and investments take 38.2 per cent of total expenditures. The 'average municipality' acquires only 19 per cent of all revenues from its own sources. These are the ones that assure autonomy to a municipality (property taxes and capital revenue).

In contrast to the 'average municipality,' the smallest municipality receives only € 465 per capita annually, and it has about 2 per cent of its own financial sources. A substantially larger share of revenues from own sources is found in the largest municipality: almost 22 per cent.

Table 19.3 Statistical representation of Slovenian municipalities

	The smallest municipality	Average municipality	The largest municipality
Total annual revenues per capita (in €)	465	712	1.867
(% of total)	100%	100%	100%
Current revenues	32.2	71.8	84.5
Tax revenues	22.5	57.9	70.2
Personal income tax	19.1	40.5	53.0
Property taxes	1.4	11.7	10.7
Taxes on goods and services	3.8	5,7	7.0
Non-tax revenues	8.3	13.9	14.3
Capital revenues	0.7	7.3	10.9
Transfers and grants	67.1	20.9	4.6
Total annual expenditures per capita (in €)	370	689	1.854
(% of total)	100%	100%	100%
Investment expenditures	28.1	38.2	62.8
Current expenditures	71.9	61.8	37.2
Education	26.8	24.8	11.9
Economic activities	20.2	25.5	28.1
Administration	17.7	15.7	12.7
Social activities	6.5	10.8	4.1
Environment	10.7	6.4	51.0
Housing and spatial development	8.1	3.5	6.4
Health	0.4	1.9	0.1
Social security	5.4	5.0	2.1
Civil and fire protection	3.7	2.3	2.5

Source: Ministry of Finance (2005).

The above-mentioned data represent analytical indicators that illustrate the fundamental problem of financing. The problem is manifested as a disparity between revenues, which are completely under municipal authority (municipalities decide on their collection as well their use), and expenditures, which are determined by law. This disproportion consequently requires massive transfers from the state budget, which implicitly reduces the autonomy of municipalities as self-governing entities, and therefore changes the fundamental concept of fiscal decentralisation.

Municipalities with revenues under the average devote twice as much of their collected revenues to current expenditures as does the municipality with the highest revenues. The small amount of income collected prevents larger investments, which is the reason for inferior transportation and capital infrastructure in smaller municipalities compared to those that are closer to the average or above it.

About 45 per cent of all municipalities achieve the mentioned € 712 revenues per capita. However, the differences between those with the lowest and those with the highest revenues are substantial. The poorest municipality acquired a meagre € 465 per capita, and the richest € 1.867. This is mostly a consequence of income tax accumulation paid by people who have their permanent residence concentrated in the rich municipality's areas.

The structure of municipal tax revenues could also be divided according to the distinction between sources that belong exclusively to municipalities and those that are *shared.* The latter are those that belong to a municipality, but their fiscal characteristics (tax basis, tax payers and marginal tax rate) are set by the state. Given this, we can divide all municipal revenues according to their significance for the financial autonomy of municipalities into the following groups:

A) own financial sources
B) shared sources (or financial sources that are ceded to municipalities by the state)
C) transfers from the state budget
D) revenues from municipal assets/property.

The above division is based on the analysis of fiscal decentralisation in OECD (see OECD, 2002). Comparing Slovenia with the members of the EU15, we find a much higher level of fiscal sovereignty in local communities in Europe. These acquire around 83 per cent of all financial sources at the local level, whereas in Slovenia this is only 34 per cent. The figure reflects a low level of decentralisation in the financing of public expenditures. Additionally, this means that Slovenian municipalities are highly dependent on transfers from the state budget. The data also suggest a direction for changes that Slovenia has to implement in order to achieve necessary convergence with other EU members regarding the fiscal autonomy of local communities.

REVENUES OF MUNICIPAL BUDGETS

In the structure of all revenues in municipal budgets, 62 per cent belong to various *tax sources* (the share has not changed much over several years). The other two large financial sources for municipalities are *non-tax revenues*, which amount to 14 per cent, and *transfers*, which account for about one-fifth of total municipal revenues.

Table 19.4 Economic structure of municipal revenues (Slovenian tolars, SIT, billion)

	2000	2001	2002	2003	2004	2005	2006
Total revenue	215.0	240.6	264.8	289.7	310.9	341.5	382.3
Current revenue	155.2	181.1	202.0	220.2	236.3	245.2	265.8
tax revenue	125.8	145.1	164.6	178.8	191.4	197.7	213.1
non-tax revenue	29.2	36.0	37.4	41.4	44.9	47.5	52.7
Capital revenue	8.8	9.2	12.8	13.5	18.1	24.9	36.0
Grants received	0.9	0.7	1.0	1.2	0.9	1.1	0.6
Transfer revenue	50.1	49.6	49.0	54.6	55.6	70.2	79.8

Source: Government Office for Local Self-Government and Regional Policy.

Table 19.4 shows that capital revenues and grants received are the two least important financial sources for municipalities. Additionally, it can be seen that tax revenues represent the most important source for municipal budgets. However, the financial structure of revenues shows that the dominant share of revenues is not rooted in the fiscal autonomy of municipalities. On the contrary, these revenues are allocated to them based on the principle of shared and assigned resources.

From the point of view of financial autonomy, we can distinguish between *own revenues* of municipalities (the municipalities independently set the tax base, tax rate, exemptions for some taxpayers, and the like); *shared taxes*, which are divided between the state and the municipality; and revenues that belong to the municipality, but their tax base, taxpayers, and the tax rates are set in various laws. These revenues are ceded to municipalities by the state and are thus called *assigned revenues* (FMA, Articles 22, 23).

The remaining financial sources include *transfers* and *grants*, the sum of which represents about one-fifth of municipal revenues.

Table 19.5 Fiscal autonomy of municipalities (in %)

Total revenues	100.00
Own and partly own revenues	34.66
Shared revenues	42.24
Transfer revenues	18.56
Assigned revenues	4.20
Grants received	0.34

Note: Data refer to 2006; calculated from Government Office for Local Self-Government and Regional Policy.

Municipalities' own Financial Sources

The Financing of Municipalities Act (Articles 21, 22) states 11 different taxes and fees that are collected by municipalities according to their right to set tax rates decide on whom the taxpayers are and what their tax obligations are. Own sources, as already has been mentioned, represent a little more than one-third of all revenues collected by municipalities. Of these, about 45 per cent are own tax revenues and 55 per cent are own non-tax revenues, which also include capital revenues.

The most important own tax revenue of municipalities, which is completely under their jurisdiction and which they should manage, is the compensation tax for the use of building land. This tax represents about 8.6 per cent of all municipal revenues and, together with participation in profits and income from property, is the most important financial source that is included in the 'own and partly own' type of municipality revenue.

In 2005, the compensation tax for the use of building land was replaced by a real estate tax, which has been in the process of preparation for quite some time. As previously mentioned, this tax represents about a tenth of own municipal revenues and is under the jurisdiction of individual municipalities. Land registers which have not been prepared or maintained with adequate accuracy (narrow and out-of-date information, changes in the intended use of land plots, differences in measuring procedures and so on) make the collection of the tax for the use of building land incomplete. There is another factor that contributes to the relatively poor collection of this tax: local authorities are not very motivated to expand the tax base for this fiscal revenue, since it would decrease the level of fiscal equalisation revenues that the municipalities receive annually from the state budget.

Other own tax revenues comprise quite a small share of own municipal revenues. This category includes communal taxes and other taxes on disposal sale and licences, with both making up about 8 per cent of all own municipal sources.

Non-tax own revenues comprised about 13.8 per cent of total municipal incomes in 2006. These sources originate from municipal property/assets, property rights, and various fees. Around 6.2 per cent of non-tax sources come from participation in profits and income from property/assets, and around 7.6 per cent are other non-tax revenues. The magnitude of non-tax revenues has been very volatile during the last five years or so. Municipalities use this source depending on the level of their current obligations. For example, these revenues increased when Slovenia implemented nine-year primary education, and many municipalities had to invest in expanding existing school facilities and other related infrastructure. For this reason, some municipalities even sold their shares in local industrial companies and commercial firms.

Capital revenues bring about 5 to 9 per cent of total revenues to municipalities (equivalent to about 14 per cent of own sources). This financial source is substantial, especially in those municipalities that, according to the new legislation, acquired territory with large numbers of manufacturing, trade, transport and financial companies. These companies are partly owned by the municipalities, which in the previous system of local self-government represented an actual, although informal, part of the state or the first level of administrative decision-making.

Shared financial sources are comprised of the financial sources set by the Financing Municipalities Act (Article 23). The state allocates them to municipalities for their unconditional use. Income tax belongs in this category. The tax is shared between municipalities, which get 35 per cent and the state, which is entitled to 65 per cent of this revenue. The share of income tax in total municipal revenues is 39 per cent; thus, it is the most important financial source for local communities in Slovenia.

The differences among municipalities in the amount of collected income tax are becoming ever greater. More than a half of all municipalities in 2005 did not reach the average income tax that was € 114 per capita. The largest amount of income tax is collected in urban municipalities, where most of the employees in manufacturing companies and lucrative service industries reside.

Transfer revenues of municipalities[3] contribute to around 20 per cent of total revenues, which is about 2.5 per cent of all public finance. However, concerning transfers received, there are very pronounced differences between individual municipalities. For example, a quarter of municipalities received less than 20 per cent of all public finance revenues, half got between 21 per cent and 50 per cent of all revenues, and a quarter had more than 50 per cent of all revenues (Oplotnik and Brezovnik, 2004, p.85).

Among transfers, there are not only external financial sources but also inter-municipal sources. Individual municipalities in some areas transfer some money to neighbouring municipalities in order to build infrastructure that is in their common interest: for example, hospitals, libraries, fire departments, and so on. During the period 2000–2005, inter-municipal transfers were between 3 and 5 per cent of all municipal transfer revenues. 'Financial equalisations' also belong among transfers.

Assigned tax sources comprise six tax categories, which represent around 5.9 per cent of total municipal revenues. The tax on real estate transactions is the most important within this category (around 70 per cent). The other relevant sources are administrative fees and a special tax on the use of gaming machines, which have about a 17 per cent share in assigned financial sources of municipalities.

Grants share in all municipal revenues is less than one-half of a percentage. Grants are not important financial revenues since they fluctuate greatly and therefore cannot be used for the medium-term or even short-run planning of local community expenditures.

FINANCIAL EQUALISATION SYSTEM

In order to perform all of the tasks required of them by the Constitution and the law, municipalities use the sources mentioned above. However, when municipalities cannot achieve a sufficient level of revenues to finance so-called appropriate expenditure levels (according to Articles 20, 22, and 23 of the Financing of Municipalities Act) they are entitled to money from the state budget. These resources are called 'financial equalisation'.

Financial equalisation thus amounts to the difference between the amount of the appropriate expenditure level and the available revenues of a municipality, which it collects following the Law on the Financing of Municipalities. This, in principle, means that the municipalities with sufficient revenue to finance the appropriate level of expenditures are not entitled to receive any financial equalisation transfers. On the other hand, a municipality that did not have any revenues (which is, of course, only an analytical assumption) would have an opportunity to acquire the total amount needed to finance its level of normatively set appropriate expenditures based on financial equalisation. The optimal solution would thus be that municipalities completely finance their expenditures from their own sources, or that there would be no difference between the appropriate level of expenditures and their own revenues. In this particular case, municipalities would enjoy complete fiscal autonomy and the financial equalisation would be zero.

As many as 173 municipalities received money from the state budget in 2005. Small and less developed municipalities, which are mostly concentrated in the north-eastern area of the country, in individual years received as much as 85 per cent of all revenues for financing their appropriate level of expenditure based on the financial equalisation scheme.

It is clear that in this kind of systemic arrangement for the financing of local communities, the latter were not stimulated to expand their tax bases and in this way assure sufficient own means to cover the appropriate level of expenditures on their territories. This has now been corrected with a new instrument. Financial equalisation can now be limited or conditional. The money that individual self-governing communities can get from the state budget depends on their financial strength. This is determined based on not only actual but also potential revenues. Potential financial power here is based on the revenue collections that did not take place, despite the fact that they could have been used according to the Constitution and laws. In this way, a new category of estimated revenues is introduced into the system of financing local communities. Estimated revenues are all the revenues that could have been brought together if a municipality had collected all the possible duties/revenues. Such an approach ensures that the amount of financial equalisation is reduced by the amount of possible revenues that were not collected. If, however, revenues exceed the estimated level, the financial equalisation remains unchanged.

Revenues of municipalities based on financial equalisation are statistically included in the category of 'transfers'. As mentioned previously, transfers represent around 20 per cent of all municipal revenues; however, financial equalisation has the largest share (65 to 80 per cent between 1997 and 2005). This money is also called general grants, as distinguished from special grants, and can be at most 35 per cent of all revenues belonging to the 'transfers' category. Municipalities can receive special grants from the state budget to help finance investments. They are allotted according to criteria that are decided upon by individual ministries.

APPROPRIATE EXPENDITURE LEVEL

According to the Financing Local Communities Act (Article 25) the appropriate per capita level of expenditures is determined by the National Assembly in the procedure of adopting the state budget for each individual budgetary year.

The appropriate expenditure level, which is determined for the country as a whole, is defined as the average amount of funds per capita that municipalities need to satisfy their legal and constitutional obligations/functions. These amounts include explicit financial funds providing for adequate current expenditures and are not intended for investment.

The amount of the appropriate expenditure level (defined by the Law of Financing Local Communities, Article 20a) is based on a rather unusual formula that includes the territory of the municipality, the length of local roads, the population under the age of 15, and the population over the age of 65. Some local specific characteristics are also added into the equation. All these indicators are calculated per capita and are expressed as a share of the reference value for the whole country. They are thus ratios with respect to Slovenian averages. In this manner, calculated numbers may not necessarily reflect the actual need of municipalities. For example, if a municipality, when established, has 'inherited' more kilometres of road, it is entitled to a larger amount based on the criterion of appropriate expenditure level. However, this does not mean that the municipality is using roads to its optimal transportation advantage. Even when the utilisation of its roads is suboptimal, the municipality is entitled to money from the financial equalisation scheme. In contrast, some municipalities are unable to perform all of the functions specified by law at an appropriate quality level since the amounts they are granted are too small.

The money for an individual municipality is determined on an equation according to which the municipality is entitled to 70 per cent of the money depending on the level of appropriate expenditures per capita, and 30 per cent depending on the correction ratio. Correction factors are the length of roads, a population that is either very young or very old, and territory of a municipality calculated as a ratio in comparison to the average for the whole state.

The following formula is used to calculate the amount of appropriate expenditures:

$$E = P \cdot N \cdot [0.70 + (0.05 \cdot C) + (0.05 \cdot T) + (0.16 \cdot M) + (0.04 \cdot S)]$$

where

E = appropriate level of expenditures for financing of local needs in an individual municipality.

P = appropriate level of per capita expenditures in the current year as set by the National Assembly.

N = number of people in the municipality as of January 1 of the current year.

C = ratio of the length of local roads per capita to the length of roads per capita for the whole country.

T = ratio of the municipal territory per capita to the territory per capita for the whole country.
M = ratio of the share of the population under the age of 15 in the individual municipality to the average share of these people in the whole country as of 1 January.
S = ratio of the share of the population over the age of 65 in the individual municipality to the average share of these people in the whole country as of 1 January.

The sum of all coefficients is 1.00. However, some exceptions are possible. For municipalities that otherwise do not have the status of urban municipalities but used to be the centres of old communities, the coefficient of 0.74 is used instead of 0.70. This gives the sum of the coefficients of 1.04. For urban municipalities, the coefficient of 0.70 is replaced by the coefficient 0.78, which gives the sum of all coefficients of 1.08.

The National Assembly determined the amount of the appropriate expenditure level per capita for 2006 to be €432, which is approximate the same as the amount of the appropriate level of municipal per capita expenditures one year earlier.

MUNICIPAL BORROWING/DEBT

Local communities in Slovenia have a very limited borrowing option. Municipalities can borrow only after they have acquired a preliminary agreement from the Ministry of Finance. This is further restricted so that they can borrow only within the Slovenian financial system and not abroad. Borrowing abroad is limited to cases that are explicitly allowed by law. During the years 1992–2006, municipalities never borrowed any money from abroad. All the loans came from home lenders (these were mostly loans by commercial banks: more than 80 per cent of all loans). Although municipalities can issue financial instruments to finance their development programs they have not issued any municipal bonds since 1999 (Ministry of Finance, 2006).

Local communities can obtain new loans under two conditions: (i) if their existing and planned debt does not exceed 10 per cent of all annual municipal revenues, and (ii) if annual payment of interest and principal does not exceed 5 per cent of their annual revenues. These restricting criteria are meant to prevent excessive municipal borrowing since in the case where municipalities are not able to meet their obligations they must be bailed out by the state budget at the expense of all taxpayers. Table 19.6 gives the ratio of borrowing to repaying municipal debt.

Table 19.6 Borrowing for repaying debt (Slovenian tolars (SIT), billion)

	2000	2001	2002	2003	2004	2005	2006
Borrowing	1.8	3.0	7.9	5.8	8.2	5.4	8.6
Debt payments	1.9	2.2	2.2	2.3	3.3	3.2	3.2

Source: Ministry of Finance, no. 12, 2006.

EXPENDITURES OF LOCAL COMMUNITIES

Slovenia adopted the EU classification that distinguishes between five basic groups of public finance expenditures, among them municipal expenditures. The criteria for such a classification are the characteristics of individual expenditures, and records in accounting. Thanks to this, there exists a unified budgetary and accounting classification for municipal expenditures (Table 19.7).

Among current expenditures are wages and other compensation to employees, social security payments based on wages, expenditures for goods and services, interest payments, and reserves.

Current transfers make up the second group of expenditures, which includes payments for which municipalities do not receive any tangible or intangible compensation from the recipients. Around one-third of this category is transfers to individuals and households. Also belonging among current transfers are subsidies to public and private enterprises; money for subsidising prices, interest, employment and covering losses.

Table 19.7 Structure of municipal expenditures (Slovenian tolars (SIT), billion)

	Total expenditures	Current expenditures	Current transfers	Investment expenditures	Investment transfers
2000	214.4	46.6	89.6	58.2	20.0
2001	242.5	53.6	97.9	67.9	23.2
2002	273.5	61.8	105.6	76.5	29.6
2003	290.8	68.7	112.8	75.9	33.3
2004	310.8	75.1	120.2	79.3	36.2
2005	328.8	78.4	126.6	90.4	33.4
2006	390.0	90.7	138.4	122.3	38.6

Note: Figures do not add due to rounding;

Source: Government Office for Local Self-Government and Regional Policy.

Investment expenditures and investment transfers represent between 33 and 37 per cent of all municipal expenditures. In contrast to investment expenditures, economic agents on the territory of individual municipalities allot investment transfers for the payment of own development projects. However, the companies have no obligation to pay these back. In this way, these are non-repayment funds (they are used to co-finance development projects in dynamic companies or vital infrastructure, both of which are of common interest to locals; various forms of help in cases of natural disasters; and so on).

In contrast to investment expenditures, investment transfers do not increase the real (physical) assets of municipalities, which mean that they do not increase the value of fixed capital in the balance sheets of local communities. Instead, they increase the real assets of recipients of transferred money. In the balance sheets of a municipality, investment transfers show up as financial investments in a public institution, company, financial institution, private firms, and so on.

The municipal expenditure structure breakdown, according to individual function, shows that the largest share is comprised of education (25 per cent) and housing and utilities (also around 25 per cent). These are followed by general public services (15 per cent) and expenditures for transportation (around 10 per cent). All other municipal activities (defence, social security, culture, recreation, and so on) account for 25 per cent of all expenditures of local communities.

CONCLUSION

The existing system of municipal financing is not well suited to the needs of the actual local community's activities or their future development within the EU. The most notable problem is insufficient decentralisation of financing public expenditures. Municipalities should enjoy a higher level of fiscal autonomy in order to fulfil their obligations, with no financial intervention of the state (which usually means administrative interference). The share of local finance in total public finance is about 12 per cent, which represents about 5 per cent of gross domestic product. For the EU, this share stands at about 26 per cent of total public finance and about 16 per cent of GDP. Own sources represent one-third of all municipal fiscal and non-fiscal revenues. The dominant element is income tax, which is shared between the municipality, which gets 35 per cent and the state, whose share is 65 per cent of this revenue. The degree of fiscal autonomy in Slovenian municipalities is therefore very low and lags substantially behind the EU average.

The formula of appropriate expenditure level, which has to be constantly adjusted and its average value is not suitable for many municipalities, does not meet new economic and social needs. The state transfers around SIT 30 billion per year from the central budget, and on the other hand some municipalities register surpluses of SIT 26 to 28 billion. Correct determination of the appropriate level of expenditures would facilitate lower government budget expenditure. Around 25 per cent of municipalities, mostly those with a small population on their territory, receive more than half of the resources being transferred by the state to the local communities within the scheme of financial equalisation.

One of the suggestions for improving the existing system of public finance is to redistribute part of the revenues from relatively rich to poor municipalities. Most urban municipalities have more people and more taxable business buildings and other infrastructures on their territory. The taxes collected are an autonomous financial source that belongs to these municipalities. Besides, they are able to set the tax rates for these buildings independently. The urban municipality of Ljubljana, for example, collects revenue large enough to cover the deficits of all other municipalities in the country. However, rich municipalities are surely not delighted with such a proposal. They respond that due to their larger population, they have to bear higher costs: there are more students in their schools, more patients in their hospitals, and they have higher outlays for cultural and sports activities, environmental protection, and so on. It is understandable that a possible recalculation of an appropriate level of expenditures would be based on these and other similar characteristics. However, the abandonment of formalised revenue distribution criteria and building of a new system of financing local communities cannot be carried out in a short time period. Besides, changes in both the consumption structure and in the list of taxpayers would affect the 'new' formula of appropriate expenditure level and would make it obsolete rather quickly.

If municipalities were to gain a larger share of fiscal revenues, this would strengthen their fiscal potential and expand their manoeuvring space in performing legally mandated functions and tasks. As we have seen, only a smaller share of total tax revenues belongs to municipalities. Thus, the changes could encompass three basic suggestions: a) increase the share of local communities in tax revenues, b) increase transfers from the central budget, and c) expand the fiscal autonomy of municipalities in a such way that they could generate their own new financial sources.

Additionally, municipalities should be granted the right to borrow, especially on long-run terms, which would allow for larger investments in public infrastructure: the road system, water supply utilities, health and recreation and sports facilities, and so on. Now the legal provisions limit borrowing by municipalities, regardless of the type of credits and the ability to pay off debt in the future.

Tax reform is under way in Slovenia. Among other modifications, it foresees the change in taxes on different forms of wealth, especially real estate. About 0.2 per cent of the market value of a plot of land is collected annually under the compensation tax for the use of building land. One of the possibilities related to this is the introduction of additional taxes for buildings of extraordinary size and quality, and for luxury buildings, the tax proceeds from which would belong to local communities. The tax revenue from this source in Slovenia at the moment is substantially lower than in other EU countries. Privatisation of real estate expanded the potential tax base and therefore also the possible tax sources for municipalities. This would be a permanent tax source with which municipalities could gain stable financial revenue, independent of business cycle fluctuations and state supporting funds.

One should note that an appropriate level of decentralisation and formation of several levels of local self-government bring the local public sector much closer to the needs of its environment and to satisfying the needs of the local population. With increasing economic, demographic, cultural, and social diversity, the demand for specific local public goods and services are growing. This requires a higher level of autonomy for local communities regarding the financing of their activities that satisfy these needs. Therefore, fiscal federalism can be regarded as a public good and an important component of the welfare state.

NOTES

1. There is a historic parallel to this. During the time of the Socialist Federal Republic of Yugoslavia, the municipality actually functioned as an integral part of the central state or as the first level of decision making. According to the Constitution of 1973, the municipalities performed around 3,000 various tasks for the state. More than two-thirds of municipal agencies were engaged in performing 'state tasks'. The federal Constitution stated that the municipality is in charge of all public matters in its territory, regardless of state or local character. In this sense the municipality was an 'extended arm' of the state.
2. At the same time, this region has the largest share of agriculture in GDP (close to 10 per cent) while the average for Slovenia is 3 per cent.
3. All of the resources that municipalities receive from other institutions of public finance, especially the state budget, belong in this category. These revenues are neither original (collected as tax or non-tax) nor capital revenues. Instead they are transfers of money from other accounts of public finance.

BIBLIOGRAPHY

Brezovnik, B. and Ž. Oplotnik, (2003), Fiskalna decentralizacija v Sloveniji: oris stanja, problematika in mednarodna primerjava, *Lex localis*, št. 3.

De Mello, L.R. (2000), Fiscal Decentralization and Intergovernmental Fiscal Relations: A Cross-Country Analysis, *World Development*, **28**(2).

Government Office for Local Self-Government and Regional Policy. Web site: http://www.svlr.gov.si/en.

Grafenauer, B. (2000), *Lokalna samouprava na Slovenskem; teritorialno-organizacijske strukture* [Local Self-government in Slovenia: territorial and organizational structures], Maribor: Pravna fakulteta.

Joumard, I. and Kongsrud, P. (2003), Fiscal relations across government levels, *OECD Economic Studies*, **36** (1), 155–229.

Ministry of Finance of RS, 'Bilten javnih financ', 2004, 2005, 2006, No. 12

Oates, W. (1999), An Essay on Fiscal Federalism, *Journal of Economic Literature*, **32**, 1120–1149.

OECD (2002), *Fiscal Decentralization in EU Applicant States and Selected EU Member States*, Paris, OECD.

Official Gazette of the RS, various issues.

Oplotnik Ž. and B. Brezovnik, (2004), Financing Local Government in Theory and Practice: Short Lesson from Slovenia, *Zagreb International Review of Economics and Business*, 7(2), 75–93.

Statistical Office of the RS, *Statistični letopis*, 2006.

Statistical Office of the RS, *Slovene Regions in Figures*, 2007.

Statistical Office of the RS *Bulletins*, various issues.

20. Funding local government in Ukraine

Sergii Slukhai

INTRODUCTION

In 1991, Ukraine began its existence as an independent state. The nation began to look for a way to build up a self-reliant economy and effective state. Much was done in the domain of the national economy: privatisation of productive assets, liberalisation of entrepreneurial activity, introduction of market institutions and so on. But the nation state itself, despite the progress in market reform, was still very slow in rebuilding a new modern way forward. This relates not only to the central government, but especially to local governments. The approval of the Constitution of the independent Ukraine in 1996 and of basic legislation on local government (Law on Local Self-Government and Law on Local State Administration) passed respectively in 1997 and 1999, has created a legal framework for public administration at both regional and local levels.

According to the Constitution, the central government bears most of the responsibilities in the delivery of public services. A portion of these is vested in locally elected bodies through a mechanism of delegation. The majority of local authorities are still far from being able to take over the role of self-reliant public service providers that could meet local voters' approval. In fact, weak popular demands for independent local authorities and long-lasting traditions of a centralistic state create, in society, a lack of any desire to devolve power from top to bottom, although the municipal bodies of large cities gained some real power in the course of ongoing reforms. After the Budget Code was adopted (2001), new possibilities for fostering local autonomy and accountability arose. However, there is still a long way to go until innovations are implemented and the reform brings about any results in terms of increasing the efficiency of local governance.

The chapter outlines an extensive overview on the development of local finance in Ukraine with a special emphasis on the prospective steps towards enhancing local fiscal autonomy and accountability.

LOCAL GOVERNMENT FINANCE LEGAL FRAMEWORK

The local finance in Ukraine is regulated by a set of national acts, comprising the Budget Code (2001), the Law on Local Self-Government (1997) and the Law on Local State Administration (1999). This legislation creates the basic legal framework for local government fiscal activity. As in many other transition countries, some secondary legal acts provide a significant input into the legal environment the local governments are coping with, especially the annual budget laws and regulations of the Ukrainian Cabinet of Ministers.

The Law on Local Self-Government provides a broad definition of local government responsibilities at the different tiers, defines their budgetary rights and the structure of the budget sheet and the declared independence of local budgets. Item 62 of this law states that the state is responsible for granting per capita minimal local budget to any local government according to nationwide standards with special allowances for the specific conditions in which the respective government operates. Item 66 of this law covers non-deficit local budgets which could be achieved with state support. The local governments received the right to impose local taxes and fees, issue securities and receive bank loans.

The Law on Local State Administration sets the framework for local state administration activities and their interaction with local self-government. These bodies represent the executive power at the territorial (*oblast* and *rayon*) level and, being directly subordinated to the President's Office, have a wide range of responsibilities, ranging from managing the delivery of basic social services to composing and executing *oblast* and *rayon* budgets. The functional departments of local state administrations are territorial departments of the respective functional ministries.

Despite these important features, these laws did not fully eliminate the soviet legacy in intergovernmental finance. The local finance was, in general, treated as a supplement to the state so the common place was the central administration of fiscal flaws. A new era has begun with the enactment of the Budget Code (2001) which substituted the old Law on the Budget System (1995) and other linked acts. The Budget Code introduced new approaches to the budgetary process; it settled the budgetary issues on solid ground, minimising the subjectivity and arbitrariness in fiscal issues; finally, local governments received clearly defined sources of revenue, together with a clear definition of what they are responsible for.

Currently, Ukraine has two types of local authorities. First are the local state administrations at the region (*oblast*) and county (*rayon*) levels. The heads of local state administration are not elected, but appointed directly by the

President of Ukraine. The second are bodies of self-government at the *oblast*, *rayon* and municipal levels. The elected councils at the *oblast* and *rayon* levels have no executive bodies and that is why they are not in a position to run the subordinated budgetary institutions.

The elected councils in cities, villages and townships form their own executive bodies so they can manage to some extent issues of local importance. The local authorities extend to jurisdictions which are based on the current administrative-territorial composition of Ukraine: 1 autonomous republic (Crimea)[1], 26 *oblasts* (including two cities of national significance, Kyiv and Sevastopol), 490 rural *rayons*, 458 cities and towns (including 179 of *oblast* significance), 118 urban districts, 886 settlements and 28,540 villages (Ukrainian State Statistical Committee, 2007). This demonstrates that the number of local communities, especially in rural areas, is quite large. But at the same time, up until now, most of them are not in a position to execute their own rights: only about one-third have formed councils. The obsolete territorial structure has many inconsistencies. For example, some territorial units such as large cities administer not only urban districts, but also other units of the same territorial level – small cities, villages and settlements, which comprise, according to the Law on Self-Government, the self-governing communities.

A large number of small jurisdictions create a situation of fragmented local government sectors that formally have some scope of legally prescribed tasks, but cannot perform them because of a lack of funding and administrative capacity. Here, the situation is quite similar to some Central European countries (Kimball, 1999). Suggestions have been made to lessen the number of *oblasts* and *rayons* and to make them more self-reliant. The most challenging issue is the amalgamating of rural communities (villages and settlements) with urban ones and thus approaching an integrated type of local government. The existing administrative structure creates duplicate fiscal statistics. This leads a student to suggest that the aggregated fiscal data on local governments' involvement in public service delivery and revenue accumulation could be misleading (see Table 20.1) – the real role of the sub-national sector of government is actually less than is shown by statistics, because in many cases, the local budgets serve as formal transit stations for funding local budgetary institutions such as schools and hospitals and so on which are actually administrated by local state administrations at the *rayon* level.

What is very important is the trend in expenditure and revenue assignment: the data above show that up until 2001, there were no clear trends to decentralise public revenues and expenditures in Ukraine due to the non-existent policy of decentralisation. Only since 2001 when the first steps to budgetary reform were undertaken, has this shaky beginning appeared to turn to decentralisation, but by the middle of the first decade of the 2000s this has quickly reversed. As a result, throughout the 2000s there is no stable growth in sub-national government (SNG) share observed, as opposed to many other post-socialist countries.

Table 20.1 Distribution of general government total expenditures and total revenues (without transfers and state pension fund outlays and revenues), in per cent

Year	Expenditures		Revenues	
	Central government	Sub-national governments	Central government	Sub-national governments
1991	68.6	31.4	54.1	45.9
1992	62.2	37.8	52.4	47.6
1993	60.5	39.5	53.3	46.7
1994	64.7	35.3	58.0	42.0
1995	52.7	47.3	47.2	52.4
1996	56.4	43.6	52.4	47.6
1997	60.1	39.9	56.8	43.2
1998	51.9	48.1	54.3	45.7
1999	54.6	45.4	60.0	40.0
2000	64.7	35.3	70.9	29.1
2001	59.7	40.3	67.7	32.3
2002	58.9	41.1	68.6	31.4
2003	58.6	41.4	70.0	30.0
2004	62.2	37.8	75.1	24.9
2005	63.3	36.7	77.4	22.6

Source: Author's calculation based on Ukrainian Ministry of Finance data.

As Table 20.2 demonstrates, the shifts in expenditure distribution among governmental tiers in Ukraine are obvious: (i) the SNGs began playing a greater role in financing the economy (first of all in subsidising industries); this is especially true for *oblast* governments; (ii) the expenditures on housing and amenities have been redistributed in favour of SNGs; (iii) the central government took over most expenditures on social protection. In other spheres of the public sector activities, there were no significant changes concerning the governmental tier shares.

Since most budgetary revenues are national revenues, the SNGs are obliged to be accountable for their spending to central government and not to the local

Table 20.2 Distribution of expenditures by function within a sector of public administration of Ukraine, in per cent

Sphere	Year	Central government	Total sub-national government	Oblast governments	Rayon governments	Cities of oblast significance	Cities of rayon significance	Settlements	Villages
Total expenditures	1992	62.2	37.8	11.5	7.7	15.5	0.7	0.7	1.7
	2005	63.3	36.7	9.4	9.7	14.7	0.5	0.6	1.8
Social protection	1992	35.0	65.0	31.7	9.3	22.9	0.4	0.3	0.4
	2005	79.1	30.9	4.1	9.0	7.7	0.0	0.0	0.0
Economy	1992	84.0	16.0	5.1	1.5	8.4	0.6	0.4	0.1
	2005	74.0	26.0	13.3	0.9	9.4	0.6	0.7	1.2
Housing and amenities	1992	5.3	94.7	15.7	4.2	65.8	4.7	3.4	1.1
	2005	3.2	96.8	12.3	4.8	69.7	3.5	2.7	3.7
Education	1992	33.9	66.1	6.6	17.0	28.1	3.0	3.1	8.3
	2005	37.1	62.9	8.2	23.5	26.6	1.3	1.2	2.3
Health care	1992	10.1	89.9	22.2	25.6	39.3	0.4	0.6	1.8
	2005	22.7	77.3	28.1	17.9	27.1	0.1	0.7	3.5

Source: Author's calculation based on Ukrainian Ministry of Finance data.

voters. Spending of money is strictly controlled by the State Treasury which holds the accounts of the SNGs. The low accountability is strengthened by the way the local administration is functioning. As was mentioned above, a high portion of expenditures are performed or directly controlled by the local state administrations.

LOCAL GOVERNMENT REVENUE SOURCES

The sources of SNGs' revenues are mostly determined by the Budget Code which delineates the public revenues between levels of government. Such taxes as VAT, EPT (except that for communal enterprises), excises and import levies are assigned to the national level. PIT and land tax are ceded national taxes that are accounted to local budgets in the full amount. The list of local taxes and duties had been enacted by Decree of the Minister's Cabinet in 1993 and is still (after small amendments) a basic document regulating own local revenues. The legislative base of local revenues is still not comprehensive. So, the Tax Code that should legally fix the vertical revenue distribution introduced by the Budget Code is still not approved. Many details concerning local revenues are not clarified because important pieces of legislation such as the Law of Local Finance, Law on Local Taxes and Duties and the Law on Donations and Subventions have not yet been drafted.

The SNGs' finance in Ukraine depicts a high reliance on central government fiscal assistance. The structure of revenues of sub-national levels is characterised by the dominance of the direct or indirect transfers. As Table 20.3 shows, the tax share in SNGs' revenues is quite high – around 44 per cent; almost all of these proceeds are national, ceded to the SNGs or shared with them. The portion of local taxes is insignificant (about 1 per cent of total revenues) with a diminishing trend. As to user charges, their potential importance is quite high, but they are not statistically assessed due to current methodology; only subventions covering the deficits of communal enterprises (transportation, water management, sanitation facilities etc.) are reflected in the budgets of the SNGs. The share of official transfers in SNGs' budgets is quite high – about half of the total revenue; the dominating majority of *rayon* governments, as well as small towns, settlements, and villages cannot perform their activities without having massive fiscal support from the state budget or budgets of upper levels.

The tax administration belongs to the national government; local governments do not have their own tax administrations. The State Tax Administration has its territorial offices up to the level of *rayon* (city district) and they are responsible for collecting both the national dues and the local ones. Although local governments do not have direct administrative instruments to deal with tax payers, the high dependence on national taxes leads them to influence the business units informally to pay taxes in their full amount and in due time mainly through administrative tools.

Table 20.3 Composition of sub-national government revenues in Ukraine

Revenue type	1999 Million UAH	1999 Million USD	1999 Per cent	2005 Million UAH	2005 Million USD	2005 Per cent
Tax revenues	10,962	2,654	55.26	23,589	4,607	43.9
Taxes on income, profit, market value increase, including	7,936	1,922	40.0	16,678	3,257	31.1
PIT	3,111	753	15.7	16,487	3,220	30.7
EPT	4,824	1,168	24.3	192	38	0.4
Property taxes	296	72	1.5	833	163	1.6
Fees for special usage of natural resources	1,171	284	5.9	2,789	545	5.2
Internal taxation of goods and services total	1,018	246	5.1	1,150	225	2.1
Other taxes, including	542	131	2.7	2,138	418	4.0
Local taxes and duties	442	107	2.2	598	117	1.1
Unified tax for small businesses	62	15	0.3	1,371	268	2.6
Non-tax revenues	552	134	2.8	3,542	692	6.6
Capital revenues	7	2	0.04	2,079	406	3.9
Earmarked funds	1,631	395	8.2	1,107	216	2.1
Revenues without transfers	13,152	3,185	66.3	30,316	5,921	56.5
Official transfers	2,942	712	33.7	23,361	4,563	43.5
Total revenues	16,095	3,897	100.0	53,677	10,484	100.0

Note: A National Bank of Ukraine's average exchange rate UAH/USD for 1999 was 4.13, 2005 – 5.12.

Source: Ukrainian Ministry of Finance.

The development of sub-national revenues over time could be characterised as non-stable. Up until 2001, the sub-national revenue share in GDP demonstrated a downward trend (by about one-quarter since independence); respectively, the central government revenue share decreased (by more than 20 per cent in 2000). This drop can be attributed mostly to a negative financial development at the sub-regional level.

The national tax sharing system delivered a dominating portion of local revenues up to the fiscal year 2000: it counted from 50 up to 80 per cent on average. The tax sharing between national and sub-national levels was generally abolished by the Budget Code in 2001, but in fact it still remains to be carried out through annual budget laws concerning national taxes such as EPT and excises. The permanent turbulence of the assignment of national taxes to the SNGs made local fiscal planning and sound fiscal management almost impossible and sub-national fiscal autonomy insignificant. Under the precondition of prevailing national tasks in SNGs' activities they preferred to piggyback national revenue sources instead of generating own revenues.

The instability of intergovernmental revenue arrangements in Ukraine can be mostly attributed to the function that was vested on tax sharing by the Ministry of Finance: minimising the number of regional budgets subsidised by the state budget. By given fluctuation in expenditures and disbursed (due to the origin principle) revenues, the mismatch has changed from year to year. It made permanent the annual reassessment of sharing rates. Since the process of reassessment touched the interests of regional governments, some kind of bargaining between central and sub-national authorities concerning the list of shared taxes and – especially – sharing rates took place. But this process was carried out in a very non-transparent way that caused significant deviations from the actual territorial revenue distribution from the legislated one. The negative results of this system for sustainable SNGs' finance, accountability and sound fiscal management resulted finally in its abolition in 2001.

Since then, PIT became a ceded tax that delivers the dominating share of sub-national revenues – it has made about half the sub-national proceeds since 2001. But this change did not solve the problem of sustainable local revenues. On the one hand, it has made sub-national budgets more vulnerable to macroeconomic performance because of the pro-cyclic development of private earnings. On the other hand, the use of this tax as a tool of macroeconomic regulation endangers local budgets. For example, the abolition in 2003 of the progressive scale and the introduction of the flat 13 per cent tax rate has led to an immediate massive loss in local revenues; together with mandated public servant salary increases, it has created an enormous fiscal shock for many local governments, especially those of small communities.

After separation of revenue sources according to the Budget Code, local governments down to the level of city and rural *rayon* enjoy independent relations from the Ukrainian Ministry of Finance. They receive more stable revenue sources to finance their delegated functions – locally collected national taxes and duties and PIT. The proceeds from these revenues are included when calculating the sum of intergovernmental transfers. To fund the own expenditures, the self-governing bodies are granted revenues that are not subject to equalisation – mostly local taxes and duties.

After enacting the Ukrainian legal act concerning local taxation in 1993, the local governments were reluctant to exploit this new source: for example in 1995, 54.7 per cent of local communities had not introduced any local tax or duty (Kyrylenko, 2000); in general, local governments were not very active in imposing local taxation: by the end of the 1990s, even in large cities, the only levy introduced in any territorial unit was the communal tax (Parhomenko, 1999).

Table 20.4 Local taxation portion in SNGs' revenues (transfers excluded)

Year	Combined local budgets	Oblasts	Rayons	Cities of oblast significance	Cities of rayon significance	Settlements	Villages
1992	0.03	0.00	0.01	0.05	1.54	0.83	0.61
1993	0.13	0.00	0.03	0.27	0.34	0.10	0.63
1994	0.51	0.02	0.12	0.83	2.54	1.56	0.49
1995	1.46	0.35	0.35	2.96	8.86	6.94	1.90
1996	2.63	0.67	0.63	5.28	13.14	12.90	4.33
1997	2.94	0.78	1.24	5.42	15.38	14.38	5.21
1998	2.97	0.41	5.80	2.40	15.66	16.43	5.93
1999	3.36	0.29	6.66	3.16	14.59	16.41	6.88
2000	3.65	0.28	3.35	5.92	12.23	14.27	5.29
2001	2.90	0.17	2.94	5.50	12.67	10.70	3.80
2002	2.80	0.11	3.11	4.28	8.57	8.23	3.23
2003	2.62	0.12	3.39	3.80	7.22	7.08	2.88
2004	2.44	0.11	0.36	3.83	6.85	6.02	2.33
2005	1.97	0.08	0.28	3.14	5.77	5.22	1.76

Source: Author's calculation based on Ukrainian Ministry of Finance data.

The competence of the SNGs in levying local taxes is formally quite broad: imposing local taxes and duties, granting tax credits, reduced rates and privileges to the payers to local budgets. But the real discretion in this field is very limited because the list of levies granted, the tax bases, and the marginal tax rates are determined centrally. Thus, SNGs do not have direct authority in administering their own taxes because the levies are collected and administered by the local offices of the State Tax Administration. Currently, the list of levies that could be imposed by SNGs in Ukraine numbers 17 (for more details see Rozputenko et al., 2000). The most important tax from this list is the communal tax that delivers about one-half of the total proceeds from local taxation; the second one by rank is the market place duty. Local taxation plays a different role depending on the SNGs' type. As Table 20.4 suggests, it delivers a rather notable portion of revenues in cities of *rayon* significance and settlements. The trend is also quite remarkable: up until 1999, the relative size of local taxation proceeds soared, then it begun rapidly to decrease (in most territorial units by 3–5 times).

The most acute problems with own local revenue bases have been in the small rural communities. The local taxation base is non-existent for many them. So called 'self-taxation' (imposing fees according to the popular vote of the community) granted by legislation, cannot be an affluent source of funding because the pecuniary personal incomes in rural communities are very low. As an alternative, they have tried to develop some commercial activities: founding communal enterprises in service delivery such as bakeries, barbers' shops, convenience stores and so on; imposing fees on mediation between processing plants and individual suppliers, especially in milk and meat production); levying fees for delivery of certain services to the local population such as cattle grazing, agricultural machinery and land and so on (Grab, 2000). The lack of feasible revenues engages the Ukrainian local authorities in seeking other, non-official revenue sources (among them pecuniary and in-kind contributions of private businesses to the respective local authority budget).

The non-tax revenues of SNGs still play a minor role in their budgets. There is not sufficient available information on the user's fees that could be an important source of local revenues. Actually, the SNGs operate public utility facilities that are run though economically independent bureaus (for transportation, sanitation, water treatment, power and gas delivery and amenities). The companies delivering these services collect the user's fees; generally, the tariffs are set in a way to make the service affordable to most of the population, so the communal services and utilities are usually subsidised by most SNGs throughout Ukraine; only a balance of fiscal flows appears in the budget sheets.

According to the data in Table 20.3, the non-tax revenues have increased very rapidly throughout the last years (they nominally grew by more than seven times in 2005 compared to 1999) and reached a relative value of about 6.6 per cent to total SNGs' revenues in 2005. The important components of this revenue category are administrative payments and penalties. A share of such revenue type as interest from bank deposits is not so very high and has been diminishing over time due to the mandatory shifting of all SNGs' accounts from commercial banks to State Treasury accounts with no interest payments.

There is no doubt that the local revenue base in Ukraine should be and could be expanded. The most promising levies to be turned into local ones are taxes on land and property, as well as motor vehicle tax. The tax on land belongs, at the moment, to national proceeds which are shared between sub-national levels; for example, motor vehicle tax is a national levy assigned to SNGs' budgets. Assigning these taxes fully to the SNGs, the centre should retain the legal determination of a tax base and marginal rates of taxation. The suggestion to make PIT and EPT local taxes as expressed by some researchers (Kyrylenko, 2000) seems to be non-applicable to current Ukrainian conditions.

A very disputable point is imposing a local property tax. There is some inconsistency in Ukrainian property taxation. Some objects of property are being taxed by the national government (land, motor vehicles), but one of the most valuable kinds of property – private housing and commercial buildings – are excluded from taxation. Taking into account the growing inequalities in society, the implementation of such a tax seems to be justified. The situation where the direct redistribution of wealth in society is excluded from the toolbox of redistribution policy is frustrating. This problem has been an object of intense discussions over many years. There have been many disputes among researchers and practitioners that concern the very important issues of property taxation: (i) who is a taxpayer? (legal personalities or individuals); (ii) what is a tax base? (building space or its market value, inventories or luxuries in possession); (iii) how to assess the value of property by given under-developed market relations; (iv) how to define the tax rates; (v) what means of social protection of disadvantaged households are justified. The draft legislation (there were at least six variants of the law on property taxation drafted) had no feasible result. No doubt this tax should be implemented and assigned to the local authorities, on the one hand, and most locally elected municipality heads see no alternative to it. On the other hand, it will make the distribution in society fairer by pressing the more fortunate social groups to make a larger contribution to funding public outlays. The introduction of the property tax assigned by the sub-national governments will benefit the urban communities in the first line. The big cities of national and *oblast* significance will receive a large source of revenues, but the rural communities will not benefit greatly from this innovation because valuable property objects are absent in the territory of their jurisdiction. Such a deficiency of local property taxation could be resolved by surtax, as proposed by some experts (Bird, 2000). The PIT could be considered as a good candidate for imposing a local surcharge because its revenue base is not so mobile in comparison to EPT or VAT. If a modest surcharge is imposed on PIT, it would give the SNGs a large (and highly flexible) additional revenue source.

TRANSFERS

Since independence, the state transfers played an equaliser role in the differentials in public institution spatial allocation. The existing net of institutions, with the application of a budgetary norm set, delivered a base to calculate the expenditure needs of a territorial unit. The Budget Code changed this situation quite significantly: a new intergovernmental transfer system, the core of which is formula-based equalisation grants, was introduced. According to the new system, each SNG, up to the city of *oblast* significance and rural *rayon*, receives fiscal support from the central government based on the assessment of its fiscal potential and expenditure needs.

Cash transfers flow from the state budget down to the local budgets, mainly in the form of (i) equalisation grants to cover the lack of funding for delegated expenditure assignments; (ii) subventions to compensate for revenue losses in carrying out own expenditure assignments that are attributable to changes in national legislation; (iii) special subventions to pay for state mandated social protection programs; (iv) local investment support grants and (v) subventions for regions with special needs. This new approach led to the abolition of transfer instruments that were non-transparent and badly predictable, such as mutual settlements between budgets of different levels and SNGs' subventions to the central government (both abolished in 2002). The dominating forms of transfers became equalisation grants and subventions for state mandated benefits for some categories of the population.

Equalisation grants are allocated according to formula, involving such factors as equalisation coefficient (the range 0.6–1.0), relevant population size and the percentage of difference between a local government's per capita expenditure needs, measured on the basis of expenditure norms and adjusted for cost-related and need-related factors, and its per capita revenue capacity for the last three years. In cases where some local governments experience a surplus of forecasted normative revenues over calculated expenditures, it should transfer this sum (adjusted for equalisation coefficient) to the state budget. The allocation of equalisation transfers for each year is elaborated by the Ukrainian Ministry of Finance and approved by Parliament as an Annex to the Annual State Budget Law of the respective year. The formula for equalisation grants can be presented as following:

$$Ti = \alpha(V_i - D_i),$$

where α is an equalisation coefficient,
V_i = estimated expenditure need,
D_i = estimated revenue capacity.

Table 20.5 Composition of state transfer funds granted to Ukrainian local governments at all levels, per cent

Year	Total transfer share in SNGs' revenues	Mutual settlements	Equalisation grants	Budgetary loans	Targeted grants (subventions)
1991	14.4	34.9	55.9	9.2	-
1992	35.3	48.5	0.1	51.4	-
1993	9.9	89.8	-	10.2	-
1994	8.0	36.5	58.7	4.7	-
1995	4.9	51.7	40.3	8.0	-
1996	5.9	33.8	60.6	5.6	-
1997	13.8	18.0	81.9	0.1	-
1998	13.9	0.0	99.7	0.3	-
1999	18.0	27.4	70.0	2.4	0.2
2000	22.9	0.2	96.5	1.9	2.4
2001	29.0	0.0	58.5	0.4	41.1
2002	31.2	0.0	52.8	-	47.2
2003	34.2	0.2	55.3	-	44.5
2004	42.5	1.0	55.4	-	43,6
2005	43.5	-	61.8	-	38.2

Source: Author's calculation based on Ukrainian Ministry of Finance data.

The philosophy behind this approach lies in the general support of SNGs which suffer a lack of cash revenues because of an insufficient revenue base. The goal is to guarantee the minimal level of budget revenues to fund the mandated public services such as secondary education, health care, social protection and cultural events at an appropriate level. The programme-based approach is applied at the national level, but not at the local level. Despite the advantages compared to the previous discretionary system, the existing procedure of untied equalisation grant allocation led to a very uneven distribution of public money between functional spheres and separate institutions at the local level.

The proportion between different grant types has changed significantly after the Budget Code enactment (Table 20.5): the portion of targeted grants increased up to almost half of the total. These grants are designated mainly for funding of mandated social benefits, but there is a part of them which is supposed to foster local economic development – investment subventions.

LOCAL GOVERNMENT EXPENDITURES

The introduction of the Budget Code (2001) brought more stability to the inter-budgetary arrangements. Prior to 2001, Ukrainian public finance suffered year after year changes in the assignment of expenditure responsibilities within levels of government. This was caused by attempts of the central Executive to manage current budgetary shortcomings. The changes in budget appropriations also used to happen during the fiscal year and led to drastic changes in funding local expenditure programmes. That, in turn, caused the growing budget arrears of local governments.

The central government's responsibilities such as education, health care, culture and sports are delegated to the local governments with full reimbursement of standard expenditures through intergovernmental equalisation grants. Thus, the expenditures of local governments are divided into own and delegated categories. The main criterion for the inclusion into local governments' own expenditure tasks is the fact of whether these services are related to maintenance and improvement of a local physical and social infrastructure or not. Delegated national expenditure tasks involve the provision of people-related public services such as education, health and social protection; these expenditures will be included while calculating the amounts of intergovernmental cash transfers.

Own expenditures of local governments (to be excluded when calculating intergovernmental cash transfers) will extend to local fire-fighting, out of school education, social welfare programs for specified categories of the local population, assisting cultural events of local importance, municipal development programs, transportation and street maintenance, debt servicing and local environment protection programmes, and so on.

The composition of SNGs' expenditure by function presented in Table 20.6 below suggests that the most important functions of the SNGs are secondary education, health care and social protection – together they currently account for about 70 per cent of the total. These functions are those delegated to the SNGs by the state. The expenditures for education and health care are funded through ceded national taxes (PIT and land tax) and expenditures on them are subject to equalisation throughout the country; expenditures on social protection – partly through earmarked subventions.

Table 20.6 Sub-national expenditures by function in Ukraine

	1999			2005		
	UAH millions	USD millions	Per cent	UAH millions	USD millions	Per cent
Public administration	493	119	3.1	2,230	435	4.2
Law enforcement and security	175	42	1.1	85	17	0.2
Education	3,471	840	21.6	16,869	3.295	31.5
Health care	3,450	835	21.5	11,968	2.338	22.4
Social care and social protection	2,166	525	13.5	8,377	1.636	15.6
Housing and amenities	1,154	279	7.2	3,804	793	7.6
Culture, sports, and media	537	130	3.3	2,176	425	4.1
Transportation and roads	1,736	420	10.8	1,705	333	3.2
Contributions to the state budget	229	55	1.4	1,463	286	2.7
Expenditures total	16,074	3,892	100.00	53.538	10.457	100.0

Source: A National Bank of Ukraine's average exchange rate UAH/USD for 1999 was 4.13, for 2005 – 5.12.

The tight fiscal situation made SNGs spend almost all revenues on current expenditures. Although the Budget Code introduced the separation of the budget items into current and capital ('current budget' and 'development budget'), the capital investments play a modest role in local expenditure policy – only about 15 per cent in 2005.

The minor role of capital investment expenditures in SNGs' budgets should not create a vision that local investments are not so important compared to national investments; in fact, just the opposite: local participation in investments within the public sector is growing. In order to support local investment activity, the state investment subventions are disbursed between *oblasts* with an allowance linked to their level of economic performance. The subventions are dedicated to construction and renovation of infrastructure objects such as schools, hospitals and so on.

Formally, the SNGs have some discretion in allocating money between functions. But in reality, this discretion is highly limited by composition of expenditures because their main components are mandated by the state (see Table 20.7). For example, staff salaries and heating expenditures belong to so-called 'protected' items – they should be funded in full. The expenditure policy of SNGs is strictly controlled by the State Treasury through budgetary accounts held there. That is why only appropriations due to the approved budget can be allowed.

Table 20.7 Economic composition of sub-national expenditures

Item	1999	2000	2001	2002	2003	2004	2005
Current expenditures, including	86.1	86.7	87.0	90.2	85.2	81.1	84.5
Expenditures on goods and services, including	61.1	65.7	54.0	56.0	52.7	57.7	61.8
Salaries including payroll taxes	37.0	38.4	32.9	35.9	36.5	38.7	43.5
Goods and services	9.2	13.4	10.7	11.2	10.8	10.9	10.9
Utilities	7.0	8.0	5.9	5.9	5.8	5.1	4.9
Interest payments	0.1	0.1	0.1	0.3	0.1	0.2	0.4
Subventions and current transfers	25.0	21.0	32.9	33.3	27.9	23.2	22.3
Capital expenditures	12.7	12.9	13.1	10.0	14.8	18.7	15.5
Non-disbursed expenditures	0.2	0.1	0.1	0.0	0.0	-	-
Net crediting	1.0	-0.2	-0.1	-0.2	0.0	0.1	0.0
State budget payments	-	0.5	-	-	-	-	-
Total	100.0	100.0	100.0	100.0	100.0	100.	100.0

Source: Ukrainian Ministry of Finance data.

Due to legal requirements, the budgets of most types of SNGs' should be balanced. So no deficit budget planning for *oblasts*, *rayons*, urban districts, townships and villages is allowed. The fiscal shortcomings occurring during the course of a fiscal year in these units could be bridged by short-term (three months) borrowing from the budget at the higher level which must be repaid by the end of the fiscal year at the latest. Some sub-national governments (AR Crimea, cities of *oblast* and *rayon* significance) are allowed to have a deficit only in their development budgets that can be bridged by borrowing on the financial market.

FINANCIAL MANAGEMENT AND SUPERVISION

The general principles of accounting for local governments are determined by item 56 of the Budget Code. They could be summarised shortly in the following way:

- The accounting of financial transactions, assets and fiscal obligations is provided according to the rules approved by the State Treasury and the MoF.
- The execution of local budgets is accounted by the State Treasury and key spending units. The local governments are not allowed to keep budgetary money on accounts in commercial banks.
- The budgetary proceeds and outlays are accounted in gross values disregarding possible mutual settlements.
- The budgetary proceeds and outlays should be put in chronological order; all the accounts should be backed up by various documents.
- The proceeds and outlays are accounted for during the period of actual realisation.

After the budgetary year ends, all the accounts opened for the current year should be closed by the State Treasury. In exceptional circumstances, the Minister of Finance personally can extend the date of the budget account closure (but for no longer than five business days after the year end). Closing of accounts is followed by an accumulation of cash residue on a local government's special account with further usage by them in the next year according to their destination. After the Law on the State Budget is enacted, the authorities have no right to take decisions which involve new budgetary obligations, since they are not backed up by other sources to cover these expenditures.

Composition, regularity and terms of report submission are determined by the State Treasury. The reports on execution of budgets are composed by the territorial offices of the State Treasury. The key expenditure units deliver detailed reports composed in compliance with unified methodology, which include balance sheets, information about execution of cost estimates, performance measures and other information. The information is delivered on a current, monthly, quarterly and annual base.

Some communal facilities operated by the local authorities (such as water management companies, sanitation units, transportation and utility companies and so on) have a status of legal persons, so their accounts are not included in local government reporting. The bodies of upper state level oversee the execution of the subordinated governments' budgets. The local self-government bodies (*radas*) which delegate the power to execute budgets to Executives (Local State Administrations), have a right to audit budget execution and to check the legitimacy of fund usage.

The state bodies (Accounting Office, Ministry of Finance, State Treasury and State Control and Revision Service) execute an external control over local government fiscal activities and penalise for budgetary offences. As the Budget Code provides, a budgetary offence is when certain official persons do not obey the rules provided by the Budget Code and by other legal acts concerning composition, reading, approval, amendment, execution and reporting of the budget. In the case of some event detected by the state controlling body, it has the right to stop budgetary appropriations for any local government. The reasons could be, for instance, not reporting on time; not obeying the rules in accounting, reporting or internal auditing; breaking the order of payments; delivering false information on budget execution; breaking the rules concerning execution of budgetary obligations and non-appropriate – thus, not in compliance with the tasks – usage of budgetary costs. The penalties for budget offences can range from administrative penalties for guilty administrators and suspension of budgetary appropriations up to criminal accusation.

LOCAL GOVERNMENT AND FINANCIAL MARKETS

Borrowing, a common source of local revenues in developed and many transition economies, has not yet had any significant role in Ukraine: its percentage in local governments' revenues is very close to zero. There are three types of borrowing allowed for local governments: (i) bank loans, (ii) short-term loans from the budgets at a higher level for covering a current budget deficit and (iii) long-term loans to cover the gap in the SNGs' development budget.

Issuance of municipal bonds is allowed to fund investment projects only. It is stipulated that local long-term borrowing is the full responsibility of the respective sub-national government. The debt servicing should be maintained by annual allotments from the current budget. The pioneer issues of municipal bonds in the years 1995–1998 (23 bond issues with about UAH 222 million total subscription value were registered) remained experimental, with no positive outcomes and no further development; many municipal bond issues were emitted to fund housing construction. For most of them, the rate of subscription was far below any appropriate level – lower than 10 per cent. The very negative case of an Odessa municipal loan (about USD 45 million) issued in 1997 and further insolvency of the issuer has caused a long-term ban of SNGs' operations on the financial markets. One of the main reasons for such a result was a very subjective, non-systematic regulation of the matter. In 2001, the Budget Code created a legal framework for regulating a procedure of local governments' borrowings on the financial markets. But only in 2003 did the central government issue regulations concerning this matter and this opened a new page in the history of Ukrainian municipal borrowings – in 2003–06 Ukrainian municipalities issued bonds nominated in UAH and euros in a total amount of UAH 1.6 billion (Slukhai, 2006).

The borrowing practice in Ukraine is subject to very strict limitations. The government of AR Crimea and local governments at a basic level (this means no *oblast*, *rayon*, urban district) are allowed to borrow money only for specified investment programmes. These units are allowed to borrow money both in external and internal financial markets (but the external funding is allowed only for AR Crimea and big cities – with a population of over 800,000 people). Debt servicing could not exceed 10 per cent of the general fund of expenditures of any fiscal year in which the servicing is planned. If the terms of the repayment schedule are not adhered to in any year, the guilty SNG will be suspended from new borrowing activities for a period of five years. Each borrowing is to be empowered by the Minister Cabinet's separate decision.

According to the Minister Cabinet Regulation #207 dated 2 February 2003, in order to receive permission to issue municipal bonds, the city council (or AR Crimea) should present documents stating the purpose of the borrowing, a statement on the execution of the city budget for the year previous to the year of borrowing, a statement on borrowing for the last five years, and information about sources of loan repayments, with the assessment of a rating agency. More precise prescriptions concerning issuing procedures are contained in the Regulation 982/8303 of the State Commission of Securities and Stock Markets dated 10 October 2003. The prospects for the SNGs' bond market at the moment are not very clear. There are several reasons for this. First, the negative experience in 1996–98 has discouraged prospective buyers both in the domestic and external markets for a long time. Second, the population prefers to deposit money in commercial banks instead of lending it to public institutions; so only commercial banks could buy local securities at their own risk. Third, the taxation does not encourage domestic investors to buy bonds.

CONCLUSION

The Ukrainian public sector demonstrates that the remains of the old (soviet) system of public administration are still deeply rooted in the current intergovernmental relations. The attempts to overcome the reluctant behaviour of the sub-national authorities that are accountable to the state, not to the population, would have no success without a critical reassessment of the current state.

The enhancement of SNGs' accountability in Ukraine requires significant changes in their revenue basis. Without implementing serious reforms in this field, it would hardly be possible to make them more responsible in meeting the local population's demand for public services. Making the locally generated revenues a significant portion of regional and local incomes will ensure the relative growth of own (not delegated) responsibility in service delivery. Recent steps in reforming intergovernmental fiscal relations, as presented in the Budget Code, do not affect many important aspects of this issue, so the own revenues still remain an insignificant part of the local budget proceeds. The portion of local revenues in the Ukrainian SNGs' budgets should and may cover up to one-third of their revenues. All these should be supported by some organisational measures, such as creating an independent local tax administration in order to give the SNGs the tools for real control over fiscal flows on the territory of their jurisdiction, accomplishing the territorial-administrative reform and enhancing sub-national government administrative and technical capacities. All these steps will bring about good results if institutional reforms take place. The most important of these is the reform of the territorial-administrative composition of the country aimed at the creation of more fiscally self-reliant territorial units. On the other hand, the institutional strengthening of regional and local authorities needs to re-introduce the link between elected bodies and the executives at the *oblast* and *rayon* level.

NOTE

1. Unlike the other territorial units at the regional level, the Autonomous Republic of Crimea has some attributes of independent governance: its own Parliament, Cabinet of Ministers, constitution and legislation (that should not contradict the national one). But in terms of public finance, its status has very little difference from that of the other units at the regional level.

BIBLIOGRAPHY

Bird, R.M. (2000), Rethinking Sub-national Taxes: A New Look at Tax Assignment, *Tax Notes International*, 8 May.

Grab, A. ed. (2000), *Місцеві податки і збори (закон, практика, проблеми)*, Київ: Парламентське Видавництво [*Local Taxes and Duties (Legislation, Practice and Problems)*].

Kimball, J.D. ed. (1999), *The Transfer of Power: Decentralization in Central and Eastern Europe*, Budapest: LGI/OSI.

Kyrylenko, O.P. (2000), *Місцеві бюджети України: теорія, практика, політика,* Київ: НІОС [*Local Budgets in Ukraine: History, Practice, Policy*].

Parhomenko, V. (1999), *Проблеми місцевого самоврядування в Україні 1990-х років.* – Київ: Інститут демократії імені Пилипа Орлика [*The Issues in Local Self-Government in Ukraine in the 1990s*].

Rozputenko, I., V. Yurchyshyn, O. Ivanytska and B. Senchuk (2000), Local and Regional Tax Administration in Ukraine, in M. Hőgye, ed., *Local and Regional Tax Administration in Transitional Countries*, Budapest: LGI/OSI, pp. 349–400.

Slukhai, S. (2006), Ukrainian Local Governments and Financial Markets, *Proceedings from the 14th NISPAcee Annual Conference 'Public Administration and Public Policy in Emerging Europe & Eurasia: For Professionalism, Impartiality and Transparency'* (11–13 May 2006, Ljubljana, Slovenia), www.nispa.sk/_portal/files/conferences/2006/papers/200604201513350.PaperSlukhai.doc

Ukrainian State Statistical Committee (2007), *Україна в цифрах 2006*, Київ: Техніка [State Committee of Statistics of Ukraine, *Ukraine in Numbers 2006*].

Index